THE CONCEPT OF EQUALITY OF ARMS IN CRIMINAL PROCEEDINGS UNDER ARTICLE 6 OF THE EUROPEAN CONVENTION ON HUMAN RIGHTS

THE CONCEPT OF EQUALITY OF ARMS IN CRIMINAL PROCEEDINGS UNDER ARTICLE 6 OF THE EUROPEAN CONVENTION ON HUMAN RIGHTS

Omkar Sidhu

intersentia
Cambridge – Antwerp – Portland

Intersentia Ltd
Sheraton House | Castle Park
Cambridge | CB3 0AX | United Kingdom
Tel.: +44 1223 370 170 | Fax: +44 1223 370 169
Email: mail@intersentia.co.uk
www.intersentia.com | www.intersentia.co.uk

Distribution for the UK and Ireland:
NBN International
Airport Business Centre, 10 Thornbury Road
Plymouth, PL6 7 PP
United Kingdom
Tel.: +44 1752 202 301 | Fax: +44 1752 202 331
Email: orders@nbninternational.com

Distribution for Europe and all other countries:
Intersentia Publishing nv
Groenstraat 31
2640 Mortsel
Belgium
Tel.: +32 3 680 15 50 | Fax: +32 3 658 71 21
Email: mail@intersentia.be

Distribution for the USA and Canada:
International Specialized Book Services
920 NE 58th Ave. Suite 300
Portland, OR 97213
USA
Tel.: +1 800 944 6190 (toll free) | Fax: +1 503 280 8832
Email: info@isbs.com

ISBN 978-1-78068-164-1
D/2017/7849/5
NUR 828

GPRC
Guaranteed
Peer Reviewed
Content

British Library Cataloguing in Publication Data. A catalogue record for this book is available from the British Library.

CONTENTS

INTRODUCTION

The plight of one subject to a criminal charge is most precarious. His reputation, livelihood and freedom are susceptible to jeopardy as the state pursues the 'general justifying aim' of the administration of criminal justice, namely the control of crime which is manifested as detecting, convicting and duly sentencing the guilty.[1] Single-minded attempts to realise this aim would be inconsistent with a civilised society's interest in also ensuring that respect be afforded the interests of those of its members – qua moral agents endowed with autonomy and rationality (dignity)[2] – against whom criminal proceedings are being conducted. Indeed, state failure to afford such respect to its citizens is seriously deleterious to the legitimacy of a process that calls them to answer for alleged criminal wrongdoing.[3] The challenge for the state, therefore, at its most basic level, is to ensure that the practices and procedures applied in its pursuit of crime control are balanced with due respect for the interests of the accused.[4]

It is an expression of this respect that an accused is granted the fundamental right to a fair trial under Article 6 of the European Convention on Human Rights (ECHR),[5] a provision which reflects a commitment to the rule of law.[6] Drawing on the spirit of Hayek's definition,[7] Raz postulates that the rule of law

---

1 AJ Ashworth, 'Concepts of Criminal Justice' [1979] Crim LR 412, 412. See also *R v Brown (Winston)* [1994] 1 WLR 1599 (CA) 1606 (Steyn LJ).

2 Ch 2 text to n 7.

3 A Duff and others, 'Introduction: Towards a Normative Theory of the Criminal Trial' in A Duff and others (eds), *The Trial on Trial (1): Truth and Due Process* (Hart, Oxford 2004) 25.

4 This tension is reflected in the competing crime control and due process models in HL Packer, *The Limits of Criminal Sanction* (Stanford UP, Stanford 1969) 153–154, 158–159, 163–164.

5 (Adopted 4 November 1950, entered into force 3 September 1953, as amended by Protocols Nos 11 and 14) ETS 5.

The Court has found more violations of Art 6 than any other article, even excluding cases on length of proceedings: European Court of Human Rights, 'Overview 1959–2013' (Council of Europe, Strasbourg 2014) <www.echr.coe.int/Documents/Overview_19592013_ENG.pdf> 5–7.

6 *Golder v UK* (App 4451/70) (1975) Series A no 18 [34]; *The Sunday Times v UK (No 1)* (App 6538/74) (1979) Series A no 30 [55]; *Salabiaku v France* (App 10519/83) (1988) Series A no 141-A [28]; *Stran Greek Refineries and Stratis Andreadis v Greece* (App 13427/87) (1994) Series A no 301-B [46]; *Kinský v the Czech Republic* (App 42856/06) ECHR 9 February 2012 [104]; *Kaçiu and Kotorri v Albania* (Apps 33192/07; 33194/07) ECHR 25 June 2013 [139].

On Art 6 and the rule of law, see M Kuijer, *The Blindfold of Lady Justice: Judicial Independence and Impartiality in Light of the Requirements of Article 6 ECHR* (EM Meijers Instituut, Leiden 2004) 79–83.

7 FA Hayek, *The Road to Serfdom* (Routledge, London 1944) 54: 'the Rule of Law ... means that government in all its actions is bound by rules fixed and announced beforehand – rules which

broadly has two aspects: people should be ruled by and obey the law; and the law must be capable of guiding the behaviour of its subjects if it is to be obeyed.[8] Crucially, both aspects require correct application of the law and '[o]pen and fair hearing, absence of bias and the like' is essential if confidence is to be had that this has been carried out.[9] Upholding the rule of law through fair trial also implies respect for the dignity of citizens since the state is constrained from exercising arbitrary or oppressive power.[10] In constraining the scope and manner of exercise of state power, the rule of law is an integral element of democratic governance. Accordingly, the right to a fair trial is also acknowledged as holding a prominent place in a democratic society.[11]

The nature of fairness in this right is procedural. The European Court of Human Rights ('Court') lacks competence to entertain cases where a national court decision is wrong on the merits (error of fact or law), unless and insofar as the error impacts upon the procedural requirements of Article 6; it is not an appeal court of fourth instance.[12] Procedures – 'the means by which standards of fair treatment are applied in legal processes'[13] – vary across Contracting States, which are inclined naturally to establish and maintain in criminal proceedings their own legal and cultural traditions.[14] These procedures constitute local variations of the broader adversarial (Anglo-American common law) and inquisitorial (Continental civil law) procedural models,[15] though most criminal

---

make it possible to foresee with fair certainty how the authority will use its coercive powers in given circumstances, and to plan one's individual affairs on the basis of this knowledge.'

See further on the meaning of the rule of law GQ Walker, *The Rule of Law: Foundation of Constitutional Democracy* (Melbourne UP, Carlton 1988) ch 1; J Waldron, 'The Concept and the Rule of Law' (2008) 43 Ga L Rev 1, 6–9.

8 J Raz, 'The Rule of Law and its Virtue' (1977) 93 LQR 195, 198. This proposition is reflected in ECHR jurisprudence: eg *S and Marper v UK* (Apps 30562/04; 30566/04) ECHR 2008 [95]; *Gillan and Quinton v UK* (App 4158/05) ECHR 2010 [76]; *Munjaz v UK* (App 2913/06) ECHR 17 July 2012 [88]; *MM v UK* (App 24029/07) ECHR 13 November 2012 [193].

9 Raz (n 8) 201.

10 A Duff and others, *The Trial on Trial (3): Towards a Normative Theory of the Criminal Trial* (Hart, Oxford 2007) 21, 95.

11 Eg *Airey v Ireland* (App 6289/73) (1979) Series A no 32 [24]; *Deweer v Belgium* (App 6903/75) (1980) Series A no 35 [44]; *Adolf v Austria* (App 8269/78) (1982) Series A no 49 [30]; *Hermi v Italy* (App 18114/02) ECHR 2006-XII [76]; *Nataliya Mikhaylenko v Ukraine* (App 49069/11) ECHR 30 May 2013 [32].

12 Eg *Kemmache v France (No 3)* (App 17621/91) (1994) Series A no 296-C [44]; *García Ruiz v Spain* (App 30544/96) ECHR 1999-I [28]; *FC Mretebi v Georgia* (App 38736/04) ECHR 31 July 2007 [31]; *Centro Europa 7 Srl and Di Stefano v Italy* (App 38433/09) ECHR 2012 [197].

13 DJ Galligan, *Due Process and Fair Procedures: A Study of Administrative Procedures* (Clarendon, Oxford 1996) 54.

14 See further S Maffei, *The European Right to Confrontation in Criminal Proceedings: Absent, Anonymous and Vulnerable Witnesses* (Europa Law, Groningen 2006) 3: 'Criminal law, procedure and evidence do not fully participate of the movement towards a unified European legal area as Member States seem almost stubbornly attached to their own way of prosecuting, judging and punishing those who have allegedly committed a criminal offence.'

15 The two classical models are contrasted in M Damaška, 'Evidentiary Barriers to Conviction and Two Models of Criminal Procedure: A Comparative Study' (1973) 121 U Pa L Rev 506,

justice systems do not conform exclusively to either model.[16] The Court must remain sensitive to this procedural diversity and, accordingly, has not sought that a particular model of criminal procedure be implemented: 'Contracting States enjoy considerable freedom in the choice of the appropriate means to ensure that their judicial systems comply with the requirements of Article 6.'[17] Instead, the Court seeks to ascertain whether the procedure chosen by the state led to results consistent with a fair trial.[18] In doing so, the procedure is considered in its entirety.[19]

The rights of Article 6 did not spring fully formed into existence in a vacuum but bear the impress of the influence of Western historical developments in criminal trial safeguards. These developments, arising from both common law and civil law jurisdictions, reveal a centuries-long evolution in standards of, and the value attributed to, procedural fairness. Accordingly, Chapter 1 aims primarily to draw attention to certain of these influential developments to establish a background for Article 6 before it was conceived. It first considers whether biblical divine law could be treated as an inspirational source of support for the basic right to be heard. Thereafter, the main thrust of the chapter is on the historical emergence and recurrence of certain trial safeguards – at national, constitutional and international levels – which bear some resemblance to those included in Article 6. It culminates with a sketch of the motivation behind and influence of the ECHR, and of the character and content of Article 6.

Inherent to and at the very core of the right to a fair criminal trial under Article 6 is the concept of equality of arms, the construct to which this

---

510–589; M Damaška, 'Structures of Authority and Comparative Criminal Procedure' (1975) 84 Yale LJ 480, 487–529.

Key distinguishing features of each model are summarised briefly in eg P Duff, 'Changing Conceptions of the Scottish Criminal Trial: The Duty to Agree Uncontroversial Evidence' in Duff and others (n 3) 30; JD Jackson, 'The Effect of Human Rights in Criminal Evidentiary Processes: Towards Convergence, Divergence or Realignment?' (2005) 68 MLR 737, 742–744; Duff and others (n 10) 220–221; P Murphy and L Baddour, 'International Criminal Law and Common Law Rules of Evidence' in KAA Khan, C Buisman and C Gosnell (eds), *Principles of Evidence in International Criminal Justice* (OUP, Oxford 2010) 97–98.

Aspects of the adversarial tradition of England and Wales are usefully compared and contrasted with the inquisitorial tradition of the Netherlands and France respectively in N Jörg, S Field and C Brants, 'Are Inquisitorial and Adversarial Systems Converging?' in P Fennell and others (eds), *Criminal Justice in Europe: A Comparative Study* (Clarendon, Oxford 1995) 44–56 and J Hodgson, 'Conceptions of the Trial in Inquisitorial and Adversarial Procedure' in A Duff and others (eds), *The Trial on Trial (2): Judgement and Calling to Account* (Hart, Oxford 2006) ch 13.

16 M Findlay, 'Synthesis in Trial Procedures? The Experience of International Criminal Tribunals' (2001) 50 ICLQ 26, 29: 'Most legal systems now operate procedural hybrids'; Duff and others (n 10) 220.

17 *Hadjianastassiou v Greece* (App 12945/87) (1992) Series A no 252 [33]; *Ryakib Biryukov v Russia* (App 14810/02) ECHR 2008 [31]; *Chorniy v Ukraine* (App 35227/06) ECHR 16 May 2013 [39].

18 *Quaranta v Switzerland* (App 12744/87) (1991) Series A no 205 [30].

19 Ch 2 text to n 39.

book is devoted. This concept is intended to ensure that parties to criminal proceedings, as far as their different roles permit, are afforded equal procedural opportunities to prepare and present their cases. It thus refers to 'procedural equality'[20] or a 'fair balance between the parties',[21] a condition to be realised irrespective of the particular model of criminal procedure adopted within a state's legal system.[22] A close association exists accordingly between procedural fairness and balance, a relationship emphasised by the International Criminal Court: 'The term "fairness" (*equité*), from the Latin "*equus*", means equilibrium, or balance. As a legal concept, equity, or fairness, "is a direct emanation of the idea of justice". Equity of the proceedings entails equilibrium between the two parties'.[23]

A thorough theoretical insight on equality of arms within a criminal context under Article 6 is offered in Chapter 2. Whereas most could readily accept as axiomatic that procedural equality should pertain between state and accused, the chapter opts instead to investigate the actual value of such equality. It also identifies a contemporary legal basis for this equality in Article 6 and in international law. Furthermore, the chapter breaks down the well-established definition of equality of arms, as formulated at Strasbourg, and elaborates on the fundamental elements thereof to clarify the nature of the concept, including its underpinning relationship with Article 6(3). The most important of these elements is the requirement that the accused have suffered 'disadvantage' for a violation to be registered. In this regard, the book argues that the Court does not equate the term with inequality in itself (unequivocal inequality), which would be a dignitarian interpretation, but with inequality that gives rise to actual or, in some circumstances, inevitable prejudice. This is the key proposition in the

20 Eg *Ofner and Hopfinger v Austria* (Apps 524/59; 617/59) (1963) 6 Yearbook 676 (EComHR) 696; *Pataki and Dunshirn v Austria* (Apps 596/59; 789/60) (1963) 6 Yearbook 714 (EComHR) 731–732; *Kuopila v Finland* (App 27752/95) ECHR 27 April 2000 [27]; *Cyprus v Turkey* (App 25781/94) ECHR 2001-IV [105], [211], [339].

21 Eg *Salov v Ukraine* (App 65518/01) ECHR 2005-VIII [87]; *Perić v Croatia* (App 34499/06) ECHR 27 March 2008 [19]; *Batsanina v Russia* (App 3932/02) ECHR 26 May 2009 [22]; *Laska and Lika v Albania* (Apps 12315/04; 17605/04) ECHR 20 April 2010 [60]; *Lagardère v France* (App 18851/07) ECHR 12 April 2012 [38].

22 See further SJ Summers, *Fair Trials: The European Criminal Procedural Tradition and the European Court of Human Rights* (Hart, Oxford 2007) 104: 'the Court does not believe this principle [of equality of arms] to be culturally specific. It has applied it in criminal and civil cases concerning, *inter alia*, the United Kingdom, France, Austria, Belgium, the Netherlands, Switzerland and Finland.'

23 *Situation in the Democratic Republic of the Congo* (Decision on the Prosecution's Application for Leave to Appeal the Chamber's Decision of 17 January 2006 on the Applications for Participation in the Proceedings of VPRS 1–6) (Pre-Trial Chamber I) ICC-01/04-135 (31 March 2006) [38] (fn omitted). See also *Situation in Uganda* (Decision on Prosecutor's Application for Leave to Appeal in Part Pre-Trial Chamber II's Decision on the Prosecutor's Applications for Warrants of Arrest under Article 58) (Pre-Trial Chamber II) ICC-02/04-01/05-20 (19 August 2005) [30]: 'Fairness is closely linked to the concept of "equality of arms", or of balance, between the parties during the proceedings.'

work, for it is the golden thread running through the analytical heart of the survey of case-law in the three subsequent chapters.

Chapters 3–5 rely on Article 6(3) as the context in which to demonstrate and assess the Court's approach to procedural equality in practice. This provision contains a catalogue of minimum rights which 'exemplify the notion of fair trial in respect of typical procedural situations which arise in criminal cases'.[24] Of the case-law concerning these rights, it is that on three rights within sub-paragraphs (b)–(d) that raises the range and depth of issues that are most conducive to getting right to the heart of the Strasbourg approach to the equality of arms doctrine. Each chapter corresponds to one of these three rights. The nexus between each right and procedural equality is established at the beginning of the corresponding chapter.

Chapter 3 considers the Court's approach to equality of arms in the light of the Article 6(3)(d) right to challenge and call witness evidence. Those who can occupy the position of witness or of examiner are defined. Analysis of the right to question adverse witnesses predominates the chapter as this component of Article 6(3)(d) attracts the most attention of the Court. In this regard, an examination model that is a benchmark of compliance with the article is outlined to serve as a point of reference for a discussion on derogations therefrom. Derogations have been permitted to secure the safety and well-being of victims and witnesses and their ability to testify freely. The Court's approach to equality of arms within the context of derogations from the benchmark examination model is discussed, focussing on three categories of witness for whom derogations have been made: absent, anonymous and vulnerable. The remainder of the analysis is devoted to the right to call witness evidence under the same conditions as the prosecution.

Chapter 4 investigates the Strasbourg approach to equality of arms when complaints of inadequate time and facilities are assessed under Article 6(3)(b). Whereas the key matters taken into account in assessing adequacy of time are identified, greater regard is had in the chapter for the right to adequate facilities which predominates the jurisprudence. Examples of several facilities necessary for procedural equality are given but it is the facility of disclosure that features most prominently in the case-law. An outline of the character of disclosure is followed with a discussion on the Court's approach to equality of arms as applied to cases of non-disclosure both of evidence and of written observations.

Chapter 5 finally examines the Court's approach to equality of arms in the application of the Article 6(3)(c) right to legal assistance. The Court's response to domestic restrictions on the right to privately retained counsel is assessed before turning to the right to legally aided assistance. Eligibility for the latter and

---

[24] *Can v Austria* (App 9300/81) EComHR Report 12 July 1984 [48]; *Mayzit v Russia* (App 63378/00) ECHR 20 January 2005 [77]; *Seleznev v Russia* (App 15591/03) ECHR 26 June 2008 [67]. See also *Artico v Italy* (App 6694/74) (1980) Series A no 37 [32]; *Meftah and others v France* (Apps 32911/96; 35237/97; 34595/97) ECHR 2002-VII [40].

whether those who are eligible are entitled to influence the selection of appointed counsel are issues addressed. Also addressed is whether states can insist upon counsel for an accused wishing to represent himself. Thereafter, the chapter considers the Court's approach to pre-trial legal assistance and to complaints of ineffective assistance.

The basic structure of this book, therefore, comprises a contextual prelude (Chapter 1), a theoretical insight (Chapter 2), and analysis of case-law (Chapters 3–5). The conclusions to each chapter provide a comprehensive summary of the findings therein, necessitating only a brief concluding overview at the end of the book. Though this work is based primarily on Article 6 decisions of the Court and, to a much lesser extent, the former European Commission of Human Rights ('Commission'),[25] references are made throughout to other contemporary and historical national and international legal instruments and judgements whenever instructive. Nonetheless, in the international fora, it is the Strasbourg organs that have articulated the most sophisticated and detailed jurisprudence on equality of arms, the influence of which has extended to other international tribunals.[26]

Given the theoretical importance and practical significance of equality of arms to procedural fairness, it is unsurprising that it is the object of much commentary.[27] This book is intended, however, to distinguish itself by offering

---

25 Abolished by ECHR Protocol No 11 (adopted 11 May 1994, entered into force 1 November 1998) ETS 155.

26 Eg *Prosecutor v Tadić* (Judgement) (Appeals Chamber) ICTY-94-1-A (15 July 1999) [44], [48]–[49]; *Prosecutor v Kayishema and Ruzindana* (Judgement: Reasons) (Appeals Chamber) ICTR-95-1-A (1 June 2001) [80]; *Prosecutor v Norman et al* (CDF Case) (Decision on *Inter Partes* Motion by Prosecution to Freeze the Account of the Accused Sam Hinga Norman at Union Trust Bank (SL) Limited or at any other Bank in Sierra Leone) (Trial Chamber) SCSL-04-14-PT (19 April 2004) text to fn 1; *Situation in the Democratic Republic of the Congo* (n 23) text to fns 47, 50.

27 Eg S Stavros, *The Guarantees for Accused Persons Under Article 6 of the European Convention on Human Rights: An Analysis of the Application of the Convention and a Comparison with Other Instruments* (Martinus Nijhoff, Dordrecht 1993) 52–54; M Wąsek-Wiaderek, *The Principle of "Equality of Arms" in Criminal Procedure Under Article 6 of the European Convention on Human Rights and its Functions in Criminal Justice of Selected European Countries: A Comparative View* (Leuven UP, Leuven 2000) 23–32, 39–42, 50–54; S Trechsel, *Human Rights in Criminal Proceedings* (OUP, Oxford 2005) 94–102; P van Dijk and M Viering, 'Right to a Fair and Public Hearing (Article 6)' in P van Dijk and others (eds), *Theory and Practice of the European Convention on Human Rights* (4th edn Intersentia, Antwerp 2006) 580–584; Summers (n 22) 103–112; D Harris and others, *Harris, O'Boyle and Warbrick: Law of the European Convention on Human Rights* (3rd edn OUP, Oxford 2014) 413–416.

There are also useful accounts on equality of arms based predominantly outside the Art 6 context: eg JS Silver, 'Equality of Arms and the Adversarial Process: A New Constitutional Right' [1990] Wis L Rev 1007, 1032–1041; G McIntyre, 'Equality of Arms – Defining Human Rights in the Jurisprudence of the International Criminal Tribunal for the former Yugoslavia' (2003) 16 LJIL 269, 271–320; J Meernik, 'Equality of Arms? The Individual vs. The International Community in War Crimes Tribunals' (2003) 86 Judicature 312, 314–319; GJA Knoops, 'The Dichotomy Between Judicial Economy and Equality of Arms Within

a greater depth of theory and jurisprudence based treatment of the subject within the realm of Article 6. Not only is this readily evident in the degree of consideration given to the value, legal basis and definition of the concept of equality of arms (Chapter 2), but also in the fact that a thorough examination of three heavily issue-laden rights within Article 6(3) is conducted distinctly from an equality of arms perspective (Chapters 3–5). Additionally, the wider context of equality of arms is not ignored, for a synthesis of a range of historical developments not found in any one account on trial rights is presented to establish a background for Article 6 (Chapter 1). On this basis, it is hoped that this work will not only forge an enhanced general understanding of procedural fairness safeguards and standards, including from a historical perspective, but also provoke, more specifically, new reflection on the concept of equality of arms in criminal proceedings under Article 6.

International and Internationalized Criminal Trials: A Defense Perspective' (2005) 28 Fordham Int'l LJ 1566; S Negri, 'The Principle of "Equality of Arms" and the Evolving Law of International Criminal Procedure' (2005) 5 Int CLR 513, 522–571; S Negri, 'Equality of Arms – Guiding Light or Empty Shell?' in M Bohlander (ed), *International Criminal Justice: A Critical Analysis of Institutions and Procedures* (Cameron May, London 2007) 16–19, 22–73; RJV Cole, 'Validating the Normative Value and Legal Recognition of the Principle of Equality of Arms in Criminal Proceedings in Botswana' (2012) 56 JAL 68; M Fedorova, *The Principle of Equality of Arms in International Criminal Proceedings* (Intersentia, Cambridge 2012).

CHAPTER 1

A BACKGROUND FOR ARTICLE 6

Historical Developments in Trial Rights

1. INTRODUCTION

Procedural rights of individuals subjected to judicial proceedings act as a restraint on the arbitrary and oppressive assertion of power by state authorities. This restraint is especially critical in criminal proceedings where life or liberty is at stake, thus '[t]he history of liberty has largely been the history of observance of procedural safeguards.'[1] The procedural rights of the accused, and his capacity to exercise them, reflect the content and standard of procedural fairness available in the particular society in which the criminal proceedings occur. The content and standard of this fairness is grounded in reason, experience and the socio-cultural environment and expectations prevailing within that society in the historical time-period of those proceedings. Accordingly, as the level of civilisation in a society develops through history, procedural rights securing this fairness exhibit an evolution: 'Fairness is a constantly evolving concept. … [S]tandards and perceptions of fairness may change, not only from one century to another but also, sometimes, from one decade to another.'[2] This progressive evolution, albeit interrupted by periods of regression, reveals the emergence and recurrence of certain trial rights, in various forms, which have been developed or adopted by legal systems through history as a useful or essential means to a just and fair adjudication.

This chapter charts this historical evolution in standards of procedural fairness, identifying certain influential developments in the trial rights of accused persons, to establish a background for Article 6 before its inception. The Article 6 catalogue of rights was not devised in a vacuum, but was informed by the past. Certain basic safeguards for the accused, resembling to a degree those included in Article 6, emerged and endured through different stages of procedural history because of their contribution to juridical activity perceived at the time as well-founded and fair. These procedural safeguards

1 *McNabb v US* 318 US 332, 347 (1943) (Frankfurter J).

2 *R v H and others* [2004] UKHL 3; [2004] 2 AC 134 [11] (Lord Bingham).

included, for example, witnesses being called and challenged, the provision of some disclosure and the allowance of legal representation, all of which are also discussed in the modern context of Articles 6(3)(b)–(d) and equality of arms in Chapters 3–5. The presence of such safeguards is indicative of historical attempts to avert some of the disadvantage between the prosecution or accuser and the accused. It is through these attempts increasingly being made in history that procedural equality would eventually become an aspiration for judicial proceedings purporting to be rational and fair.

The influential historical developments in trial safeguards for the accused traced in this chapter are features of practice and procedure at national, constitutional and international levels. This practice and procedure is of the Western legal tradition, for Article 6 is a construct of liberal Western democracies.[3] Since the development of Western civilisation has undoubtedly been influenced by the Bible, section 2 addresses briefly whether divine law could be treated as an inspirational source of support for the fundamental right of the accused to be heard before pronouncement of judgement. Section 3 turns to influential developments at national level, where safeguards were implemented as instrumental to attaining a correct trial outcome. It discusses, in particular, the rights of the accused in classical antiquity; medieval trials by oath, ordeal and combat; ecclesiastical inquisitorial procedure; heresy inquisitions; the French Criminal Ordinance 1670; English jury trials; and the French Napoleonic Code of Criminal Procedure 1808. Nevertheless, the historical implementation of safeguards was not concerned exclusively with reaching a correct outcome. Procedural fairness also became relevant at constitutional level, implying that it was acknowledged to be an important component of securing some form of good governance, particularly since it helps advance the rule of law and foster a societal perception of criminal process legitimacy. Section 4 thus draws attention to the rights of the accused in influential instruments of constitutional significance, focussing on Magna Carta and American and French instruments born of revolution. It was not until the aftermath of the Second World War that this concern to protect the accused from oppressive or arbitrary state action moved meaningfully on to the international plane. Certain enduring safeguards at national and constitutional levels impressed themselves in various formulations upon the Nuremberg war crimes trials and the fair trial clauses of the Universal Declaration of

---

3 See further AH Robertson and JG Merrills, *Human Rights in the World: An Introduction to the Study of the International Protection of Human Rights* (4th edn Manchester UP, Manchester 1996) 2: 'When we consider the philosophical foundations of the concept of human rights, it is clear that the mainstream has its origins in the liberal democratic tradition of Western Europe – a tradition which is itself the product of Greek philosophy, Roman law, the Judeo-Christian tradition, the humanism of the Reformation and the Age of Reason.'

Human Rights (UDHR),[4] the International Covenant on Civil and Political Rights (ICCPR)[5] – whose early drafts preceded the ECHR – and the ECHR. These three human rights instruments were testament that procedural fairness had evolved to become more than just an aid to correct outcomes or to good governance; it was also a manifestation of respect in international law for the dignity of the individual. Section 5 accordingly has regard to procedural fairness in the Nuremberg trials, the UDHR and the ICCPR, before culminating in an overview of the rationale for and influence of the ECHR, and of the character and content of Article 6.

2. DIVINE LAW AND THE *AUDI ALTERAM PARTEM* PRINCIPLE

The Bible has historically been a profoundly influential feature of the fabric and development of Western civilisation. Divine law as expressed therein – 'that law which God has set to the actions of men'[6] – was treated by some as an inspirational source of support for a cardinal principle of natural justice:[7] *audi alteram partem* ('hear the other side'). This principle, from which the concept of equality of arms is derived,[8] entitles the accused to a reasonable opportunity to state his case before judgement is passed. Justice Fortescue, reiterating a view earlier enunciated by the fourth century bishop Lucifer of Cagliari[9] and influential canonists Paucapalea, Stephen of Tournai, Guillaume Durand and Johannes Monachus between the twelfth and fourteenth centuries,[10] derived divine authority for the principle from the Garden of Eden account:

> The laws of God and man both give the party an opportunity to make his defence … [E]ven God himself did not pass sentence upon Adam before he was called upon to make his defence. "Adam" (says God) "where art thou? Hast thou not eaten from the tree whereof I commanded thee that thou shouldest not eat?" And the same question was put to Eve also.[11]

---

4 (Adopted 10 December 1948) UNGA Res 217 A(III) UN Doc A/810 71.

5 (Adopted 16 December 1966, entered into force 23 March 1976) 999 UNTS 171.

6 J Locke, *An Essay Concerning Human Understanding* (Samuel Marks, New York 1825) vol 1 book 2 ch 28 s 8.

7 On natural justice, see HH Marshall, *Natural Justice* (Sweet & Maxwell, London 1959) chs 1–3; P Jackson, *Natural Justice* (Sweet & Maxwell, London 1979) chs 1–3.

8 Ch 2 s 4.3.2 defines the relationship.

9 JM Kelly, '*Audi Alteram Partem*' (1964) 9 Nat LF 103, 109.

10 K Pennington, *The Prince and the Law, 1200–1600: Sovereignty and Rights in the Western Legal Tradition* (California UP, Berkeley 1993) 142–144, 161–162.

11 *R v The Chancellor, Masters and Scholars of the University of Cambridge* (1723) 93 ER 698 (CKB), 704.

It thus appears that, on this view, even God's omniscience is not such as to override the hearing principle.[12]

Yet, in contrast, the Bible also reveals numerous examples in which the opportunity provided to Adam and Eve to be heard in their defence was not extended by divine law to others. This inconsistency is even evident in the Garden of Eden account as the offending serpent was condemned unheard.[13] In the Cain and Abel story, rather than allowing Cain to make a defence to the killing of his brother, God invites an explanation from him only rhetorically: "What have you done? Hark! Your brother's blood … is crying out to me from the ground. Now you are accursed, and banished".[14] At King Belshazzar's feast, a divine hand inscribed that he had 'been weighed in the balance and found wanting',[15] judgement thus having been passed without a hearing.[16] Similarly, in the Last Judgement scene, condemnation to eternal punishment is not preceded by an opportunity to render a defence.[17]

It is in view of the inconsistency between the apparent respect for the *audi alteram partem* principle in the case of Adam and Eve and the lack thereof in other biblical instances that renders it unconvincing to treat divine law as an inspirational source of support for this principle.

3. DEVELOPMENTS AT NATIONAL LEVEL

A historical sketch of influential developments in criminal practice and procedure at national level illuminates the emergence and recurrence of certain trial rights for an accused bearing some resemblance to those included in Article 6. These safeguards were developed or adopted as instrumental to reaching a correct trial outcome. Their implementation was also suggestive of a recognition that realisation of this end necessitated attempts to mitigate some of the disadvantage between the prosecution or accuser and the accused, though not to a standard intended to secure equality of arms in the proceedings as a whole. The application of safeguards did not translate into a purely progressive and linear evolution in standards of procedural fairness; standards also suffered periods of regression. Nevertheless, even in periods of regression, the accused still enjoyed some procedural rights, albeit their practical value was diluted by other adverse aspects of the proceedings. Both progressive and regressive historical developments inform the standards of fair treatment set by subsequent

12 Pennington (n 10) 143.

13 *Genesis* 3:14–15: CH Dodd (ed), *The New English Bible: Old Testament* (OUP, Oxford 1970).

14 *Genesis* 4:10–11: ibid.

15 *Daniel* 5:27: ibid.

16 RFV Heuston, *Essays in Constitutional Law* (2nd edn Stevens & Sons, London 1964) 185.

17 *Matthew* 25:41–46: CH Dodd (ed), *The New English Bible: New Testament* (OUP, Oxford 1961); Kelly (n 9) fn 38.

generations of architects of criminal procedure. Progressive developments introduce or reaffirm procedural rights which are considered or proven at the time to be fundamental, or at least useful, to well-founded and fair juridical activity. Regressive developments serve to expose the negative consequences of the absence of certain rights on the reliability of trial outcomes, the dignity of accused persons, and societal perceptions of the quality of state governance, thereby discouraging future recurrence of the same.

3.1. CLASSICAL ANTIQUITY

Recognition that some regard be had for the procedural protection of the accused when being judged is rooted in ancient Athens and Rome.

3.1.1. Athens

The principle of *audi alteram partem* is reflected in classical Grecian thought. Rather than regarding the principle merely as a precept of justice, however, the Greeks also considered it a pragmatic construct for good decision-making.[18] Although justice and good decision-making both entail reaching a correct outcome and treating similar cases alike, they are distinguishable notions. The former refers to the effect of an outcome as perceived by the affected actors; the latter is associated with the 'quality of mind' of the decision-maker.[19]

Several examples demonstrate the application of the hearing principle either in the pursuit of justice or as an aid for wise decision-making. In respect of justice, the orator Demosthenes referred to the prescription in Athenian law that both prosecutor and defendant should be equally heard in his speech in *On the Crown*.[20] In his speech at the prosecution of Timocrates in *Against Timocrates*, Demosthenes also highlights the Heliastic judicial oath which requires judges to ensure that a hearing is enjoyed by prosecutor and defendant alike.[21] Additionally, *Wasps* by Aristophanes, based on the Athenian passion for court proceedings, involves attention being drawn to the hearing principle by the character Bdelycleon: "In the gods' name, father, don't prejudge him guilty; wait till you've heard both sides".[22] Within the same work, one also finds the hearing principle associated with wise decision-making when the chorus

18 Kelly (n 9) 103.

19 Ibid.

20 CA Vince and JH Vince (trs), *Demosthenes: De Corona and De Falsa Legatione* (Heinemann, London 1926) [1]–[2], [6]–[7].

21 JH Vince (tr), *Demosthenes: Against Meidias, Androtion, Aristocrates, Timocrates, Aristogeiton* (Heinemann, London 1935) [149]–[151].

22 AH Sommerstein (ed) (tr), *Aristophanes: Wasps* (Aris & Phillips, Warminster 1983) [919]–[920].

leader pronounces that '[t]ruly it seems he was a wise man who said, "Until you have heard the tale of both parties, you should not judge"'.[23] Similarly, in *The Children of Heracles*, Euripides refers to the hearing principle in a manner more suggestive of its close relationship with good decision-making than justice: "Who can decide a plea or judge a speech until he has heard a clear statement from both sides?"[24] He reinforces this close relationship in *Andromache* when Orestes tells Hermione, "[w]ise was the advice of him who taught men to listen to reports from their enemies".[25]

The prevalence of the hearing principle in classical Athens should not be underestimated. Whilst most contemporary Western defendants may be inclined to take the principle for granted, even allowing the other side to be heard at all is a significant step for any society to take towards ensuring procedural fairness. Indeed, the establishment of this right evidences one of the earliest efforts by a civilisation to limit the possibility for arbitrary decision-making.

Despite the provision of an opportunity to be heard, the relativist nature of fairness, in the light of modern proceedings, is evident in other aspects of the Athenian judicial process.

A permanent, professional judicial body did not exist and, instead, Athens was served by a judiciary of 6,000 citizens, appointed annually by lot, sitting in committees of 200 to 2,000.[26] Whilst such a degree of public participation in the adjudicatory process may, prima facie, display a keenness to uphold public confidence in the legal system, the judiciary did not enjoy a reputation for independence and impartiality. The distinction between the judicial and legislative bodies was extremely blurred, resulting in a justice system tainted by politically motivated prosecutions and judgements.[27] In addition to the challenges to impartiality by self-interest,[28] judges were often familiar with the parties pre-trial[29] and, as demonstrated in Aeschines's oration *Against Timarchus*, were called upon to make judgements based on their own knowledge and extra-judicial investigations rather than solely on evidence presented at trial.[30] Decisions made on these grounds were lawful.[31] Due to the size and non-professional make-up of court membership, life and death decisions were made in an environment more prone to fickleness and sentimentality than upholding the interests of justice.[32]

---

23 Ibid [725]–[726].
24 D Kovacs (ed) (tr), *Euripides* (Harvard UP, Cambridge 1995) vol 2 [179]–[180].
25 Ibid [957]–[958].
26 J Macdonell, *Historical Trials* (Clarendon, Oxford 1927) 6.
27 Ibid 6–7; JW Jones, *The Law and Legal Theory of the Greeks* (Clarendon, Oxford 1956) 128–130.
28 Jones (n 27) 135.
29 Macdonell (n 26) 6.
30 CD Adams (tr), *Aeschines: The Speeches* (Heinemann, London 1919) [92]–[93].
31 Jones (n 27) 135–136.
32 Ibid 122; Macdonell (n 26) 6.

With respect to evidence, Athenian law did not permit defendants to provide evidence on their own behalf, other than that extracted during prosecutorial questioning.[33] Witnesses were not subject to verbal examination[34] and, consequently, their evidence was read from written statements, the veracity of which the authors were summonsed to confirm.[35] Although hearsay evidence was inadmissible, unless extenuating circumstances existed,[36] evidence procured through the torture of slaves, despite its inherent unreliability, was admissible.[37]

Further unfavourable conditions to defendants included the ambiguity of indictments, a prime example of which is found in a trial rank with political passions – that of Socrates in 399 BC. His brief indictment stipulated that he 'does not believe in the gods whom the city believes in, but introduces other new deities. He corrupts the youth'.[38] The absence of precise particulars of offences would, of course, adversely affect a defendant's ability to refute formal charges effectively.[39]

It was with the aim of challenging charges effectively that defendants sought representatives, from relatives to professional orators, to advocate on their behalf.[40] Whilst representation was permitted, professional advocates, because of the absence of blood-ties or friendships with their clients, were sometimes viewed in courts as legal mercenaries skilled in oratory, thus untrustworthy, disinterested in justice and a potential liability for clients.[41] Of course, in an environment where representation was not deemed essential to ensuring fairness at trial, a formal system of legal aid did not exist and defendants were compelled to use their own initiative in seeking assistance. Nevertheless, allowing self-acquired representation and an opportunity to be heard before the passing of judgement reflected at least a modicum of protection for the accused in the Athenian legal system's pursuit of correct outcomes.

---

33 Demosthenes, *Apollodorus Against Stephanus 2* in AT Murray (tr), *Demosthenes: Private Orations* (Heinemann, London 1939) vol 5 [9]–[10].

34 Demosthenes, *On the False Embassy* in Vince and Vince (n 20) [176].

35 Lycurgus, *Against Leocrates* in JO Burtt (tr), *Minor Attic Orators* (Heinemann, London 1962) vol 2 [19]–[20].

36 Demosthenes (n 33) [7]. Extenuating circumstances included a witness that was dead, sick or absent from the country.

37 Jones (n 27) 141.

38 Macdonell (n 26) 9.

39 Ibid. See also R Allen, 'The Trial of Socrates: A Study in the Morality of the Criminal Process' in ML Friedland, *Courts and Trials: A Multidisciplinary Approach* (Toronto UP, Toronto 1975) 18: 'the charges provided no standard by which empirically ascertainable fact could be adduced either to support or refute them; they admitted neither proof or disproof.'

40 Jones (n 27) 144–145; R Pound, 'What is a Profession? The Rise of the Legal Profession in Antiquity' (1944) 19 Notre Dame L 203, 212–214.

41 Jones (n 27) 145–146; Lycurgus (n 35) [138].

3.1.2. Rome

The principle of *audi alteram partem* was also entrenched in the mindset of ancient Romans. The Athenian conception of this principle as serving justice and good decision-making, both of which imply attaining correct outcomes, was shared in Rome, though justice received stronger emphasis.[42] Application of the principle as a means to justice was evident in positivist law. One thus finds in the *Digesta* 533 AD (code of law compiled from juristic works) the rules that a 'father cannot kill his son without giving him a hearing'[43] and that defendants should not be condemned in absentia because 'justice does not permit of a person's being condemned without his case being heard'.[44] Reference to the principle as a rule of law was also made by Seneca the Elder in regard to Iphicrates on trial: "Everything the law prescribed was carried out. The accuser spoke in his turn, the defendant replied in his; the trial was completed in all its details".[45] Outside positivist law, upholding the hearing principle for justice was also customary.[46] Suetonius in *Divus Claudius* refers accordingly to a representative's remark that "it is usual" for a client to be allowed to present a defence.[47] Apuleius's *Metamorphoses* describes magistrates, facing an imminent act of mob justice against an accused, advising that "a verdict ought to be rendered with due process and customary procedure" and that "the allegations of both sides should be examined". They add that the crowd must not "condemn a man unheard".[48] Furthermore, Tacitus recounts, in respect of the informer Faustus, the Senate opine that "no matter how odious and guilty the defendant might be, yet he must be heard according to precedent".[49] 'Precedent' in this context is synonymous with customary practice. Tacitus did not, however, regard the hearing principle merely as a rule of justice, but also as a rule of good decision-making: "What man of ordinary prudence ... would force death upon a son whose defence was unheard ...?"[50] Cicero also makes this association in a letter concerning a grievance over a debt owed by his brother to his friend by observing that both

42 Kelly (n 9) 103, 105.
43 A Watson (ed) (tr), *The Digest of Justinian* (Pennsylvania UP, Philadelphia 1998) vol 2 book 48 [8.2].
44 Ibid [17.1].
45 M Winterbottom (tr), *The Elder Seneca: Declamations: Controversiae Books 1–6* (Harvard UP, Cambridge 1974) vol 1 book 6 [5].
46 Kelly (n 9) 106.
47 JC Rolfe (tr), *Suetonius* (Harvard UP, Cambridge 1998) vol 2 book 5 [15].
48 JA Hanson (ed) (tr), *Apuleius: Metamorphoses Books 7–11* (Harvard UP, Cambridge 1989) vol 2 book 10 [6].
49 CH Moore (tr), *Tacitus: The Histories Books 1–3* (Heinemann, London 1980) vol 2 book 2 [10]. See also the remark by Festus, the Roman procurator of Judea: "It is not Roman practice to hand over any accused man before he is confronted with his accusers and given an opportunity of answering the charge": *Acts* 25:16: Dodd (n 17).
50 J Jackson (tr), *Tacitus: The Annals Books 4–6, 11–12* (Heinemann, London 1986) vol 4 book 4 [11].

sides should be heard before he judges the situation.[51] Pliny the Younger further exemplifies the same: "you can hear both sides of the case and be better able to decide what is to be done."[52]

Beyond the basic provision of a hearing, Roman imperial, inquisitorial criminal procedure was progressive in its application of certain safeguards for defendants in an effort to secure correct outcomes.

Foremost amongst these safeguards was the requirement of an impartial decision-maker, which reflects the second fundamental principle of natural justice: *nemo iudex in sua causa* ('no man shall be judge in his own cause'). Thus, a magistrate or judge was considered to have acted improperly if he arranged for false evidence to be given against a defendant or accepted a bribe to find the defendant guilty.[53] In *A Dialogue on Oratory*, Tacitus refers to a remark by Secundus promoting impartiality: "I shall follow the usual practice of upright and conscientious judges, who ask to be excused from acting in cases where it is obvious that one of the two parties stands higher in their good graces than the other".[54] Even previously under the Republic, the Twelve Tables 449 BC, a foundation instrument of Roman law, stipulated that a judge would incur capital punishment if he accepted a bribe for his decision.[55] An impression existed, however, that infringements of the impartiality requirement in Imperial Rome were rife.[56] Further to the dwindling of jury courts, politically-appointed single judges, special senatorial court proceedings and the judicial supremacy of the Emperor took prominence in an inquest-based process.[57] The absence of a strict separation of powers was an affront to independent decision-making, particularly in view of the Emperor's jurisdiction and law creating capacity. Moreover, a defendant's social status impacted on his procedural treatment by the decision-maker,[58] and provincial decision-making assumed an arbitrary character.[59] Whilst impartiality was not therefore always upheld in practice, the fact remains that it was a procedural requirement.

---

51 DR Shackleton Bailey (ed) (tr), *Cicero: Letters to Atticus* (Harvard UP, Cambridge 1999) vol 2 book 7 [18.4]: 'I like to follow the maxim … "judge not a cause …,"[3]' (fn 3: '"Do not judge a case until you hear both sides"').

52 B Radice (tr), *Pliny: Letters and Panegyricus* (Harvard UP, Cambridge 1975) vol 2 book 10 [59].

53 Watson (n 43) book 48 [8.1]–[8.1.1].

54 M Hutton and W Peterson (trs); RM Ogilvie, EH Warmington and M Winterbottom (revised), *Tacitus: Agricola; Germania; Dialogus* (Harvard UP, Cambridge 1980) vol 1 [5].

55 Table IX.3. Reprinted in C Pharr (ed) and others, *Ancient Roman Statutes: A Translation with Introduction, Commentary, Glossary, and Index* (Texas UP, Austin 1961) 12.

56 J Harries, *Law and Empire in Late Antiquity* (CUP, Cambridge 1999) ch 8. See further JM Kelly, *Roman Litigation* (Clarendon, Oxford 1966) chs 2, 5.

57 Harries (n 56) 53, 101; JL Strachan-Davidson, *Problems of the Roman Criminal Law* (Clarendon, Oxford 1912) vol 2, 156–159.

58 P Garnsey, *Social Status and Privilege in the Roman Empire* (Clarendon, Oxford 1970) 95–100.

59 WL Burdick, *The Principles of Roman Law and their Relation to Modern Law* (Lawyers Co-Operative, Rochester New York 1938) 699–700.

Safeguards were also implemented in respect of the basis of a charge. The *Digesta* reveals that, in addition to defendants being notified pre-trial of the alleged offence and its factual basis,[60] accusers were required to ensure the credibility of the allegation by disclosing their identity and rendering themselves susceptible to punishment if the charge was unmeritorious.[61] It was with the integrity of the allegation in mind that, earlier in the Principate, Emperor Trajan professed that anonymous accusations should not be admissible as "[t]hey create the worst sort of precedent and are quite out of keeping with the spirit of our age".[62] Indeed, accusers were obliged to be in the defendant's presence in court for their assertions to have effect.[63] Additionally, it was decreed in the *Codex Justinianeus* 529 AD (compilation of imperial legislation) that charges should only be pressed if supported 'by proper witnesses or by conclusive documents, or by circumstantial evidence which amounts to indubitable proof and is clearer than day.'[64] Once charges were pressed, the combined effect of the accuser having the burden of proof,[65] the defendant not being condemned in absentia and, in cases of factual doubt, the more generous interpretation being preferred[66] supports the view that the presumption of innocence was a notion familiar to imperial Roman law.[67] Freedom from self-incrimination, however, despite its close link to the presumption of innocence, was not a recognised principle.[68]

Competent witnesses were compellable[69] and required to testify in the presence of the judge.[70] Defendant and accuser were afforded an opportunity to hear this testimony in their presence[71] but cross-examination by the parties became an obsolete procedure.[72] It was permissible for the testimony of slaves to be adduced at trial through torture, with the qualification that such

---

60 Watson (n 43) book 48 [2.3]; Burdick (n 59) 698.

61 Watson (n 43) book 48 [2.7]–[2.7.1].

62 Radice (n 52) book 10 [97].

63 'If anything should be spoken by an accuser alone against an absent person, the accusation must not immediately be considered true, as though spoken against a person present and convicted': *Codex Theodosianus* 438 AD (pre-Justinian compilation of imperial legislation) 11.39.9. Reprinted in C Pharr (tr), *The Theodosian Code and Novels and the Sirmondian Constitutions* (Princeton UP, Princeton 1952) 340–341.

64 Book 4 [20.25] cited in *Coffin v US* 156 US 432, 454 (1895) (White J).

65 Burdick (n 59) 693; 'Proof lies on him who asserts, not on him who denies': Watson (n 43) vol 1 book 22 [3.2].

66 Watson (n 43) book 50 [17.56], [17.155] ('the milder interpretation is to be adopted'), [17.192] ('to follow the milder interpretation is no less just than safe').

67 *Coffin* (n 64) 454 (White J).

68 Burdick (n 59) 694.

69 Watson (n 43) vol 1 book 22 [5.1.1]. Individuals not considered competent are identified throughout book 22 [5].

70 *Novellae Constitutiones* 535–564 AD (legislation supplementing *Codex Justinianeus*) 90.5. Reprinted in SP Scott (tr), *The Civil Law* (Central Trust, Cincinnati 1932) vol 16, 340.

71 Ibid respectively 90.9; 342.

72 FR Herrmann and BM Speer, 'Facing the Accuser: Ancient and Medieval Precursors of the Confrontation Clause' (1994) 34 Va J Int'l L 481, 488–490.

testimony should be treated cautiously and not be relied upon as a sole basis of conviction.[73] Such caution also extended to hearsay evidence, which was generally inadmissible.[74]

Defendants were also permitted to benefit from representation.[75] In the Dominate, advocates assumed professional status and laid the foundations of modern advice provision and advocacy.[76]

3.2. MEDIEVAL TRIAL BY OATH, ORDEAL AND COMBAT

Rather than improving upon the progressive standard of procedural fairness of Imperial Rome, subsequent medieval accusatorial criminal procedure of Germanic origin took in Western Europe a primitive and superstitious stance. Riding the expanding wave of Latin Christendom, this regressive procedure sought to reach correct outcomes by appealing to divinity through trial by oath and/or ordeal or battle.

The widespread practice of trial by oath and/or ordeal[77] peaked in the ninth to thirteenth centuries. Following an accuser's plea to the court by corroborated oath, the defendant was required to take an exculpatory oath either on his own or supported by compurgators attesting to his good character.[78] Taking an oath was to invoke God as a witness and invite divine wrath if it was knowingly false. Guilt was determined upon whether or not the defendant was of good status and his oath was properly taken.[79] If these conditions were met, the defendant was acquitted; if not, he was referred to the ordeal.[80] The procedure was not devoid of all procedural merit for defendants: accusers were confronted, written evidence was examined and, by the early thirteenth century, accusers were obliged to support allegations with a minimum of two witnesses liable to defence cross-examination.[81] Nevertheless, if on formal accusation the defendant was known to be of ill-repute, or he could not rally a sufficient number of compurgators or produce

---

73 Watson (n 43) book 48 [18.1]–[18.1.2], [18.1.23].

74 CA Morrison, 'Some Features of the Roman and the English Law of Evidence' (1959) 33 Tul L Rev 577, 587.

75 Burdick (n 59) 698.

76 Pound (n 40) 223, 228; JA Crook, *Legal Advocacy in the Roman World* (Duckworth, London 1995) 45.

77 R Bartlett, *Trial by Fire and Water: The Medieval Judicial Ordeal* (Clarendon, Oxford 1986) 25, 42–49.

78 D Pollitt, 'The Right of Confrontation: Its History and Modern Dress' (1959) 8 J Pub L 381, 385. Examples of corroborated and exculpatory oaths are provided in JF Stephen, *A History of the Criminal Law of England* (Macmillan, London 1883) vol 1, 70.

79 Stephen (n 78) 70.

80 Ibid.

81 Pollitt (n 78) 385–386.

supporting evidence, oaths were considered improper and he faced trial by ordeal at first instance.[82]

Recourse to the ordeal was designed to test publicly the defendant's innocence by requiring divine intervention.[83] Common ordeals included a defendant holding a hot iron or putting a hand in boiling water, his innocence being acknowledged if the injuries healed after three days,[84] or a bound defendant being lowered into water, whereby sinking indicated innocence and thus an honourable death.[85] Whichever form of ordeal was applied, the legitimacy of outcomes attracted gradual distrust since administrators were susceptible to interpreting physical signs in such a way as to generate the outcome that they considered to be correct.[86]

Appeals to divine judgement also took the form of trial by battle. This practice, from which vindication was achieved when an opponent yielded or suffered death, was prevalent amongst the Germanic peoples and was imported to England by the Normans in 1066.[87] Cases involving odious and surreptitious crimes, such as treason and arson, and those involving heavily clashing evidence came within the remit of judicial combat, which reinforced the preceding oaths taken by the parties.[88] Defendants could challenge accusers and witnesses, the norm being that one could only contest another of equal social status.[89] Unlike in civil cases, the parties fought in person and could not be represented by champions fighting in their stead.[90] Strict rules were in place to ensure that neither combatant carried an advantage in weapons and armour.[91] Since parties contested the case from procedurally equal positions, judicial combat was an early expression of the concept of equality of arms.

The use of judicial combat, ordeals and oaths seems to the modern eye an irrational means of determining guilt, particularly given the obvious scope for miscarriages of justice. The standard of procedural fairness was at one of its lowest points in history. Yet, in societies that 'believed emphatically in divine

---

82 Bartlett (n 77) 26–27, 30.

83 Stephen (n 78) 73.

84 Pollitt (n 78) 385.

85 Ibid; Stephen (n 78) 73.

86 A Duff and others, *The Trial on Trial (3): Towards a Normative Theory of the Criminal Trial* (Hart, Oxford 2007) 23.

87 Bartlett (n 77) 104–105. See also 111 for an example of a judicial combat. The procedural steps for an English trial by battle are described in MJ Russell, 'Trial by Battle Procedure in Writs of Right and Criminal Appeals' (1983) 51 Tijdschrift voor Rechtsgeschiedenis 123, 129–134.

88 Bartlett (n 77) 106.

89 Ibid 109–110.

90 G Neilson, *Trial by Combat* (W Hodge, Glasgow 1890) 46–47; TFT Plucknett, *A Concise History of the Common Law* (5th edn Butterworth, London 1956) 116–117.

91 JS Silver, 'Equality of Arms and the Adversarial Process: A New Constitutional Right' [1990] Wis L Rev 1007, 1007.

revelation, appeals to divinity were entirely rational.'[92] Their understanding was that trial procedures only needed to be such as to justify and facilitate the submission of the accused to the judgement of God, which would reveal the correct outcome. However, clerical challenges to the legitimacy of ordeals by fire and water led to their eventual abandonment after 1215.[93] These challenges were repeated to erode gradually the practice of trial by battle, which became almost obsolete by the fifteenth century.[94] As this erosion occurred, the use of alternative procedures such as trial by jury or inquisition grew.[95] Divine revelation was thus being supplanted by reason and attempts by man – now the determiner of guilt – to establish facts based principally on oral and written evidence.

3.3. ECCLESIASTICAL INQUISITORIAL PROCEDURE

Trial by inquisition had already been implemented in European ecclesiastical courts in 1198 as a means of arriving at correct outcomes. The ecclesiastical procedure provided an influential model for the subsequent evolution in Continental secular courts from accusatorial to inquisitorial modes of trial.

Originally instituted by Pope Innocent III to investigate efficiently clerical corruption, the essence of the *inquisitio* procedure was that judges could ex officio, without accusers and relying on the strength of public rumours of guilt (*infamia*), act independently to investigate offences, amass evidence and prosecute suspects.[96]

The procedure was divided into two inquiries, the preliminary one of which was to establish *infamia*. Witnesses were examined by a judge and evidence gathered, in the absence of the suspect, to attest to the presence of public suspicion against the latter.[97] This testimony was disclosed thereafter to the summoned suspect, who was entitled to refute it, adduce witness evidence of his good reputation and demand that adverse witnesses be re-examined.[98]

92 JD Jackson, 'Managing Uncertainty and Finality: The Function of the Criminal Trial in Legal Inquiry' in A Duff and others (eds), *The Trial on Trial (1): Truth and Due Process* (Hart, Oxford 2004) 130.

93 Bartlett (n 77) 77, 81, 83, 86, 88, 100. England abandoned ordeals of this type in 1219. Canon 18 of the Fourth Lateran Council 1215 (ecumenical council) cemented ecclesiastical opinion by prohibiting the involvement of clerics in ordeals. Reprinted in HJ Schroeder, *Disciplinary Decrees of the General Councils: Text, Translation, and Commentary* (B Herder, St Louis 1937) 258.

94 Bartlett (n 77) 116–118, 120, 122–123. The final judicial combat in England was in 1492: Neilson (n 90) 203.

95 Bartlett (n 77) 126, 137–142.

96 Herrmann and Speer (n 72) 523.

97 A Esmein, *A History of Continental Criminal Procedure* (J Murray, London 1914) 89.

98 Ibid 89, 92.

If *infamia* was proved, the suspect faced a second inquiry to determine guilt and was afforded certain procedural safeguards. He was entitled to be present at the hearing and was notified of and given time to peruse the charges.[99] A not guilty plea resulted in the judge producing evidence and interrogating the defendant, who was permitted the aid of counsel.[100] Although adverse witnesses were examined in secret, their names and depositions were disclosed to the defendant, who was entitled to respond, request re-examination and call witnesses in defence.[101] Whereas disclosure of the names of adverse witnesses later became a matter for judicial discretion during the papacy of Pope Innocent IV, this safeguard was abolished in the ecclesiastical courts by sixteenth century Popes Paul III and Pius IV.[102] Nonetheless, defendants were very often granted the opportunity to confront these witnesses during the reading out of testimony, though a right of the same was not available.[103] Surprisingly, despite clerical opposition to ordeals and judicial combat, both of which caused physical harm, the use of torture in ecclesiastical courts after the mid-thirteenth century was a lawful mode of proof.[104]

Despite the application of torture in some cases, the inclusion in ecclesiastical inquisitorial procedure of witness confrontations and several rights important to an effective defence represents a procedure that was otherwise generally progressive in its standard of fairness.

3.4. HERESY INQUISITIONS

The standard of procedural fairness prescribed by the medieval Catholic Church in the ordinary ecclesiastical courts did not extend in thirteenth century Western Europe to its prosecution of suspected heretics. Constituting a crime against both church and state, heresy involved proactive rejection of orthodox Catholic doctrine. New intellectual enlightenment spread heretical thought, posing an intolerable challenge to the established church order and, by virtue of their interdependence with that order,[105] states themselves. Further to the codification of existing heresy legislation in the third canon of the Fourth Lateran Council,[106] Pope Gregory IX provided the momentum for the adoption and adaptation of the *inquisitio* procedure of the ecclesiastical

99 Ibid 89; eighth canon of the Fourth Lateran Council: reprinted in Schroeder (n 93) 248–250.
100 Esmein (n 97) 90–91.
101 Ibid; eighth canon of the Fourth Lateran Council: reprinted in Schroeder (n 93) 248–250.
102 Esmein (n 97) 92.
103 Ibid 93.
104 Ibid 91–92; FL Cheyette, 'Inquest, Canonical and French' in JR Strayer (ed), *Dictionary of the Middle Ages* (Scribner, New York 1985) vol 6, 479.
105 M Bévenot, 'The Inquisition and its Antecedents, II' (1966) 7 Heythrop J 381, 384–389; B Hamilton, *The Medieval Inquisition* (E Arnold, London 1981) 16–17.
106 Reprinted in Schroeder (n 93) 242–244.

courts to identify heretics more effectively. Consequently, a decentralised set of special inquisitorial tribunals were established to prosecute and suppress heresy.[107]

Tasked with presiding over these tribunals, usually as single inquisitors and under direct papal authority, were members of the Franciscan or Dominican Orders.[108] Their appointment was made with a view to ensuring some impartiality. Inquisitors were not local to the tribunals, thereby limiting any possible receptiveness to community prejudices.[109] Obliged to poverty, inquisitors of the mendicant orders were also less susceptible to bribery.[110] Indeed, bias was taken sufficiently seriously so as to warrant an inquisitor's deposition and excommunication.[111] The requirement of impartiality stretched to the taking of witness and defendant testimony, which required the presence of two impartial individuals unconnected to the tribunal.[112]

Notwithstanding this appreciation in principle for a degree of impartiality, trial proceedings were held in camera[113] and assumed an authoritarian character, affording scant protection for the defendant in practice. Stronger opportunities for defence were considered unnecessary since, in the vast majority of cases, correct outcomes as perceived by inquisitors were reached when admissions of guilt were extracted and defendants were reconciled with the Church.[114]

Even opportunities for defence made available in principle were found by defendants to be ineffective in practice. Proper tribunal procedure, for example, dictated that defendants be informed before trial of the nature of the charge and be provided with a written statement of the incriminating evidence.[115] However, this safeguard was habitually ignored in practice and defendants at trial were questioned on their beliefs and coerced into speculating the rationale for their summons, the aim being to support prevailing suspicions or provide grounds for alternative charges.[116] Furthermore, although suspects were entitled in principle to instruct trial counsel,[117] the entitlement was rendered entirely illusory in practice. If a suspect was convicted, advocates faced prosecution for abetting

---

107 As to the background of the tribunals, see M Bévenot, 'The Inquisition and its Antecedents' (1966) 7 Heythrop J 257 (pt 1), 381 (pt 2); (1967) 8 Heythrop J 52 (pt 3), 152 (pt 4).

108 HC Lea, *A History of the Inquisition of the Middle Ages* (Macmillan, London 1908) vol 1, 299–302, 374; Hamilton (n 105) 36–39.

109 AL Maycock, *The Inquisition: From its Establishment to the Great Schism* (Constable, London 1926) 130.

110 Hamilton (n 105) 38.

111 Maycock (n 109) 127–128.

112 Lea (n 108) 376.

113 Hamilton (n 105) 43.

114 Lea (n 108) 443; Maycock (n 109) 152–154.

115 Maycock (n 109) 148–149.

116 HA Kelly, *Inquisitions and Other Trial Procedures in the Medieval West* (Ashgate, Aldershot 2001) 449 (essay 1).

117 Hamilton (n 105) 44.

their heretical clients.[118] Such a powerful disincentive ensured that advocates chose not to act in heresy cases.[119]

The opportunities for defence were also severely limited with respect to witnesses. Defendants were neither confronted with adverse witnesses nor informed of their identities, the primary rationale being to protect the lives of informers.[120] In recognition of the danger of false witnesses, defendants were permitted to name individuals bearing mortal enmity towards them; if the named individual was an accusing witness, the associated testimony was withdrawn after investigation.[121] However, save for proving enmity, defence witnesses could not be called.[122] Additionally, witnesses considered in the medieval era to be incompetent to testify were compellable to give evidence against suspected heretics.[123]

Nevertheless, it was not the tribunals' approach towards witnesses, the charges or counsel that most negatively affected the standard of procedural fairness. To induce confessions, the greatest infamy in the trial process was protracted detention without conviction and the lawful[124] administration of torture. If an acceptable confession could not be obtained at the initial trial hearing, defendants could be remanded to deliberately harsh prison conditions, sometimes for three, five or ten years, until a confession was made on further hearing.[125] If all other inducements failed, the most obstinate defendants that refused to confess and denounce their accomplices could be tortured until they were willing to cooperate at hearing.[126]

Thus, the procedural position of defendants in this special inquisitorial process for heresy prosecutions was manifestly weak, where the only effective form of defence rested on proving enmity. Yet, even this regressive process was not absent in principle of a small measure of defence safeguards. It was, nonetheless, almost inevitable that this process, which was dependent upon strict adherence to Catholicism throughout Europe, became inactive in the sixteenth century as the Protestant reform movement, advocating doctrinal, administrative and legal reforms of church and state, spread.

---

118 Lea (n 108) 444–445.
119 Hamilton (n 105) 44.
120 Lea (n 108) 437–439; Maycock (n 109) 149–151.
121 Lea (n 108) 436, 446; Hamilton (n 105) 44.
122 Hamilton (n 105) 44.
123 Lea (n 108) 434–435. Categories of witnesses incompetent to testify in regular criminal proceedings are outlined in W Ullmann, 'Medieval Principles of Evidence' (1946) LQR 77, 80–82.
124 By virtue of Pope Innocent IV's bull of 1252, *Ad extirpanda*: Lea (n 108) 421–422.
125 Ibid 418–421; J Given, 'The Inquisitors of Languedoc and the Medieval Technology of Power' (1989) 94 Am Hist Rev 336, 344–347.
126 Maycock (n 109) 157–161.

3.5. FRENCH CRIMINAL ORDINANCE 1670

The *inquisitio* procedure of the ecclesiastical courts not only influenced the procedure for heresy prosecutions, but was also adapted and applied in the secular criminal courts. In the thirteenth century, the exposure and prosecution of crime, formerly by private initiative in accusatorial proceedings, became a matter of public interest; crimes could not tolerably remain unpunished for want of a private accuser.[127] Inquisitorial procedure was considered the most effective means of catering for this newfound concern and delivering correct outcomes. Whereas this style of procedure was introduced into the secular jurisprudence of Italy, Spain, Germany and the Netherlands,[128] France deserves particular prominence because '[n]owhere had the forms become better settled, or the rules more clearly and firmly established'.[129] Subsequent to the continuous development of French inquisitorial practice from the thirteenth to sixteenth centuries,[130] the codifying and authoritative Criminal Ordinance of 1670 ('Ordinance')[131] introduced in France a precise and comprehensive statement of inquisitorial procedure.

Pre-trial proceedings opened with a preparatory inquiry, the first component of which was for judges to conduct a crime scene investigation to establish the nature of the offence committed and gather real and witness evidence.[132] Witnesses were later summonsed to be heard separately and secretly.[133] Thereafter, suspects could be summonsed or arrested for secret interrogation by the judge to determine whether formal accusation would be justified.[134] Suspects remained unacquainted, however, with the exact allegations against them or the sources thereof.[135] Although suspects were granted the essential safeguard of an interpreter if required,[136] the assistance of counsel was prohibited in capital cases throughout the entire trial procedure.[137] This was not considered to be a hindrance to the defence as the judge was responsible for both defending and directing the prosecution of suspects.[138] Nonetheless, consultation with counsel

127 RM Fraher, 'The Theoretical Justification for the New Criminal Law of the High Middle Ages: "Rei Publicae Interest, Ne Crimina Remaneant Impunita"' [1984] U Ill L Rev 577, 581–589.
128 Esmein (n 97) 288–322.
129 Ibid 288.
130 Ibid 94–99, 104–161.
131 Reproduced in JP Doucet, '*Ordonnance Criminelle du Mois D'Août 1670*' (Le Droit Criminel) <http://ledroitcriminel.fr/la_legislation_criminelle/anciens_textes/ordonnance_criminelle_de_1670.htm>.
132 RM Andrews, *Law, Magistracy, and Crime in Old Regime Paris 1735–1789* (CUP, Cambridge 1994) vol 1, 425.
133 Ibid.
134 Ibid 427–428.
135 Ibid 428.
136 Ibid.
137 Esmein (n 97) 227.
138 Ibid 229.

after interrogation could be permitted by judicial discretion for non-capital offences, though counsel could not speak for their clients.[139] Adverse real evidence was put before suspects and explanations could be given in defence.[140] Endorsing a principle established earlier in medieval inquisitions, suspects could not in the great majority of cases be condemned at this stage, irrespective of the strength of the evidence of guilt.[141]

If the preparatory inquiry resulted in formal accusation, the accused proceeded to definitive inquiry, the main body of the trial procedure. To encourage testimonial accuracy, witnesses were heard anew, separately and in secret, to provide final depositions.[142] Thereafter, adverse witnesses were confronted by the defendant who could object to their inclusion in the proceedings and challenge their written testimony, inconsistencies in which were grounds for indictment for perjury, a capital offence.[143] The inclination existed, consequently, for witnesses not to concede that a sincere error in their testimony had been made and, instead, support their original claims with untruths to avoid indictment.[144] This consequence compromised the defendant's right of challenge. Also compromised was the effectiveness of the defendant's preparation for confrontation since it was only at this stage that he became fully cognisant of the nature and sources of the charges against him.[145] He was entitled, however, to submit written challenges post-confrontation.[146] The defendant was also offered an opportunity to react to any adverse real evidence.[147] Upon completion of confrontation, civil parties to the proceedings could make written recommendations for the trial outcome, to which defendants were able to respond in writing.[148]

The final part of the definitive inquiry involved a trial review by an assembly of judges unfamiliar with the case, before whom the defendant was heard once more.[149] Rather than conduct re-examinations of witnesses, the bench relied on depositions. Though these depositions also included those which were either generally neutral or favourable to the defendant, the defendant had neither seen them nor confronted their authors.[150] Accordingly, defendants were denied an opportunity to provoke from these witnesses crucial evidence not already

139 Ibid 227.
140 Andrews (n 132) 428.
141 Ibid 431; W Ullmann, 'Some Medieval Principles of Criminal Procedure' (1947) 59 Jur Rev 1, 20.
142 Andrews (n 132) 432.
143 Ibid 433.
144 AL Lowell, 'The Judicial Use of Torture' (1897) 11 Harv L Rev 220, 227.
145 Esmein (n 97) 230.
146 Andrews (n 132) 433.
147 Ibid.
148 Ibid 434.
149 Ibid.
150 Ibid 433.

elicited by judicial questioning and comment thereon or, if required, repair any damage unexpectedly done by them. The assembled bench also considered the public prosecutor's written submissions and the potential outcomes suggested by civil claimants and the original judge.[151] Prosecutors were not entitled to cross-examine defendants or be present during witness examinations, trial review and judgement; their submissions were informed principally by case documentation.[152] Accordingly, judges, with whom procedural equality was not possible, dominated every stage of the proceedings.

From review, the trial procedure advanced to either definitive or interlocutory judgement. Most cases proceeded immediately to definitive judgement where the three review judges concluded the trial and rendered judgement by vote.[153] Interlocutory judgements were delivered in a minority of cases when it was concluded from the review that there was insufficient proof to justify either a guilty or not guilty verdict.[154]

Three types of interlocutory judgements could be made, the first of which was to order that certain facts arising from the preceding stages be proved by further definitive inquiry.[155] The facts to be investigated were selected at the defendant's request or by judges themselves and communicated to the former, who could call supporting witnesses to testify out of his presence.[156] Again, the absence of confrontation with favourable witnesses potentially limited the opportunities for defence. The court moved to definitive inquiry following the prosecutor's submissions.[157]

Constituting a customary measure rather than one expressly specified in the Ordinance, the second type of interlocutory judgement deferred definitive judgement for periods from one month to indefinitely to allow for further evidence to materialise.[158] Compelling evidence did not emerge in most cases[159] and, by prolonging the trial process in this manner, procedural fairness suffered; little consideration was given to conducting the trial within a reasonable time. Whilst prosecutors sought evidence to progress the procedure to definitive judgement, defendants were imprisoned or released with an undertaking to return to court on summons, or both, during the extendible deferred period.[160] Although both situations entailed dishonourable stigma, detention was applicable only to the most serious offences, amongst which were capital

151 Ibid 434–435.
152 Ibid 434.
153 Ibid 473, 475.
154 Ibid 436.
155 Ibid.
156 Esmein (n 97) 234, 236.
157 Andrews (n 132) 436.
158 Ibid 437.
159 Ibid 438–439.
160 Ibid 437–438.

crimes.[161] Andrews maintains that the deferral procedure 'filled the gap between considerable evidence of guilt and formal proof of guilt, in a manner that was prudent and scrupulous'.[162] However, one may observe that by filling this 'gap', the procedure invited the protracted anxiety of being in legal limbo and involved possible imprisonment, which effectively amounted to imposing on defendants punitive consequences through the backdoor for probable but unproven guilt; the presumption of innocence did not prevail. The 'gap' should have been filled by acquittal. Yet, the procedure was prudent admittedly insofar as its availability ensured that judges could opt to spare defendants in capital cases from the alternative recourse: torture.[163]

Judicial torture, the most odious procedural measure, represented the third form of interlocutory judgement. Confessions were considered the 'queen of proofs' earlier in the Middle Ages and torture a legitimate means to extort them.[164] Under the Ordinance, however, the probative value of confessions, whether obtained under duress or otherwise, was treated with greater caution given the inherent risk of partial or absolute unreliability.[165] Accordingly, the probative value of confessions was dependent on preceding corroborative proofs. Torture, applicable exclusively to capital cases, could be sanctioned to extract a confession only if the occurrence of the offence had been proved and there was a sufficient alliance of testimonial, real, circumstantial and character evidence to conclude that a defendant's guilt was very likely but unproven.[166] The defendant was subjected to three interrogations, only one of which could be under torture, before the case proceeded to definitive judgement.[167]

Although torture considerably weakened the standard of procedural fairness in the Ordinance, several mitigating safeguards were incorporated therein. First, torture could not be administered without authorisation from the relevant *parlement* (appeal court), which received the defendant and case bundle for hearing and review.[168] *Parlements* were competent to uphold the decision to torture or reverse it and instruct inferior courts to move to definitive or an alternative provisional judgement, or render final judgement themselves.[169] Second, if a confession was retracted after torture or not provided at all, the defendant could not face the death penalty.[170] Third, confessions had to coherently include the particulars of a defendant's guilt in relation to the evidence, rather

161 Ibid.
162 Ibid 439.
163 Ibid.
164 Herrmann and Speer (n 72) 522.
165 Andrews (n 132) 445.
166 Ibid 445–446.
167 Ibid 447.
168 Ibid 446.
169 Ibid 446–447.
170 Ibid 446, 449.

than consist merely of a guilty plea.[171] Fourth, if torture unearthed new evidence on an issue, the defendant could not be tortured again on the same issue; neither could the defendant be tortured again if already withdrawn from it.[172]

In this example of early modern inquisitorial procedure, correct outcomes were sought from a judge-dominated process which offered some important and progressive opportunities for defence from pre-trial to trial review. The value of these opportunities, however, suffered some significant dilution. For example, the accused enjoyed a right of confrontation at trial but could not confront favourable witnesses; consultation with counsel was possible but only in non-capital cases and after interrogation, and counsel could not answer on behalf of the accused; and at all stages the accused was heard and shown the physical evidence against him, yet he only became informed of the charges during trial. In a minority of cases, the standard of procedural fairness could be further diluted by interlocutory judgement. Although many features of the Ordinance's inquisitorial procedure were shared elsewhere in Western Europe, a different approach was pursued across the English Channel.

3.6. ENGLISH JURY TRIALS

As primitive modes of trial fell into desuetude, Continental European enthusiasm for the inquisitorial process as a means of securing correct outcomes was not shared in England where, instead, the institution of trial by jury evolved and prevailed in an accusatorial system. Continental rulers in the High Medieval Ages had succumbed to Romano-canonical influences partly because the associated inquisitorial practices offered an additional mechanism to assert and legitimise their political supremacy in an era of power struggles.[173] Whilst these struggles raged, however, the royal government of England was in the eleventh and twelfth centuries the most centralised in Europe.[174] Consequently, royal justice reigned supreme throughout the entire country, superseding the local courts and ensuring that Romano-canonical influences could not achieve an overwhelming foothold in the judicature.[175]

The power of the Crown was exerted through royal judges accompanied by fact-determining juries and, accordingly, the jury system spread as rapidly and widely as the common law making royal courts.[176] Indeed, the spread of this system was hastened by early views as to its relative fairness when

171 Ibid 449.
172 Esmein (n 97) 234.
173 WS Holdsworth, *A History of English Law* (3rd edn Little, Brown and Co, Boston 1922) vol 1, 315–316; Given (n 125) 341.
174 Holdsworth (n 173) 316.
175 Ibid.
176 Ibid.

contrasted with primitive ordeals.[177] The classic Brunner thesis as to the origin of the English jury derives from inquisitions initiated by ninth century Carolingian kings, in which the most distinguished and credible inhabitants of a relevant district were summoned and compelled to disclose upon oath any information connected with the Crown interest at issue as a means of proof. This mode of inquest was, apparently, inherited and retained by the Normans following their invasion of Neustria (Normandy), from where it was imported to England in the Conquest of 1066.[178] This thesis, however, has attracted significant criticism and alternative theories, including English juries being of indigenous, Anglo-Saxon derivation.[179] Whatever its origins, Glanvill confirmed in the twelfth century that there was only minor engagement of the jury in the English criminal justice system; by the fourteenth century, the jury achieved greater penetration.[180]

Criminal juries were divided into accusing (grand) and trial (petty) juries in a justice system in which the standard of procedural protection afforded to the defence grew in sophistication over a long process of evolution.

Early accusing juries, the general applicability of which in criminal justice matters was first provided for in the Assize of Clarendon 1166,[181] were a large selected body of representatives from the relevant hundred (subdivision of a county) obliged to assert from their own knowledge or from information received from others whether an individual was suspected by common repute of having committed a specified offence.[182] However, the function of the grand jury had changed by the 1700s, as had its composition which was likely considered impractical for effective investigations.[183] The Crown presented a proposed indictment, on its own initiative or by private request, to a convened panel of 12 to 23 jurors who were to return a majority decision of 12 on whether there was a case to answer at trial, not on the basis of their own knowledge or inquiries, but only on the adequacy of prosecution evidence.[184] Since evidence was not heard

177 JB Thayer, *A Preliminary Treatise on Evidence at the Common Law* (Little, Brown and Co, Boston 1898) 60.

178 Ibid 47–48, 50; F Pollock and FW Maitland, *The History of English Law before the Time of Edward I* (2nd edn CUP, London 1898) vol 1, 140–141, 143.

179 W Forsyth, *History of Trial by Jury* (JW Parker, London 1852) ch 1; M Macnair, 'Vicinage and the Antecedents of the Jury' (1999) 17 Law & Hist Rev 537.

180 Thayer (n 177) 67–68; R de Glanvill and GDG Hall (ed) (tr), *The Treatise on the Laws and Customs of the Realm of England* (Nelson, London 1965) book 14 [1], [3].

181 Clause 1. Reprinted in EF Henderson (ed) (tr), *Select Historical Documents of the Middle Ages* (G Bell and Sons, London 1905) 16. The accusing jury was first introduced in criminal cases but given only limited application by the Constitutions of Clarendon 1164. Accusing juries could be employed in cases where no individual wished or dared to accuse a suspected layman (clause 6). Reprinted in ibid 13.

182 Pollock and Maitland (n 178) vol 2, 642, 648; Holdsworth (n 173) 321–322.

183 W Blackstone, *Commentaries on the Laws of England* (13th edn A Strahan, London 1800) vol 4 [302]–[303].

184 Ibid [302]–[303], [308]–[309].

on behalf of suspects, they could rely only on the jury's scrutiny and conscience to screen out oppressive prosecutions.

Nonetheless, the English grand jury was not to last. In the early nineteenth century, the police became the principal authority for conducting criminal inquiries, displacing justices of the peace who had previously assumed most of that burden after jurors ceased their investigatory function.[185] The justices acquired thereafter a purely judicial character in a preliminary examination procedure designed to determine on the evidence put before them whether or not a prima facie case for trial existed.[186] The magisterial examination in the mid-nineteenth century reflected an evolution in pre-trial protection for the accused by exhibiting several important features associated with procedural fairness: it was held in the presence of the accused and usually, but not necessarily, in public; a right to silence could be exercised; the accused could make a statement; prosecution witnesses could be cross-examined by the accused or his counsel; and defence witnesses could be called.[187] Following the preliminary examination, the grand jury heard prosecution evidence at an independent inquiry held in camera.[188] The jury rarely did not return an indictment[189] and by merely serving to duplicate, in an expensive and inconvenient process, the purpose of the magisterial examination, its existence could not be justified on the ground that it may very occasionally reach a conclusion different from that of the examining magistrate.[190] Consequently, the grand jury became redundant, suffering eventual abolishment in 1933.[191]

Moving beyond the pre-trial context, it falls next to chart some developments in safeguards at trial for an accused facing the petty jury. The petty jury was originally composed of men from the neighbourhood in which the offence occurred but gradually became drawn in practice, and thereafter formally in 1826, from the county at large.[192] It was established practice that some of the trial jurors were those that sat and indicted the defendant as part of the grand jury.[193] However, by the thirteenth century, the defendant was entitled to object to the presence of a juror considered a personal enemy and, by the fourteenth century, he was allowed to object to the presence on the trial jury of grand jurors who indicted him.[194] This opportunity of challenge reflected increasing efforts to ensure impartiality at trial. It was also in the fourteenth century that

185 P Devlin, *The Criminal Prosecution in England* (OUP, London 1960) 4–5, 7.
186 Ibid 6–7.
187 FW Maitland, *Justice and Police* (Macmillan, London 1885) 129–130.
188 Ibid 139.
189 Ibid.
190 Devlin (n 185) 7–9.
191 Administration of Justice (Miscellaneous Provisions) Act 1933 s 1.
192 Thayer (n 177) 90–91; Holdsworth (n 173) 332.
193 Thayer (n 177) 82–83.
194 Holdsworth (n 173) 324–325.

the requirement of 12 jurymen became a settled principle.[195] This number was probably set because of the necessity of reducing the large and cumbersome numbers of jurors in past juries, thereby maintaining feelings of personal responsibility, and because grand jurors, in essence, numbered 12.[196] The intended protection for defendants was that verdicts would rely on the wisdom of a collective group rather than on a single decision-maker, lessening the scope for the integrity of the latter to be compromised. Further protection was provided by the eventual requirement in the second half of the fourteenth century for a unanimous verdict, a majority verdict having sufficed in the past.[197]

More remarkably, for a substantial period of its development, trial by jury could only be proceeded with in felony cases upon the express consent of the accused.[198] This requirement did not, however, manifest itself properly in early practice and some accused persons were tried by jury and punished without consent.[199] When the requirement became a settled principle that was adhered to, consent was granted in most cases[200] but malicious refusal to consent would result in offenders remaining unconvicted and unpunished, an unendurable outcome which necessitated relief. Whilst the simplest solution is to abolish the requirement of consent, this was not feasible in the context of a people long accustomed to primitive modes of trial. The introduction of criminal juries was viewed initially as 'an impertinence, an intrusion into private rights, popular privilege, and individual honour'.[201] Formal consent was viewed as legitimising the procedure and confirming the renunciation by the accused of the right to trial by battle,[202] which was not formally abolished until 1819. Refusal of consent was, consequently, remedied by inducing consent by duress, beginning with 'strong and hard imprisonment' in 1275 and developing thereafter into *peine forte et dure*, in which the accused was pressed under progressively heavy weights.[203] Torture was thus a procedural characteristic shared by both Continental inquisitions and English jury trials. The issue of consent would become part of the gradual evolution in procedural fairness. In 1772, the practice of torture was abolished and the accused, in refusing to consent to trial by not

195 Thayer (n 177) 88–90.

196 CL Wells, 'The Origin of the Petty Jury' (1911) 27 LQR 347, 356–357.

197 Thayer (n 177) 86–90.

198 Stephen (n 78) 297. In cases of treason or misdemeanours, however, refusal to consent resulted in automatic conviction (298).

199 Thayer (n 177) 69–70.

200 Ibid 81.

201 CL Wells, 'Early Opposition to the Petty Jury in Criminal Cases' (1914) 30 LQR 97, 101. Wells also highlights the author of the *Mirror of Justices* – 'a fair representative of the average conservative opinion of the day' – who regarded the use of juries as 'an abuse' when men 'had offered to defend themselves by their bodies' (100).

202 Esmein (n 97) 333.

203 Thayer (n 177) 74–77. In one 1726 case, a suspected murderer refused to plead and was pressed for an hour and 45 minutes with nearly 400 pounds of iron, after which he pleaded not guilty, was convicted by jury and hung: Stephen (n 78) 298.

entering a plea, was to be treated as if convicted by verdict or confession.[204] By 1827, however, if the accused remained silent on plea, an automatic plea of not guilty was entered and the trial proceeded with.[205] Five centuries thus passed before the implementation of this logical and procedurally fair rule.

A long period would also pass before juries assumed, by virtue of developments in the use of witnesses, their sole function as judges of fact, acting only upon evidence presented at public trial, the consequence of which was a greater standard of procedural fairness for defendants. Originally, the petty jury had returned its verdict solely on the basis of its own knowledge and investigations, rather than on witness or other evidence presented in court.[206] They were not expected to be eye-witnesses but were chosen as being likely to be already cognisant of some of the relevant circumstances of a case, the means by which they acquired such information deemed irrelevant in law.[207] Given the susceptibility of human nature to form prejudice and accept hearsay or rumours as truth in these circumstances, this was far from a fair and impartial decision-making process.

However, societal growth and development in the late Middle Ages rendered jurors less likely to have adequate personal knowledge of an incident and, consequently, voluntary witnesses were admitted in court.[208] The increasing importance of witness testimony ensured that by 1555, prosecution witnesses could be compelled to testify against and in the presence of defendants.[209] The defendant's capacity to challenge adverse testimony was severely restricted in treason cases until the early seventeenth century when the right to confront and cross-examine witnesses was made available.[210] Defence witnesses were not permitted to be heard, the restriction then considered proper because conviction required a high standard of proof: clearer than the light.[211] This procedural inequality was eventually seen by the courts in the 1600s as unreasonable and oppressive and, consequently, it became practice that defence witnesses were heard, but not under oath.[212] The effect of this lesser procedural inequality, since prosecution witnesses were heard under oath, was that greater credence was assigned to prosecution evidence.[213] This too was remedied eventually as

204 Thayer (n 177) 77–78 and accompanying fn 1.
205 Ibid.
206 Esmein (n 97) 326–327, 334.
207 Holdsworth (n 173) 333–334.
208 WR Cornish, *The Jury* (Penguin, Harmondsworth 1971) 12.
209 Holdsworth (n 173) 335 fn 2; Plucknett (n 90) 436.
210 Pollitt (n 78) 388–389.
211 '*in criminalibus, probationes debent esse luce clariores*': E Coke, *The Third Part of the Institutes of the Laws of England* (6th edn W Rawlins, London 1680) 210; Esmein (n 97) 342.
212 Blackstone (n 183) [359]–[360].
213 Ibid [360].

defence witnesses could be sworn from 1696 in certain cases of treason[214] and from 1702 in all cases of felony and treason.[215] Inevitably, the steady rise in the admission and importance of witness testimony transformed the manner in which trial juries reached verdicts. Though it was acknowledged that jurors were permitted to rely solely upon their own knowledge for a verdict in 1670 without fear of penal consequences,[216] this was no longer acceptable in the nineteenth century and, instead, jurors were to rely solely upon evidence presented in open court.[217] This completed the transformation of jurors to judges of fact, entitling defendants to be tried before an impartial verdict-rendering audience.

This audience would also eventually see the scope of the right to be heard extended to allow the defendant himself to give evidence on oath. In trials of the 1500s and 1600s, the statements of a defendant putting his case before the court were unsworn, since an oath was regarded as giving these statements undue gravitas, and his responses to judicial questioning were not sworn evidence as questioning defendants under oath was viewed as invoking compulsion.[218] The prosecution, in contrast, enjoyed the advantage of presenting sworn evidence. After the Revolution of 1688, however, the accused was no longer made to undergo judicial questioning at trial, and from 1848 he could not be subjected to magisterial interrogation at the pre-trial stage.[219] Though oral defence statements could still be made at the pre-trial and trial stages,[220] the protection against judicial questioning was in practice often detrimental to indigent accused persons lacking competent and well-prepared representation, since the most appropriate defence was not necessarily brought to light fully or at all, leading to inaccurate outcomes.[221] Strengthening the opportunity for defence, the solution adopted in 1898 was to allow the accused to give evidence on oath by making him a competent, though not compellable, witness in his own defence.[222]

Also serving the interests of the accused was the promotion of judicial independence and impartiality. Parliament in the eighteenth century sought to limit the Crown's control over royal judges, who held their tenure at the pleasure of the Crown and were seen not as impartial servants of the law, but

---

214 Treason Act 1696 s 1. Reprinted in EN Williams, *The Eighteenth-Century Constitution 1688–1815: Documents and Commentary* (CUP, London 1960) 53.

215 An Act for Punishing of Accessories to Felonies, and Receivers of Stolen Goods, and to Prevent the Wilful Burning and Destroying of Ships 1701 s 3. Reprinted in J Raithby (ed), *The Statutes at Large, of England and of Great-Britain: From Magna Carta to the Union of the Kingdoms of Great Britain and Ireland* (G Eyre and A Strahan, London 1811) vol 6, 383.

216 *Bushell's Case* (1670) 124 ER 1006 (CCP), 1011–1012.

217 Thayer (n 177) 170 and accompanying fn 1.

218 JH Wigmore, *A Treatise on the Anglo-American System of Evidence in Trials at Common Law* (3rd edn Little, Brown and Co, Boston 1940) vol 8, 293–294 and fn 81; Plucknett (n 90) 437.

219 Plucknett (n 90) 437.

220 Ibid.

221 Stephen (n 78) 444–445; Plucknett (n 90) 437.

222 Plucknett (n 90) 437.

as agents of the sovereign's will.[223] Parliament accordingly prescribed through the Act of Settlement 1701 that judges' commissions should be held during good behaviour, their salaries should be ascertained and established by law, and they may be removed from office only on an address from both Houses of Parliament.[224] This enactment marked the first effective step in the development of the concept of judicial independence in England. Also at this time, the principle expressed earlier in seventeenth century cases that no man shall be judge in his own cause[225] was reaffirmed by Chief Justice Holt: 'it is impossible that one should be Judge and party, for the Judge is to determine between party and party, or between the Government and the party'.[226] The principle, however, was interpreted to require recusal only when the judge had a direct pecuniary interest in the case outcome.[227] As Blackstone observed, the accused in the eighteenth century could not make a challenge for recusal of a judge for bias, '[f]or the law will not suppose a possibility of bias or favour in a judge, who is already sworn to administer impartial justice'.[228] Nevertheless, the importance of an impartial tribunal was well-established, hence bias or partiality in a judge 'would draw down a heavy censure from those to whom the judge is accountable for his conduct'[229] and jurors could be challenged on suspicion of the same.[230]

Also important to increasing the standard of procedural fairness at trial for the accused was that legal representation was eventually permitted in cases concerning serious crimes. Defence counsel had already been allowed in misdemeanour cases by the early seventeenth century.[231] However, it was a long-standing rule that counsel could not generally be instructed in treason or felony cases as it was for the judge, the dominant presence at trial, to act as counsel for the accused and ensure for him procedural regularity.[232] An exception

223 M Shapiro, 'Judicial Independence: The English Experience' (1977) 55 NC L Rev 577, 619, 621; IR Kaufman, 'The Essence of Judicial Independence' (1980) 80 Colum L Rev 671, 676, 678; JN Rakove, 'The Original Justifications for Judicial Independence' (2007) 95 Geo LJ 1061, 1063.

224 S 3. Reprinted in Williams (n 214) 59.

225 Eg *Dr Bonham's Case* (1610) 77 ER 646 (CKB), 652; *Earl of Derby's Case* (1613) 7 ER 1390 (CKB), 1390; *Day v Savadge* (1614) 80 ER 235 (CKB), 237.

226 *City of London v Wood* (1701) 88 ER 1592 (CKB), 1602.

227 JP Frank, 'Disqualification of Judges' (1947) 56 Yale LJ 605, 609–612.

228 Blackstone (n 183) vol 3 [361].

229 Ibid.

230 Ibid [363].

231 CW Brooks, *Pettyfoggers and Vipers of the Commonwealth: The 'Lower Branch' of the Legal Profession in Early Modern England* (CUP, Cambridge 2004) 190. See also JH Langbein, 'The Prosecutorial Origins of Defence Counsel in the Eighteenth Century: The Appearance of Solicitors' (1999) 58 Cambridge LJ 314, 316, who suggests that one reason for allowing defence counsel in misdemeanour cases, but not in cases concerning serious crimes, may have been the essentially civil character of some matters within the misdemeanour category: 'it would have been awkward to forbid counsel because an archaic form had characterised … [such matters] as misdemeanour.' Legal representation was permitted in civil litigation.

232 Coke (n 211) 29, 137; Blackstone (n 183) [355]; JM Beattie, *Crime and the Courts in England 1660–1800* (Princeton UP, Princeton 1986) 342–343, 345, 352. Additionally, putting the

stemming from the late fifteenth century was that counsel could be engaged to argue questions of law.[233] Though there was no rule barring the instruction of prosecuting counsel, this option until the early eighteenth century was only taken up in a few cases, amongst which were important state trials; the vast majority of felony prosecutions were conducted by the accuser himself.[234] Important state trials included those for treason in the 1680s, from which arose particular concern regarding, inter alia, the advantage enjoyed by the Crown in engaging counsel against the unassisted accused whose life was at stake.[235] Addressing this inequality of arms, the Treason Act 1696 introduced a right to defence counsel in cases of high treason.[236] Accompanying this right was an entitlement to a copy of the indictment at least five days before trial,[237] and in 1708 it was enacted that the accused be supplied the indictment and a list of the jury and prosecution witnesses ten days before trial,[238] thereby enabling more effective defence preparation. Outside of treason cases, it was with a view to more effective prosecution of felonies that the 1730s witnessed the increasing engagement of prosecuting counsel at trial.[239] This development, coupled with solicitors having been increasingly employed in the pre-trial phase to build and manage prosecutions, created a prosecutorial advantage which judges attempted to counterbalance in the 1730s by beginning to allow defendants to instruct counsel to examine and cross-examine witnesses.[240] Though the appearance of defence counsel became commonplace by the late eighteenth century,[241] it was not until 1836 that the Prisoners' Counsel Act secured for accused felons the right to a full defence by counsel, authorising the latter to not merely examine witnesses, but also to address the jury on the evidence.[242]

The involvement of defence counsel at trial after the early eighteenth century presented a stronger challenge to the factual accuracy of prosecution cases which, in turn, began shifting the onus of proof from the accused to the prosecution and encouraging a presumption of innocence.[243] Before this period, the mindset

---

accused in a position of having to speak without counsel's interference was, as Beattie observes, thought justified 'not merely as an aid to the court's discovery of the truth but as the means whereby the innocent prisoner might most readily exculpate himself' (353).

233 Coke (n 211) 29, 137; Blackstone (n 183) [355]; Plucknett (n 90) 434–435.

234 Beattie (n 232) 353.

235 Ibid 357–358; Langbein (n 231) 317.

236 S 1. Reprinted in Williams (n 214) 53. On the origins of the Act, see AH Shapiro, 'Political Theory and the Growth of Defensive Safeguards in Criminal Procedure: The Origins of the Treason Trials Act of 1696' (1993) 11 Law & Hist Rev 215.

237 Treason Act 1696 s 1.

238 An Act for Improving the Union of the Two Kingdoms 1708 s 11. Reprinted in Raithby (n 215) vol 7, 52–53.

239 Beattie (n 232) 354–356, 359.

240 Langbein (n 231) 317–321, 325–329, 332–338, 347–356, 360–364.

241 Beattie (n 232) 361.

242 Langbein (n 231) 318.

243 Beattie (n 232) 375.

within the courts was such that once prosecution evidence had been presented, the emphasis lay on the accused to satisfactorily prove himself innocent.[244] This attitude was at least accompanied by an understanding, evidenced by Hale in the seventeenth century and Blackstone in the mid-eighteenth century, that presumptive evidence against the accused should be admitted cautiously since it would be better that five[245] or even ten[246] guilty persons escape unpunished than one innocent person be condemned. Although the late eighteenth century saw the notion being articulated that the accused ought to be actively treated as innocent until convicted, only in the nineteenth century with the increasing involvement of defence counsel did the notion become firmly established.[247] In 1811, for example, jurors were urged to heed the axiom '[e]very man is presumed to be innocent till he has clearly been proved to be guilty; the onus of the proof of guilt lies therefore on the accuser, and no man is bound, required, or expected to prove his own innocency.'[248] In *McKinley's Case* in 1817, Lord Gillies responded emphatically to the prosecutor's denial of the existence of a presumption of innocence:

> I cannot listen to this. I conceive that this presumption is to be found in every code of law which has reason and religion and humanity for a foundation. It is a maxim which ought to be inscribed in indelible characters in the heart of every judge and juryman, and I was happy to hear from Lord Hermand he is inclined to give full effect to it. To overturn this, there must be legal evidence of guilt, carrying home a degree of conviction short only of absolute certainty.[249]

These early nineteenth century acknowledgements of the existence of the presumption of innocence were reinforced in 1890 by Stephen, who observed that the presumption pervaded the whole administration of the criminal law and implied that 'the commission of a crime … must be proved beyond all reasonable doubt. The burden of proving that any person has been guilty of a crime … is on the person who asserts it'.[250]

---

244 Ibid 341, 349.

245 M Hale and S Emlyn (ed), *The History of the Pleas of the Crown* (E and R Nutt and R Gosling, London 1736) vol 2, 289.

246 Blackstone (n 183) [358].

247 Beattie (n 232) 341, 349, 375.

248 R Phillips, *On the Powers and Duties of Juries, and on the Criminal Laws of England* (2nd edn Sherwood, Neely and Jones, London 1813) 385 r 6. See also, to similar effect, Lord Campbell's charge to the jury in A Bennett, *The Queen v Palmer: Verbatim Report of the Trial of William Palmer at the Central Criminal Court, Old Bailey, London, May 14, and Following Days, 1856* (J Allen, London 1856) 307–308, 324.

249 (1817) 33 State Tr 275, 506 cited in *Coffin* (n 64) 457 (White J). See also W Forsyth, *Hortensius: or, The Advocate: An Historical Essay* (J Murray, London 1849) 367, who describes the presumption of innocence as a 'maxim of our law'.

250 JF Stephen, *A General View of the Criminal Law of England* (2nd edn Macmillan, London 1890) 183.

The treatment of the presumption of innocence as an active doctrine and all the other above-mentioned adjustments effected to safeguard the accused represent a gradual evolution in the standard of procedural fairness in jury trials. For a long period, the process of trial by jury remained heavily weighted against the defendant, whose 'vulnerability in court was calculated to reveal truth.'[251] This process, however, underwent a crucial and progressive transformation in the eighteenth and nineteenth centuries, whereby the jury itself came to be viewed as a bulwark of liberty[252] and the greater opportunities for defence decreased significantly the imbalances between the parties. A prominent catalyst for this reform appears to have been the disaffection in the late seventeenth century stemming from the procedural unfairness associated with politically charged treason trials.[253]

3.7. FRENCH NAPOLEONIC CODE OF CRIMINAL PROCEDURE 1808

The standard of procedural fairness exhibited by English jury trials in the eighteenth century contrasted favourably with the inquisitorial procedure of the 1670 Ordinance and, consequently, served as an inspirational model for radical reform of French criminal procedure at a time of political upheaval. The standard of procedural fairness associated with the Ordinance in the eighteenth century bred philosophic discontentment[254] and provoked wider appeals for reform disseminated principally through a series of influential memorials,[255] and the Revolution of 1789 provided fertile ground for the implementation of a more liberal procedure. Consequently, both the Law of 16 September 1791 – which introduced in France the inquisitorial form of trial by jury – and its more precise and expansive replacement, the Code of Offences and Punishments 1795, increased defence safeguards and the orality of the proceedings.[256] However, revolution-induced social instability attracted a far-reaching plague of criminality which the new procedure could not effectively repress.[257] As part of the effort to restore social order, the level of protection for accused persons was reduced in certain respects through the Law of 7th Pluviôse Year IX (27 January 1801), which revived the secret character of the preliminary examination in

251 Shapiro (n 236) 222.

252 Eg Blackstone (n 183) [349]; Phillips (n 248) 1.

253 Beattie (n 232) 357.

254 Esmein (n 97) 362–369. Voltaire, for example, in a philosophic movement also headed by Montesquieu and Beccaria, argued that the Ordinance 'seems on several points to have been directed only towards the destruction of those accused. … Should it not be as favourable to the innocent as it is terrible to the guilty?' (365).

255 Ibid 382–390.

256 Ibid 408–419, 426–435, 507–508.

257 Ibid 437, 447–451.

the Ordinance, whereby witnesses were heard secretly and the accused was interrogated without being properly informed, at the outset, of the witness evidence and accusations against him.[258]

In the light of all the aforementioned legislation, it is unsurprising that the Napoleonic Code of Criminal Procedure 1808 ('Code')[259] was intended to secure correct outcomes through a compromised blend of pre-revolutionary and revolutionary procedure. Not only did it remain in force with amendments until 1958 and serve as an influential model for much of the criminal procedure worldwide[260] but, having already discussed the position of the accused in the 1670 Ordinance, it is instructive to chart the next seminal stage in the evolution of French trial procedure for serious crimes.

In the Code, the preliminary examination to determine whether there was a case to answer bore a strong resemblance to the pre-revolutionary procedure of the Ordinance. The accused was, nonetheless, provided the safeguard of a prompt hearing; following a summons or a warrant, he was to appear before the *juge d'instruction* (investigating magistrate) at once or within 24 hours respectively.[261] Other aspects of the procedure, however, placed the accused in a weak position. The magistrate, searching for and scrutinising incriminatory and exculpatory evidence with equal conviction, first summoned witnesses familiar with the circumstances of the alleged offence to be heard secretly without the accused being present.[262] The latter was also interrogated in secret by the magistrate and was not entitled, unless judicial discretion was applied, to be informed of the charges, or see any witness statements or other evidence against him.[263] This interrogation could take place as often as required and the magistrate had a discretionary power to place the accused in solitary confinement indefinitely during the examination period.[264] Thus, whilst torture had been abolished in the 1780s, it had been replaced by another means of inducing the accused to cooperate. He could also neither call his own witnesses, unless judicial discretion was exercised, nor challenge court-appointed expert witnesses.[265] Written submissions to the magistrate could be made but there was no right to representation.[266] Essentially, therefore, the preliminary examination was a procedure tainted by secrecy, where only the prosecuting authority was

---

258 Ibid 439–440, 508.

259 Reproduced in JP Doucet, '*Code d'Instruction Criminelle de 1808*' (Le Droit Criminel) <http://ledroitcriminel.fr/la_legislation_criminelle/anciens_textes/code_instruction_criminelle_1808.htm>.

260 J Hatchard, B Huber and R Vogler (eds), *Comparative Criminal Procedure* (BIICL, London 1996) 8–9. Belgium is an apt example.

261 Stephen (n 78) 531.

262 Ibid.

263 Esmein (n 97) 507–508; Stephen (n 78) 533–534.

264 Stephen (n 78) 533.

265 Esmein (n 97) 505–506.

266 Stephen (n 78) 533–534.

familiar with the evidence, and the standard of fairness applied was at the mercy of judicial discretion.

An important amendment to the examination was made eventually in respect of legal assistance. By the Law of 8 December 1897, the accused could have or be assigned counsel.[267] Counsel was permitted to communicate freely with his client, familiarise himself with the case documents before any interrogation and be present therein, though he could only address the bench when authorised to do so.[268]

If the accused was not discharged by the investigating magistrate, the Napoleonic Code required him to undergo a further preliminary stage involving the *Chambre d'Accusation* (Chamber of Indictment), rather than a grand jury. Consisting of at least five judges, the purpose of the Chamber was to consider, independently of the investigating magistrate, whether the accused should be discharged or tried.[269] Having perused the case bundle from the investigating magistrate, the *procureur-général* (Attorney-General) made a verbal or written report to the Chamber detailing his recommendations.[270] Only he appeared before the Chamber, though not during its deliberations; the accused, the civil party and witnesses were never confronted or examined.[271] The accused was allowed to provide written submissions, and the Chamber could inform itself of the written evidence in the case and order further inquiries.[272] It was thus the written word, rather than orality, that dominated the Chamber's decision-making. If trial was considered justified, the subsequent indictment was communicated to the accused, allowing him to finally become fully aware of the nature and cause of the accusation.[273] The Chamber's role in the preliminary phase of proceedings, however, was not to last; the Law of 17 July 1856 gave the investigating magistrate sole responsibility for determining whether the case ought to be referred to trial.[274]

It is in the subsequent procedure of the Code, beginning with an intermediate transitional stage, that a higher standard of procedural fairness begins to emerge. Within 24 hours of being notified of the indictment, the accused was transferred to the courthouse.[275] Within 24 hours of his arrival, he faced judicial questioning, during which he could air any complaints and was to be advised of his right to challenge the validity of the proceedings before the Court of Cassation.[276] Thereafter, the accused could confer freely with counsel and, if he

267 Esmein (n 97) 555.
268 Ibid.
269 Stephen (n 78) 536–537.
270 Ibid 536.
271 Ibid; Esmein (n 97) 509.
272 Stephen (n 78) 536.
273 Ibid 537–538.
274 Esmein (n 97) 541.
275 Ibid 511.
276 Ibid.

did not have representation, counsel was assigned by the court, a practice not mirrored in England at that time.[277] Furthermore, there was full disclosure, entitling the defence to copies of all case documents, official reports and witness statements.[278] By allowing disclosure and engagement of counsel, the intermediate stage recognised that a prepared defence would render the ensuing trial more conducive to reaching a correct outcome.

At the trial before the Assize Court, the outcome was decided by jury. The institution of the jury was thought during the Revolution to reflect democratic ideals.[279] From a general list of qualifying individuals, a panel of at least 30 jurymen was convened, the identities of whom were disclosed to the defendant a day before trial.[280] Their names were randomly drawn at trial and the defendant could exercise his right of challenge until 12 jurors remained,[281] the aim being to secure an independent and impartial decision-making body. Whereas jurors were solely judges of fact in both the Code and nineteenth century English criminal procedure, French juries differed in that the lesser protection of a mere majority verdict, rather than unanimity, was considered sufficient for conviction.[282]

The mere majority verdict could be influenced heavily by the president of the court. Rather than acting as umpire between opposing parties, the president, accompanied by associate judges, played a more active role and could interrogate defendants himself at trial.[283] Although impartiality was requisite in judges, a balanced judicial interrogation of the defendant could not be assured in practice, especially when seen in the light of many trial reports which suggested that defendants were 'cross-examined with the utmost severity, and with continual rebukes, sarcasms, and exhortations'.[284] The president also performed a summing up after the parties' cases concluded, reminding the jury of the main evidence for and against the defendant.[285] This summing up ought to have been impartial but was not always formulated in an even-handed and impartial manner, a consequence of the president having interrogated the defendant himself.[286] The potential scope for impartiality to be compromised in

---

277 Ibid.

278 Ibid 511–512.

279 JM Donovan, *Juries and the Transformation of Criminal Justice in France in the Nineteenth and Twentieth Centuries* (North Carolina UP, Chapel Hill 2010) 28. Donovan provides a useful account of the development of the French jury in its foundational period 1791–1814 in ch 1.

280 Stephen (n 78) 540.

281 Ibid 540–541.

282 Esmein (n 97) 513.

283 Stephen (n 78) 543. The Law of 4 March 1831 eventually reduced the number of accompanying judges from four to two: Donovan (n 279) 56.

284 Stephen (n 78) 543.

285 Ibid 553.

286 Ibid 544, 553; Esmein (n 97) 534.

the president's summing up appears to have been acknowledged by the Law of 19 June 1881, which abolished his right to perform it.[287]

Accompanying the impartiality requirement under the Code were certain other important defence safeguards at trial. The secrecy associated with the preliminary examination was not replicated at trial, which was held in public.[288] Defence counsel could also fully represent his client at the hearing.[289] A list of witnesses appearing at trial was to be supplied to the accused at least 24 hours beforehand,[290] though, as mentioned above, witness statements had been disclosed earlier at the intermediate stage. Whilst there was scope for a written witness statement or part thereof to be read out at the hearing, and for other case documentation to be submitted to the jury, the trial maintained an oral character, relying strongly on the evidence of witnesses appearing and testifying in court.[291] Witnesses could be called for the defence but direct examinations of them and prosecution witnesses were generally the preserve of the president; the defence, like the civil party, could nevertheless question a witness through the medium of the president.[292]

Such safeguards within the Code for those accused of serious crimes thus provided a standard of procedural fairness at trial that contrasted significantly from that at the preliminary stages. The influence of the 1670 Ordinance certainly impressed itself upon the preliminary examination and the proceedings before the *Chambre d'Accusation*, both of which restricted severely the opportunities for defence and kept the accused largely uninformed of the case against him. However, the progressive post-revolutionary spirit for implementing a higher standard of procedural fairness to secure correct outcomes took firm hold after the interrogation at the intermediate stage and continued into the trial. This spirit was manifested in the entitlement of defendants to mount a full, informed and legally assisted defence, and to call and examine witnesses, before a court mandated to maintain a public, oral and impartial character.

4. DEVELOPMENTS AT CONSTITUTIONAL LEVEL

The historical development in Western legal systems of procedural rights for the accused, which hold some resemblance to those contained in Article 6, was not preoccupied exclusively with securing correct trial outcomes. Certain of these rights also developed to become associated with instruments of constitutional significance, elevating their status to that of constitutional requirements.

287 Ibid respectively 544; 534.
288 Esmein (n 97) 510–511.
289 Ibid 511; Stephen (n 78) 541, 549–552.
290 Stephen (n 78) 544.
291 Esmein (n 97) 510, 514–515, 534–535 and accompanying fn 2.
292 Stephen (n 78) 547.

This constitutional status testifies that an 'added value' was attached to the protection of those rights, as compared to simply common law or ordinary statutory rights.[293] It also implies that sustaining an acceptable standard of procedural fairness, to which those rights contribute, was recognised as being of fundamental importance to achieving some form of good governance. Procedural fairness is important to good governance because it reflects the state's respect for the rule of law and effort to secure a societal perception of criminal process legitimacy. Indeed, a perceived lack of procedural fairness may contribute strongly to inducing the disaffected to resort to rebellion against the existing government.

4.1. MAGNA CARTA

It was with the intention of placating the open revolt arising from baronial grievances against the King of England that Magna Carta – a statement guaranteeing certain rights and liberties of free subjects of the realm – was first issued in 1215.[294] The Charter was a constitutional document in two important respects. First, it was treated as fundamental law. It was looked upon as 'different from the common law although it guaranteed it, and superior to statute law although it was itself an enactment',[295] and became 'a sacred text, the nearest approach to an irrepealable "fundamental statute" that England has ever had.'[296] In particular, it was implicitly evident that the Charter was assumed to be fundamental law not only because it 'was used as a yardstick of legality against which new measures could be assessed, and accepted or rejected', but also because 'the sense of the Charter was repeatedly re-interpreted to ensure that it conformed to new social and political conditions'.[297] Second, the Charter was a proclamation of the principle that a ruler, and thus the state, is subordinate to the rule of law.[298] This commitment to government bound by law was a foundation stone of constitutional government[299] and signalled to the governed

293 *Allie Mohammed v The State* [1999] 2 AC 111 (PC) 123 (Lord Steyn).

294 Reissued and revised in 1216, 1217 and 1225, Magna Carta became statute law in 1297. Definitive 1297 text reprinted in M Evans and RI Jack, *Sources of English Legal and Constitutional History* (Butterworths, Sydney 1984) 51–55.

295 RL Mott, *Due Process of Law: A Historical and Analytical Treatise of the Principles and Methods Followed by the Courts in the Application of the Concept of the "Law of the Land"* (Bobbs-Merrill, Indianapolis 1926) 45.

296 Pollock and Maitland (n 178) 173.

297 JC Holt, *Magna Carta* (2nd edn CUP, Cambridge 1992) 14.

298 Ibid 338; Pollock and Maitland (n 178) 173.

299 I Jennings, *Magna Carta and its Influence in the World Today* (HMSO, London 1965) 15. See also GB Adams, *The Origin of the English Constitution* (2nd edn Yale UP, New Haven 1920) 244: 'the steady development of the limited monarchy and constitutional government … dates from Magna Carta'; WS Holdsworth, *A History of English Law* (3rd edn Methuen, London 1923) vol 2, 210 ('the Charter was regarded as the pledge and the symbol [of constitutional

the intention to respect their rights and liberties. Lord Denning thus venerated the Charter as 'the greatest constitutional document of all times – the foundation of freedom of the individual against the arbitrary authority of the despot.'[300]

Its chapter 29[301] was directed specifically at addressing grievances stemming from acts sanctioned by the King against accused persons, including disseisins, outlawries, and arrests and imprisonments, without lawful or any judicial process:

> No free man shall be taken or imprisoned or disseised of his freehold, liberties or free customs or outlawed or exiled or in any way ruined, nor will we go or send against him, except by the lawful judgement of his peers or by the law of the land. To no one will we sell, to no one will we deny or delay right or justice.

At its heart, the clause was a rule that lawful judgement must first be rendered against the accused before carrying out on behalf of the Crown any punitive action against his person or property. Judgement by peers or by the law of the land have been interpreted convincingly by Powicke as non-rigid alternatives.[302] The latter entailed being judged by some process other than that involving a judgement of peers[303] which was consonant with the established laws and customs of England[304] (the law of the land). Its broad scope thus comprehended, for example, the process of trial by combat or the process of outlawry if an accused was formally charged and failed to appear in person before the court.[305] Judgement by peers referred to a distinct proceeding in which judgement was

government]'), 216; Lord Irvine, 'The Spirit of Magna Carta Continues to Resonate in Modern Law' (2003) 119 LQR 227, 230: 'Magna Carta emerged as the rock upon which the constitution would gradually be built and the fulcrum upon which the constitutional balance would be struck'; Lord Woolf and C Campbell-Holt (ed), *The Pursuit of Justice* (OUP, Oxford 2008) 108: 'Magna Carta … has played the most critical role in developing our form of democratic government subject to the rule of law.'

300 Cited in SF Wiltshire, *Greece, Rome, and the Bill of Rights* (Oklahoma UP, Norman 1992) 56.

301 Ch 29 (1297) was originally chs 39–40 (1215).

302 FM Powicke, 'Per Judicium Parium vel per Legem Terrae' in HE Malden (ed), *Magna Carta Commemoration Essays* (Royal Historical Society, London 1917) 99. This interpretation is supported by Holt (n 297) 328.

Contrast WS McKechnie, *Magna Carta: A Commentary on the Great Charter of King John* (J Maclehose, Glasgow 1914) 379, 381–382 and accompanying fn 3, 391, 393, who argues that the terms 'judgement by peers' and 'law of the land' must be combined. The peers, he suggests, appointed a mode of trial that was in accordance with the law of the land (battle, ordeal or compurgation), presided over it as umpires and delivered the final judgement. This view relies on construing the word '*vel*', which connects the two terms in their original form ('*per legale judicium parium suorum vel per legem terrae*'), as 'and'. It may, however, also be translated legitimately as 'or' or as 'and/or': Holdsworth (n 173) 61; RV Turner, *Magna Carta* (Pearson Education, Harlow 2003) 72.

303 Powicke (n 302) 97, 100–103.

304 CH McIlwain, 'Due Process of Law in Magna Carta' (1914) 14 Colum L Rev 27, 49; P Vinogradoff, 'Magna Carta, C. 39: Nullus Liber Homo, etc' in Malden (n 302) 84.

305 Powicke (n 302) 100–101, 105–107; Holdsworth (n 173) 62.

delivered by men equal to the accused in social status;[306] 'the king's justices are no peers for earls or barons.'[307] This proceeding was not synonymous with trial by jury,[308] which was still in its infant stage in the thirteenth century[309] and 'was exactly what the barons did not want.'[310] It was the normal form of trial in many cases, including those before the *Curia Regis* (King's Court), and was particularly desirable in cases of alleged treason and felony[311] or when the accused was of some importance.[312] Its role, however, was not only that of an alternative in some circumstances to judgement by the law of the land. It was also employed as an ultimate resort in cases where judgement by the law of the land had failed to deliver justice or resolve an uncertainty in the law.[313] The law of the land was the law that peers were duty bound to observe in rendering judgement.[314] The free men upon whom the protection of judgement by peers or by the law of the land was conferred in 1215 were free tenants (freeholders);[315] only in 1354 did 'free man' become construed as any man, irrespective of estate or condition.[316] In addition, a free man could only rely on this protection in a case concerning the Crown, not when he was the subject of a private prosecution.[317]

Chapter 29, on account of the term 'the law of the land', has long been associated with the concept of due process of law, most notably by Coke in the seventeenth century.[318] Due process is formed of two parts: substantive and procedural. The substantive part requires the substantive law to be upheld and correctly applied, and implies limitations on the state, stemming from its

306 McIlwain (n 304) 43; McKechnie (n 302) 377–379; Holt (n 297) 328.

307 Pollock and Maitland (n 178) 173.

308 Ibid 173 fn 3; LO Pike, *A Constitutional History of the House of Lords from Original Sources* (Macmillan, London 1894) 169–170; McIlwain (n 304) 31, 43; McKechnie (n 302) 134, 138, 392–393; W Clark, 'Magna Carta and Trial by Jury' (1924) 58 Am L Rev 24.

309 Ch 1 text to n 180; Holdsworth (n 299) 215; Holt (n 297) 10.

310 Holdsworth (n 173) 59. See also McKechnie (n 302) 393: 'The barons would have repudiated trial by jury if they had known it.'

311 Pike (n 308) 173.

312 Powicke (n 302) 99–100, 102, 120.

313 Ibid 107, 120.

314 Ibid 102; McIlwain (n 304) 50.

315 McKechnie (n 302) 115 and accompanying fn 2; Powicke (n 302) 109–110; Vinogradoff (n 304) 80–81.

316 Statute of 28 Edward III (1354) ch 3. Reprinted in AJ Wood (ed), *The Statutes: Revised Edition* (Eyre & Spottiswoode, London 1870) vol 1, 196. See also F Thompson, *Magna Carta: Its Role in the Making of the English Constitution 1300–1629* (Minnesota UP, Minneapolis 1948) 69, 92.

317 Pike (n 308) 217; McKechnie (n 302) 382.

318 E Coke, *The Second Part of the Institutes of the Laws of England* (6th edn W Rawlins, London 1681) 50. 'The law of the land' was first equated with 'due process of law' in the fourteenth century: Statute of 28 Edward III (1354) ch 3; Thompson (n 316) 69, 92. See further Holdsworth (n 173) 61–63; Mott (n 295) 4–5; Holt (n 297) 10, 331. The terms were also regarded as equivalents in eighteenth and nineteenth century America: RE Riggs, 'Substantive Due Process in 1791' [1990] Wis L Rev 941, 950, 991–995. In respect of the nineteenth century, see also *Walker v Sauvinet* 92 US 90, 93 (1875); *Hurtado v California* 110 US 516, 535, 543, 551–553 (1884).

constitutional and political values, in respect of the type, authorship and content of the law it makes.[319] Substantive due process is implied in chapter 29: accused persons were to be treated in accordance with established law – the law of the land – and the Crown did not enjoy the legal authority to alter or violate this law at will.[320] The procedural part requires the state to adhere to certain procedures necessary for the fair treatment of persons.[321] The emergence of an embryonic sense of procedural due process is also discernible in the clause: accused persons were to be treated fairly to at least the extent that punitive action had to be preceded by a trial process that conformed to certain procedures established by the law of the land. Proper compliance with these procedures entailed respect for the defence safeguards implemented within them. Although the clause largely refrains from identifying any of these procedural safeguards, it does include expressly the safeguard of the right not to suffer delayed justice, implying that cases were to be tried without undue delay. The right is reflected in the Article 6(1) entitlement of an accused to a hearing within a reasonable time.[322]

Although the right is in itself important, for 'justice delayed is justice denied', the key importance of chapter 29 to the evolution of standards of protection for an accused remains that it was a germinal expression of the concept of due process in both a substantive and procedural sense. As such, the clause was fundamental in protecting the liberty and property of the accused from the arbitrary exercise of executive power and thereby bolstered the Charter's constitutional significance. The baronial framers of the clause were conscious, particularly amidst a climate of revolt, that binding the exercise of that power to the rule of law was a necessary prerequisite to some form of good governance and a perception of criminal process legitimacy.

4.2. AMERICAN AND FRENCH CONSTITUTIONAL INSTRUMENTS BORN OF REVOLUTION

More than five centuries after Magna Carta, certain safeguards for the accused were also prominently entrenched in constitutional instruments born of the American and French Revolutions of 1776 and 1789. Constitutionalising safeguards not only strongly precluded their arbitrary modification or repeal in the corpus of domestic law, but also limited in practice the scope of state action

319 DJ Galligan, *Due Process and Fair Procedures: A Study of Administrative Procedures* (Clarendon, Oxford 1996) 172–173.

320 Ibid 173.

321 Ibid 74, 172, 191. Procedural due process, now most readily associated with the American constitutional tradition, is an early English common law predecessor to the wider concept of procedural fairness (73–74, 170–171, 189).

322 Irvine (n 299) 242–243. See further *Klopfer v North Carolina* 386 US 213, 223 (1967), where the US Supreme Court traced the right to a speedy trial in the Sixth Amendment to Magna Carta ch 29.

against an accused, including to such an extent as could serve to protect him against even 'the tyranny of the majority'.[323] This bulwark of protection for the accused reflected a strong commitment to the rule of law and to developing a public perception of criminal process legitimacy, a commitment that was essential if some form of good governance was to be secured by the American and French peoples.

Before turning to France, it falls first to highlight certain American constitutional developments in safeguarding the accused. The American constitutional experience is relevant not only because it was a particularly influential source of inspiration for constitution makers across the world,[324] but also because it contributed to forging the Anglo-American legal and philosophical tradition which, in turn, helped shape the Western liberal legal and philosophical tradition, the dominant influence[325] in the framing of the UDHR and ICCPR. In the background to the Anglo-American perspective stands the legacy of Magna Carta, which was highly influential to the American constitutional experience of limiting the power of the legislative, executive and judicial authorities.[326] The influence of its chapter 29, in particular, was discernible in equivalent law of the land or due process clauses in colonial legislative enactments of the seventeenth century[327] and in the late eighteenth

---

323 The term refers to a situation whereby the societal majority operates through the acts of the state authorities to deliberately oppress individuals or minorities: JS Mill, *On Liberty* (2nd edn Ticknor and Fields, Boston 1863) 13. See also A Hamilton, 'On Maintaining a Just Partition of Power Among the Necessary Departments' in A Hamilton, J Jay and J Madison, *The Federalist* (The Colonial Press, New York 1901) No L 287, who emphasised the 'importance in a republic not only to guard the society against the oppression of its rulers, but to guard one part of the society against the injustice of the other part.'

324 AP Blaustein, 'Our Most Important Export: The Influence of the United States Constitution Abroad' (1987) 3 Conn J Int'l L 15, 16–24; DS Law and M Versteeg, 'The Declining Influence of the United States Constitution' (2012) 87 NYU L Rev 762, 764–766.

325 MG Johnson, 'A Magna Carta for Mankind: Writing the Universal Declaration of Human Rights' in MG Johnson and J Symonides (eds), *The Universal Declaration of Human Rights: A History of its Creation and Implementation 1948–1998* (UNESCO, Paris 1998) 39–40, 42–48; M Mutua, *Human Rights: A Political and Cultural Critique* (Pennsylvania UP, Philadelphia 2002) 154; S Joseph and M Castan, *The International Covenant on Civil and Political Rights: Cases, Materials, and Commentary* (3rd edn OUP, Oxford 2013) 4–7.

326 HD Hazeltine, 'The Influence of Magna Carta on American Constitutional Development' in Malden (n 302) 180–226. See further AED Howard, *The Road from Runnymede: Magna Carta and Constitutionalism in America* (Virginia UP, Charlottesville 1968).

327 Eg Maryland Act for the Liberties of the People 1638: Inhabitants 'Shall not be imprisoned nor disseised or dispossessed of their freehold goods or Chattels or be out Lawed Exiled or otherwise destroyed fore judged or punished then according to the Laws of this province'; Massachusetts Body of Liberties 1641 Art 1: 'No mans life shall be taken away, ... no mans person shall be arested, restrayned, banished, dismembred, nor any wayes punished, ... no mans goods or estaite shall be taken away from him ... unlesse it be by vertue or equitie of some expresse law of the Country warranting the same'; Rhode Island Acts and Orders of 1647: 'no person, in this Colonie, shall be taken or imprisoned, or be disseized of his Lands or Liberties, or be Exiled, or any other otherwise molested or destroyed, but by the Lawfull judgment of his Peeres, or by some known Law'; Connecticut Code of Laws 1650 (almost identical wording to

century state[328] and federal[329] constitutions born of the revolutionary struggle for independence. Nevertheless, the state and federal constitutions went

---

that of Massachusetts); the Charter or Fundamental Laws of West New Jersey 1676 ch XVII: 'no Proprietor, freeholder or inhabitant … shall be deprived or condemned of life, limb, liberty, estate, property or any ways hurt in his or their privileges, freedoms or franchises, upon any account whatsoever, without a due tryal, and Judgment passed by twelve good and lawful men of his neighborhood first had'; New York Charter of Liberties and Privileges 1683: 'Noe freeman shall be taken and imprisoned or be disseized of his ffreehold or Libertye or ffree Customes or be outlawed or Exiled or any other wayes destroyed nor shall be passed upon adjudged or condemned But by the Lawfull Judgment of his peers and by the Law of this province'; Act Declaring Rights and Privileges of Subjects of East New Jersey 1698 (very similar wording to that of New York). Reprinted in A Leaming and J Spicer (eds), *The Grants, Concessions, and Original Constitutions of the Province of New Jersey* (2nd edn Honeyman, Somerville 1881) 371 (East New Jersey), 395 (West New Jersey); DS Lutz (ed), *Colonial Origins of the American Constitution: A Documentary History* (Liberty Fund, Indianapolis 1998) docs 22 (Massachusetts), 39 (Rhode Island), 52 (Connecticut), 56 (New York), 67 (Maryland).

328 Maryland Declaration of Rights 1776 Art XXI: 'no freeman ought to be taken, or imprisoned, or disseized of his freehold, liberties, or privileges, or outlawed, or exiled, or in any manner destroyed, or deprived of his life, liberty, or property, but by the judgment of his peers, or by the law of the land'; North Carolina Declaration of Rights 1776 Art XII: 'no freeman ought to be taken, imprisoned, or disseized of his freehold, liberties or privileges, or outlawed, or exiled, or in any manner destroyed, or deprived of his life, liberty, or property, but by the law of the land'; Pennsylvania Declaration of Rights 1776 Art IX: 'nor can any man be justly deprived of his liberty except by the laws of the land, or the judgment of his peers'; Virginia Bill of Rights 1776 s 8 (very similar wording to that of Pennsylvania); New York Constitution 1777 Art XIII: 'no member of this State shall be disfranchised, or deprived of any the rights or privileges secured to the subjects of this State by this constitution, unless by the law of the land, or the judgment of his peers'; Vermont Declaration of Rights 1777 Art X (identical wording to that of Pennsylvania); South Carolina Constitution 1778 Art XLI (almost identical wording to that of Maryland); Massachusetts Declaration of Rights 1780 Art XII: 'no subject shall be arrested, imprisoned, despoiled, or deprived of his property, immunities, or privileges, put out of the protection of the law, exiled, or deprived of his life, liberty, or estate, but by the judgment of his peers, or the law of the land'; New Hampshire Bill of Rights 1784 Art XV (identical wording to that of Massachusetts); Delaware Constitution 1792 Art I s 7: 'nor shall [he] be deprived of life, liberty, or property, unless by the judgment of his peers or the law of the land'; Kentucky Constitution 1792 Art XII [10] (almost identical wording to that of Delaware); Tennessee Declaration of Rights 1796 s 8 (almost identical wording to that of Maryland). Reprinted in FN Thorpe (ed), *The Federal and State Constitutions, Colonial Charters, and Other Organic Laws of the States, Territories, and Colonies Now or Heretofore Forming the United States of America* (Government Printing Office, Washington 1909) vol 1, 569 (Delaware); vol 3, 1275 (Kentucky), 1688 (Maryland), 1891 (Massachusetts); vol 4, 2455 (New Hampshire); vol 5, 2632 (New York), 2788 (North Carolina), 3083 (Pennsylvania); vol 6, 3257 (South Carolina), 3422 (Tennessee), 3741 (Vermont); vol 7, 3813 (Virginia).

329 Fifth Amendment 1791 to the US Constitution 1787: 'No person shall be … deprived of life, liberty, or property, without due process of law'. In *Murray's Lessee v Hoboken Land & Improvement Co* 59 US 272, 276 (1856), the US Supreme Court opined that '[t]he words, "due process of law" were undoubtedly intended to convey the same meaning as the words "by the law of the land," in Magna Charta' (Curtis J). See also n 318. A similar clause, directed against state rather than federal government action, was adopted in s 1 of the Fourteenth Amendment 1868: 'No state shall … deprive any person of life, liberty, or property, without due process of law'. The term 'due process of law' was ascribed the same meaning in both amendments: *Malinski v New York* 324 US 401, 415 (1945) (Frankfurter J Concurring Op). Amendments reprinted in Thorpe (n 328) vol 1, 29 (Fifth), 31 (Fourteenth).

further than chapter 29 by also incorporating expressly a number of other specific safeguards. A notable example was the Bill of Rights in the Virginia Constitution 1776 – 'the first true Bill of Rights in the modern American sense'[330] – which specified for the accused the rights to demand the cause and nature of his accusation, to confront accusers and witnesses, to call for evidence in his favour, to a speedy trial before an impartial jury, and to not be compelled to give evidence against himself.[331] It proved to be an influential model,[332] for other states subsequently included all or several of these or similar rights in their revolutionary constitutions, though specified additionally the rights to counsel and/or to a public trial, and/or to protection from double jeopardy.[333] Virginia's Bill of Rights was, furthermore, an influential precursor to the national Bill of Rights 1791,[334] which contained the first ten amendments to the federal Constitution 1787, the latter marking the establishment of a new political order in the United States. While the Fifth Amendment accompanied its due process clause with prohibitions against double jeopardy and compelled self-incrimination, the Sixth Amendment secured for the accused the rights to a speedy and public trial, to an impartial jury, to be informed of the nature and cause of the charge, to confront witnesses against him, to call witnesses in his favour, and to have legal representation.

Two years before the ratification of these amendments, the French had adopted their own bill of rights as an early step in their revolutionary movement. The Declaration of the Rights of Man and of Citizens 1789[335] was an enunciation of the natural rights of the individual and of the foundational principles of the

---

330 B Schwartz, *The Great Rights of Mankind: A History of the American Bill of Rights* (Rowman & Littlefield, Lanham 1992) 67.

331 S 8. Reprinted in Thorpe (n 328) vol 7, 3813.

332 RA Rutland, *The Birth of the Bill of Rights, 1776–1791* (North Carolina UP, Chapel Hill 1955) 48; RC Pittman, Book Review (1960) 68 Va Mag Hist & Biog 109, 110–111; JE Selby, *The Revolution in Virginia, 1775–1783* (Colonial Williamsburg, Williamsburg 2007) 103.

333 Maryland Declaration of Rights 1776 Arts XIX–XX (counsel included); North Carolina Declaration of Rights 1776 Arts VII, IX (public trial included); Pennsylvania Declaration of Rights 1776 Art IX (counsel and public trial included); Vermont Declaration of Rights 1777 Art X (counsel and public trial included); Massachusetts Declaration of Rights 1780 Arts XII, XXIX (counsel included); New Hampshire Bill of Rights 1784 Arts XV–XVII (counsel and double jeopardy included); Delaware Constitution 1792 Art I ss 7–8 (counsel, public trial and double jeopardy included); Kentucky Constitution 1792 Art XII [10], [12] (counsel, public trial and double jeopardy included); Tennessee Declaration of Rights 1796 ss 9–10 (counsel, public trial and double jeopardy included). Reprinted in Thorpe (n 328) vol 1, 569 (Delaware); vol 3, 1274–1275 (Kentucky), 1688 (Maryland), 1891, 1893 (Massachusetts); vol 4, 2455–2456 (New Hampshire); vol 5, 2787 (North Carolina), 3083 (Pennsylvania); vol 6, 3422 (Tennessee), 3741 (Vermont).

334 Pittman (n 332) 111; JAL Lemay, 'John Mercer and the Stamp Act in Virginia, 1764–1765' (1983) 91 Va Mag Hist & Biog 3, 37; Wiltshire (n 300) 93; L Banning, *Jefferson and Madison: Three Conversations from the Founding* (Madison House, Lanham 1995) 104. US Bill of Rights reprinted in Thorpe (n 328) vol 1, 29–32.

335 Reprinted in T Paine, *The Rights of Man; Being an Answer to Mr Burke's Attack on the French Revolution* (Sherwin, London 1817) 65–67.

new political order: popular sovereignty (the will of the people is the source of legitimate political authority), the equality of all citizens, and the rule of law. It assumed the mantle of a constitutional instrument, for it was prefixed to the 1791 Constitution[336] and reaffirmed subsequently in the 1852, 1946 and 1958 Constitutions.[337] The significance of the Declaration was not confined merely to its deep entrenchment within the French legal and political tradition. As a significant articulation of liberal thinking on rights and freedoms, it also exerted a powerful influence on the introduction of similar bills of rights into most of the constitutions of the other European states in the nineteenth century.[338] Lord Acton thus observed that 'this single page of print ... outweighs libraries, and is stronger than all the armies of Napoleon'.[339] Furthermore, the Declaration was looked at as a precedent when the concept of an international bill of rights was being defined in 1947[340] and has been well acknowledged as a landmark document in the development towards the ECHR,[341] the creation of which was

336 Reprinted in National Constituent Assembly, *The French Constitution, Revised, Amended, and Finally Decreed, by the National Assembly* (W Young, Philadelphia 1791) 4–5.

337 1852 Constitution Art 1: 'The Constitution admits, confirms, and guarantees the great principles proclaimed in 1789, and which are the bases of the public rights of Frenchmen.' Reprinted in F Lieber, *On Civil Liberty and Self-Government* (Lippincott, Grambo and Co, Philadelphia 1853) vol 2, 310; 1946 Constitution Preamble: 'the people of France ... solemnly reaffirm the rights and freedoms of man and the citizen enshrined in the Declaration of Rights of 1789'. Reproduced in Conseil Constitutionnel, 'Preamble to the Constitution of 27 October 1946' <www.conseil-constitutionnel.fr/conseil-constitutionnel/english/constitution/preamble-to-the-constitution-of-27-october-1946.105306.html>; 1958 Constitution Preamble: 'The French people solemnly proclaim their attachment to the Rights of Man and the principles of national sovereignty as defined by the Declaration of 1789, confirmed and complemented by the Preamble to the Constitution of 1946'. Reproduced in Conseil Constitutionnel, 'Constitution of 4 October 1958' <www.conseil-constitutionnel.fr/conseil-constitutionnel/english/constitution/constitution-of-4-october-1958.25742.html>.

338 G Jellinek and M Farrand (tr), *The Declaration of the Rights of Man and of Citizens: A Contribution to Modern Constitutional History* (Holt and Co, New York 1901) 4–5.

339 JEE Dalberg-Acton; JN Figgis and RV Laurence (eds), *Lectures on the French Revolution* (Macmillan, London 1910) 107.

340 Johnson (n 325) 34. See also L Hunt, 'Introduction: The Revolutionary Origins of Human Rights' in L Hunt (ed) (tr), *The French Revolution and Human Rights: A Brief Documentary History* (Bedford/St Martin's, Boston 1996) 3: 'The framers of the UN declaration of 1948 closely followed the model established by the French Declaration of the Rights of Man and Citizen of 1789'.

341 Eg AH Robertson, *Human Rights in Europe* (Manchester UP, Manchester 1963) 177; US Congress, *The French Declaration of the Rights of Man and of the Citizen and the American Bill of Rights: A Bicentennial Commemoration Issued Pursuant to SJ Res 317, 100th Congress* (Government Printing Office, Washington 1989) 13; Árpád Göncz, opening ceremony speech in Council of Europe, *8th International Colloquy on the European Convention on Human Rights* (Council of Europe, Strasbourg 1996) 30; T Lansford, 'Declaration of the Rights of Man and of the Citizen' in G Fremont-Barnes (ed), *Encyclopedia of the Age of Political Revolutions and New Ideologies, 1760–1815* (Greenwood, Westport 2007) 194; RCA White and C Ovey, *Jacobs, White, & Ovey: The European Convention on Human Rights* (5th edn OUP, Oxford 2010) 3.

championed in 1949–1950 by, inter alia, France.[342] Interestingly, the Declaration itself bore the impress of the influence of the constitutional experience of the American states of the late eighteenth century. Collected translations of the constitutions of six states and of all thirteen states were published and circulated in France in 1778 and 1783 respectively,[343] thus before the outbreak of revolution. The example set by the bills of rights, or similar guarantees, in these state constitutions influenced the drafting of the Declaration,[344] a process which also involved some input from Founding Fathers Jefferson, Madison, Gouverneur Morris, Hamilton, Franklin and Thomas Paine.[345] Article 7 of the Declaration, in particular, bore a resemblance to the law of the land or due process clauses in these constitutions,[346] protecting accused persons against state action conducted outside the framework of a legal process and its safeguards: 'No man should be accused, arrested, or held in confinement, except in cases determined by the law, and according to the forms which it has prescribed.' Nevertheless, this influence was not such as to distract French drafters from enshrining in Article 9 the presumption of innocence, a principle which was not expressly laid down in the American state constitutions.

Articles 9 and 7 thus sat alongside the above-mentioned rights in the American instruments to represent progressive and influential developments in the Western constitutionalisation of fundamental safeguards for the accused against encroachments of governmental power. This constitutionalisation created a binding covenant between government and the governed that certain rights of accused persons would be respected as a matter of supreme law of the land. Whereas both American and French Revolutions had given due process a constitutional platform, it is from the American experience that one can discern stronger constitutional efforts to reduce the potential scope of procedural inequality between prosecution and defence, manifested through the rights

---

342 E Bates, *The Evolution of the European Convention on Human Rights: From its Inception to the Creation of a Permanent Court of Human Rights* (OUP, Oxford 2010) 78.

343 CA Régnier (ed), *Recueil des Loix Constitutives des Colonies Angloises, Confédérées sous la Dénomination d' États-Unis de l'Amérique-Septentrionale* (Cellot & Jombert, Paris 1778) 53–130 (Pennsylvania), 131–150 (New Jersey), 151–186 (Delaware), 187–257 (Maryland), 265–293 (Virginia), 294–323 (South Carolina); LA de La Rochefoucauld (tr), *Constitutions des Treize États-Unis de l'Amérique* (Pierres & Pissot, Paris 1783) 3–415.

344 Jellinek and Farrand (n 338) 18, 20, 25–43, 89; HE Bourne, 'American Constitutional Precedents in the French National Assembly' (1903) 8 Am Hist Rev 466, 473, 476; VR Johnson, 'The Declaration of the Rights of Man and of Citizens of 1789, the Reign of Terror, and the Revolutionary Tribunal of Paris' (1990) 13 BC Int'l & Comp L Rev 1, 9, 12–13, 35–45; RR Ludwikowski, 'The French Declaration of the Rights of Man and Citizen and the American Constitutional Development' (1990) 38 Am J Comp L Supp 445, 451–452, 453 fn 34, 457.

The influence, in particular, of Virginia's Bill of Rights has often been emphasised: eg Pittman (n 332) 110; Wiltshire (n 300) 91; AED Howard, 'The Values of Federalism' (1993) 1 New Eur L Rev 143, 143; Banning (n 334) 103–104; Selby (n 332) 103.

345 AP Blaustein, 'The Influence of the United States Constitution Abroad' (1987) 12 Okla City U L Rev 435, 451–452.

346 Ch 1 text to n 328.

to be informed of the nature and cause of the accusation, to confront adverse witnesses, to call defence witnesses, and to instruct counsel. In affording the accused this respect, both revolutions had sought to embrace the ideal of the rule of law and to enhance the perceived legitimacy of the criminal process in their efforts to achieve some form of good governance.

5. DEVELOPMENTS AT INTERNATIONAL LEVEL

Although the issue of trial safeguards for accused persons had long held much significance at national and constitutional levels, it was not until the aftermath of the Second World War that states were propelled into addressing with progressive and meaningful developments the issue at international level. The traditional assumption before the war was that procedural fairness in criminal proceedings was a matter that ought to belong exclusively within the domestic jurisdiction of states. Against the backdrop of the totalitarian atrocities committed on the eve of and during the war, however, came the curtailment of unfettered national sovereignty and the emergence of the modern human rights movement. In 1942, alongside Churchill's conviction that the war ought to end with the 'enthronement of human rights',[347] 26 state signatories to the Declaration by United Nations affirmed that victory over the Axis powers was essential to the preservation of 'human rights and justice' in their own and other lands.[348] In 1945, the Charter of the United Nations established that a fundamental purpose of the organisation was '[t]o achieve international cooperation in … promoting and encouraging respect for human rights and for fundamental freedoms for all'.[349] All UN members pledged under Articles 55(c) and 56 to take action to achieve 'universal respect for, and observance of, human rights and fundamental freedoms for all'. The Charter thus reflected a developing global determination, as part of a conflict and atrocity prevention agenda, 'to reaffirm faith in fundamental human rights, in the dignity and worth of the human person'.[350] Dignity – inherent in the human person and derived from his capacity as a rational and moral agent[351] – was now affirmed prominently at international level as a value that states should seek to protect and enhance through human rights. Accordingly, it underpinned the subsequent UDHR and ICCPR – whose fair trial provisions were, in their definitive or draft formulations, influential precursors to Article 6 – and the ECHR. Procedural

347 *The Times* (London, 30 October 1942) cited in H Lauterpacht, *International Law and Human Rights* (Archon, Hamden 1968) 78.

348 (Adopted and entered into force 1 January 1942) 204 LNTS 381. By 1945, 21 additional states had acceded to the Declaration.

349 (Adopted 26 June 1945, entered into force 24 October 1945) 1 UNTS 16 Art 1(3).

350 UN Charter Preamble.

351 'Dignity' is defined more fully in Ch 2 s 2.2.

fairness had therefore become, after the war, more than a contributor to correct outcomes or to good governance; it also reflected respect in international law for inherent human dignity.

Yet the UDHR and early drafts of the ICCPR were not the earliest occasions upon which specific concern for the accused was demonstrated at international level. Certain important procedural safeguards had been applied previously at the Nuremberg trials of perpetrators of wartime atrocities. Significantly, certain safeguards that had emerged and endured in various formulations throughout the ages at national and constitutional levels had now found their way into the Nuremberg trials and the fair trial provisions of the UDHR, ICCPR and ECHR. The historical contribution of these safeguards to procedural fairness at national and constitutional levels was such as could not be ignored by lawmakers setting minimum fair trial standards at international level.

5.1. NUREMBERG TRIALS

Before the right to a fair trial featured in major international human rights instruments, some concern to ensure fairness to the accused at international law level was earlier evident in the Nuremberg trials of war criminals of the European Axis. In the first of these trials, 22 high-ranking defendants were tried before the International Military Tribunal (IMT) in the period 1945–1946 pursuant to the quadripartite London Agreement 1945 and the IMT Charter annexed thereto.[352] A subsequent series of 12 trials of 177 lesser-ranking defendants were held before the US Nuremberg Military Tribunal (NMT) between 1946 and 1949 pursuant to Allied Control Council Law No 10 1945.[353] Some effort to accord fair treatment to defendants was acknowledged as requisite to allay potential fears of victor's justice. Chief Prosecutor Jackson, for example, addressed the IMT thus:

> There is a dramatic disparity between the circumstances of the accusers and of the accused that might discredit our work if we should falter ... in being fair and temperate. ... We must never forget that the record on which we judge these defendants today is the record on which history will judge us tomorrow. To pass these defendants a poisoned chalice is to put it to our own lips as well. We must summon such detachment and intellectual integrity to our task that this Trial will commend itself to posterity as fulfilling humanity's aspirations to do justice.[354]

352 Agreement for the Prosecution and Punishment of Major War Criminals of the European Axis, and Charter of the International Military Tribunal (adopted and entered into force 8 August 1945) 82 UNTS 279. France, UK, US and USSR were signatories to the Agreement.

353 Reprinted in T Taylor, *Final Report to the Secretary of the Army on the Nuernberg War Crimes Trials Under Control Council Law No 10* (Government Printing Office, Washington 1949) 250–253.

354 *US and others v Hermann Wilhelm Göring and others* (1947) 2 IMT 1, 101.

A similar view was expressed in the NMT case of *US v Friedrich Flick and others*: 'There may well be misgivings as to the fairness of such a trial. These considerations have made the judges … keenly aware of their grave responsibility and of the danger to the cause of justice if the conduct of the trial and the conclusions reached should even seem to justify these misgivings.'[355] The procedural framework implemented in the Nuremberg trials with the intention of providing defendants with fair treatment was derived largely from the Anglo-American adversarial tradition.[356]

An effort to provide this fair treatment was discernible in the safeguards adopted in the IMT's procedural regime. Article 16 of the IMT Charter afforded the accused the rights to a detailed indictment in a language he understands within reasonable time before trial, to give any explanation relevant to the charges, to have the proceedings conducted in or translated into a language he understands, to conduct his own defence or have legal assistance, to present evidence, and to cross-examine prosecution witnesses. Additionally, the presumption of innocence was recognised[357] and the accused was entitled under Article 24(j) of the Charter to make a final statement to the court after the closing speeches. Despite these safeguards, however, the proceedings revealed some significant limitations on the standard of procedural fairness. The Charter did not include, even implicitly, a right to silence for defendants, whose statements during pre-trial interrogation were admissible at trial.[358] Defendants could also be tried in absentia,[359] as occurred in the case of Bormann, who could not be located. Concerning disclosure, not only were defence counsel excluded from the prosecution's evidentiary archives,[360] but also the prosecution was not duty bound to provide early disclosure, resulting in some incriminating documents being disclosed, dramatically, during the cross-examination of defendants or their witnesses.[361] In addition, the IMT was not 'bound by technical rules of evidence', allowing it to admit any evidence of probative value.[362] Consequently, it established a practice of admitting hearsay evidence – generally inadmissible

---

355 (1952) 6 TWC 1, 1189 (Presiding Judge Sears).

356 *US v Oswald Pohl and others* (1950) 5 TWC 193, 959 (Tribunal II): 'The trial was conducted generally along the lines usually followed by the trial courts of the various States of the United States, except as to the rules of evidence'; EJ Wallach, 'The Procedural and Evidentiary Rules of the Post-World War II War Crimes Trials: Did They Provide an Outline for International Legal Procedure?' (1999) 37 Colum J Transnat'l L 851, 853–854.

357 *Friedrich Flick and others* (n 355) 1188.

358 JD Jackson and SJ Summers, *The Internationalisation of Criminal Evidence: Beyond the Common Law and Civil Law Traditions* (CUP, Cambridge 2012) 118.

359 IMT Charter Art 12.

360 T Taylor, *The Anatomy of the Nuremberg Trials: A Personal Memoir* (AA Knopf, New York 1992) 627.

361 'Contemporaneous and Captured Documents' (1953) 15 TWC 632, 639; R May and M Wierda, 'Trends in International Criminal Evidence: Nuremberg, Tokyo, The Hague, and Arusha' (1999) 37 Colum J Transnat'l L 725, 756.

362 IMT Charter Art 19.

in common law jurisdictions – in affidavit form to shorten the proceedings.[363] Nevertheless, whenever the affidavit evidence of an available witness was admitted, it was not relied upon heavily by the Tribunal unless a subsequent cross-examination of that witness, which the defence could apply for,[364] was conducted.[365] If the defendant was convicted, the judgement was 'final and not subject to review.'[366] Despite these limitations, the aforementioned procedural safeguards were still sufficient to indicate that a genuine concern for fairness guided the IMT. Indeed, the proceedings in 1945–1946 'were the fairest that defendants of vanquished powers might have had at that time.'[367]

This effort to ensure defendants some procedural fairness also extended to the NMT proceedings, albeit certain shortcomings were once again apparent. From November 1946, suspects were to be informed of their right to silence during interrogation; however, the many incriminating statements already made before this date remained admissible in evidence.[368] The Tribunal was, nevertheless, prepared to exclude from evidence incriminating pre-trial statements obtained under duress.[369] At least 30 days before trial,[370] the accused was entitled to a copy of the indictment in a language he understood.[371] This 30-day period, which in practice was extended to an average of nine weeks,[372] gave the defence more preparation time than that prescribed by German or American law.[373] The

---

363 *Hermann Wilhelm Göring and others* (n 354) 352; 'Affidavits and Interrogatories – IMT Case' (1953) 15 TWC 746, 747–748.

364 'Affidavits and Interrogatories – IMT Case' (n 363) 747–748.

365 May and Wierda (n 361) 751–752; Jackson and Summers (n 358) 118.

366 IMT Charter Art 26.

367 Jackson and Summers (n 358) 119. See also Taylor (n 360) 635: 'So the International Military Tribunal began and finished, with general approval and little criticism from the world public. There were no charges that the defendants were being railroaded, the disclosures of Nazi atrocities were appalling, and the judges appeared to be fair and humane men. Thus the Tribunal accomplished what it had been established for'; V Morris and MP Scharf, *An Insider's Guide to the International Criminal Tribunal for the Former Yugoslavia: A Documentary History and Analysis* (Transnational, Irvington-on-Hudson 1995) vol 1, 9–10: 'The proceedings … were generally viewed as providing the defendants with the essentials of due process and a fair trial'; KN Calvo-Goller, *The Trial Proceedings of the International Criminal Court: ICTY and ICTR Precedents* (Martinus Nijhoff, Leiden 2006) 13: 'from a procedural perspective the Nuremberg trials … were seen as generally fair.'

368 KJ Heller, *The Nuremberg Military Tribunals and the Origins of International Criminal Law* (OUP, Oxford 2011) 166, 178.

369 Eg *US v Ulrich Greifelt and others* (1950) 5 TWC 1, 88; 'Farben Case – Various Extracts from the Record Concerning the Admissibility of Pre-Trial Affidavits by Defendants' (1953) 15 TWC 854, 868 (*US v Carl Krauch and others*).

370 Uniform Rules of Procedure, Military Tribunals, Nuernberg, Revised to 8 January 1948 r 4. Reprinted in (1953) 15 TWC 70, 70–78.

371 Military Government Ordinance No 7 1946 Art 4(a). Reprinted in Taylor (n 353) 286–291.

372 Heller (n 368) 173. A further three to four weeks of defence preparation time was also usually provided after the prosecution's case-in-chief, as well as shorter recesses whenever necessary (173–174).

373 BB Ferencz, 'Nurnberg Trial Procedure and the Rights of the Accused' (1948) 39 J Crim L & Criminology 144, 148.

trial itself was open to the public[374] and conducted in a language understood by the accused,[375] who was entitled to be present throughout it[376] and be presumed innocent.[377] He also enjoyed the right to conduct his own defence or be represented by self-chosen or appointed counsel.[378] In this regard, each accused could instruct two counsel and a secretary, and had access to an American legal consultant at all times, with the Tribunal appointing additional counsel and staff as necessary.[379] However, suspects were denied counsel until formally indicted,[380] hence found themselves disadvantaged during interrogation.

Significant resources were made available to the defence to facilitate case preparation, including payment of remuneration to the defence team and alleviating many of their living costs, providing office space, furniture and supplies, allowing unlimited domestic phone calls and the free sending of cables outside of Germany, providing transportation, authorising international evidence gathering trips, and providing translation, photocopying and mimeographing facilities on equal terms with the prosecution.[381] Also intended to facilitate defence preparation was the requirement on the prosecution, at least 24 hours in advance of offering into evidence any documents, to file copies of those documents for the defence to peruse.[382] Although this 24-hour notice period fell well short of early disclosure, most prosecution documents were in practice disclosed soon after the arraignment.[383] The defence could also request that the Tribunal obtain particular documents on its behalf.[384] Nevertheless, the prosecution did withhold documents intended for use on cross-examination as the 24-hour rule was inapplicable to such documents.[385]

Defendants could cross-examine prosecution witnesses through counsel,[386] and represented defendants possessing special knowledge were even occasionally permitted to cross-examine expert witnesses themselves.[387] Defendants could

374 Ibid 145.

375 Ordinance No 7 (n 371) Art 4(b).

376 Ibid Art 4(d).

377 *US v Alfried Krupp and others* (1950) 9 TWC 1, 405; *Friedrich Flick and others* (n 355) 1188–1189.

378 Ordinance No 7 (n 371) Art 4(b); Uniform Rules of Procedure (n 370) r 7(a).

379 Taylor (n 353) 297–344; 'Final Report of the Defense Center' (1953) 15 TWC 187, 190; Heller (n 368) 174.

380 Heller (n 368) 167.

381 'Interim Report on The Secretariat for the Military Tribunals, 30 September 1949, Submitted by the Secretary General of the Military Tribunals to the United States High Commissioner for Germany' (1953) 15 TWC 155, 173–175; 'Final Report of the Defense Center' (n 379) 189–190; Ferencz (n 373) 147–148.

382 Uniform Rules of Procedure (n 370) r 17.

383 Taylor (n 353) 87.

384 Ordinance No 7 (n 371) Art 4(f); Uniform Rules of Procedure (n 370) r 12.

385 Taylor (n 353) 87; 'Contemporaneous and Captured Documents' (n 361) 639.

386 Ordinance No 7 (n 371) Art 4(e).

387 'Occasional Provision for the Examination of Witnesses by Defendants in Addition to the Right of Examination through Counsel' (1953) 15 TWC 342, 343–351. In contrast, the IMT

also request the Tribunal to procure witnesses for their defence.[388] Although the Tribunal made considerable efforts in this regard, both in respect of witnesses located within and outside Germany, defendants complained of the greater opportunities available to the prosecution to obtain affidavits or witnesses from abroad, particularly given the difficulties of arranging travel for German defence counsel and the dependence of the defence on the willingness of military authorities or foreign governments to cooperate with its requests.[389] Witness affidavits were particularly important as the Tribunal could admit any document deemed to be of probative value.[390] The Tribunal demonstrated a willingness to admit over defence objection even the affidavits of witnesses not produced for cross-examination,[391] albeit significantly there was a marked reduction in the weight accorded to such evidence[392] and the practice was not followed in every case.[393]

After the evidentiary phase of the trial and closing arguments, the accused was allowed to make a final statement before the Tribunal delivered its judgement.[394] Although the judgement, which had to be reasoned, was not open to appeal,[395] the accused could during trial call for a review of any rulings on points of law that were inconsistent with rulings in the Tribunal's other cases.[396] Additionally, the sentence could be reduced or amended subsequently by the Military Governor, but he could not increase its severity.[397]

Whereas the procedural shortcomings were not insignificant, the NMT overall demonstrated a strong effort to ensure that adequate opportunities

held that represented defendants could not put questions directly to prosecution witnesses: *US and others v Hermann Wilhelm Göring and others* (1947) 3 IMT 1, 31–33.

388 Ordinance No 7 (n 371) Art 4(f).

389 'Procurement of Witnesses for the Defense' (1953) 15 TWC 363, 364–368, 379, 384–385; Heller (n 368) 171.

390 Ordinance No 7 (n 371) Art 7.

391 '[T]hese affidavits ... are admissible, and that would be true ... whether or not the affiants are available for cross-examination': 'Affidavits, Interrogatories, and Statements Not Under Oath – Selections from the Record of Cases Other Than the IMT and Medical Cases' (1953) 15 TWC 807, 841 (*US v Wilhelm von Leeb and others*) (Presiding Judge Young). See also 'Affidavit of Deceased Affiants and Interrogations of Deceased Persons' (1953) 15 TWC 879, 880 (*US v Ernst von Weizsaecker and others*; *US v Otto Ohlendorf and others*), 886, 892 (*US v Karl Brandt and others*), 892–893 (*US v Erhard Milch*).

392 Eg *US v Otto Ohlendorf and others* (1949) 4 TWC 1, 579; *US v Ernst von Weizsaecker and others* (1949) 14 TWC 1, 357, 445, 541 (conviction cannot rest upon such an affidavit alone); 'Affidavit of Deceased Affiants and Interrogations of Deceased Persons' (n 391) 880.

393 Eg *Alfried Krupp and others* (n 377) 1328; *US v Wilhelm von Leeb and others* (1950) 11 TWC 1, 1259; *US v Carl Krauch and others* (1952) 8 TWC 1, 1084; 'Affidavits, Interrogatories, and Statements Not Under Oath – Selections from the Record of Cases Other Than the IMT and Medical Cases' (n 391) 818 (*US v Oswald Pohl and others*).

394 Ordinance No 7 (n 371) Art 11(i).

395 Ibid Art 15.

396 Military Government Ordinance No 11 1947 Arts 2(a)–(b). Reprinted in Taylor (n 353) 292–293.

397 Ordinance No 7 (n 371) Art 17(a).

for defence were available, with Fritz Sauter, defence counsel in three trials, attesting that even the defendants themselves would not have preferred trial before a different court.[398] The NMT and IMT had attempted to secure fairness between the parties and, in doing so, served to put certain trial safeguards on an international platform, upon which the eyes of the world were focussed given the nature of the crimes committed. This progressive development laid a firm foundation for the subsequent further strengthening of the standard of procedural fairness at international law level.

5.2. UDHR AND ICCPR

Following the Nuremberg trials, respect for procedural fairness also became entrenched in the UDHR and ICCPR – multilateral instruments forming part of the UN's International Bill of Rights – as part of the collective postwar effort to foster a more peaceful and secure international political order and to promote and protect fundamental human rights. These instruments were framed under the dominant influence of the Western liberal legal and philosophical tradition[399] and grounded in respect for the dignity inherent in the human person.

Adopted without dissent by the UN General Assembly in 1948, the UDHR marked a historic milestone in the postwar human rights movement. The President of the Assembly hailed it as 'a step forward in a great evolutionary process. It was the first occasion on which the organised community of nations had made a declaration of human rights and fundamental freedoms.'[400] Yet, conceived only 'as a common standard of achievement for all peoples and all nations',[401] the UDHR was neither intended[402] to be nor is in itself legally binding, though arguably it is an authoritative interpretation of the human rights provisions of the UN Charter (Articles 55(c) and 56)[403] or has become in part an

---

398 Heller (n 368) 178 referring to a July 1948 interview by Sauter. See also PM Hebert, 'The Nurnberg Subsequent Trials' (1949) 16 Ins Counsel J 226, 231: 'The judges of the American tribunals at Nurnberg exhibited deep concern over protecting the rights of the defendants to fair trial in accordance with Anglo-American concepts.'

399 Ch 1 text to n 325.

400 UN GAOR, 3rd Session, 183rd Plenary Meeting (10 December 1948) UN Doc A/PV.183 (1948) 934.

401 UDHR Preamble.

402 H Lauterpacht, 'The Universal Declaration of Human Rights' (1948) 25 Brit YBIL 354, 356–363, 365; Johnson (n 325) 62–64.

403 'Montreal Statement of the Assembly for Human Rights, March 22–27, 1968' (1968) 9 J Int'l Comm Jurists 94, 95; MGK Nayar, 'Human Rights: The United Nations and United States Foreign Policy' (1978) 19 Harv Int'l LJ 813, 817; MS McDougal, HD Lasswell and L-C Chen, *Human Rights and World Public Order: The Basic Policies of an International Law of Human Dignity* (Yale UP, New Haven 1980) 325; International Law Association, 'Report of the Sixty-Sixth Conference' (Buenos Aires 1994) cited in H Hannum, 'The Status of the Universal

expression of customary international law.[404] Notwithstanding its intrinsically non-binding character, the UDHR was of further significance for expressly underpinning its catalogue of rights with respect for inherent human dignity. Its Preamble thus asserts that 'recognition of the inherent dignity and of the equal and inalienable rights of all members of the human family is the foundation of freedom, justice and peace in the world', and reaffirms 'faith in fundamental human rights, in the dignity and worth of the human person'. Article 1 acknowledges man's 'reason and conscience' and proclaims that '[a]ll human beings are born free and equal in dignity and rights.' Furthermore, Article 22 adds that '[e]veryone … is entitled to realization … of the economic, social and cultural rights indispensable for his dignity'.[405] Included within the catalogue of rights sharing this dignitarian foundation is the right to a fair trial enshrined in Articles 10–11(1), which entitles the accused to be presumed innocent, to full equality at a fair and public hearing before an independent and impartial tribunal, and to all the guarantees necessary for the defence. More detailed fair trial provisions were not included for it was understood that the UDHR, as the first component of the International Bill of Rights, would establish only general principles or standards of human rights.

Instead, it was for the ICCPR to give greater specificity to the right to a fair trial and to embody legally binding obligations for ratifying or acceding states. Adopted by the UN General Assembly in 1966, this treaty entered into force in 1976 and has 168[406] states parties from all regions of the world. Like the UDHR, the ICCPR was keen to emphasise the preservation of human dignity as a key factor motivating its rights catalogue. Its Preamble recognises 'the inherent dignity … of all members of the human family' and declares that their inalienable rights 'derive from the inherent dignity of the human person'. Additionally, in cases of deprivation of liberty, Article 10(1) holds that individuals should be treated 'with respect for the inherent dignity of the human person.' Amongst the articles underpinned by the ICCPR's respect for human dignity was Article 14, which represented an increased and shared expectation amongst states that accused persons around the world ought to be treated in a

Declaration of Human Rights in National and International Law' (1995–1996) 25 Ga J Int'l & Comp L 287, 323.

404 JP Humphrey, 'The International Bill of Rights: Scope and Implementation' (1976) 17 Wm & Mary L Rev 527, 529, 540; Nayar (n 403) 817; McDougal, Lasswell and Chen (n 403) 274; LB Sohn, 'The New International Law: Protection of the Rights of Individuals Rather than States' (1982) 32 Am U L Rev 1, 17; RB Lillich, 'Civil Rights' in T Meron (ed), *Human Rights in International Law: Legal and Policy Issues* (Clarendon, Oxford 1984) vol 1, 116; P Thornberry, *International Law and the Rights of Minorities* (Clarendon, Oxford 1991) 237.

405 See also Art 23(3): 'Everyone who works has the right to just and favourable remuneration ensuring for himself and his family an existence worthy of human dignity'.

406 Treaty Section, 'Multilateral Treaties Deposited with the Secretary-General: Status of Treaties: International Covenant on Civil and Political Rights' (UN, New York 2016) <https://treaties.un.org/Pages/Treaties.aspx?id=4&subid=A&clang=_en>.

manner consistent with minimum international fair trial standards. Article 14 affords the accused the rights to equality before the courts, to a fair and public hearing by a competent, independent and impartial tribunal without undue delay, to be presumed innocent, to be informed of the charge, to adequate time and facilities to prepare a defence, to be present at trial, to self-representation or legal assistance, to examine and call witnesses, to an interpreter, to silence and not to incriminate himself, to an appeal, to compensation for wrongful conviction, and to freedom from double jeopardy.

Article 14 and UDHR Articles 10–11(1) were testament that the interest in ensuring at international law level procedural fairness for the accused had spilled beyond the confines of the Nuremberg trials and assumed a more global scale. Their presence in the UDHR and ICCPR also reflected recognition by the world community that procedural fairness was valuable to protecting human dignity, hence it had become more than a means to a correct outcome or to good governance. These provisions were furthermore significant for serving as inspirational models for ECHR Article 6. The ECHR Preamble refers to the UDHR on three occasions, one of which states that contracting parties are resolved 'to take the first steps for the collective enforcement of certain of the rights stated in the Universal Declaration'. Such rights include those in Articles 10–11(1), which are recalled with greater elaboration in ECHR Article 6. The framers of Article 6 were also able in 1949 to draw upon early drafts of the ICCPR.[407]

5.3. ECHR

Whereas the UDHR and ICCPR are global instruments, the ECHR is a regional instrument, applicable to all persons within the jurisdiction of its 47 contracting states. Each such state is a member of the Council of Europe – founded in 1949 to achieve greater postwar unification of the peoples of Europe – and must, as a condition of membership, 'accept the principles of the rule of law and of the enjoyment by all persons within its jurisdiction of human rights and fundamental freedoms'.[408] These rights and freedoms are defined in the ECHR, which the Council created in 1950 to function not only as an alarm that would alert the European democracies of systematic, large-scale human rights violations in time for intervening remedial action to be taken, but also

---

407 D Harris, 'The Right to Fair Trial in Criminal Proceedings as a Human Right' (1967) 16 ICLQ 352, 353; P van Dijk, 'Universal Legal Principles of Fair Trial in Criminal Proceedings' in A Rosas and J Helgesen (eds), *Human Rights in a Changing East-West Perspective* (Pinter, London 1990) 109; JG Merrills and AH Robertson, *Human Rights in Europe: A Study of the European Convention on Human Rights* (4th edn Manchester UP, Manchester 2001) 7.

408 Statute of the Council of Europe (adopted 5 May 1949, entered into force 3 August 1949) ETS 1 Art 3.

as a rampart against the spread of communism into Western Europe.[409] The treaty was thus envisaged primarily, as described by Bates, as a 'collective pact against totalitarianism',[410] entitling under Article 24 (now Article 33) every contracting state to refer to the Strasbourg enforcement machinery alleged violations by another contracting state. However, since entry into force of the ECHR in 1953, inter-state cases have numbered only 20;[411] the overwhelming majority of cases have been brought to Strasbourg under the right of individual petition in Article 34[412] (formerly Article 25). Acceptance of this right and the jurisdiction of the European Court of Human Rights, whose judgements are final and binding on the respondent state,[413] was originally optional but became compulsory for all contracting states in 1998.[414] This development was part of the evolution in the primary function of the ECHR from being an inter-state pact against totalitarianism to being increasingly, especially from the 1970s onwards, a type of European Bill of Rights,[415] providing through an international court a remedy for individual victims of isolated human rights infringements by states generally committed to democracy, the rule of law and human rights. In both regards – collective pact against totalitarianism or European Bill of Rights – the ECHR was 'designed to maintain and promote the ideals and values of a democratic society.'[416]

The ECHR is now widely hailed as having established the most developed and effective international legal regime in existence for the protection of human rights,[417] the judgements generated from which exercise an influence not confined solely to the parties to a particular case. The Court's judgements, besides providing individual relief, serve to elucidate, safeguard and develop ECHR norms,[418] with an expectation that contracting states not involved in the

409 D Harris and others, *Harris, O'Boyle and Warbrick: Law of the European Convention on Human Rights* (3rd edn OUP, Oxford 2014) 3. See also Merrills and Robertson (n 407) 3–5.

410 Bates (n 342) 8, 75, 104.

411 European Court of Human Rights, 'Inter-States Applications' (Council of Europe, Strasbourg 2016) <http://www.echr.coe.int/Documents/InterStates_applications_ENG.pdf>.

412 'The Court may receive applications from any person, non-governmental organisation or group of individuals claiming to be the victim of a violation by one of the High Contracting Parties of the rights set forth in the Convention'.

413 ECHR Arts 44(1)–(2), 46(1).

414 ECHR Protocol No 11 (adopted 11 May 1994, entered into force 1 November 1998) ETS 155.

415 Bates (n 342) 8, 10–25. See also Harris and others (n 409) 4.

416 *Kjeldsen, Busk Madsen and Pedersen v Denmark* (Apps 5095/71; 5920/72; 5926/72) (1976) Series A no 23 [53]; *United Communist Party of Turkey and others v Turkey* (App 19392/92) ECHR 1998-I [45]; *Ždanoka v Latvia* (App 58278/00) ECHR 2006-IV [98]; *Svinarenko and Slyadnev v Russia* (Apps 32541/08; 43441/08) ECHR 2014 [118].

417 Eg A Moravcsik, 'The Origins of Human Rights Regimes: Democratic Delegation in Postwar Europe' (2000) 54 Int'l Org 217, 218, 243; Merrills and Robertson (n 407) 1; Harris and others (n 409) 34; Bates (n 342) 2; H Lovat and Y Shany, 'The European Court of Human Rights' in Y Shany, *Assessing the Effectiveness of International Courts* (OUP, Oxford 2014) 253.

418 *Ireland v UK* (App 5310/71) (1978) Series A no 25 [154]; *Karner v Austria* (App 40016/98) ECHR 2003-IX [26]; *Konstantin Markin v Russia* (App 30078/06) ECHR 22 March 2012 [89];

proceedings ought to take such judgements into account.[419] Accordingly, certain judgements have prompted other contracting states to change their law or practice to ensure compliance with the ECHR,[420] thereby reinforcing the idea of the ECHR as an 'instrument of European public order'.[421] Strasbourg judgements and the ECHR text have additionally inspired several hundred constitutional court decisions,[422] and many constitutions have drawn on the ECHR text for their human rights guarantees.[423] On the international stage, the text served as a reference model for two other regional human rights treaties[424] and, more interestingly, in the specific context of procedural fairness, Strasbourg case-law on equality of arms has informed the decisions of international tribunals.[425]

Also of significance is that the ECHR shares with the UDHR and ICCPR respect for inherent human dignity as a foundational value, albeit dignity is not expressly mentioned in the European text. Teitgen, a founding father of the ECHR, submitted in 1949 that the ECHR as proposed would set forth 'a list of

---

Centre for Legal Resources on behalf of Valentin Câmpeanu v Romania (App 47848/08) ECHR 17 July 2014 [105].

419 *Opuz v Turkey* (App 33401/02) ECHR 9 June 2009 [163].

420 Eg *Benthem v the Netherlands* (App 8848/80) (1985) Series A no 97: Austria (establishment of independent administrative tribunals); *Scordino v Italy (No 1)* (App 36813/97) ECHR 29 July 2004: Czech Republic (just satisfaction for non-pecuniary damage); *Luedicke, Belkacem and Koç v Germany* (Apps 6210/73; 6877/75; 7132/75) (1978) Series A no 29: France (interpretation costs); *Hirst v UK (No 2)* (App 74025/01) ECHR 2005-IX: Cyprus, Ireland (prisoners' voting rights); *Brogan and others v UK* (App 11209/84 et seq) (1988) Series A no 145-B: Netherlands (time-limit between arrest and appearance before a judge); *Campbell v UK* (App 13590/88) (1992) Series A no 233, *Klamecki v Poland (No 2)* (App 31583/96) ECHR 3 April 2003: Ukraine (correspondence of detainees and prisoners). These examples are elaborated upon in Parliamentary Assembly of the Council of Europe: Committee on Legal Affairs and Human Rights, 'Strengthening Subsidiarity: Integrating the Strasbourg Court's Case Law into National Law and Judicial Practice' AS/Jur/Inf (2010) 04, 17, 20–21, 24, 37.

421 *Loizidou v Turkey (Preliminary Objections)* (App 15318/89) (1995) Series A no 310 [75], [93]; *Cyprus v Turkey* (App 25781/94) ECHR 2001-IV [78]; *Neulinger and Shuruk v Switzerland* (App 41615/07) ECHR 6 July 2010 [133]; *Amirov v Russia* (App 51857/13) ECHR 27 November 2014 [67]. See further R Ryssdal, 'The Coming of Age of the European Convention on Human Rights' [1996] EHRLR 18, 18: 'as far as the democratic protection of individuals and institutions is concerned, the Convention has become the single most important legal and political common denominator of the States of the continent of Europe in the widest geographical sense.'

422 M Delmas-Marty, *Towards a Truly Common Law: Europe as a Laboratory for Legal Pluralism* (CUP, Cambridge 2002) 67. See also Parliamentary Assembly of the Council of Europe (n 420), which cites as examples constitutional court decisions from Croatia (17, 19), Poland (25), Russia (27), Slovenia (29–30), Slovakia (34), Turkey (35) and Ukraine (36); B Emmerson and others, *Human Rights and Criminal Justice* (3rd edn Sweet & Maxwell, London 2012) 6: Strasbourg judgements 'have been cited with approval by the constitutional courts of Canada, New Zealand, South Africa, Hong Kong, India, Zimbabwe and Mauritius, amongst others'.

423 Ryssdal (n 421) 27, referring to constitutions in Eastern and Central Europe; Emmerson and others (n 422) 5–6, referring to constitutions in Commonwealth Africa and the Commonwealth Caribbean.

424 Ryssdal (n 421) 22: American Convention on Human Rights (adopted 22 November 1969, entered into force 18 July 1978) 1144 UNTS 123; African Charter on Human and Peoples' Rights (adopted 27 June 1981, entered into force 21 October 1986) 1520 UNTS 217.

425 Examples in Introduction n 26.

rights and fundamental freedoms, without which personal independence and a dignified way of life cannot be ensured'.[426] This intention to protect dignity is also implied in the ECHR Preamble's express endorsement of the UDHR; the latter, as above-mentioned, refers to dignity in its Preamble and Articles 1, 22 and 23(3). Furthermore, Strasbourg case-law acknowledges that respect for dignity underlies the ECHR. The Court has often stated that the 'very essence of the Convention is respect for human dignity and human freedom',[427] with Judges Spielmann and Jebens similarly adding that 'the concept of dignity prevails throughout the European Convention'.[428] Amongst the Convention articles most prominently associated with upholding dignity is Article 6,[429] under which the dignitarian value specifically of equality of arms is explained in Chapter 2. Accordingly, as is the case under the UDHR and ICCPR, procedural fairness under the ECHR is valued as conducive to maintaining dignity, hence its value is not limited merely to its contribution to correct outcomes or to good governance.

Procedural fairness in criminal proceedings under Article 6 is tied principally to adequate observance, having regard to the proceedings as a whole, of various express and implied fundamental safeguards for the accused. Certain of these safeguards had featured, in various formulations, in Western historical legal practice and procedure at national, constitutional and international levels. Article 6 is in large part the product of this historical experience in safeguarding the accused in judicial proceedings. Article 6(1) secures the general right to a fair trial. Reflecting the cardinal principles of natural justice, it guarantees the rights to a hearing and to an impartial tribunal.[430] It specifies that this hearing must be fair, public and held within a reasonable time, and that the tribunal should furthermore be independent and established by law. It stipulates additionally that judgement must be pronounced publicly. Thus, Article 6(1) 'enunciates

426 'Presentation of the Report of the Committee on Legal and Administrative Questions' in Council of Europe, *Collected Edition of the "Travaux Préparatoires" of the European Convention on Human Rights* (Martinus Nijhoff, The Hague 1975) vol 1, 272.

427 Eg *Pretty v UK* (App 2346/02) ECHR 2002-III [65]; *Christine Goodwin v UK* (App 28957/95) ECHR 2002-VI [90]; *Jehovah's Witnesses of Moscow v Russia* (App 302/02) ECHR 10 June 2010 [135]; *Al Nashiri v Poland* (App 28761/11) ECHR 24 July 2014 [538].

428 *Vereinigung Bildender Künstler v Austria* (App 68354/01) ECHR 25 January 2007 Joint Diss Op [8].

429 Other articles include Arts 3 (prohibition of torture), 4 (prohibition of slavery and forced labour), 8 (right to respect for family and private life), 9 (freedom of thought, conscience and religion), 11 (freedom of assembly and association), 12 (right to marry and found a family) and 14 (prohibition of discrimination), and Art 2 (right to education) of ECHR Protocol No 1 (adopted 20 March 1952, entered into force 18 May 1954, as amended by Protocol No 11) ETS 9: D Feldman, 'Human Dignity as a Legal Value: Part 1' [1999] PL 682, 690–696; C Gearty, *Principles of Human Rights Adjudication* (OUP, Oxford 2004) 91–92.

430 'The common law principles of natural justice anticipated by many years the concept of a fair trial which has been elaborated by the European Court of Human Rights under article 6(1) of the Convention': *Bow Spring (Owners) v Manzanillo II (Owners)* [2004] EWCA Civ 1007; [2005] 1 WLR 144 [57] (Clarke LJ).

rights which are distinct but stem from the same basic idea and which, taken together, make up a single right not specifically defined in the narrower sense of the term.'[431] Article 6(2) guarantees the presumption of innocence. Article 6(3) contains the following minimum rights: (a) to prompt and detailed notification of the charge; (b) to adequate time and facilities for defence preparation; (c) to defend oneself or through legal assistance of one's own choosing, or to legal aid if one has insufficient means and the interests of justice so require; (d) to examine or have examined adverse witnesses and to obtain the attendance and examination of defence witnesses under the same conditions as adverse witnesses; and (e) to free interpreter assistance, if necessary. Articles 6(2)–(3) represent specific components of, but do not exhaust, the 'fair hearing' guarantee in Article 6(1),[432] thus a hearing as a whole may be unfair even if Articles 6(2)–(3) are respected.[433] Other essential safeguards have been recognised as implicit in this open-ended guarantee, including the right to remain silent and the privilege against self-incrimination;[434] the right of access to a court;[435] the right in some or all circumstances not to be subject to the use of evidence acquired through torture or inhuman or degrading treatment contrary to ECHR Article 3,[436] or entrapment;[437] the right to be present[438] and participate effectively[439] in the hearing; the right to have one's submissions, arguments and evidence properly examined;[440] the principle of equality of arms;[441] the right to adversarial proceedings, entailing that the defence be afforded the opportunity to know about and comment on observations filed or evidence adduced by the other party;[442] the right to a reasoned judgement;[443] and the right not to be

431 *Golder v UK* (App 4451/70) (1975) Series A no 18 [28].

432 *Nielsen v Denmark* (App 343/57) (1961) 4 Yearbook 494 (EComHR) 548; *Deweer v Belgium* (App 6903/75) (1980) Series A no 35 [56].

433 *Nielsen* (n 432) 548; *Barberà, Messegué and Jabardo v Spain* (App 10590/83) (1988) Series A no 146 [67], [80], [89], [91].

434 *Saunders v UK* (App 19187/91) ECHR 1996-VI [68]; *Bykov v Russia* (App 4378/02) ECHR 10 March 2009 [92].

435 *Deweer* (n 432) [49]; *Kart v Turkey* (App 8917/05) ECHR 2009 [79]–[80].

436 *Gäfgen v Germany* (App 22978/05) ECHR 2010 [166]–[167], [173], [178]; *El Haski v Belgium* (App 649/08) ECHR 25 September 2012 [85].

437 *Ramanauskas v Lithuania* (App 74420/01) ECHR 2008 [54], [60], [73]; *Bannikova v Russia* (App 18757/06) ECHR 4 November 2010 [34]–[35], [56].

438 *Sejdovic v Italy* (App 56581/00) ECHR 2006-II [81], [84]; *Hermi v Italy* (App 18114/02) ECHR 2006-XII [58]–[59].

439 *Stanford v UK* (App 16757/90) (1994) Series A no 282-A [26]; *V v UK* (App 24888/94) ECHR 1999-IX [85], [91].

440 *Krasulya v Russia* (App 12365/03) ECHR 22 February 2007 [50]; *Lazariu v Romania* (App 31973/03) ECHR 13 November 2014 [168].

441 *Neumeister v Austria* (App 1936/63) (1968) Series A no 8 [22] ('The Law'); *Jelcovas v Lithuania* (App 16913/04) ECHR 19 July 2011 [106].

442 *Eskelinen and others v Finland* (App 43803/98) ECHR 8 August 2006 [31]; *Schädler-Eberle v Liechtenstein* (App 56422/09) ECHR 18 July 2013 [85] (civil).

443 *Hadjianastassiou v Greece* (App 12945/87) (1992) Series A no 252 [33]; *Taxquet v Belgium* (App 926/05) ECHR 2010 [91].

expelled or extradited to a country where one would risk suffering a flagrant denial of justice.[444] The 'fair hearing' guarantee does not, however, imply a right to trial by jury,[445] but jury trials are in principle acceptable under Article 6.[446] Nor does it imply a right of appeal, though where domestic law includes this right, the Article 6 guarantees continue to apply to the appeal proceedings.[447] Nevertheless, the right of appeal is included in ECHR Protocol No 7 – which has been ratified by 44 states – along with the right to compensation for wrongful conviction and the prohibition on double jeopardy.[448]

While specific rights within Article 6, whether express or implied, are capable of being subject to limited restrictions where justified,[449] the overarching right to a fair trial in Article 6(1) is an absolute right,[450] in the absence of a derogation. Certain ECHR rights are non-derogable under Article 15(2), hence cannot be restricted or suspended even in times of national emergency (Articles 2–4(1) and 7), while certain others include express general public interest qualifications (Articles 8–11). The general right to a fair trial falls into neither of these two classifications; it is a derogable and unqualified right. Ashworth and Redmayne consequently identify it as a 'strong right', sitting between non-derogable rights and qualified rights in terms of importance in the hierarchy of ECHR rights.[451]

Regardless of the classifications of ECHR rights, it should be borne in mind that such rights constitute minimum standards. The guarantee of a fair trial entitles the defence to a minimum of procedural protection, not to the most favourable procedures imaginable. Minimum standards for procedural fairness raise a realistic prospect of general compliance across all contracting states,

---

444 *Ahorugeze v Sweden* (App 37075/09) ECHR 27 October 2011 [113]–[114]; *Othman (Abu Qatada) v UK* (App 8139/09) ECHR 2012 [258]–[259].

445 *X and Y v Ireland* (App 8299/78) (1980) 22 DR 51, 73; *Callaghan and others v UK* (App 14739/89) (1989) 60 DR 296 [1] ('The Law'); *Twomey, Cameron and Guthrie v UK* (Apps 67318/09; 22226/12) ECHR 28 May 2013 [30].

446 *Taxquet* (n 443) [83]–[84], [90]; *Legillon v France* (App 53406/10) ECHR 10 January 2013 [52].

447 *Delcourt v Belgium* (App 2689/65) (1970) Series A no 11 [25]; *Evrenos Önen v Turkey* (App 29782/02) ECHR 15 February 2007 [28].

448 (adopted 22 November 1984, entered into force 1 November 1988, as amended by Protocol No 11) ETS 117 Arts 2(1), 3, 4(1).

449 *Van Mechelen and others v the Netherlands* (App 21363/93 et seq) ECHR 1997-III [58]; *Rowe and Davis v UK* (App 28901/95) ECHR 2000-II [61].

450 *R v Forbes* [2001] 1 AC 473 (HL) [24]; *Brown v Stott* [2003] 1 AC 681 (PC) 704, 719; *DS v HM Advocate* [2007] UKPC D1; 2007 SC (PC) 1 [17]; *Secretary of State for the Home Department v MB* [2007] UKHL 46; [2008] 1 AC 440 [91]; *O'Halloran and Francis v UK* (Apps 15809/02; 25624/02) ECHR 2007-III [53].

The public hearing component of Art 6(1) is, however, subject specifically to an express qualification: 'the press and public may be excluded from all or part of the trial in the interests of morals, public order or national security in a democratic society, where the interests of juveniles or the protection of the private life of the parties so require, or to the extent strictly necessary in the opinion of the court in special circumstances where publicity would prejudice the interests of justice.'

451 A Ashworth and M Redmayne, *The Criminal Process* (4th edn OUP, Oxford 2010) 38.

though it is obviously open to such states to set higher standards than the ECHR in their domestic law.

These states enjoy considerable freedom in the design of their criminal procedure system, albeit the system must not contravene minimum standards for a fair trial.[452] This procedural freedom is important for sustaining states' support for the ECHR regime given that criminal procedure systems are tied to individual states' history, tradition and legal culture. Indeed, the Court has emphasised that it is not its function to standardise the different procedural systems in Europe.[453] The generality of the fair trial safeguards of Article 6 allows for the Court to interpret them in a manner conducive to accommodation within these different systems, whether the system is common law or civil law in origin. Importantly, the Court does not approach Article 6 cases with the presumption that the common law approach to a fair trial is superior to the civil law approach, or vice versa;[454] each is capable of meeting the requirements of Article 6. Furthermore, the Court's approach has also been such that no model of criminal procedure – accusatorial, inquisitorial or mixed – is immune from censure.[455]

Whatever a state's choice of criminal procedure system, the Court will in principle have regard to the proceedings as a whole in determining whether the fair trial safeguards of Article 6 have been respected.[456] Accordingly, as regards the specific guarantees in Article 6(3), it has commented thus: 'their intrinsic aim is always to ensure, or contribute to ensuring, the fairness of the criminal proceedings as a whole. The guarantees ... are therefore not an end in themselves, and they must accordingly be interpreted in the light of the function which they have in the overall context of the proceedings.'[457] This holistic approach entails that the pre-trial[458] and appellate[459] stages of the proceedings, alongside the trial hearing itself, are relevant in determining compliance with

452 *Taxquet* (n 443) [83]–[84]. See also Introduction, text to n 17.

453 *Taxquet* (n 443) [83]; *Nejdet Şahin and Perihan Şahin v Turkey* (App 13279/05) ECHR 20 October 2011 [68].

454 B Swart and J Young, 'The European Convention on Human Rights and Criminal Justice in the Netherlands and the United Kingdom' in P Fennell and others (eds), *Criminal Justice in Europe: A Comparative Study* (Clarendon, Oxford 1995) 85.

455 M Delmas-Marty, 'Toward a European Model of the Criminal Trial' in M Delmas-Marty (ed), *The Criminal Process and Human Rights: Toward a European Consciousness* (Martinus Nijhoff, Dordrecht 1995) 196.

456 *Taxquet* (n 443) [84], [93]; *Horncastle and others v UK* (App 4184/10) ECHR 16 December 2014 [130].

457 *Mayzit v Russia* (App 63378/00) ECHR 20 January 2005 [77]; *Seleznev v Russia* (App 15591/03) ECHR 26 June 2008 [67]. See also *Can v Austria* (App 9300/81) EComHR Report 12 July 1984 [48]; *Al-Khawaja and Tahery v UK* (Apps 26766/05; 22228/06) ECHR 2011 [143]: 'the Court has always interpreted Article 6 § 3 in the context of an overall examination of the fairness of the proceedings.'

458 *Salduz v Turkey* (App 36391/02) ECHR 2008 [50]; *Duško Ivanovski v the former Yugoslav Republic of Macedonia* (App 10718/05) ECHR 24 April 2014 [41].

459 *Hermi* (n 438) [60]; *Cipleu v Romania* (App 36470/08) ECHR 14 January 2014 [30]. Art 6 is also relevant to leave to appeal proceedings: *Monnell and Morris v UK* (Apps 9562/81; 9818/82) (1987) Series A no 115 [54].

the guarantees of Article 6. If, on consideration of the proceedings as a whole, the applicant has been convicted in breach of these guarantees, the Court takes the view that there should be *restitutio in integrum*: putting the applicant, as far as possible, in the same situation as he enjoyed prior to the breach.[460] Although the Court is not empowered to direct a state to open a new trial or to set aside a conviction,[461] it has indicated repeatedly that a retrial or a reopening of the case, if requested by the applicant, would in principle constitute the most appropriate form of *restitutio in integrum*.[462] In addition, the Court may award just satisfaction under Article 41 in the form of pecuniary and/or non-pecuniary damages,[463] or declare that the finding of a violation of Article 6 is in itself sufficient just satisfaction.[464]

As a precondition to consideration of the proceedings as a whole under the criminal head of Article 6, the Court must satisfy itself that the applicant was the subject of a 'criminal charge'. All types of criminal offence are covered by Article 6, 'from the most straightforward to the most complex.'[465] Rather than relying decisively on domestic law definitions or classifications, the Court has interpreted the terms 'criminal' and 'charge' as having autonomous meanings,[466] thwarting states from evading improperly the applicable scope of Article 6. It formulated in *Engel and others v the Netherlands* three criteria for evaluating whether an offence is 'criminal':[467]

1) Classification in domestic law: If the law of the respondent state classifies the offence as criminal, Article 6 is automatically applicable. Otherwise, the second and third criteria, which are alternative and not necessarily cumulative,[468] are relevant.

460 *Sakhnovskiy v Russia* (App 21272/03) ECHR 2 November 2010 [112]; *Efendiyev v Azerbaijan* (App 27304/07) ECHR 18 December 2014 [64].

461 *Saïdi v France* (App 14647/89) (1993) Series A no 261-C [46]–[47]; *Lyons and others v UK* (App 15227/03) ECHR 2003-IX ('The Law').

462 Eg *Somogyi v Italy* (App 67972/01) ECHR 2004-IV [86]; *Krasniki v the Czech Republic* (App 51277/99) ECHR 28 February 2006 [93]; *Sakhnovskiy* (n 460) [112]; *Cēsnieks v Latvia* (App 9278/06) ECHR 11 February 2014 [78]. See also Recommendation No R (2000) 2 on the Re-examination or Reopening of Certain Cases at Domestic Level Following Judgments of the European Court of Human Rights (adopted by Committee of Ministers 19 January 2000) (2000) 43 Yearbook 290, 291, 293, in which the Committee (supervises the execution of judgments) encourages states to provide for the possibility of reopening criminal proceedings in instances where the Court has found serious procedural shortcomings that contravene the ECHR.

463 Eg *Kudła v Poland* (App 30210/96) ECHR 2000-XI [165]; *Al-Khawaja and Tahery* (n 457) [169].

464 Eg *Hanif and Khan v UK* (Apps 52999/08; 61779/08) ECHR 20 December 2011 [155]; *Aras v Turkey (No 2)* (App 15065/07) ECHR 18 November 2014 [62].

465 *Ramanauskas* (n 437) [53]; *Bannikova* (n 437) [33].

466 *Adolf v Austria* (App 8269/78) (1982) Series A no 49 [30].

467 (App 5100/71 et seq) (1976) Series A no 22 [82].

468 *Pákozdi v Hungary* (App 51269/07) ECHR 25 November 2014 [18]. See also *Jussila v Finland* (App 73053/01) ECHR 2006-XIV [31], which elaborates that '[i]t is enough that the offence

2) Nature of the offence: Indicators pointing to the criminal nature of the offence include that the legal provision infringed is of general application to all citizens and not solely a limited group with a special status;[469] the proceedings are brought by a state authority under statutory powers of enforcement;[470] the offence carries a deterrent and punitive penalty;[471] the penalty can only be imposed pursuant to a finding of guilt;[472] and the offence is classified as criminal in other contracting states.[473] The minor nature of an offence does not in itself exclude its classification as criminal.[474]
3) Severity of the penalty: Severity is measured by reference primarily to the maximum potential penalty legally available, not the actual penalty imposed.[475] A punishment of deprivation of liberty is generally a criminal penalty, unless it cannot be considered 'appreciably detrimental' given its 'nature, duration or manner of execution'.[476] A fine that is substantial[477] or entails imprisonment for default of payment[478] may also constitute a criminal penalty. Even a modest fine, despite its relative lack of seriousness, can indicate that an offence is criminal in nature if its purpose is deterrent and punitive.[479] Other penalties qualifying as criminal may include, for example,

---

in question is by its nature to be regarded as criminal or that the offence renders the person liable to a penalty which by its nature and degree of severity belongs in the general criminal sphere.' If either criterion is not in itself conclusive on the matter, a cumulative approach may be adopted: *Bendenoun v France* (App 12547/86) (1994) Series A no 284 [47]; *Balsytė-Lideikienė v Lithuania* (App 72596/01) ECHR 4 November 2008 [55].

469 *Öztürk v Germany* (App 8544/79) (1984) Series A no 73 [53]; *Bendenoun* (n 468) [47]; *Lauko v Slovakia* (App 26138/95) ECHR 1998-VI [58].

470 *Benham v UK* (App 19380/92) ECHR 1996-III [56].

471 *Öztürk* (n 469) [53]; *Janosevic v Sweden* (App 34619/97) ECHR 2002-VII [68]. The withdrawal of a driving licence or the imposition of a drink-driving rehabilitation course, for example, are not considered punitive but principally preventative measures aimed at securing the safety of road users: *Escoubet v Belgium* (App 26780/95) ECHR 1999-VII [37]; *Blokker v the Netherlands* (App 45282/99) ECHR 7 November 2000 [1] ('The Law').

472 *Benham* (n 470) [56].

473 *Öztürk* (n 469) [53]; *Maaouia v France* (App 39652/98) ECHR 2000-X [39].

474 *Öztürk* (n 469) [53]; *Ezeh and Connors v UK* (Apps 39665/98; 40086/98) ECHR 2003-X [104]; *Sergey Zolotukhin v Russia* (App 14939/03) ECHR 2009 [55].

475 *Ezeh and Connors* (n 474) [120]; *Sergey Zolotukhin* (n 474) [56].

476 *Engel and others* (n 467) [82] (two days' strict arrest for military indiscipline held too short to be a criminal penalty); *Ezeh and Connors* (n 474) [126] (awards of 40 and seven additional days' detention by prison governor were criminal sanctions). See further *Campbell and Fell v UK* (Apps 7819/77; 7878/77) (1984) Series A no 80 [72], where a substantial loss of remission was considered a criminal penalty since it caused the prisoner's detention to continue beyond the period legitimately expected; *Štitić v Croatia* (App 29660/03) ECHR 8 November 2007 [56], where solitary confinement, which did not extend the applicant's prison term, was held to be a disciplinary, not a criminal, sanction.

477 *Janosevic* (n 471) [69], [71].

478 *Weber v Switzerland* (App 11034/84) (1990) Series A no 177 [34]; *Bendenoun* (n 468) [47]; *Schmautzer v Austria* (App 15523/89) (1995) Series A no 328-A [28]. Contrast *Ravnsborg v Sweden* (App 14220/88) (1994) Series A no 283-B [35].

479 *Lauko* (n 469) [58].

a lengthy prohibition from holding public office,[480] the deduction of points from a driving licence with a resulting possibility of disqualification,[481] or a confiscation measure.[482]

Alongside this understanding of 'criminal', the Court understands 'charge' to mean not only the formal notification to a person of an allegation that he has committed a criminal offence, but also any official measure which implies such an allegation and substantially affects his situation.[483] The Court thus looks behind the domestic conception of 'charge' to the substantive reality of the individual's situation.[484] Accordingly, it has held that an individual may be considered subject to a charge – the point at which Article 6 comes into play – when, for example, a preliminary investigation has been opened and he officially learns of the investigation or begins to be affected by it;[485] he is questioned by the police and makes a confession or self-incriminating statement;[486] he is arrested or his arrest is ordered;[487] he is first questioned as a suspect;[488] he is notified that he is being charged;[489] a search of his home and offices is conducted;[490] evidence is seized from him;[491] his business is ordered provisionally closed pending payment of a fine to avoid prosecution;[492] or the prosecuting authorities have requested the lifting of his parliamentary immunity.[493]

6. CONCLUSION

It has been said that 'everything which has power to win the obedience and respect of men must have its roots deep in the past'.[494] Article 6 is no exception

480 *Matyjek v Poland* (App 38184/03) ECHR 2006-VII [55]–[58].
481 *Malige v France* (App 27812/95) ECHR 1998-VII [39]–[40].
482 *Balsytė-Lideikienė* (n 468) [60]–[61].
483 *Corigliano v Italy* (App 8304/78) (1982) Series A no 57 [34]; *Kravtas v Lithuania* (App 12717/06) ECHR 18 January 2011 [35].
484 *Deweer* (n 432) [44]; *Šubinski v Slovenia* (App 19611/04) ECHR 18 January 2007 [62]–[63].
485 *Eckle v Germany* (App 8130/78) (1982) Series A no 51 [74]; *Kangasluoma v Finland* (App 48339/99) ECHR 20 January 2004 [26].
486 *Aleksandr Zaichenko v Russia* (App 39660/02) ECHR 18 February 2010 [43]; *Yankov and others v Bulgaria* (App 4570/05) ECHR 23 September 2010 [23].
487 *Wemhoff v Germany* (App 2122/64) (1968) Series A no 7 [19] ('The Law'); *Boddaert v Belgium* (App 12919/87) (1992) Series A no 235-D [35]; *Heaney and McGuinness v Ireland* (App 34720/97) ECHR 2000-XII [42].
488 *Hozee v the Netherlands* (App 21961/93) ECHR 1998-III [45].
489 *Pedersen and Baadsgaard v Denmark* (App 49017/99) ECHR 2004-XI [44].
490 *Coëme and others v Belgium* (App 32492/96 et seq) ECHR 2000-VII [133].
491 *Marpa Zeeland BV and Metal Welding BV v the Netherlands* (App 46300/99) ECHR 2004-X [55]; *TK and SE v Finland* (App 38581/97) ECHR 31 May 2005 [27].
492 *Deweer* (n 432) [45]–[46].
493 *Frau v Italy* (App 12147/86) (1991) Series A no 195-E [14].
494 J Bryce, *The American Commonwealth* (Macmillan, New York 1914) vol 1, 28.

to this rule and, accordingly, this chapter set out primarily to establish a background for the provision before it came into being. Its catalogue of rights did not spring from sudden inspiration, but has profited from Western historical developments in criminal trial safeguards which mark an evolution over time in standards of procedural fairness in both common law and civil law traditions. Standards and expectations of procedural fairness evolve in response to reason, historical experience and the socio-cultural environment within which the particular trial proceedings occur. Different historical stages in Western legal practice and procedure at national, constitutional and international levels reveal the emergence and recurrence of certain trial safeguards, in various formulations, which present some resemblance to those included in Article 6.

At national level, procedural safeguards were implemented as instrumental to securing correct trial outcomes. Such safeguards include the right to be heard, which lacks a convincing inspirational basis in divine law but can be traced concretely back to ancient Athens. From ancient Athens onwards, the evolution in standards of procedural fairness was not exclusively progressive and linear. Standards also suffered regression, most notably in medieval trials by oath, ordeal and combat and in heresy inquisitions, albeit even under these proceedings the accused enjoyed at least a modicum of procedural protection. Regressive developments are instructive because they unveil the adverse consequences of the absence of certain safeguards on the soundness of trial outcomes, the dignity of the accused, and societal perceptions of the quality of state governance, thereby discouraging later generations of procedural lawmakers from following suit. Also instructive to later generations, of course, are progressive developments because they introduce or reaffirm (in varied formulations) procedural rights which are envisaged or proven at the time to be important to maintaining or strengthening the opportunities for a fair defence. This chapter identified progressive historical developments concerning classical antiquity, ecclesiastical inquisitorial procedure, the French Criminal Ordinance 1670, English jury trials, and the French Napoleonic Code of Criminal Procedure 1808, that afforded the accused crucial rights pertaining to, for example, judicial impartiality, notice of the charge, facilities for case preparation, legal assistance, and witnesses. Whilst, admittedly, progressive rights were marred by other serious procedural shortcomings, including the use of torture, the existence of such rights in the first place indicates that the seeds for the content of Article 6 were long sown.

The historical development of progressive procedural rights was not disposed exclusively towards securing correct trial outcomes. Certain of these rights, which contribute to procedural fairness, evolved to become identified with influential instruments of constitutional significance, impressing upon them the added value of the stamp of constitutionality. This evolution implies that procedural fairness was understood to be of vital importance to effectuating some form of good governance, particularly since it reflects state support for the rule of law and helps secure a public perception of criminal process legitimacy. Magna Carta subjugated the exercise of executive power to the rule of law. Chapter 29 expressed in germinal form the rule that the Crown could no longer act punitively against the accused without due process of law in both a substantive and procedural sense. Its influence resonated in America in equivalent clauses in seventeenth century enactments and in the late eighteenth century state and federal constitutions born of revolution. These state and federal constitutions notably went further by also including several other specific safeguards that correspond to certain ones in Article 6. The late eighteenth century additionally saw due process and presumption of innocence clauses given a constitutional footing in the French Declaration of the Rights of Man. French and Anglo-American legal and philosophical thinking was a powerful contributor in shaping the overarching Western liberal legal and philosophical tradition – the dominant tradition behind the composition of the UDHR and ICCPR and the tradition in which the ECHR is grounded.

Having long been a significant issue at national and constitutional levels, it was not until the aftermath of the Second World War that the fair treatment of accused persons also moved meaningfully onto the international agenda. The remit of international law, which had traditionally confined itself to the protection of states, experienced postwar expansion to include the protection of the rights of individuals. It had thus come to recognise that 'the individual human being – his welfare and the freedom of his personality in its manifold manifestations – is the ultimate unit of all law.'[495] The protection of individuals included the protection of war crimes defendants at the Nuremberg trials, which represented an early milestone in the development of minimum standards of procedural fairness at international law level. Although the proceedings involved some significant procedural deficiencies, the important safeguards enjoyed by defendants were indicative of a strong and sincere overall commitment to procedural fairness by the IMT and NMT. Beyond Nuremberg, procedural fairness also featured in the UDHR and ICCPR as part of a global postwar movement, stemming from the UN Charter, to promote and protect human rights and the inherent dignity of the individual. In serving to protect human dignity, procedural fairness had evolved to become recognised as more than just a contributor to correct outcomes or to good governance. Like the Nuremberg safeguards, the general fair trial principles of UDHR Articles 10–11(1) and the more specific fair trial rights of ICCPR Article 14 included various formulations of certain key protections that had emerged and endured at national and constitutional levels. The UDHR and early drafts of

[495] H Lauterpacht, 'The Law of Nations, the Law of Nature and the Rights of Man' (1943) 29 Transactions Grotius Society 1, 31.

the ICCPR provided an inspirational and influential point of reference for the framers of the ECHR.

Whilst these framers envisaged the ECHR as an inter-state pact against totalitarianism, it increasingly evolved to function primarily as a type of European Bill of Rights, predominantly employed by individuals seeking redress through an international court for isolated state infringements of their human rights. This instrument and its Court constitute the most developed, effective and influential international legal regime in existence for upholding human rights, which has proved an asset to maintaining a peaceful and democratic European public order. Like the UDHR and ICCPR, the ECHR is also underpinned by respect for human dignity, a manifestation of which includes the right to a fair trial. This dignitarian aspect reaffirms that the value of procedural fairness is not confined to just assisting the securing of correct outcomes or of good governance. Procedural fairness in criminal proceedings is principally understood under Article 6 as adequate observance of the express and implied safeguards therein. These safeguards constitute minimum standards which, in large part, carry the experience of Western historical legal practice and procedure at national, constitutional and international levels. Although certain of these safeguards are susceptible to justified limitations, the general right to a fair trial in Article 6(1) is unqualified, albeit derogable. This article also warrants re-mentioning for its 'fair hearing' aspect, the open-ended nature of which has allowed important safeguards, such as equality of arms, to be implied into it. Indeed, it has considerably broadened the capacity of Article 6 to evolve its standard of procedural fairness in response to new developments in states' criminal procedure systems, reinforcing the character of the ECHR as 'a living tree capable of growth and expansion within its natural limits.'[496] Whilst states must not contravene Article 6 standards, it is not for the Court to impose upon them a standardised design of criminal procedure system. Rather, Article 6 safeguards can be reconciled with the variety of legal systems existing in Europe, whether common law or civil law based, which is important for encouraging continued support for ECHR standards from states inclined naturally to remain faithful to their historical legal traditions. In ascertaining a state's compliance with Article 6 safeguards, the Court will in principle take account of the criminal proceedings in their entirety, including the pre-trial and appeal phases. The 'criminal' character of proceedings derives from the involvement of a 'criminal charge', to which the Court has rightly assigned an autonomous meaning to ensure that the applicability of Article 6 under its criminal head is not undermined by any unduly restrictive domestic interpretations.

---

496 *Edwards v Attorney-General for Canada* [1930] AC 124 (PC) 136 (Lord Sankey LC). See also *Tyrer v UK* (App 5856/72) (1978) Series A no 26 [31], where the ECHR was described as 'a living instrument which ... must be interpreted in the light of present-day conditions.'

Whilst the procedural position of persons under a criminal charge now benefits from Article 6 protection, the provision of trial safeguards through different stages of Western procedural history represents that attempts have always been made – though to considerably varying degrees – to lessen the extent to which such persons suffer a position of procedural disadvantage vis-à-vis the prosecution or accuser. These historical attempts were reflected, for example, in the provision of time and facilities for case preparation, the allowance of legal representation, and the opportunities for calling and examining witnesses. Modern aspirations for procedural equality between the parties can rely upon the support of Article 6 jurisprudence, which has specifically formalised this idea. It falls to the next chapter to explore the value, legal basis and definition of the concept of equality of arms in Article 6.

CHAPTER 2
EQUALITY OF ARMS
Value, Legal Basis and Definition

1. INTRODUCTION

This chapter approaches equality of arms in criminal proceedings under Article 6 from a predominantly theoretical standpoint. Whilst procedural equality between parties to proceedings appeals to our intuitive sense of procedural fairness, a deeper exploration of its actual value is deserved. Section 2 reveals its two principal values, accompanied with an assessment of which of these has theoretical primacy, and reveals its secondary, collateral value. In order for the value of procedural equality to manifest itself practically, such equality must first be given effect in law. Section 3 identifies a contemporary legal foundation for equality of arms in Article 6 and in international law. The legal obligation assumed in criminal proceedings under the concept of equality of arms in Article 6 has been enunciated recurrently as requiring that 'each party must be afforded a reasonable opportunity to present his case under conditions that do not place him at a disadvantage vis-à-vis his opponent'.[1] Section 4 defines each essential element of this formula to elucidate in detail the nature of the concept, before its application is assessed critically in the chapters hereafter.

2. THE VALUE OF PROCEDURAL EQUALITY

The value of procedural equality in its modern form is multi-faceted. It has two principal values – it contributes to attaining a correct trial outcome and it reflects respect for the dignity of the individual – as well as a secondary value as a component of securing some form of good governance. The latter is referred to

1 Eg *Bulut v Austria* (App 17358/90) ECHR 1996-II [47]; *Foucher v France* (App 22209/93) ECHR 1997-II [34]; *Josef Fischer v Austria* (App 33382/96) ECHR 17 January 2002 [18]; *Lanz v Austria* (App 24430/94) ECHR 31 January 2002 [57]; *Öcalan v Turkey* (App 46221/99) ECHR 2005-IV [140].

as a secondary value because it is a collateral consequence of the principal values being present.

2.1. CORRECT TRIAL OUTCOME

A correct trial outcome entails that the defendant should be found guilty if he has undoubtedly committed the offence as charged and that the innocent should not be wrongfully convicted. It requires that the judgement of the court is accurate and reliable in its finding of facts on the evidence and in its application of the law to those facts. Procedural rights and principles facilitate the communicative engagement of the parties with the decision-maker as to facts, evidence and law, consequently influencing the trial outcome. Procedural equality has an instrumental value in rendering more probable the achievement of a correct trial outcome. A guarantee of the same is unattainable since procedural equality and other trial safeguards cannot escape Rawls's notion of 'imperfect procedural justice', whereby an incorrect trial outcome may be reached despite strict observance of procedural fairness and regularity.[2] Neither can one guarantee that an incorrect outcome will necessarily follow from procedural inequality, especially if a particular inequality is minor in nature. Nevertheless, the prospect of reaching a correct trial outcome is greater under conditions of procedural equality because there is equality of opportunity for the parties to prepare and present their cases and, in turn, exert influence over the decision-maker. Such equality with the prosecution enhances the ability of the accused to participate effectively in the proceedings before a decision is reached. This creates balance in, as well as increases, the flow of information from the parties to the decision-maker, making it more likely that he will form an accurate and reliable account of the situation.

2.2. RESPECT FOR HUMAN DIGNITY

The second principal value is not instrumental in character, for procedural equality is valuable for its own sake, irrespective of its contribution to achieving a correct trial outcome. This intrinsic value is dignitarian: procedural equality is an expression of due respect for the dignity of the individual. The atrocities of the Second World War created the impetus at international law level to promote and protect human dignity, a value which reverberates not only through the ECHR, but also many other regional and international human rights instruments.[3]

---

2 J Rawls, *A Theory of Justice* (OUP, Oxford 1999) 74–75.

3 Ch 1 links human dignity to the UN Charter (text to n 350), the UDHR and ICCPR (s 5.2), and the ECHR (s 5.3). Other examples include:

Although a definition of human dignity remains elusive in such instruments, perhaps to the advantage of facilitating political consensus and providing scope for evolutionary development,[4] the eighteenth century Kantian interpretation of this abstract concept provides an instructive point of reference upon which to draw. Kant identified dignity as the intrinsic worth of a human being, absolute

---

International Convention on the Elimination of All Forms of Racial Discrimination (adopted 21 December 1965, entered into force 4 January 1969) 660 UNTS 195 Preamble.

International Covenant on Economic, Social and Cultural Rights (adopted 16 December 1966, entered into force 3 January 1976) 993 UNTS 3 Preamble, Art 13(1) ('education shall be directed to the full development of the human personality and the sense of its dignity').

American Convention on Human Rights (adopted 22 November 1969, entered into force 18 July 1978) 1144 UNTS 123 Arts 5(2), 6(2), 11(1) ('Everyone has the right to have his honor respected and his dignity recognized'); Additional Protocol to the ACHR in the Area of Economic, Social and Cultural Rights (adopted 14 November 1988, entered into force 16 November 1999) (1989) 28 ILM 156 Preamble, Art 13(2).

Convention on the Elimination of All Forms of Discrimination against Women (adopted 18 December 1979, entered into force 3 September 1981) 1249 UNTS 13 Preamble: 'discrimination against women violates the principles of equality of rights and respect for human dignity'.

African Charter on Human and Peoples' Rights (adopted 27 June 1981, entered into force 21 October 1986) 1520 UNTS 217 Preamble, Art 5 ('Every individual shall have the right to the respect of the dignity inherent in a human being').

Convention against Torture and Other Cruel, Inhuman or Degrading Treatment or Punishment (adopted 10 December 1984, entered into force 26 June 1987) 1465 UNTS 85 Preamble.

Convention on the Rights of the Child (adopted 20 November 1989, entered into force 2 September 1990) 1577 UNTS 3 Preamble, Arts 23(1), 28(2), 37(c) ('Every child deprived of liberty shall be treated with humanity and respect for the inherent dignity of the human person'), 39–40(1).

International Convention on the Protection of the Rights of All Migrant Workers and Members of Their Families (adopted 18 December 1990, entered into force 1 July 2003) 2220 UNTS 3 Arts 17(1) ('Migrant workers and members of their families who are deprived of their liberty shall be treated … with respect for the inherent dignity of the human person'), 70.

Convention on the Rights of Persons with Disabilities (adopted 13 December 2006, entered into force 3 May 2008) 2515 UNTS 3 Preamble, Arts 1 ('The purpose of the present Convention is to promote, protect and ensure the full and equal enjoyment of all human rights and fundamental freedoms by all persons with disabilities, and to promote respect for their inherent dignity'), 3(a), 8(1)(a), 16(4), 24(1)(a), 25(d).

Charter of Fundamental Rights of the European Union (adopted 12 December 2007, entered into force 1 December 2009) (2010) OJ C83/389 Preamble, Arts 1 ('Human dignity is inviolable. It must be respected and protected'), 25, 31(1).

Standard Minimum Rules for the Treatment of Prisoners (the Nelson Mandela Rules) (adopted 17 December 2015) UNGA Res 70/175 UN Doc A/Res/70/175 (2015) Preamble, rr 1 ('All prisoners shall be treated with the respect due to their inherent dignity and value as human beings'), 5(1), 50, 58(2), 72, 76(1)(b).

4 D Shultziner, 'Human Dignity: Functions and Meanings' in J Malpas and N Lickiss (eds), *Perspectives on Human Dignity: A Conversation* (Springer, Dordrecht 2007) 78: 'human dignity is used as a linguistic symbol that can represent different outlooks, thereby justifying a concrete political agreement on a seemingly shared ground. … [T]he content of human dignity is a corollary of a political agreement and compromise set in each legal document by the cultural, political, constitutional and other conditions, which can evolve and change in the course of history.'

in character.[5] Pritchard adds that 'having a sense of dignity includes concern to achieve and maintain various forms of integrity, as well as attitudes of self-respect, self-esteem, pride, shame, resentment, and indignation.'[6] Within the Kantian tradition, dignity resides without exception in all human beings because of man's capacity, as an intelligible (moral) being, for autonomous rational agency, a trait that elevates him above all other animals.[7] It is by virtue of his dignity that man is entitled to respect and to not be used merely as a means to others' ends; he is to be treated as an end in himself.[8] On this basis, in criminal proceedings, the accused should not be reduced to the status of an instrument of the will of the state, but rather treated as a valued subject of the process, irrespective of the character of the charges laid against him. Whilst such proceedings by their very nature pose an acute limitation on the accused's capacity for autonomous self-determination, and to this extent compromise necessarily an aspect of his dignity, he must not be faced by arbitrariness. To accord him fair treatment is to acknowledge and uphold his innate dignity and sense of worth.[9]

Fair treatment includes observance of procedural equality, which is a measure demonstrating commitment to respecting individual dignity through its contribution to upholding dignitarian process values. These values 'refer to standards of value by which we may judge a legal process to be good *as a process*, apart from any "good result efficacy" it may have.'[10] Given the width of this definition, any catalogue of process values is non-exhaustive but the following values may qualify as examples: procedural legality; process peacefulness; humaneness; individual autonomy; personal privacy; procedural predictability, transparency and rationality; timeliness and finality; revelation

5 I Kant and M Gregor (ed) (tr), *The Metaphysics of Morals* (CUP, Cambridge 1996) [435], [462]; J Hruschka, 'Kant and Human Dignity' in BS Byrd and J Hruschka (eds), *Kant and Law* (Ashgate, Aldershot 2006) 70, 82.

6 MS Pritchard, 'Human Dignity and Justice' (1972) 82 Ethics 299, 300.

7 Kant and Gregor (n 5) [213]–[214], [239], [392], [418], [420], [434]–[435], [462]–[463]; Hruschka (n 5) 70–76, 79–81. See also Pritchard (n 6) 303: 'The connection between autonomy and dignity is shown in the resentment often felt when one believes his autonomy is being interfered with'; O Schachter, 'Human Dignity as a Normative Concept' (1983) 77 AJIL 848, 851: Human dignity 'includes recognition of a distinct personal identity, reflecting individual autonomy and responsibility.'

8 Kant and Gregor (n 5) [434]–[435], [462]; Hruschka (n 5) 70, 81–82.

9 DJ Galligan, *Due Process and Fair Procedures: A Study of Administrative Procedures* (Clarendon, Oxford 1996) 75–76. See also Pritchard (n 6) 308: 'One's genuine conviction that others are entitled to fair treatment in itself shows that he regards others as having dignity, as being worthy of respect. Taking positive steps to promote justice for others (or prevent injustice) can indicate respect for their dignity'; R Dworkin, *Taking Rights Seriously* (Duckworth, London 1977) 198: 'the vague but powerful idea of human dignity … supposes that there are ways of treating a man that are inconsistent with recognizing him as a full member of the human community, and holds that such treatment is profoundly unjust.'

10 RS Summers, 'Evaluating and Improving Legal Processes – A Plea for "Process Values"' (1974) 60 Cornell L Rev 1, 3.

(of reasons for unfavourable treatment); and participation.[11] It is especially the latter value[12] that is promoted and enhanced by procedural equality between the parties. This equality does not merely invite the participation of the accused in the criminal process, but admits participation on equal terms with his opponent in respect of opportunities for preparing and presenting his case and, in turn, for influencing the decision-maker. This enables the accused to become an empowered and effective participant in the process by which his fate will be determined. Equal opportunities for effective participation can enable the accused to feel that he has some control in that process and that attention will be paid to his side of the case by the decision-maker, irrespective of the actual effect on outcome. They also send the message to the accused that he remains an equal within society and need not feel powerless against the prosecutorial machinery of the state. These are effects that reinforce dignity and sense of worth.

Participation on equal terms can also be seen as reinforcing dignity when considered from a sporting perspective. The balance of power and resources between the individual and the state is inherently unequal in a criminal case. Redressing this imbalance by making both sides (the players) participate on an equal procedural footing ensures that the criminal proceedings (the game) do not involve an undue advantage for either side. This is reflected in the idea of maintaining a 'level playing field' between both sides, an often used Anglo-American metaphor for fair procedures.[13] Levelling the playing field can enable the accused to feel that he is afforded a sporting chance against his opponent. This spirit of sportsmanship has been referred to by Wigmore as the 'instinct of giving the game fair play', by Bentham as the 'fox hunter's reason', and by Pound as the 'sporting theory of justice'.[14] It is a spirit that urges procedural equality between opponents for its own sake. Indeed, such equality is an acknowledgement of the dignity of the accused and affords him a sporting chance of expressing it.

11 Ibid 20–27; FI Michelman, 'Formal and Associational Aims in Procedural Due Process' in JR Pennock and JW Chapman (eds), *Due Process* (New York UP, New York 1977) 127; RB Saphire, 'Specifying Due Process Values: Toward a More Responsive Approach to Procedural Protection' (1978) 127 U Pa L Rev 111, 122; JL Mashaw, *Due Process in the Administrative State* (Yale UP, New Haven 1985) 175–181; MD Bayles, *Procedural Justice: Allocating to Individuals* (Kluwer, Dordrecht 1990) 130–134, 139.

12 '[T]o be a *person*, rather than a *thing*, is at least to be *consulted* about what is done with one': LH Tribe, *American Constitutional Law* (2nd edn Foundation Press, Mineola New York 1988) 666.

13 Eg *United States v O'Keefe* 128 F3d 885, 897 (5th Cir 1997); GP Fletcher, *The Grammar of Criminal Law: American, Comparative, and International* (OUP, New York 2007) vol 1, 136.

14 JH Wigmore, *A Treatise on the System of Evidence in Trials at Common Law* (Canada Law Book Co, Toronto 1905) vol 1, 127; J Bentham, *Rationale of Judicial Evidence* (Hunt and Clarke, London 1827) vol 5, 238–239 (hunted fox must be given a fair chance to escape with its life); R Pound, 'The Causes of Popular Dissatisfaction with the Administration of Justice' (1906) 40 Am L Rev 729, 738–739.

2.3. PRIMACY OF VALUE: CORRECT TRIAL OUTCOME V RESPECT FOR HUMAN DIGNITY

Admitting the co-existence of the two principal values of procedural equality is not to accord them equal import. The question of which of these values has theoretical primacy begs consideration.

Galligan is a particularly keen exponent of the subordinacy of non-outcome values to procedural instrumentalism: dignitarian values are to be respected but procedural rights are first and foremost a means for securing correct outcomes.[15] Alternatively, the thrust of the dignitarian account asserts that procedures intrinsically upholding dignitarian values are justified, irrespective of contribution to outcome; correctness of outcome is not more than ancillary to these values.[16] Galligan evinces a scepticism towards this 'dignitarian challenge', resting on alleged failures to establish a direct link between respect for individuals and certain procedures, and to recognise that correctness of outcome is itself an important aspect of respect for the individual, thus is unduly depreciated.[17]

Although in response one may refer to the link between dignity and procedural equality presented in section 2.2 above, there is further scope to strengthen the dignitarian cause. The superiority of a dignitarian rather than instrumental foundation for procedural equality possesses intuitive merit. Human intuition is such that '[w]e all feel that process matters to us irrespective of result.'[18] Relying on survey-based research, Tyler found the same in his examination of the psychology of procedural fairness: people value fair process for its own sake, independently of its influence on outcome.[19] Indeed, he concluded that, in judging fairness, people place greater weight on the value of procedures in themselves than on outcomes.[20] A prohibition against a process involving torture, for instance, is compelled by the affront to the dignity of coerced individuals, despite the possibility of obtaining reliable evidence; the former concern takes precedence over the latter. Procedural inequality between opponents can offend the disadvantaged party's sense of worth and generate, intuitively, a feeling of unfair treatment, regardless of the outcome reached. His legitimate and intuitive expectation to equal treatment, born of his dignity, remains unfulfilled.

---

15 A recurrent proposition throughout Galligan (n 9), eg 55, 72, 81, 92–94, 131–143, 349–351. Another instrumentalist is TC Grey, 'Procedural Fairness and Substantive Rights' in Pennock and Chapman (n 11) 184, 204–205 fn 17.

16 Eg Summers (n 10) 3, 14, 21–27; Mashaw (n 11) 158–160, 204.

17 Galligan (n 9) 77–78, 81 and eg 135–140.

18 Mashaw (n 11) 162.

19 TR Tyler, *Why People Obey the Law* (Princeton UP, Princeton 2006) 116, 127, 133, 146–147, 150, 175, 178, 276.

20 Ibid 97, 101, 126, 138–139, 146–147.

Beyond this intuitive level, the relationship between procedural equality and human dignity may be explained by reference to two further arguments. Duff first argues the following: as the law recognises the rational agency of individuals, obligations imposed upon them are required to be justified to earn acceptance; the criminal trial must respect this rational agency to adhere to the law and also purports to be a rational enterprise itself; accordingly, the court's verdict must be justified to the accused affected by it.[21] This idea of the trial as a process that seeks to justify an adverse verdict to the accused is also taken up by Ho: 'The court must strive, in the manner in which it reaches the verdict, to acquire the moral authority to say to the [accused] that [he] should accept it'.[22] This moral authority will be lacking when there is insufficient regard for his dignity or interests.[23] If the accused suffers procedural inequality, hence his status as a responsible agent has not been adequately recognised, the court has not acquired the moral authority to adequately justify an adverse decision to him. This is the case even if the outcome is correct, thus it is the dignitarian rather than instrumental value of procedural equality that comes to the fore. The requirement of justification, within the context of procedural fairness, puts more emphasis and value on the process employed to justify the outcome – a dignitarian focus – than on the correctness of the outcome itself.

Duff's second line of argument is that the indictment addressed to the accused is a charge which *he must answer* to society through its courts; to deny him the opportunity to respond is to reject his very status as an accused.[24] In other words, the trial is not just about establishing guilt or innocence, but also about calling the accused to account:

> It is to give the defendant a central, and at least ideally an active, role in the trial – as the person to whom the criminal charge is addressed; who is summoned to answer that charge, and to answer for his conduct if it is proved to be criminal; and who is expected to accept responsibility for what he has done, and to accept the condemnation that a conviction expresses if his guilt is proved.[25]

Calling the accused to account reflects respect for his dignity as a responsible agent, particularly since it allows him to respond – give an account of himself.[26] He can only be expected to give an account of himself in an effective manner if

---

21 RA Duff, *Trials and Punishments* (CUP, Cambridge 1986) 115–116. See also A Duff and others, *The Trial on Trial (3): Towards a Normative Theory of the Criminal Trial* (Hart, Oxford 2007) 227: 'state power must be justified *to* the defendant through the appropriate kind of communicative process, treating him as a responsible agent.'

22 HL Ho, *A Philosophy of Evidence Law: Justice in the Search for Truth* (OUP, Oxford 2008) 81.

23 Ibid 80–81.

24 Duff (n 21) 116–118.

25 A Duff and others, 'Introduction: Judgement and Calling to Account' in A Duff and others (eds), *The Trial on Trial (2): Judgement and Calling to Account* (Hart, Oxford 2006) 3.

26 Ibid 4.

procedural equality is maintained between the parties. Since the idea of 'calling to account' puts its central focus on the accused himself, rather than on the trial outcome, the implication is that it gives more prominence to the dignitarian, rather than instrumental, value of procedural equality.

To these arguments one may also add that Galligan's principal claim is certainly not in consonance with the human rights ideal forged in the aftermath of the Second World War to protect, above all, the dignity of the individual. As aforementioned, respect for dignity underpins modern human rights instruments, including the ECHR. The jurisprudence of the ECHR, nevertheless, presents somewhat of a paradox in this regard, diverting from the dignitarian ideal to requiring evidence of prejudice (outcome-orientated) for a violation of the concept of equality of arms.[27] A strictly dignitarian approach would dictate that a procedural inequality in itself is sufficient for a breach, irrespective of the occurrence of prejudice. The second component of Galligan's view is much more readily acceptable: correct outcomes are demonstrative of respect. However, what he fails to recognise is that process values such as participation are a superior expression of respect because they exist to directly benefit the accused, whereas a correct outcome can either be to his favour or detriment.

In the light of these arguments, it is submitted that the value of procedural equality in its modern form lies theoretically foremost in its contribution to upholding individual dignity. Indeed, procedural equality between the parties would be justified even if it was a measure incapable of having a bearing on outcome.

2.4. GOOD GOVERNANCE

As a collateral consequence of its two principal values, procedural equality also has a secondary value as an ingredient in securing some form of good governance. It contributes to good governance – the achievement of which is in the interest of everyone in a civilised society – in two respects. First, it reflects the state's respect for the rule of law, 'one of the basic principles of a democratic society enshrined in the Convention'.[28] Adherence to the rule of law requires the correct application of the law,[29] which Fuller describes as 'congruence between official action and the law';[30] procedural equality contributes to the achievement of a correct trial outcome; a correct trial outcome entails necessarily that the law has been applied correctly, enabling one's action to be guided by the law. Additionally, Waldron identifies the rule of law as resting upon 'respect for the

27 Ch 2 ss 4.4.1–4.4.3.

28 *Gillan and Quinton v UK* (App 4158/05) ECHR 2010 [77]; *Roman Zakharov v Russia* (App 47143/06) ECHR 2015 [247]. The ECHR Preamble refers expressly to the 'rule of law'.

29 Introduction, text to n 9.

30 LL Fuller, *The Morality of Law* (Yale UP, New Haven 1969) 81.

freedom and dignity of each person as an active center of intelligence.'[31] As a contributor to upholding this dignity, procedural equality exemplifies the state's willingness to limit in law the exercise of state power – which otherwise could be oppressive or arbitrary – at least to the extent that the accused ought to be able to express his dignity and not suffer the indignity of disadvantage vis-à-vis his opponent. Second, procedural equality is a manifestation of the state's effort to secure a societal perception of criminal process legitimacy. Legitimacy refers to societal confidence in and support for the criminal process. This confidence and support is important to securing public compliance with the law and the decisions and policies of legal authorities.[32] This is even more so because each member of society can be subject potentially to criminal proceedings, hence can identify with the accused and will only accept proceedings that are fair: 'from the moment the offender is perceived as a surrogate self, this identification calls for a "fair trial" for him before he is punished, as we would have it for ourselves.'[33] Indeed, a perception of legitimacy is fundamental to democratic rule as the right to a fair trial holds a prominent place in a democratic society.[34] Procedural equality bolsters this perception because of its contribution to increasing significantly the prospect of the trial outcome being correct. Furthermore, as Duff and others note, 'legitimacy can be established only if the trial is governed by norms that require defendants to be treated as citizens of a liberal polity, not as mere subjects of power.'[35] As such a norm, procedural equality further bolsters criminal process legitimacy because it demonstrates a fraternal concern for protecting the dignity of all members of society who stand accused.

3. A CONTEMPORARY LEGAL BASIS FOR PROCEDURAL EQUALITY

Having explored the value of the concept of equality of arms, it falls now to also identify a contemporary legal basis for it. A basis in Article 6 and thereafter in international law is considered.

3.1. BASIS IN ARTICLE 6

The inclusion of the concept of equality of arms in Convention jurisprudence was realised by the willingness of the Strasbourg authorities to interpret Article 6(1)

31 J Waldron, 'The Concept and the Rule of Law' (2008) 43 Ga L Rev 1, 60.

32 Tyler (n 19) 19. See also LB Solum, 'Procedural Justice' (2004) 78 S Cal L Rev 181, 278–279.

33 AS Goldstein, 'The State and the Accused: Balance of Advantage in Criminal Procedure' (1960) 69 Yale LJ 1149, 1150.

34 Introduction, text to n 11.

35 Duff and others (n 21) 287–288.

with a broad construction, an enlightened approach, in keeping with the spirit of the instrument, which continues to reverberate in modern judgements.[36] The inherent ambiguity of the content of the 'fair hearing' guarantee in this provision presented the authorities with scope for positive exploitation. Articles 6(2) and (3) contain specific guarantees that form a constituent part of the 'fair hearing' guarantee without exhausting its content,[37] thus a hearing may be unfair despite observance of the articles.[38] A determination of whether or not the guarantee has been complied with must be made in the light of the overall context of the proceedings ('trial as a whole'),[39] which can include pre-trial[40] and appellate stages.[41] On this basis, the content of the 'fair hearing' requirement has been continually and prudently open to a flexible and evolutionary interpretation, depending on new developments in national criminal procedure systems, and enabled the Convention institutions to incorporate implicit procedural safeguards therein beyond the rights expressly specified in Article 6. Thus, despite the absence of an express reference to the concept of equality of arms in Article 6, both Commission and Court adjudged it from an early stage to be an inherent element of the Article 6(1) 'fair hearing' obligation,[42] thereby specifically formalising the concept. By virtue of this inextricable link, disregard

---

36 Eg *Perez v France* (App 47287/99) ECHR 2004-I [64]; *Gregačević v Croatia* (App 58331/09) ECHR 10 July 2012 [49]; *Javor and Javorová v Slovakia* (App 42360/10) ECHR 15 September 2015 [59]: 'the right to a fair trial holds so prominent a place in a democratic society that there can be no justification for interpreting Article 6 § 1 restrictively.'

37 *Nielsen v Denmark* (App 343/57) (1961) 4 Yearbook 494 (EComHR) 548; *Deweer v Belgium* (App 6903/75) (1980) Series A no 35 [56].

38 *Nielsen* (n 37) 548; *Barberà, Messegué and Jabardo v Spain* (App 10590/83) (1988) Series A no 146 [67], [80], [89], [91].

39 *Vidal v Belgium* (App 12351/86) (1992) Series A no 235-B [33]. See also eg *Isgrò v Italy* (App 11339/85) (1991) Series A no 194-A [31]; *Edwards v UK* (App 13071/87) (1992) Series A no 247-B [34]; *Van Mechelen and others v the Netherlands* (App 21363/93 et seq) ECHR 1997-III [50]; *Schatschaschwili v Germany* (App 9154/10) ECHR 2015 [116].

40 Eg *Imbrioscia v Switzerland* (App 13972/88) (1993) Series A no 275 [36], [38]; *John Murray v UK* (App 18731/91) ECHR 1996-I [62]–[63]; *Brennan v UK* (App 39846/98) ECHR 2001-X [45]; *Öcalan* (n 1) [131].

41 Eg *Delcourt v Belgium* (App 2689/65) (1970) Series A no 11 [25]; *Monnell and Morris v UK* (Apps 9562/81; 9818/82) (1987) Series A no 115 [54]; *Ekbatani v Sweden* (App 10563/83) (1988) Series A no 134 [24]; *Belziuk v Poland* (App 23103/93) ECHR 1998-II [37]; *Evrenos Önen v Turkey* (App 29782/02) ECHR 15 February 2007 [28]; *Tudor-Comert v Moldova* (App 27888/04) ECHR 4 November 2008 [35] (civil).

42 *X v Sweden* (App 434/58) (1959) 2 Yearbook 354 (EComHR) 370, 372 (civil); *X v Germany* (App 1169/61) (1963) 6 Yearbook 520 (EComHR) 574; *Neumeister v Austria* (App 1936/63) (1968) Series A no 8 [22] ('The Law').

In *Ofner and Hopfinger v Austria* (Apps 524/59; 617/59) (1963) 6 Yearbook 676 (EComHR) 696 and *Pataki and Dunshirn v Austria* (Apps 596/59; 789/60) (1963) 6 Yearbook 714 (EComHR) 731–732, the Commission acknowledged that the legal basis of the concept could, instead, possibly derive from Arts 6(3)(b) and (c). It refused, however, to offer a conclusive view on this issue because, in any case, it was beyond doubt that the wider and general provision for a fair trial in Art 6(1) embodied the concept of equality of arms. This approach is understandable given the absence of any discernible benefit arising from the alternative legal basis. A strict attachment of the concept to these articles would impose a

for the concept in itself amounts to an infringement of Article 6(1).[43] Regard must be had for it from pre-trial to appellate level proceedings, whether such proceedings are rooted in the adversarial or the inquisitorial tradition. Yet, quite reasonably, adherence to it does not automatically assure fulfilment of the 'fair hearing' requirement because the former comprises only one subsidiary feature of the overarching latter.[44] Nevertheless, the concept is the feature most crucial to an evaluation of whether or not a hearing is fair:[45] it impacts on the balance of procedural opportunities between the parties to prepare and present their cases to influence the outcome, thus lies at the very core of the trial structure and the fair trial guarantee.

3.2. BASIS IN INTERNATIONAL LAW

It is, therefore, unsurprising that jurisprudential recognition of a requirement for procedural equality as an implied component of a fair hearing is not exclusive to the Strasbourg organs. It also finds acceptance in international law.

The concept of equality of arms has featured in the jurisprudence of the Human Rights Committee (HRC) and of other international adjudicatory bodies for human rights protection. In its interpretation of the 'fair hearing' guarantee in Article 14(1) ICCPR, the HRC has oft-reiterated that respect for equality of arms is included therein.[46] Sometimes equality of arms is also associated with the right to be 'equal before the courts' in the same provision,[47] though the latter

greater limitation on its potential scope of application. Interestingly, these cases were the first at Strasbourg to employ the term 'equality of arms'.

Equality of arms is also implied in the fair hearing requirement as applied to civil litigation: *Dombo Beheer BV v the Netherlands* (App 14448/88) (1993) Series A no 274 [33].

43 *De Haes and Gijsels v Belgium* (App 19983/92) ECHR 1997-I [58]–[59].

44 *Delcourt* (n 41) [28]. See also eg *Monnell and Morris* (n 41) [62].

45 A view shared by M Nowak, *UN Covenant on Civil and Political Rights: CCPR Commentary* (Engel, Kehl 1993) 246 and the Trial Chamber in *Prosecutor v Delalic* (Decision on the Prosecution's Motion for an Order Requiring Advance Disclosure of Witnesses by the Defence) ICTY-96-21 (4 February 1998) [45].

46 Eg *Morael v France* (Comm 207/1986) UN Doc Supp No 40 (A/44/40) 210 (1989) [9.3]; *Wolf v Panama* (Comm 289/1988) UN Doc CCPR/C/44/D/289/1988 80 (1992) [6.6]; *John Campbell v Jamaica* (Comm 307/1988) UN Doc CCPR/C/47/D/307/1988 (1993) [6.4]; *Fei v Colombia* (Comm 514/1992) UN Doc CCPR/C/53/D/514/1992 (1995) [8.4]; *Jansen-Gielen v the Netherlands* (Comm 846/1999) UN Doc CCPR/C/71/D/846/1999 (2001) [8.2]; *Äärelä and Näkkäläjärvi v Finland* (Comm 779/1997) UN Doc CCPR/C/73/D/779/1997 (2001) [7.4].

47 Eg *Frank Robinson v Jamaica* (Comm 223/1987) UN Doc CCPR/C/35/D/223/1987 (1989) [10.4]; D Weissbrodt, *The Right to a Fair Trial Under the Universal Declaration of Human Rights and the International Covenant on Civil and Political Rights* (Martinus Nijhoff, The Hague 2001) 130–131; L Doswald-Beck and R Kolb, *Judicial Process and Human Rights: United Nations, European, American and African Systems: Texts and Summaries of International Case Law* (NP Engel, Kehl 2004) 144; HRC, 'General Comment No 32: Article 14: Right to Equality before Courts and Tribunals and to Fair Trial' (2007) UN Doc CCPR/C/GC/32 [8], [13].

is predominantly a specific application of the non-discrimination stipulation in Article 26.[48] Equality of arms concerns prevention of the improper difference in procedural treatment of parties arising from their opposing roles; discrimination practices, on the other hand, relate to undue distinctions made on non-role grounds, including race, colour, sex or religion. Similarly, the entitlement of an accused to minimum defence guarantees 'with full equality' in Article 8(2) of the American Convention on Human Rights is more strongly allied to the anti-discrimination provisions of Articles 1(1) and 24[49] than the principle of equality of arms. This principle is, nevertheless, acknowledged within the inter-American human rights system. It has been applied by the Inter-American Court most prominently in relation to its own practice and procedure and that of the Inter-American Commission, rather than in respect of its analysis of domestic proceedings.[50] The African Commission on Human and Peoples' Rights has also exercised its interpretative function in ascribing equality of arms to the concept of fair trial in Article 7 of the associated African Charter:

> the right to fair trial involves fulfilment of certain objective criteria, including the right to equal treatment ... The right to equal treatment ... means ... that both the defence and the public prosecutor shall have equal opportunity to prepare and present their pleas and indictment during the trial. Simply put, they should argue their cases before the jurisdiction on an equal footing.[51]

The precedence set by the human rights bodies has found acceptance within ad hoc tribunals exercising competence in international criminal law: the International Criminal Tribunals for Rwanda (ICTR) and the former

---

48 Art 26: 'All persons are equal before the law and are entitled without any discrimination to the equal protection of the law'; Nowak (n 45) 238–239. See also HRC, 'General Comment No 18: Non-discrimination' (1989) UN Doc A/45/40 [3], [10]; S Trechsel, *Human Rights in Criminal Proceedings* (OUP, Oxford 2005) 94–95 who considers that the right to equality before the courts refers exclusively to the principle of non-discrimination.

49 Art 1(1): States parties are obliged to ensure that all persons are able to exercise their 'rights and freedoms, without any discrimination'; Art 24: 'All persons are equal before the law. Consequently, they are entitled, without discrimination, to equal protection of the law.'

50 S Negri, 'The Principle of "Equality of Arms" and the Evolving Law of International Criminal Procedure' (2005) 5 Int CLR 513, 532. See eg *Gangaram Panday Case* (Preliminary Objections) Inter-Am Ct HR Series C No 12 (4 December 1991) [18], [8] (Concur Op Judge AA Cançado Trindade); *Cayara Case* (Preliminary Objections) Inter-Am Ct HR Series C No 14 (3 February 1993) [13]; *Castillo Petruzzi et al Case* (Judgment) Inter-Am Ct HR Series C No 52 (30 May 1999) [60]; *Barrios Altos Case* (Interpretation of Judgment on the Merits: Art 67 ACHR) Inter-Am Ct HR Series C No 83 (3 September 2001) [6]; *Cantoral Benavides Case* (Reparations: Art 63(1) ACHR) Inter-Am Ct HR Series C No 88 (3 December 2001) [31]; *19 Merchants Case* (Preliminary Objections) Inter-Am Ct HR Series C No 93 (12 June 2002) [28], [31].

51 *Avocats Sans Frontières (on behalf of Bwampamye) v Burundi* (Comm 231/99) African Comm Hum & Peoples' Rights (2000) [26]–[27].

Yugoslavia (ICTY). Entrenched in Articles 20(1) and 21(2) of the ICTY Statute,[52] and in corresponding Articles 19(1) and 20(2) of the ICTR Statute,[53] is the general fair trial guarantee. In *Prosecutor v Tadić*, the ICTY Appeals Chamber held that 'the principle of equality of arms falls within the fair trial guarantee under the Statute',[54] a theme recurrent in the Tribunal's jurisprudence.[55] In so doing, the Chamber exhibited a willingness to consider international case-law, including that of the Strasbourg Court, as an authoritative point of reference for its assessment.[56] Not only does this approach, oft-employed by the ICTY, offer clarity with respect to defining a concept, but it supports the legitimacy of the Tribunal's conclusions and ensures a basic level of consistency with other international practice of significance.[57] Such international practice includes that of the ICTR which has also attributed a legal basis to the concept of equality of arms through the fair trial guarantee in its Statute.[58]

The degree of international acceptance of equality of arms as an aspect of procedural fairness is given greater width in the context of inter-state disputes before the International Court of Justice (ICJ), its former president Shi Jiuyong professing that states are to be guaranteed equality of arms before the Court.[59] Absent an express reference to a right to a fair hearing within its Statute and Rules of Court, several clauses remain as indicators of a requirement that parties be placed on an equal footing in their case preparation and presentation.[60] The

---

52 (Adopted and entered into force 25 May 1993, as amended 7 July 2009) <www.icty.org/sid/135>.

53 (Adopted and entered into force 8 November 1994, as amended 16 December 2009) <http://unictr.unmict.org/en/documents/statute-and-creation>.

54 (Judgement) ICTY-94-1-A (15 July 1999) [44].

55 Eg *Delalic* (n 45) [45]; *Prosecutor v Milutinović* (Decision on Interlocutory Appeal on Motion for Additional Funds) (Appeals Chamber) ICTY-99-37-AR73.2 (13 November 2003) [26] (Diss Op Judge Hunt); *Prosecutor v Halilović* (Decision on Motion for Prosecution Access to Defence Documents Used in Cross-Examination of Prosecution Witnesses) (Trial Chamber) ICTY-01-48-T (9 May 2005) [7]–[8].

56 *Tadić* (n 54) [44]: 'there is no reason to distinguish the notion of fair trial under Article 20(1) of the Statute from its equivalent in the ECHR and ICCPR, as interpreted by the relevant judicial and supervisory treaty bodies under those instruments', [48]–[50]. See also *Prosecutor v Delalic* (Judgement) (Appeals Chamber) ICTY-96-21-A (20 February 2001) [24]: 'the Appeals Chamber will necessarily take into consideration other decisions of international courts'.

57 A Cassese, 'The Influence of the European Court of Human Rights on International Criminal Tribunals – Some Methodological Remarks' in M Bergsmo (ed), *Human Rights and Criminal Justice for the Downtrodden* (Martinus Nijhoff, Leiden 2003) 24–26, 31–45.

58 Eg *Prosecutor v Kayishema and Ruzindana* (Judgement: Reasons) (Appeals Chamber) ICTR-95-1-A (1 June 2001) [67]; *Prosecutor v Bagilishema* (Judgement) (Trial Chamber) ICTR-95-1A-T (7 June 2001) [14]; *Prosecutor v Nahimana* (Decision on the Motion to Stay the Proceedings in the Trial of Ferdinand Nahimana) (Trial Chamber) ICTR-99-52-T (5 June 2003) [4].

59 UN General Assembly, 'Report of the International Court of Justice: 1 August 2003–31 July 2004' 59th Session Supp No 4 UN Doc A/59/4 (2004) [288].

60 ICJ Statute (adopted 26 June 1945, entered into force 24 October 1945) <www.icj-cij.org/documents/index.php?p1=4&p2=2&p3=0>: eg Arts 35(2) (conditions under which the Court

ICJ has, accordingly, endeavoured to ensure equality of arms in contentious cases,[61] including *Military and Paramilitary Activities in and against Nicaragua*:

> the Court has to emphasize that the equality of the parties to the dispute must remain the basic principle for the Court. … [N]either party should be placed at a disadvantage … The Court is careful … to give each of them the same opportunities and chances to produce their evidence; … [it] regards it as essential to guarantee as perfect equality as possible between the parties.[62]

Similarly, the presence of a fundamental requirement for the ICJ to observe equality of arms in its binding advisory capacity has also been acknowledged. This was particularly evident when tasked with reviewing employment cases.[63]

---

is accessible to states not party to the Statute must not 'place the parties in a position of inequality before the Court'); 39(3) ('The Court shall, at the request of any party, authorize a language other than French or English to be used by that party'); 42(2) (parties 'may have the assistance of counsel or advocates before the Court'); 43(4) ('A certified copy of every document produced by one party shall be communicated to the other party').

ICJ Rules of Court (adopted 14 April 1978, entered into force 1 July 1978, as amended 14 April 2005) <www.icj-cij.org/documents/index.php?p1=4&p2=3&p3=0>: eg Arts 56(3) (on production of a late document, 'the other party shall have an opportunity of commenting upon it and of submitting documents in support of its comments'); 57 ('each party shall communicate to the Registrar, in sufficient time before the opening of the oral proceedings, information regarding any evidence which it intends to produce or which it intends to request the Court to obtain. … A copy of the communication shall also be furnished for transmission to the other party'); 72 (any submissions or evidence by a party 'received by the Court after the closure of the oral proceedings, shall be communicated to the other party, which shall be given the opportunity of commenting upon it'); 76(3) (if a party requests revocation or modification of a provisional measures decision, 'the Court shall afford the parties an opportunity of presenting their observations on the subject').

See also *Military and Paramilitary Activities in and against Nicaragua (Nicaragua v US)* (Merits: Judgement) [1986] ICJ Rep 14 [59]: 'The Court is bound by the relevant provisions of its Statute and its Rules relating to the system of evidence, provisions devised to guarantee the sound administration of justice, while respecting the equality of the parties.'

61 Eg *Maritime Delimitation and Territorial Questions between Qatar and Bahrain (Qatar v Bahrain)* (Jurisdiction and Admissibility: Judgement) [1994] ICJ Rep 112 [39]; *Request for an Examination of the Situation in Accordance with Paragraph 63 of the Court's Judgment of 20 December 1974 in the Nuclear Tests (New Zealand v France) Case* (Order) [1995] ICJ Rep 288 [28]; *Application of the Convention on the Prevention and Punishment of the Crime of Genocide (Bosnia and Herzegovina v Yugoslavia)* (Counter-Claims: Order) [1997] ICJ Rep 243 [42], 296 (Diss Op Vice-President Weeramantry); *Oil Platforms (Islamic Republic of Iran v US)* (Counter-Claim: Order) [1998] ICJ Rep 190 [45]; *Land and Maritime Boundary between Cameroon and Nigeria (Cameroon v Nigeria)* (Order) [1999] ICJ Rep 983, 986.

62 *Military and Paramilitary Activities* (n 60) [31], [59].

63 Eg *Judgements of the Administrative Tribunal of the ILO upon Complaints made against the UNESCO* (Advisory Opinion) [1956] ICJ Rep 77, 86: 'The principle of equality of the parties follows from the requirements of good administration of justice'; *Application for Review of Judgement No 158 of the United Nations Administrative Tribunal* (Advisory Opinion) [1973] ICJ Rep 166 [92]: Equality of arms is one of the 'well recognized' criterions of procedural fairness; *Application for Review of Judgement No 273 of the United Nations Administrative Tribunal* (Advisory Opinion) [1982] ICJ Rep 325 [59]: 'elementary principles of judicial procedure' include equality of arms.

Accordingly, it opined that '[g]eneral principles of law and the judicial character of the Court do require that, even in advisory proceedings, the interested parties should each have an opportunity, and on a basis of equality, to submit all the elements relevant to the questions which have been referred to the review tribunal.'[64]

It is particularly interesting that the ICJ had recourse to 'general principles of law' as recognised in Article 38(1)(c) of its Statute in sourcing a legal basis for the concept of equality of arms. 'General principles' have been confirmed widely as representing doctrines underlying the international legal system and/or domestic law.[65] Prevalent articulation of the basic right to a fair trial on the international plane and in major national legal systems is indicative of its status as an accepted general principle of law.[66] Given that the concept of equality of arms is a cogent deduction from this right and fundamental to its effective realisation, it is plausible to afford the concept the same status.

This is not, however, to exclude the concept from possible customary norm status within the meaning of Article 38(1)(b) of the same statute ('general practice accepted as law') for there is considerable overlap between custom and general principles: 'customary practice may emerge from or be based on pre-existing "principles." *Mutatis mutandi*, customs, when consistently practiced, become "principles."'[67] Reflecting this article, the formation of international custom traditionally requires 'extensive and virtually uniform' state practice accompanied by *opinio juris*: 'a belief that this practice is rendered obligatory by the existence of a rule of law requiring it.'[68] Playing a supplementary role are multilateral conventions whose function extends to 'recording and

---

64 *Application for Review of Judgement No 158* (n 63) [36], [38] ('The Court is ... concerned to ensure that the interested parties shall have a fair and equal opportunity to present their views to the Court').

65 Eg NK Hevener and SA Mosher, 'General Principles of Law and the UN Covenant on Civil and Political Rights' (1978) 27 ICLQ 596, 602; MC Bassiouni, 'A Functional Approach to "General Principles of International Law"' (1990) 11 Mich J Int'l L 768, 768, 771–772; B Simma and P Alston, 'The Sources of Human Rights Law: Custom, Jus Cogens, and General Principles' (1992) 12 Aust YBIL 82, 102; MC Bassiouni, 'Human Rights in the Context of Criminal Justice: Identifying International Procedural Protections and Equivalent Protections in National Constitutions' (1993) 3 Duke J Comp & Int'l L 235, 238–239; A Cassese, *International Law* (OUP, Oxford 2001) 86–88, 158; H Thirlway, 'The Sources of International Law' in MD Evans (ed), *International Law* (2nd edn OUP, Oxford 2006) 128.

66 American Law Institute, *Restatement of the Law Third: The Foreign Relations Law of the United States* (American Law Institute, St Paul Minnesota 1987) vol 1, 28–29; Bassiouni 1993 (n 65) 265–286, 292; Cassese (n 65) 104; CJM Safferling, *Towards an International Criminal Procedure* (OUP, Oxford 2001) 27.

67 Bassiouni 1990 (n 65) 801. For further acknowledgement of the overlap, see eg American Law Institute (n 66) 29; T Meron, *Human Rights and Humanitarian Norms as Customary Law* (Clarendon, Oxford 1989) 89; Simma and Alston (n 65) 102; Thirlway (n 65) 128.

68 *North Sea Continental Shelf Cases (Germany v Denmark; Germany v Netherlands)* (Judgement) [1969] ICJ Rep 3 [74], [77].

defining rules deriving from custom, or indeed in developing them.'[69] The crystallisation of the right to a fair trial into customary international law has recurrently been asserted, including by the ICTY and ICTR.[70] Neither of these tribunals are partnered with a treaty and, accordingly, principally apply custom in rendering judgement. Their express recognition of the concept of equality of arms, therefore, serves to evidence a belief that it is part of customary international law. As with general principles, it is the cogency of the deduction from the fair trial right that lends credence to this belief, in addition to the common acceptance of procedural equality in all the international tribunals mentioned hitherto and *in foro domestico*. Of course, one must accept that there will be instances of state conduct infringing upon this requirement of equality. This does not deny the requirement from acquiring customary status, providing a consistent pattern of infringements do not occur within a wide number of states. The establishment of a customary rule is not dependent upon absolute conformity thereto.[71] If, alternatively, one is to postulate that sufficient state practice and *opinio juris* endorsing procedural equality does not exist, the concept of equality of arms still remains suited to classification as a general principle of law: 'the concept of a "recognised" general principle seems to conform more closely than the concept of custom to the situation where a norm invested with strong inherent authority is widely accepted even though widely violated.'[72] Nevertheless, the view to be preferred tentatively is that the requisite *opinio juris* confirmed by state practice exists to confer customary status upon the concept of equality of arms. Beyond treaty law, therefore, this concept may be ascribed to both custom and general principles of law,[73] thereby imposing upon states not party to relevant treaties a legally binding obligation in international law to implement equality of arms in their judicial proceedings.

---

69 *Continental Shelf (Libyan Arab Jamahiriya/Malta)* (Judgement) [1985] ICJ Rep 13 [27].

70 Eg *Prosecutor v Aleksovski* (Judgement) (Appeals Chamber) ICTY-95-14/1-A (24 March 2000) [104]; *Kayishema and Ruzindana* (n 58) [51]; American Law Institute (n 66) vol 2, 166–167; Meron (n 67) 96–97; H Hannum, 'The Status of the Universal Declaration of Human Rights in National and International Law' (1995–1996) 25 Ga J Int'l & Comp L 287, 345–346.

71 *Military and Paramilitary Activities* (n 60) [186].

72 Simma and Alston (n 65) 102 in reference to American Branch of the International Law Association, Report of the Committee on the Formation of Customary International Law: 'The Role of State Practice in the Formation of Customary and *Jus Cogens* Norms of International Law' (19 January 1989) 10.

73 S Negri, 'Equality of Arms – Guiding Light or Empty Shell?' in M Bohlander (ed), *International Criminal Justice: A Critical Analysis of Institutions and Procedures* (Cameron May, London 2007) 69–70.

4. THE FUNDAMENTAL ELEMENTS OF EQUALITY OF ARMS DEFINED

The definition of the concept of equality of arms, mentioned in the introduction above, provides a mandate for partially symmetrical procedural treatment of adversaries in the preparation and presentation of their cases. It exposes four fundamental elements requiring elaboration.

4.1. OPPONENTS

The concept of equality of arms is by definition applicable only to opposing parties ('his opponent').

4.1.1. Accused and the Prosecution

The prosecution and the accused are predominantly the only parties to criminal proceedings. They are natural adversaries and occupy inherently unique positions in relation to each other. The role of the prosecution and its counsel is to assist the court in arriving at the objective truth and ensure the effective delivery of justice on behalf of the community, rather than endeavouring merely to secure a conviction,[74] by prosecuting cases in which there is sufficient evidence, both in respect of admissibility and weight, to reasonably indicate that a conviction is

---

[74] Eg in the English legal system: *R v Puddick* (1865) 176 ER 662, 663 (Crompton J): 'counsel for the prosecution … are to regard themselves as ministers of justice, and not to struggle for a conviction' (affirmed by Avory J in *R v Banks* [1916] 2 KB 621 (CCA) 623); S Rogers, 'The Ethics of Advocacy' (1899) 15 LQR 259, 259: Prosecuting counsel 'should regard himself not as a mere advocate for a party, striving to win a verdict, but as an assistant to the Court in … ascertaining the truth according to the law. He is … "a kind of minister of justice filling a *quasi*-judicial position"'; *Randall v The Queen* [2002] UKPC 19; [2002] 1 WLR 2237 [10] (Lord Bingham): 'The duty of prosecuting counsel is not to obtain a conviction at all costs but to act as a minister of justice'; Crown Prosecution Service (CPS), *The Code for Crown Prosecutors* (7th edn, London 2013) [2.4]: 'Prosecutors must always act in the interests of justice and not solely for the purpose of obtaining a conviction.'

In Germany: Criminal Procedure Code 1987 (as amended) (StPO) ss 160(2): Prosecutors 'shall ascertain not only incriminating but also exonerating circumstances, and shall ensure that evidence, the loss of which is to be feared, is taken'; 296(2): Prosecuting counsel 'may also make use of [appellate remedies] for the benefit of the accused.' Translated in B Duffett and others (trs), 'The German Code of Criminal Procedure' (Federal Ministry of Justice, 2014) <https://www.gesetze-im-internet.de/englisch_stpo/englisch_stpo.html>.

In France: Code of Criminal Procedure 1958 (as amended) Art 33: 'The public prosecutor … is free to make such oral submissions as it believes to be in the interest of justice.' Translated in JR Spencer (tr), 'Code of Criminal Procedure' (Legifrance, 2006) <https://www.legifrance.gouv.fr/Traductions/en-English/Legifrance-translations>.

more likely than not to ensue and when public interest considerations permit.[75] This evidence is the result of a joint enterprise between the prosecution and the police. The opponent status of the prosecution not only derives from its capacity to prosecute criminal offences, but also from its capacity to discredit the merits of the case for the accused to an extent impacting upon the decision of the court. The accused, by contrast, is the subject of the criminal action, hazarded involuntarily by the possible imposition of punitive measures, and his position is reactionary and effectively one of self-interest. His adversariness is exhibited in his dedication to frustrating by counterargument the prospects of success of his antagonist's cause, either through legal representation or pro se.

4.1.2. Avocat Général or Similar Officer

Accused persons within civil law based systems have argued before the Court that an opponent relationship can also exist at appellate level between themselves and an *avocat général* or his equivalent. An *avocat général* or similar officer in such cases is distinct from a conventional prosecutor, though remains affiliated with the prosecuting authority, and is tasked with advising the court objectively on the law, in some jurisdictions with a view to ensuring the consistency of judicial precedent. *Delcourt v Belgium*[76] and *Borgers v Belgium*[77] evidence a marked evolution in the response of the Court to such officers. Both concerned an *avocat général* who had made submissions, without an opportunity of reply for the accused, that the appeal be dismissed and attended, without voting rights, the court's deliberations. An opponent relationship was not recognised in *Delcourt* where the Court regarded the *avocat général* merely as an independent and impartial adviser on the law and not concerned with establishment of guilt or innocence, a position it viewed as not unfairly disadvantageous to the accused.[78] Also influential to the Court was that the challenged procedure formed part of a long-standing and unquestioned tradition.[79]

Whereas *Delcourt* attracted substantial criticism throughout the 1970s,[80] it was not until 1991 that an opportunity arose for the Court to reassess the

---

75 Eg in England and Wales: CPS (n 74) [4.4]–[4.12]. In Germany: StPO (n 74) ss 152(2), 153(1), 153a(1), 153c(1)–(3), 153d(1), 153e(1), 203, 376.

76 *Delcourt* (n 41).

77 (App 12005/86) (1991) Series A no 214-B.

78 *Delcourt* (n 41) [33]–[35]. See further *Ofner and Hopfinger* (n 42) 704 where the EComHR did not view the *Generalprokurator* (Attorney-General) as an opponent as he merely stamped the report of the Judge-Rapporteur as 'agreed', an act not prejudicial to the accused. However, it observed that an inequality of arms may have occurred had the *Generalprokurator* attempted to influence the court's decision to the disadvantage of the accused without the latter being heard.

79 *Delcourt* (n 41) [36].

80 Eg Comments, 'Human Rights – Equality of Arms – Presence of Attorney General at Deliberations of Belgian Court of Cassation Held Not Violative of Article 6(1) of the European Court of Human Rights: *Delcourt* Case' (1971) 4 NYU J Int'l L & Pol 124, 130–131, 133;

procedure and depart from its earlier decision. In *Borgers*, the Court reaffirmed the objectivity of the *avocat général* but now considered that, by recommending that the appeal be dismissed, he became objectively speaking an opponent and it was thus an inequality of arms for the accused not to have a right of response.[81] This procedural inequality was increased more so by the *avocat général's* participation in the deliberations which afforded him an additional opportunity to promote an opinion unfavourable to the accused.[82] An additional feature of the case was the importance attached to 'appearances'.[83] Recourse to appearances is associated predominantly with the requirement of an impartial tribunal and grounded in the maxim that 'justice should not only be done, but should manifestly and undoubtedly be seen to be done.'[84] Objectively justified fears[85] could be generated as to the neutrality of a legal officer who makes submissions adverse to a party.[86] Whilst regard for appearances in this context has met both praise[87] and criticism,[88] the opponent status of the *avocat général* was certainly justified. Though he was objective, he was associated with the prosecuting authority and clearly expressed opposition to the defence whilst in a position to influence the court. He essentially assumed, or appeared to have assumed, a prosecutorial role. Also justified was the Court not sharing the reticence demonstrated in *Delcourt* to attach a status to the *avocat général* that conflicted with that afforded pursuant to long-established tradition. The Convention is, after all, 'a living instrument to be interpreted in the light of

---

KH Nadelmann, 'Due Process of Law before the European Court of Human Rights: The Secret Deliberation' (1972) 66 AJIL 509, 513–514, 517, 519, 522–524; M Cappelletti and JA Jolowicz, *Public Interest Parties and the Active Role of the Judge in Civil Litigation* (Oceana, Dobbs Ferry New York 1975) 31 fn 54; SA Cohn, 'International Adjudication of Human Rights: A Survey of its Procedural and Some of its Substantive Holdings' (1977) 7 Ga J Int'l & Comp L 315, 377.

81 *Borgers* (n 77) [24], [26]–[27], [29].

82 Ibid [28].

83 Ibid [24], [29]. Subsequently, the Court has on several occasions mentioned that it will consider 'appearances' when assessing compliance with the concept of equality of arms: eg *Bulut* (n 1) [47]; *Josef Fischer* (n 1) [18]; *Lanz* (n 1) [57]; *Öcalan* (n 1) [140]; *Stadukhin v Russia* (App 6857/02) ECHR 18 October 2007 [28]; *Moiseyev v Russia* (App 62936/00) ECHR 9 October 2008 [203], [207]. It does not in practice, however, rely upon the mere appearance of an inequality, but upon the presence of a substantive inequality to register an inequality of arms.

84 *R v Sussex Justices ex p McCarthy* [1924] 1 KB 256, 259 (Lord Hewart CJ). The maxim was first referred to in *Delcourt* (n 41) [31] and is linked to appearances and impartiality in several judgements: eg *De Cubber v Belgium* (App 9186/80) (1984) Series A no 86 [26]; *Mežnarić v Croatia* (App 71615/01) ECHR 15 July 2005 [32]; *Olujić v Croatia* (App 22330/05) ECHR 5 February 2009 [63]; *Micallef v Malta* (App 17056/06) ECHR 15 October 2009 [98].

85 For the purposes of the appearances doctrine, '[w]hat is decisive is whether the doubts raised by appearances can be held objectively justified': *Brandstetter v Austria* (Apps 11170/84; 12876/87; 13468/87) (1991) Series A no 211 [44]; *Stoimenov v the former Yugoslav Republic of Macedonia* (App 17995/02) ECHR 5 April 2007 [40].

86 *Kress v France* (App 39594/98) ECHR 2001-VI [81].

87 Eg Trechsel (n 48) 100; D Harris and others, *Harris, O'Boyle and Warbrick: Law of the European Convention on Human Rights* (2nd edn OUP, Oxford 2009) 252.

88 *Borgers* (n 77) Diss Ops Judges Cremona; Martens [3.3]–[3.9]; Storme [10]–[11]; *Kress* (n 86) Joint Partly Diss Op Judge Wildhaber and others [7]–[8], [13].

current conditions' and domestically unquestioned traditions, however old, cannot justify non-compliance with prevailing European law.[89] Subsequent cases have also reinforced the fact that those assuming a quasi-judicial function are not necessarily immune from opponent status.[90]

One cannot but conclude, therefore, that an opponent of the accused in criminal proceedings may be defined as one who is not judge, juror or witness[91] but is directly part of the prosecution team or, like an *avocat général* or similar officer, is a party joined to the proceedings whose position or observations cannot be regarded as neutral.[92] Those falling within the latter category become allies of the prosecution if not already affiliated hierarchically with it.

4.2. ARMS

The 'arms' aspect of the concept of equality of arms refers to the 'opportunity to present his case' component of the established definition.

Whereas the definition expressly mentions case presentation rather than preparation, the latter is implicit therein; trial advocacy and case preparation are natural and necessary bedfellows, hence its inclusion in this discussion. Effective

---

89 *Kress* (n 86) [70].

90 Eg ibid [81]–[83]; *Bulut* (n 1) [48]–[50]; *Reinhardt and Slimane-Kaïd v France* (Apps 23043/93; 22921/93) ECHR 1998-II [103], [105]; *Josef Fischer* (n 1) [21]–[22]; *Lanz* (n 1) [60], [64]; *APBP v France* (App 38436/97) ECHR 21 March 2002 [28]–[29].

91 Judges and jurors are independent and neutral decision-makers who are part of the court itself, and lay or expert witnesses are evidential sources called by opposing parties or the court.

The justices' clerk in the magistrates' court (England and Wales) also acts solely as part of the tribunal itself, hence is not an opponent: *Mort v UK* (App 44564/98) ECHR 2001-IX s B(1)(b) ('The Law'): 'There is no question of the justices' clerk enjoying any role in the proceedings independent of the justices, or in having any duty with regard to influencing a decision in any particular direction. In that respect, the clerk's position can be distinguished from officers such as the *procureur général*, *avocat général* or *commissaire du gouvernement*, who make submissions to the courts concerning their personal views on the outcome of particular cases.'

92 A party may be joined to the proceedings without being a state representative. Amnesty International was granted leave to intervene fully in the proceedings concerning Pinochet before the former House of Lords, the latter dealing purely with points of law of general public importance. This intervener was thereby rendered an additional party to the proceedings, independent of the prosecuting authority. Its position, by virtue of its adverse interests to the merits of Pinochet's case, was that of an opponent: *R v Bow Street Metropolitan Stipendiary Magistrate, ex p Pinochet Ugarte* [2000] 1 AC 61 (HL); *R v Bow Street Metropolitan Stipendiary Magistrate, ex p Pinochet Ugarte (No 2)* [2000] 1 AC 119 (HL); *R v Bow Street Metropolitan Stipendiary Magistrate, ex p Pinochet Ugarte (No 3)* [2000] 1 AC 147 (HL).

Intervention, nevertheless, is restricted. Affirming that the opposing parties in criminal proceedings are generally the prosecution and defence, the Divisional Court subsequently held that an overwhelming reason for intervention by an interested party would be required for leave to be granted in cases other than those which strictly concerned points of law, which might merit being handled differently: *Re Pinochet Ugarte (No 4)* [1999] All ER (D) 1371 (QB).

preparation breeds an effective response to disputed facts and aids in the delivery of convincing legal argument when facing an opponent at trial. This relationship is acknowledged by Article 6(3), the specific guarantees of which are intended to facilitate both case preparation and presentation.

'Opportunity', in the aforementioned extract from the definition, equates to procedural rights for it is the latter that generate the former. Procedural rights constitute the 'arms' that make available an 'opportunity' and medium for the parties to prepare their cases and participate proactively throughout the entire proceedings; law, facts and evidence provide the ammunition. Thus, '[w]hile a criminal trial is not a game in which the participants are expected to enter the ring with a near match in skills, neither is it a sacrifice of unarmed prisoners to gladiators.'[93] Incorporated within the term 'procedural rights' is access by the parties to the powers of the court, including available remedies. Accordingly, for example, where the parties are permitted to apply for leave to appeal, this is to be regarded as a procedural right. The procedural rights afforded the defence enabling case preparation and presentation must, of course, comply with the standards of the Article 6 catalogue. The 'arms' element, therefore, has a simplistic significance. It indicates merely that the concept of equality of arms is applicable to procedural rights or opportunities designed for case preparation and presentation within a judicial decision-making scheme for opposing parties.

4.3. EQUALITY

4.3.1. Procedural Equality

The 'conditions that do not place him at a disadvantage vis-à-vis his opponent' feature of the definition of the concept of equality of arms introduces a comparative element questioning whether the procedural rights afforded a party to prepare and present his case were equal to those extended to his opponent. It is by virtue of this feature that the notion of 'equality' is fused with the above-mentioned procedural 'arms' aspect of the definition, inferring equality of opportunity for case preparation and presentation. Implicit in equality is also the principle of reasonableness: the procedural scheme must be such that a reasonable man would adjudge the procedural rights to have been allocated to the parties in equal measure. Equality of arms, therefore, is a construct demanding that the procedural rights made available to parties to enable case preparation and presentation be preserved, as far as the parties' different roles permit, in a reasonably symmetrical balance to ensure equal treatment throughout the proceedings. To observe this balance de facto and de jure is to promote a relationship of reciprocity between the parties. In consequence

93 *Williams v Twomey* 510 F2d 634, 640 (7th Cir 1975) (Wyzanski J).

of its manifestly procedural cast, the concept of equality of arms is concerned essentially with equality of procedural position before the court in an attempt to redress the natural power and resource differentials between the state and the individual. The term 'equality of the parties' can be used as a synonym for 'equality of arms'. The latter term, nevertheless, reflects more aptly the substance of the concept it designates, readily implying that the parties are to be equally armed (in procedural opportunities), rather than be equal in a more substantive sense, and should be favoured.

4.3.2. *Equality Distinguished*

It is the condition of equality that distinguishes the concept of equality of arms from the principle from which it originally derives. It is an evolutionary development of the natural justice principle *audi alteram partem*, which calls for all parties to be given an opportunity to be heard before judgement is rendered. Fawcett, Nowak, and Jackson and Summers unconvincingly equate both principles.[94] Equality of arms, however, is a wider and more sophisticated concept. It conveys that it is insufficient merely to hear the other side; the other side must be heard on equal terms.

Cheng, nonetheless, constructs a contrasting proposition, advancing that the rule *audi alteram partem* is a derivative of the principle of equality of arms, the latter being a corollary of the right to an impartial tribunal.[95] His proposition is unpersuasive. As aforementioned, the introduction of an 'equality' requirement in hearings represents a transition from the basic to the more sophisticated. To be heard on equal terms, one must first have the right to be heard. Accordingly, logic indicates that the principle to originate first was not equality of arms. The link presented between procedural equality and the impartiality of the tribunal is also defective. The former does not stem from the latter. The issue of impartiality relates to improper influences on the composition of the court. A procedural inequality indicates that the process (pre-trial, trial and appeal procedures), rather than the decision-maker, is biased unduly against the unequal party. The procedural relationship between the parties, rather than the relationship between a party and the decision-maker, is at issue.

Whereas the concept of equality of arms is also distinguishable from the adversarial procedure principle, a close relationship remains between them in criminal proceedings. It is thus useful first to be informed of this relationship.

---

94 JES Fawcett, *The Application of the European Convention on Human Rights* (Clarendon, Oxford 1987) 154; Nowak (n 45) 246; JD Jackson and SJ Summers, *The Internationalisation of Criminal Evidence: Beyond the Common Law and Civil Law Traditions* (CUP, Cambridge 2012) 83 fn 35.

95 B Cheng, *General Principles of Law as Applied by International Courts and Tribunals* (CUP, Cambridge 1993) 290–291.

The right to adversarial proceedings is harboured implicitly in the Article 6(1) requirement of a fair hearing and entails that 'each party must in principle have the opportunity ... to have knowledge of and comment on all evidence adduced or observations filed with a view to influencing the court's decision.'[96] It is, essentially, a right of informed response and extends to submissions on points of procedure.[97] This does not, however, render it synonymous with the principle of *audi alteram partem*. It is a specific elaboration thereof because each party is also entitled to be cognizant of the information upon which the other relies in putting forward his case. It is, furthermore, a right that is feasibly reciprocal and, by nature, essential for case preparation and presentation. Accordingly, the adversarial principle is rightly oft-conceived as embraced within the umbrella concept of equality of arms.[98] Such was the case, for example, in the Trial Chamber of the Special Court for Sierra Leone which considered that the 'effect' of the concept of equality of arms was to generate a right of the parties to respond.[99] Indeed, even in 1963, the Commission viewed the lack of an opportunity to respond to constitute an inequality of arms, though the term 'adversarial proceedings' or a similar characterisation ('adversarial trial'; 'adversarial argument') did not feature.[100] Such characterisation was first used by the Court in *Barberà, Messegué and Jabardo v Spain*[101] and the adversarial principle has been frequently accompanied thereafter by reference to the concept

96 *Eskelinen and others v Finland* (App 43803/98) ECHR 8 August 2006 [31]. See also eg *Brandstetter* (n 85) [66]–[67]; *JJ v the Netherlands* (App 21351/93) ECHR 1998-II [43]; *Meftah and others v France* (Apps 32911/96; 35237/97; 34595/97) ECHR 2002-VII [51]; *Abbasov v Azerbaijan* (App 24271/05) ECHR 17 January 2008 [30].

97 *Kamasinski v Austria* (App 9783/82) (1989) Series A no 168 [102]; *Edwards and Lewis v UK* (Apps 39647/98; 40461/98) ECHR 2004-X [46], [48].

98 Eg Fawcett (n 94) 154; P Plowden and K Kerrigan, *Advocacy and Human Rights: Using the Convention in Courts and Tribunals* (Cavendish, London 2002) 408; Doswald-Beck and Kolb (n 47) 144; E Brems, 'Conflicting Human Rights: An Exploration in the Context of the Right to a Fair Trial in the European Convention for the Protection of Human Rights and Fundamental Freedoms' (2005) 27 HRQ 294, 296; Negri (n 50) 517; P van Dijk and M Viering, 'Right to a Fair and Public Hearing (Article 6)' in P van Dijk and others (eds), *Theory and Practice of the European Convention on Human Rights* (4th edn Intersentia, Antwerp 2006) 580–581.

99 *Prosecutor v Norman et al* (CDF Case) (Decision on *Inter Partes* Motion by Prosecution to Freeze the Account of the Accused Sam Hinga Norman at Union Trust Bank (SL) Limited or at any other Bank in Sierra Leone) SCSL-04-14-PT (19 April 2004) text to fn 1.

See also eg *Delalic* (n 45) [47]: 'Very closely associated with the concept of equality of arms is the related concept of a judicial process, affectionately referred to as the right to have an adversarial trial'; HRC (n 47) [13]: 'The principle of equality between parties ... demands, inter alia, that each side be given the opportunity to contest all the arguments and evidence adduced by the other party.'

100 *Pataki and Dunshirn* (n 42) 732. Such characterisation eventually became the norm, eg *Belziuk v Poland* (App 23103/93) EComHR Report 26 February 1997 [39]: 'the principle of equality of arms ... also includes the fundamental right that criminal proceedings should be adversarial.'

101 *Barberà, Messegué and Jabardo* (n 38) [78].

of equality of arms.[102] Indeed, the Court has observed that the adversarial principle is implied from the latter concept.[103] There is considerable overlap between them because a breach of the adversarial principle creates a detrimental imbalance or exacerbates an existing one between the parties. Amongst several cases illustrative to this effect is *Lanz v Austria*: 'a party which is not informed about written submissions of the opposing party and thus deprived from reacting thereto is put at a substantial disadvantage vis-à-vis its opponent.'[104]

Despite this significant overlap, distinctions may be drawn between the adversarial and equality of arms principles. The former by definition offers greater specificity because it focuses solely on matters of disclosure and the opportunity to respond, whereas the applicability of the latter not only includes these aspects but also extends to a wider catalogue of procedural conditions in criminal proceedings. Whilst the adversarial principle is narrower in this sense, it is wider to the extent that, unlike the concept of equality of arms, its applicability is not restricted to the procedural relationship between *opponents*. It is applicable whenever *anyone* presents evidence or files observations which may influence the outcome of the proceedings. This includes, for example, victims who are not witnesses[105] or a trial judge who authors a statement to a superior court disputing an accused's factual allegations.[106] In effect, therefore, the right to adversarial proceedings prevents non-adversaries from creating an undue imbalance which tilts

---

102 Eg *Jasper v UK* (App 27052/95) ECHR 16 February 2000 [51]; *Georgios Papageorgiou v Greece* (App 59506/00) ECHR 2003-VI [36]; *Laukkanen and Manninen v Finland* (App 50230/99) ECHR 3 February 2004 [34]; *Koval v Ukraine* (App 65550/01) ECHR 19 October 2006 [113]; *Sidorova (Adukevich) v Russia* (App 4537/04) ECHR 14 February 2008 [24].

103 *Fretté v France* (App 36515/97) ECHR 2002-I [47]; *Užukauskas v Lithuania* (App 16965/04) ECHR 6 July 2010 [45]; *Zhuk v Ukraine* (App 45783/05) ECHR 21 October 2010 [25]; *Eftimov v the former Yugoslav Republic of Macedonia* (App 59974/08) ECHR 2 July 2015 [38].

104 *Lanz* (n 1) [62]. See also eg *Borgers* (n 77) [26]–[27]; *Bulut* (n 1) [49]–[50]; *Werner v Austria* (App 21835/93) ECHR 1997-VII [67] (civil); *Reinhardt and Slimane-Kaïd* (n 90) [103], [105]–[106]; *Kuopila v Finland* (App 27752/95) ECHR 27 April 2000 [38].

105 The accused should at the sentencing stage be entitled under the adversarial principle to respond to a victim impact statement (outlines the physical, emotional, psychological and financial impact of the crime). Such statements may be made, for example, by bereaved close relatives who did not appear as witnesses at trial.

106 *Kamasinski* (n 97) [102]. See also *Nideröst-Huber v Switzerland* (App 18990/91) ECHR 1997-I [31] (civil) where the applicant was unable to inspect and comment on observations of a lower court which the Federal Court reproduced in its judgement.

Unlike in criminal cases, with some exceptions (*JJ* (n 96) [43]; *Meftah* (n 96) [51]–[52]; *Şahin Çağdaş v Turkey* (App 28137/02) ECHR 11 April 2006 [28]–[30]), the Court has not generally in civil cases pursued an approach based on equality of arms, by classifying an independent member of the national legal service as an opponent, but has relied instead on the adversarial principle to find a breach of Article 6(1) when there was no opportunity to reply to his opinion: *Lobo Machado v Portugal* (App 15764/89) ECHR 1996-I [31]; *Vermeulen v Belgium* (App 19075/91) ECHR 1996-I [33]; *Van Orshoven v Belgium* (App 20122/92) ECHR 1997-III [41]–[42]; *KDB v the Netherlands* (App 21981/93) ECHR 1998-II [44]; *Göç v Turkey* (App 36590/97) ECHR 2002-V [55], [58]. An exception is *APEH Üldözötteinek Szövetsége and others v Hungary* (App 32367/96) ECHR 2000-X [42]–[44].

proceedings in favour of the prosecution without fear of response from an accused. It is this distinguishing feature that further renders the adversarial principle indispensable to Article 6(1).

4.3.3. *Degree of Equality*

It is instructive to a greater understanding of the degree of procedural equality insisted upon by the concept of equality of arms to outline and rebut criticism of the same in a US appeals case. *United States v Turkish*[107] explored the issue of equality of arms with respect to securing grants of 'use immunity' for defence witnesses, a procedural device used to ensure that a reluctant witness asserting the privilege against self-incrimination can be compelled to respond but no use, direct or indirect, may be made of the compelled testimony or evidence derived therefrom in a subsequent prosecution against that individual.[108] Accordingly, an immunised witness remains adequately protected[109] in the absence of the self-incrimination privilege in exchange for the surrender of potentially incriminating but useful evidence which may be relied upon by the calling party. Use immunity could be conferred upon prospective prosecution witnesses who invoked their privilege against self-incrimination but it was not accessible to the defence, thereby advantaging the prosecution in its ability to present its case and denying the accused an opportunity to possibly elicit truthful exculpatory evidence. The defence contended unsuccessfully that this unequal treatment of its witnesses was irreconcilable with the requirements of a fair trial. The court maintained that a 'criminal prosecution … is in no sense a symmetrical proceeding.'[110] It reasoned that the implementation of such a proceeding would involve the withdrawal of rights unique to the accused, thereby lowering the level of protection available to him, and imposing upon him the procedural burdens and restrictions assumed usually by the prosecution; an unfeasible proposition. Moreover, the court asserted that the public interest would not be served by extending to accused persons the powers of investigation and enforcement at the disposal of the state.[111] It determined, therefore, that operating an asymmetrical procedure was the correct approach by which to secure a fair trial: 'in the context of criminal investigation and criminal trials, where accuser and accused have inherently different roles, with entirely different

---

107 623 F2d 769 (2nd Cir 1980).

108 18 United States Code 2012 (as amended) s 6002. Available at Office of the Law Revision Counsel, 'United States Code' <http://uscode.house.gov/>.

109 *Kastigar v United States* 406 US 441, 459 (1972) (Powell J): 'This protection coextensive with the privilege [against self-incrimination] is the degree of protection that the Constitution requires, and is all that the Constitution requires'.

110 *Turkish* (n 107) 774 (Newman J).

111 Ibid.

powers and rights, equalization is not a sound principle on which to extend any particular procedural device.'[112]

This interpretation of the concept of equality of arms is certainly misguided. The true nature of the concept was not reflected accurately therein. The concept does not seek to equalise the material resources of the parties[113] or establish proceedings that are procedurally symmetrical *in toto*, with equal procedural rights, obligations and constraints throughout. It is relative and proportionate rather than absolute equality that it seeks to achieve; '[e]quality of arms means equality "as far as possible".'[114] The realisation of fairness in criminal proceedings, by implication also an attempt to redress the natural advantages of the state, requires essentially a hybrid procedure involving the co-existence of degrees of symmetry and asymmetry. Indeed, the concept of equality of arms recognises that entirely procedurally symmetrical criminal proceedings would be inappropriate and impracticable in view of the naturally different roles of the parties and its scope of application is restricted accordingly.[115]

The consequence of the dissimilar positions of prosecution and defence is implicit acceptance within the Convention that a procedural scheme incorporating some asymmetric features, resulting in the different treatment of opposing parties, is necessary and remains consistent with the requirement of procedural fairness. Procedural asymmetry operates on the premise that non-reciprocal rights between prosecution and defence will counteract each other. The most significant advantage afforded the prosecution, acting in partnership with the police, is its exclusive access to the unrivalled investigative, evidence gathering and enforcement assets of the state, which employs powers of, inter alia, interrogation, entry, search, surveillance and seizure. Consequently, it harbours a potent ability to assemble information adverse to the defence to substantiate a charge. Pragmatic considerations, nevertheless, tend against making these powers and resources available to accused persons. Conversely,

---

112 Ibid 774–775. Support for this analysis is provided by K Goldwasser, 'Limiting a Criminal Defendant's Use of Peremptory Challenges: On Symmetry and the Jury in a Criminal Trial' (1989) 102 Harv L Rev 808, 825–826: 'any argument that our criminal justice system equates fairness with symmetry would be … untenable. The system, adversary though it is, operates on the premise that fairness can be achieved only by recognizing the differences between prosecution and defence.'

113 *Kayishema and Ruzindana* (n 58) [69]: 'equality of arms between the Defence and the Prosecution does not necessarily amount to the material equality of possessing the same financial and/or personal resources'; *Bagilishema* (n 58) [14]: 'present human rights case law does not require that both parties in a case shall be granted the same level of material means and resources'.

114 *Korellis v Cyprus* (App 60804/00) ECHR 3 December 2002 ('The Law'). This is reflected in the idea of equality of arms requiring a 'fair', rather than an 'exact', balance between the parties: Introduction, text to n 21.

115 Safferling (n 66) 265: 'Equality [of arms] … does not mean equity of powers and rights but rather the balancing of the powers and rights of each participant according to the specific differences in their procedural roles.'

certain shielding devices are exclusively reserved for the accused, all of which are intended to mitigate the disparity of resources between the parties and/or are, by their very nature, unsuited to the role of the prosecution. Thus, for example, accused persons do not generally bear the burden of proof (presumption of innocence); are incompetent as witnesses for the prosecution; are not obliged to disclose inculpatory evidence, whereas the prosecution is bound ethically and legally to disclose exculpatory evidence; should have the benefit of an interpreter if unfamiliar with the language of the court; and are entitled to a trial within a reasonable time.

Consequently, the concept of equality of arms exists in conjunction with necessarily asymmetrical aspects of criminal proceedings and can thus be associated only with partial procedural symmetry. It has already been indicated that it is also associated only with procedural rights that are essential to facilitating the effective preparation and conduct of the case at hearing. Silver, accordingly, presses that the concept does not impact upon procedural rights that are naturally or necessarily non-reciprocal; only procedural rights that can feasibly and desirably be reciprocal and are a necessary means of enabling case preparation and/or presentation are situated within its remit.[116] This remit thereby extends to procedural possibilities including, for example, the rights to submit real evidence and written arguments, to make oral representations to the judge regarding the admissibility of disputed evidence, to present opening and closing speeches, to challenge a juror on cause shown, and to avail oneself of available judicial remedies. It would be unconvincing simply to contend that fairness does not require securing the enjoyment of these rights in equal measure for both parties. It is demonstrated in the following sub-section, however, that the remit is even broader than Silver suggests.

4.3.4. Equality and Article 6(3) ECHR

The concept of equality of arms pervades and underlies the provisions of Article 6(3), *Jespers v Belgium* providing a vividly pertinent attestation thereto: 'It is, in order to establish equality, as far as possible, between the prosecution and the defence that … the "rights of the defence", of which Article 6, paragraph 3 … gives a non-exhaustive list, have been instituted.'[117]

---

116 JS Silver, 'Equality of Arms and the Adversarial Process: A New Constitutional Right' [1990] Wis L Rev 1007, 1039.

117 (App 8403/78) (1981) 27 DR 61 [55]. The overlap between the concept of equality of arms and Art 6(3) is also acknowledged widely in legal scholarship: eg B Byfield, 'The Right to a Fair Trial: Article 6 of the European Convention' in AD Byre and BY Byfield (eds), *International Human Rights Law in the Commonwealth Caribbean* (Martinus Nijhoff, Dordrecht 1991) 93; J Coppel, *The Human Rights Act 1998: Enforcing the European Convention in the Domestic Courts* (J Wiley & Sons, Chichester 1999) [9.38]; R Clayton and H Tomlinson, *Fair Trial Rights* (2nd edn OUP, Oxford 2010) [11.430]; A Jennings, 'Fair Trial' in K Starmer and others, *Criminal Justice, Police Powers and Human Rights* (Blackstone, London 2001) 154; JG Merrills

The rights of Article 6(3) are not merely those of the accused, but also those of his representative.[118] The rights to adequate time and facilities, to legal representation and to call and examine witnesses included therein certainly accord with Silver's proposition, they all being feasibly reciprocal and essential for case preparation and/or presentation. Yet, his proposition harbours a significant error: the remit he attributes to the concept of equality of arms is excessively restrictive and, in contrast to *Jespers*, results in the exclusion of the two remaining Article 6(3) rights to prompt notification of the charge and to an interpreter. To be informed of the accusation is necessary for the preparation and presentation of effective and relevant arguments in response. The assistance of an interpreter capacitates the accused to communicate with the court and the prosecuting authorities, and if necessary with his own counsel, and to understand the evidence and proceedings against him. Both rights are clearly essential to effective case preparation and presentation. Nonetheless, equivalent rights are not logically required by the prosecution, which is inherently familiar with the charge and the language of the court. Therefore, the exclusion of these rights from Silver's proposition is grounded solely upon their non-reciprocal nature. The essence of procedural equality, however, does not merely represent qualified reciprocity. It seeks to remove disadvantage to secure equality of position and the rights to prompt notification of the charge and to an interpreter, for example, contribute to the realisation of this aim. Accordingly, and contrary to Silver's premise, it is possible for non-reciprocal rights necessary for case preparation and/or presentation to contribute to equality of procedural standing before the court, thereby becoming encompassed within the equality of arms remit.

It is certainly a remit not exhausted by the rights of Article 6(3), for it encompasses all procedural rights throughout the proceedings that are relevant to securing a fair balance between the parties. Also of importance is that the concept of equality of arms does not pose a restrictive influence over potential interpretations of Article 6(3) guarantees. Such an influence would merely serve to dilute the scope for dynamic, yet reasonable, interpretations which act as beacons for the evolution of domestic criminal justice systems to a higher standard of human rights protection. This appears to have been recognised by the Court and evidenced, for example, in its observation that the concept of equality of arms does not exhaust the content of Article 6(3)(d).[119] Thus, as with

---

and AH Robertson, *Human Rights in Europe: A Study of the European Convention on Human Rights* (4th edn Manchester UP, Manchester 2001) 119; Negri (n 73) 20; D Harris and others, *Harris, O'Boyle and Warbrick: Law of the European Convention on Human Rights* (3rd edn OUP, Oxford 2014) 414, 467.

118 *Ofner v Austria* (App 524/59) (1960) 3 Yearbook 322 (EComHR) 352; *Ensslin, Baader and Raspe v Germany* (Apps 7572/76; 7586/76; 7587/76) (1978) 14 DR 91, 115.

119 Eg *Vidal* (n 39) [33]; *Solakov v the former Yugoslav Republic of Macedonia* (App 47023/99) ECHR 2001-X [57]; *Popov v Russia* (App 26853/04) ECHR 13 July 2006 [178].

respect to the content of Article 6(1), the concept of equality of arms does not exhaust the content of any Article 6(3) guarantee. Nor does it always find itself referred to expressly in cases on Article 6(3); it is an underlying doctrine.

4.4. DISADVANTAGE

4.4.1. Disadvantage Defined

The concept of equality of arms, as defined, requires the accused to have suffered a 'disadvantage' for an infringement to be registered. The inherent ambiguity in the term allows for two distinct and credible interpretations thereof. The first refers to unequivocal inequality: a procedural inequality is inherently disadvantageous, regardless of its actual or inevitable prejudicial effect. The second is discerned from Convention case-law as the interpretation actually applied in practice: 'disadvantage' equates predominantly to de facto prejudice but can, in some circumstances, also refer to inevitable prejudice. Accordingly, when proceedings are viewed in their entirety, a disadvantage is suffered if the procedural inequality actually or inevitably had an adverse and material effect on the defence case and thus influenced the reliability of the outcome. Yet, implicit in this prejudice proviso is that detriment occasioned by the inequality may be offset or overcome by other procedural safeguards,[120] thereby rendering the proceedings nevertheless fair. Thus, in essence, it is not the fact of undue asymmetrical treatment itself that will give rise to a violation, but the actual or inevitable effect thereof within the context of the trial as a whole.

4.4.2. Actual Prejudice

Treatment of 'disadvantage' as synonymous with actual prejudice predominates the approach of the Strasbourg organs to equality of arms. A requirement of prejudice has been applied also to Article 6 in general[121] and Trechsel seems to

---

120 *Matyjek v Poland* (App 38184/03) ECHR 24 April 2007 [55]: 'in order to ensure that the accused receives a fair trial any difficulties caused to the defence by a limitation on its rights must be sufficiently counterbalanced by the procedures followed by the judicial authorities'. See also eg *Doorson v the Netherlands* (App 20524/92) ECHR 1996-II [72].

121 Eg Art 6(1): *Harper v UK* (App 11229/84) EComHR 10 November 1986 quoted in S Stavros, *The Guarantees for Accused Persons Under Article 6 of the European Convention on Human Rights: An Analysis of the Application of the Convention and a Comparison with Other Instruments* (Martinus Nijhoff, Dordrecht 1993) 44: 'Where the procedural flaw is not central to the notion of a fair hearing, as it would be in a situation where the defence was not allowed to put its case, a violation will only be registered if the shortcoming in question caused actual prejudice to the defence'; *Nielsen* (n 37) 550, 568: The applicant alleged that the court-appointed expert witness made remarks at trial dealing in an inadmissible manner with his guilt. Although the EComHR considered the statements objectionable, it concluded that both the public prosecutor and the trial president significantly contributed to

imply that it is the most natural interpretation of 'disadvantage'.[122] Application of the prejudice proviso in an equality of arms context was illustrated, for example, in *Kremzow v Austria*[123] where the Court confirmed that the applicant

neutralising the influence of the remarks on the jury, resulting in a fair trial; *Campbell v UK* (App 12323/86) (1988) 57 DR 148, 155–156: The EComHR considered that being handcuffed throughout an appeal hearing in which the accused represented himself did not hamper him from presenting adequately his submissions; *Stanford v UK* (App 16757/90) (1994) Series A no 282-A [24]–[25], [30], [32]: The applicant complained that the courtroom acoustics at trial were such that he was unable to hear evidence effectively therein. Admitting that he had encountered difficulties, the Court still maintained that the trial was fair on grounds, inter alia, that the applicant was represented ably and his representatives had the opportunity to discuss with him any evidential points arising.

Art 6(3)(b): *Köplinger v Austria* (App 1850/63) (1969) 12 Yearbook 438 (EComHR) 488: The applicant alleged that because of the seven changes of lawyers and their late appointment, they did not have the necessary time to prepare his defence effectively. The circumstances were not considered prejudicial and unlawful because the lawyer assisting the applicant at the decisive regional court stage was undisputedly provided adequate preparatory time and facilities, and the lawyer who prepared the appeal also represented him before the Supreme Court; *X v UK* (App 4042/69) (1970) 13 Yearbook 690 (EComHR) 696: 'whereas it is possibly true that the applicant met and instructed the lawyer who finally represented him only for ten minutes on the actual day of his trial ... the applicant has failed to show that, as a result, he suffered any prejudice in his representation'; *F v UK* (App 11058/84) (1986) 47 DR 230, 234–236: The applicant argued that he had been deprived of the right to privileged documents in the preparation of his defence as the documents had been seized and examined by police submitting evidence at trial. As use was not made of the documents at trial, the EComHR held that the hearing was fair, the applicant having suffered no actual prejudice.

Art 6(3)(c): *Pobornikoff v Austria* (App 28501/95) ECHR 3 October 2000 [31], [33]: The applicant complained, inter alia, of his exclusion from an appeal against sentence in which the Supreme Court carried out an assessment of his personality and character. The European Court, taking into account that a possible reduction in sentence had been at stake, did not consider that the case could have been properly examined without gaining a personal impression of the applicant. Accordingly, the applicant's exclusion was prejudicial.

See further Harris and others (n 87) 204.

122 Trechsel (n 48) 99: 'some sort of detrimental effect on the defence will have to be shown. This does not give cause for concern – after all, the very definition of the principle [of equality of arms] refers to the fact that the defence has suffered some type of "disadvantage".'

123 (App 12350/86) (1993) Series A no 268-B. See also eg *Kuopila* (n 104) [36]–[38]: The applicant complained that vital evidence had been submitted by the prosecution to the Court of Appeal without disclosure. This evidence was accompanied by a letter from the prosecutor communicating his view that the evidence was not relevant for the outcome of the case. The European Court considered that the prosecutor's opinion was intended to influence the appeal court and that the applicant should have been granted the opportunity to assess the relevance and weight of the evidence and submit comments. Consequently, the applicant was prejudiced in her ability to present her case and the principle of equality of arms was breached; *Coëme and others v Belgium* (App 32492/96 et seq) ECHR 2000-VII [101]–[103]: The applicant complained that he had been tried by the Court of Cassation without the rules governing the procedure having been established beforehand. The European Court found that the trial was infected by prejudicial uncertainty since the applicant 'could not ascertain in advance all the details of the procedure which would be followed' and 'could not foresee in what way the Court of Cassation would amend or modify the provisions governing the normal conduct of a criminal trial'. As a result, the applicant suffered an inequality of arms vis-à-vis the prosecution; *Solakov* (n 119) [57], [59]–[62], [65]–[67]: The applicant first alleged that he had been unable to cross-examine witnesses in the US whose statements served as

had encountered two instances of procedural inequality upon filing a plea of nullity before the Austrian Supreme Court. Whilst the applicant was required to introduce his submissions within strict time-limits, no time-limit had been imposed on the submission of the Attorney-General's *croquis* (consultation document outlining his position), resulting in the former being given less time in advance of the hearing to formulate his counterarguments. Additionally, unlike the applicant, the Attorney-General's office was advised of the identity of the reporting judge, thereby divulging which chamber would deal eventually with the case. Holding that the time and facilities granted to the applicant to prepare his response to the *croquis* were nevertheless adequate – three weeks and it was open to his lawyer to inspect it before its transmission – the Strasbourg Court did not consider the differences sufficient to prejudice the defence and overshadow the overall fairness of the proceedings, hence rejecting the applicant's complaint of inequality of arms.[124] The finding should not be construed as implying that all inequalities in themselves of inconsiderable import have no bearing on the fairness of the proceedings. Where more than one such example of inequality exists within a case, the firmly established trial as a whole approach ensures that it should be logical for the Court to consider not the individual effects of

important grounds for his conviction. The Court observed that the applicant's lawyers had been summoned to the US but failed to take reasonable steps to attend the hearing and examine the witnesses, or request postponement to ensure their attendance. Moreover, at trial, the applicant did not register a complaint in this respect, request that the witnesses be summoned or contest the contents of their statements. The Court highlighted the fact that the domestic courts made a comprehensive and careful analysis of the witnesses' statements and examined corroborating evidence. In view of the circumstances of the trial as a whole, it was satisfied that the applicant was given an adequate and proper opportunity to present his defence unprejudiced. The applicant's second complaint related to his inability to obtain the attendance and examination of two defence witnesses. Having regard to the reasons cited by him for summoning these witnesses and to the trial in its entirety, the Court found that the refusal to summon them did not restrict his defence rights to a prejudicial extent. Consequently, equality of arms was held to have been observed in respect of both complaints; *Ashot Harutyunyan v Armenia* (App 34334/04) ECHR 15 June 2010 [138]–[139]: The Court held that the placement of the applicant in a metal cage during the appeal proceedings was not prejudicial since he was still able to communicate confidentially and freely with his lawyers, and communicate freely with the court, hence was able to defend his case effectively. Consequently, there was no inequality of arms.

For the operation of the de facto prejudice proviso in the former EComHR, see also eg *Ofner and Hopfinger* (n 42) 700–706: The EComHR, particularly Mr Castberg, in its assessment of whether there was an inequality of arms, considered, inter alia, the position of the applicant at the outcome of the proceedings, specifically whether a *reformatio in peius* (to be placed in a worse position), a manifestation of actual prejudice, had occurred. There was held to be no such occurrence and equality of arms had been maintained; *U v Luxembourg* (App 10142/82) (1985) 42 DR 86, 96–97: The EComHR considered whether the fact that the prosecuting authorities had 30 days in which to enter an appeal, whereas the applicant had only 10 days, was contrary to the principle of equality of arms. The fundamental question, in its opinion, was whether, viewing the trial in its entirety, this inequality had a decisive influence on the proceedings. It declared the application inadmissible as the trial outcome could not be explained by the longer time granted to the prosecuting officer.

124 *Kremzow* (n 123) [48]–[50], [75].

the inequalities, but their cumulative effect.[125] This overall effect may be such as to effectively prevent the proper development of a party's case, rendering the inequalities, taken as a whole, prejudicial and accordingly upsetting procedural fairness.

An approach to equality of arms based upon a requirement of actual prejudice certainly meets the preference of states. They are more predisposed to accepting the unlawfulness of their conduct if it inflicts actual harm on the defence case and compromises the reliability of the outcome. Discerning actual harm naturally requires an examination of the entire proceedings, hence the application of the prejudice proviso is wholly consistent with the Court's ever present focus on the 'fairness of the trial as a whole'. This presents states with the opportunity, therefore, to offset the effect of inequalities with additional procedural safeguards before final judgement is reached and thus avoid an inequality of arms being registered. The prejudice approach, accordingly, accepts that an affront to individual dignity occasioned by inequality can sometimes be compensated for. It is also an approach indicative of a balancing of interests between state and individual: where the preparation and/or presentation of the defence is not affected by the inequality, the inequality is overlooked and the proceedings are still held to be fair, but if a prejudicial effect is present, a finding is made in favour of the accused.

The prejudice proviso raises concerns from a defence perspective. It evidences tolerance of a degree of unequal treatment and of the consequent offence to the dignity of the individual. It can also in some cases present an especially challenging burden for the applicant to prove that such treatment had an adverse and material effect on the defence case and thus influenced the reliability of the outcome of the proceedings. This is particularly so if the state implemented remedial measures in an attempt to offset the inequality or the inequality is borderline prejudicial. The restricted competence of the Court heightens the challenge; it is not an appeal court of fourth instance.[126] Linking an inequality with prejudice requires inevitably some appraisal of the merits of both sides of the case as presented during the domestic proceedings. Such an appraisal by the Court would conflict with the general fourth instance doctrine and, accordingly, it relies upon for guidance the pronouncements of higher domestic courts concerning the effect of the inequality in relation to the merits of the charge.[127]

---

125 This proposition accords logically with the holistic approach adopted and aptly demonstrated in *Barberà, Messegué and Jabardo* (n 38) [68], [89], where the Court held that an array of procedural deficiencies, whilst individually not of decisive importance, could cumulatively render the trial, 'as a whole', violative of Art 6(1). Procedural shortcomings comprised defendants being tried almost immediately after an overnight road transfer of over 600 km; a late and unexpected change in bench membership; the brevity of the trial; and crucial evidence not being adduced and discussed orally in the defendants' presence.

126 Introduction, text to n 12.

127 Stavros (n 121) 45, 47.

Consequently, the case for the state can become more forceful and any reasonable uncertainties are more likely to fall in its favour. A distribution of the burden of proof could mitigate the extent of the hurdle the applicant must overcome if an actual prejudice approach is used. If the Court reasonably speculates that, in the case circumstances, prejudice was likely, though not inevitable, the state should bear the burden of proving the absence thereof; alternatively, if the Court does not reasonably expect on the facts that the inequality could have prejudiced the applicant, the latter could be required to prove the link between the inequality and the alleged detriment to the defence case.[128]

4.4.3. *Inevitable Prejudice*

A procedural inequality is in some circumstances such that prejudice is manifestly inevitable. Only when it is not, such as is the situation in most cases, is proof of prejudice requisite. The Court has been willing to accept inevitable prejudice as synonymous with 'disadvantage', rather than requiring prejudice to be proven, in its treatment of certain inequalities relevant to the right to legal assistance in Article 6(3)(c).[129] Such was the case in *Artico v Italy*[130] where the Court considered it impracticable to prove indubitably that a lack of legally aided assistance actually prejudiced the presentation of the defence.[131] It consequently took the view that prejudice is intrinsic to the absence of legal aid when it appears 'plausible' on the facts that the interests of justice did demand the assistance of counsel and he would have added to the effectiveness of the accused's defence.[132] Prejudice has also been assumed where states have placed undue restrictions on counsel visits[133] or insisted unjustifiably that counsel–client consultations be conducted within the hearing of the authorities.[134] The same is further evident when an accused suffers ineffective legal assistance attributable to the state.[135] One cannot but conclude that certain types of interference with the right to legal assistance or the absence of effective legal assistance will engender a disadvantage vis-à-vis the prosecution impacting upon many or all aspects of the proceedings and, in turn, upon the outcome thereof. Such interference or ineffectiveness is inevitably prejudicial because it prevents an adequate representation of the defence case. Equality of arms is certainly a stronger concept when the applicant need not prove that the inequality occasioned actual prejudice, particularly in instances where it is impracticable to do so. Given that

128 Ibid 47–48, 186.
129 Ch 5 ss 4.1.2, 6.2–7.
130 (App 6694/74) (1980) Series A no 37.
131 Ibid [35].
132 Ibid [34]–[35], [37].
133 Ch 5 s 6.2.
134 Ibid.
135 Ch 5 s 7.

the actual prejudice proviso dominates the approach of the Court to equality of arms, the Court's acceptance of inevitable prejudice in some scenarios as tantamount to 'disadvantage' is progressive.

4.4.4. *Unequivocal Inequality*

Even more progressive is to interpret 'disadvantage' as unequivocal inequality, an interpretation which does not carry a requirement of actual or inevitable prejudice: it is the fact of a procedural inequality in itself that is sufficient to constitute an inequality of arms.

An approach based on unequivocal inequality is lent deceptive authority by a remark made in some cases: 'the principle of the equality of arms does not depend on further, quantifiable unfairness flowing from a procedural inequality.'[136] However, the misleading quality of the remark is evident in the link between the rationale of the judgements in those cases and the de facto prejudice proviso. The cases concerned the submission of written observations by the state authorities to the courts without communication to the applicants.[137] The remark is directed specifically to the contents of the observations, indicating that they are not a decisive factor in finding a violation of the concept of equality of arms; the contents are further to the actual inequality. The decisive element of inequality was that the authorities had the benefit of an additional opportunity to assert their position and influence the outcome without the possibility of a response from the applicants that may have been material, the latter thereby suffering a prejudicial inequality.[138] The approach evidenced in practice in these cases is, therefore, consistent with the requirement of actual prejudice.

Despite this eventual reliance on the prejudice proviso, it remains valid textually to interpret 'disadvantage' as unequivocal inequality. To do so is acutely dignitarian, whereby any inequality is an affront to the dignity of the affected party and thereby a violation. Minor inequalities clearly not impacting on the outcome would still register a breach. To reject an unequivocal inequality based approach is to hold as acceptable some inequalities beyond those which are necessary by virtue of the roles of the opposing parties. Such inequalities in the 'arms' available to the parties offends against an intuitive sense of fair contest, regardless of outcome. Accordingly, the unequivocal inequality approach bestows the accused with a degree of protection far surpassing that of the prejudice approach, the latter limiting inherently the potential power of the concept of equality of arms. Though he acknowledges the dominance

136 *Bulut* (n 1) [49]; *APEH* (n 106) [42]; *Josef Fischer* (n 1) [19]; *Lanz* (n 1) [58].

137 Ch 4 s 4.2.2.2.

138 *Bulut* (n 1) [49]–[50]; *APEH* (n 106) [42]–[44]; *Josef Fischer* (n 1) [19], [21]–[22]; *Lanz* (n 1) [58], [60], [62]–[64].

of the actual prejudice proviso within Strasbourg case-law, the unequivocal inequality approach is favoured by Stavros.[139] If such an approach were taken, however, it would certainly not assist in acquiring the continued consent of Member States to the Convention, upon which the instrument's sustainability relies. States would feel aggrieved if their conduct was highlighted adversely on the international stage and they were compelled to amend existing rules of procedure even though particular inequalities, especially if minor, did not occasion actual prejudice to the defence case. Yet, the concept of equality of arms is more than about avoiding incorrect trial outcomes. If it is to express in practice its intrinsic value as strongly as possible – that is, protect the dignity of the individual as much as practicable – 'disadvantage' must equate to unequivocal inequality. Whilst perhaps appearing idealistic, it is not an unrealistic standard of equality for states to uphold in most cases. This dignitarian interpretation of 'disadvantage', it is submitted, should be preferred in most instances to that applied by the Court in practice requiring actual or inevitable prejudice.

4.4.5. Substantial Disadvantage

Several judgements incorporate the standard definition of the concept of equality of arms but with the exception that the reference to 'disadvantage' is immediately preceded by the term 'substantial'.[140] Their use of 'substantial', fortunately, does not expose the operation in practice of two severities of prejudice (some prejudice and substantial prejudice) in criminal proceedings. Indeed, the distinction between 'disadvantage' and 'substantial disadvantage' has not attracted judicial comment and appears to be purely illusory and without practical significance in the case-law.[141] If a requirement to demonstrate substantial prejudice in order to register a violation was applied in practice, it would imply simply that some procedural inequality harming the defence case, albeit less than substantially, is excusable. Such a consequence would be undesirable. Given that the Convention is a 'living instrument',[142] it is reasonable that definitions concerning rights

139 Stavros (n 121) 53: 'It is suggested … that the principle of the equality of arms goes to the heart of the right to be heard and that prejudice should be normally seen as inherent in the breach of this principle'.

140 Eg *Coëme and others* (n 123) [102]; *GB v France* (App 44069/98) ECHR 2001-X [58]; *MS v Finland* (App 46601/99) ECHR 22 March 2005 [30]; *Klimentyev v Russia* (App 46503/99) ECHR 16 November 2006 [95]; *Matyjek v Poland* (n 120) [55]. The definition was similarly specified by the EComHR in *Struppat v Germany* (App 2804/66) (1968) 27 CD 61, 73 and *Kaufman v Belgium* (App 10938/84) (1986) 50 DR 98, 115 (civil cases making reference also to criminal proceedings).

141 Trechsel (n 48) 97, who also highlights *Lanz* (n 1) [57] in which the Court omitted 'substantial' from the definition of equality of arms but cited as authority *Dombo Beheer BV* (n 42), a case in which 'substantial' was used.

142 *Tyrer v UK* (App 5856/72) (1978) Series A no 26 [31].

therein are subject to evolutionary modification. However, where a particular modification has no practical relevance, it should in subsequent case-law be avoided in favour of previous consistency. Accordingly, in future cases on equality of arms, the omission of the term 'substantial' when referring to 'disadvantage' would constitute a welcome development.

4.4.6. Shared Deprivation of a Procedural Right: No Disadvantage

Recognising a disadvantageous procedural position for the purposes of equality of arms complaints is a contrastive exercise; a disadvantage cannot exist in the absence of an undue contrast between the parties. Accordingly, if both parties are denied the opportunity to exercise the same procedural right, they are in theory treated equally and their positions in this respect cannot be contrasted; a position of disadvantage is thereby absent. Strasbourg proceedings have often given rise to cases in which prosecution and defence were jointly deprived of a particular procedural right and a disadvantageous position was consequently found lacking, rendering, by definition, equality of arms a concept that cannot be relied upon by an applicant in such circumstances. Many of these cases concern the right to be represented at leave to appeal or appeal proceedings. Echoing the approach of the Commission,[143] the Court in *Monnell and Morris v UK*[144] and *Ekbatani v Sweden*,[145] for example, found that the concept of equality of arms was respected at appellate level because the presence of both prosecution and defence was not permitted. This approach has been applied also with respect to disclosure. Whereas the defence alleged that it had been disadvantaged because the product of a telephone intercept had not been disclosed to it in *Jasper v UK*, the Court held procedural equality to have been realised as both prosecution and defence were prohibited from adducing the evidence in question.[146] The civil arena also further illustrates the relative character of equality and its impact on detecting disadvantage. In *Nideröst-Huber v Switzerland*, the applicant complained that the observations of a lower court calling for the dismissal of his case had been communicated to the Federal Court at appeal but not to him. The concept of equality of arms was not considered infringed because the observations were also not communicated to

143 Eg *X v Germany* (App 3139/67) (1968) 26 CD 77, 78–79; *X v UK* (App 5871/72) (1974) 1 DR 54, 54; *X v UK* (App 7413/76) (1977) 9 DR 100, 100–101; *Brown v UK* (App 11129/84) (1985) 42 DR 269, 271–272.

144 *Monnell and Morris* (n 41) [62].

145 *Ekbatani* (n 41) [30].

146 *Jasper* (n 102) [57]. See also *Sofri and others v Italy* (App 37235/97) ECHR 2003-VIII [1] ('The Law') in which certain evidence had never been made available to the defence because it had been lost or destroyed. As the prosecution were unable to forensically test the evidence, they too were unable to rely upon it at trial. Consequently, the parties were considered to be on an equal footing.

the respondent.[147] Similarly, in *Krčmář and others v the Czech Republic*, there was no disadvantage because the documentary evidence in issue, gathered by the appeal court on its own initiative, was not sent to either of the litigating parties.[148]

Criticism has, however, been levelled at the approach taken in all the aforementioned cases. Denouncing this approach as 'erroneous' and 'procedural equality at the lowest level', Stavros rightly asserts that '[a] right that might appear dispensable for the prosecution could be of fundamental importance to the defence.'[149] In such an event, the prosecution case can still find itself advantaged and this should be taken into account whenever the Court assesses whether the accused was placed on an equal footing. Nevertheless, if both parties are deprived of the same procedural right necessary for case preparation or presentation, possible relief resides within the Convention for the accused. The concept of equality of arms represents only a single component of the fair trial guarantee. Accordingly, observance of procedural equality does not preclude the finding of a breach of another fundamental fair trial right in the alternative. Such was evidenced, for instance, in *MS v Finland* where the applicant had alleged an inequality of arms because an adverse letter was submitted to the appeal court without communication to him. As the prosecution was also not privy to it, the Court did not consider procedural equality to have been compromised.[150] Instead, acknowledging that the letter was capable of influencing the appellate decision, it found a violation of the fair trial guarantee by relying on the accused's implied right to be aware of and comment on all evidence submitted with a view to influencing the decision-maker(s).[151]

4.4.7. The Disadvantaged Prosecutor

A strictly notional view of equality of arms would seem to suggest that a 'disadvantage' in criminal proceedings could relate not only to an inequality suffered by the accused, but also to an inequality suffered by the prosecution. Indeed, the very definition of the concept of equality of arms from Strasbourg refers to 'each party' being afforded a reasonable opportunity to present his case under non-disadvantageous conditions, relative to his opponent. Beyond this definition, the Court has often used language giving the appearance that neither party should suffer disadvantage. In *Ekbatani*, for instance, it commented that '[i]t is true that the Court of Appeal observed the principle of "equality of arms". In particular, neither Mr Ekbatani nor the prosecutor was allowed to appear

147 *Nideröst-Huber* (n 106) [23].
148 (App 35376/97) ECHR 3 March 2000 [39].
149 Stavros (n 121) 53–54.
150 *MS* (n 140) [31].
151 Ibid [32]–[34], [36]–[37].

in person before it and both were given equal opportunities to present their cases in writing.'[152] In *Barberà, Messegué and Jabardo*, the Court observed that Article 6(3)(d) 'entails equal treatment of the prosecution and the defence'.[153]

Recognition of the prosecutor as a potential sufferer of inequality has also come from the ICTY. The Trial Chamber in *Prosecutor v Delalic* pronounced that 'procedural equality means what it says, equality between the Prosecution and the Defence. … [A]n inclination in favour of the Defence is tantamount to a procedural inequality in favour of the Defence and against the Prosecution, and will result in inequality of arms.'[154] The Appeals Chamber reinforced this position in *Prosecutor v Aleksovski*, maintaining that equality of arms cannot be realised where the accused is favoured, beyond observance of his fundamental protections, to the disadvantage of the prosecution.[155] It found the same in *Tadić* relying on Convention jurisprudence: 'equality of arms obligates a judicial body to ensure that neither party is put at a disadvantage when presenting its case.'[156] This stance recognises that trials are arenas not only for an accused, but also for the interests of the community; as the community is represented by prosecutors, the latter are deserving of even-handed treatment in their case presentation,[157] insofar as their role permits. In *Delalic*, for example, the disadvantage was expressed as an unreasonable pre-trial failure to disclose to the prosecution the list of defence witnesses.[158] It makes conceptual sense, therefore, that procedural equality should not be solely the preserve of accused persons.

Whilst this may be accepted in theory by the European Court, an inherent restriction on its competence prevents it from applying in practice the principle of equality of arms to a disadvantaged prosecutor. The prosecution, as an agency of the state, cannot under Article 34 claim to be the victim of a violation.[159] In criminal proceedings, therefore, the Court is competent to redress a procedural imbalance only for accused persons. Interestingly, Judge Vohrah, relying on the actual practice of the European Court, took the view that the concept of equality of arms in the ICTY 'should be inclined in favour of the Defence acquiring parity with the Prosecution in the presentation of the Defence case … to preclude any

---

152 *Ekbatani* (n 41) [30].

153 *Barberà, Messegué and Jabardo* (n 38) [78].

154 *Delalic* (n 45) [49].

155 (Decision on Prosecutor's Appeal on Admissibility of Evidence) ICTY-95-14/1 (16 February 1999) [25].

156 *Tadić* (n 54) [48], [52]. See also eg *Milutinović* (n 55) [24]: 'The principle of equality of arms would be violated only if either party is put at a disadvantage when presenting its case'; *Halilović* (n 55) [8]: 'the principle of "equality of arms" should be interpreted in favour of both parties and not only in favour of the accused'.

157 *Aleksovski* (n 155) [25]; *Halilović* (n 55) [8].

158 *Delalic* (n 45) [49].

159 'The Court may receive applications from any person, *non-governmental organization* or group of individuals claiming to be the victim of a violation' (emphasis added).

injustice against the accused.'[160] He seems to apply the practical restriction imposed on the European Court to the ICTY, but fails to acknowledge that the role of the Tribunal is, in part, to assist both parties in the preparation of their cases,[161] the prosecution not being the organ of any state. Consequently, unlike the European Court, the ICTY is competent to redress any procedural disadvantage suffered by the prosecution. Therefore, despite the view of Judge Vohrah, it remains that the concept of equality of arms is applicable notionally in criminal proceedings to the position of the prosecutor but is enforceable, in this particular respect, only in fair trial regimes in which the competence of the court or tribunal allows.

5. CONCLUSION

This discussion set out to offer a thorough theoretical insight on the concept of equality of arms within a criminal context under Article 6.

It revealed that the value of this concept in its modern form is multi-faceted. It has two principal values, instrumental and intrinsic. Its instrumental value lies in its contribution to rendering more likely the achievement of a correct trial outcome. Its intrinsic value is that it reflects due respect for the dignity of the accused, enabling him to feel like an empowered and effective participant – for participation is a dignitarian process value – in the process by which his fate will be decided. It is submitted that this value rather than the former has theoretical primacy of importance, thus procedural equality would be a justified measure even if it was incapable of impacting on the trial outcome. It is a collateral consequence of the two principal values that procedural equality also has a secondary value as an element in realising some form of good governance because it is an expression of the state's respect for the rule of law and effort to secure a public perception of criminal process legitimacy.

A contemporary legal basis for procedural equality exists in Article 6 and in international law. Despite the lack of an express reference to the concept of equality of arms in Article 6, it is a well-established implied element of the Article 6(1) 'fair hearing' requirement and can apply to all stages of the proceedings. The concept is further accepted as an element of procedural

160 *Prosecutor v Tadić* (Separate Opinion of Judge Vohrah on Prosecution Motion for Production of Defence Witness Statements) (Trial Chamber) ICTY-94-1 (27 November 1996).

161 *Tadić* (n 54) [52]: 'the Chamber shall provide every practicable facility it is capable of granting under the Rules and Statute when faced with a request by a party for assistance in presenting its case.' See also ICTY Rules of Evidence and Procedure (adopted 11 February 1994, entered into force 14 March 1994, as amended 8 July 2015) UN Doc IT/32/Rev.50 (2015) r 54: 'At the request of either party or *proprio motu*, a Judge or a Trial Chamber may issue such orders, summonses, subpoenas, warrants and transfer orders as may be necessary for the purposes of an investigation or for the preparation or conduct of the trial.'

fairness in international law by human rights bodies, ad hoc criminal tribunals, and the ICJ. Indeed, it may also be considered both a general principle of law and part of customary international law.

The well-established Strasbourg definition of equality of arms has four fundamental elements which were elaborated upon in the above discussion to elucidate the nature of the concept.

Equality of arms as defined is applicable only to opposing parties. The opponent of the accused is predominantly the conventional prosecutor. The Court in *Borgers*, however, justifiably opened the door to opponent status being distributed more widely to avert procedural disadvantage. Rather than succumb to the influence of old-established national traditions, the Court relied on both an appearance of and actual lack of neutrality to establish opponent status for an individual not directly part of the prosecution team. Accordingly, a party joined to the proceedings, such as an *avocat général* or similar quasi-judicial officer, whose position or observations cannot be regarded as neutral can attract opponent status. It is thus that '[t]he principle of equality of arms has required civil law countries to make a sharper differentiation between those exercising judicial functions and those exercising "party" functions.'[162]

The 'arms' element of equality of arms relates to the 'opportunity to present his case' aspect of the established definition. It is implicit that this 'opportunity' refers also to case preparation, for it is a natural and necessary precursor to case presentation. 'Opportunity', whether in the context of case preparation or presentation, equates to procedural rights (arms). Equality of arms, therefore, concerns procedural rights formulated to afford parties an opportunity for case preparation and presentation in judicial proceedings.

The 'conditions that do not place him at a disadvantage vis-à-vis his opponent' component of the definition represents the requirement for 'equality' in the parties' procedural opportunities, as far as their different roles permit, to prepare and present their cases. This requirement is an evolutionary development of the principle of *audi alteram partem* and not a corollary of the right to an impartial tribunal. It also embraces the adversarial principle, though the latter can be applied additionally whenever a non-opponent presents evidence or files observations which may influence the outcome of the proceedings. The degree of procedural equality called for does not require criminal proceedings that are procedurally symmetrical *in toto*, for this would be inappropriate and impracticable given the naturally dissimilar roles of the parties; it requires only partial procedural symmetry. The content of this partial symmetry is not restricted only to procedural rights that can feasibly and desirably be reciprocal. Non-reciprocal rights – those not logically required by the prosecution – necessary for case preparation and/or presentation, such as the rights to prompt notification of the charge and to an interpreter, can also

162 Jackson and Summers (n 94) 101.

be encompassed within the equality of arms remit since they are intended to remove disadvantage. Article 6(3) contains reciprocal and non-reciprocal rights intended to establish procedural equality between prosecution and defence. The concept of equality of arms thus underlies these rights, albeit the nexus is not referred to expressly in every Article 6(3) case.

The fourth fundamental element of the definition of equality of arms is the requirement that the accused have suffered 'disadvantage' for a violation to be registered. In several cases, the term is prefixed with the word 'substantial' but this has no practical relevance and should be omitted in future case-law. Strictly notionally, 'disadvantage' can refer to an inequality of arms suffered by the prosecution; the Court, however, has competence only to redress disadvantage suffered by the accused. Two possible interpretations of 'disadvantage' exist.

The interpretation actually applied in practice is that the term equates predominantly to de facto prejudice but can, in some circumstances, also refer to inevitable prejudice. Thus, a disadvantage occurs if the procedural inequality actually or inevitably had an adverse and material effect on the defence case and, in turn, influenced the reliability of the outcome of the proceedings. This interpretation is consistent with the Strasbourg emphasis on considering the proceedings as a whole and accords states the opportunity in some circumstances to offset, through additional procedural safeguards, the effect of inequalities to prevent them from becoming prejudicial and constituting an inequality of arms. A requirement of actual prejudice not only evidences tolerance of some inequality, but also presents applicants with a sometimes especially challenging burden of proving causation. Moreover, reasonable uncertainties over causation are more likely to fall in favour of states given the restraints on the Court from the fourth instance doctrine. It is submitted that, if an actual prejudice approach is to be used, applicants should only be required to bear the burden of proof in cases where the Court does not reasonably expect on the facts that the inequality could have been prejudicial. In respect of certain inequalities relevant to the right to legal representation in Article 6(3)(c), however, the Court has taken a progressive approach, having accepted that prejudice was manifestly inevitable, and not required prejudice to be proven.

The second interpretation of 'disadvantage' is that a procedural inequality is sufficient in itself to satisfy the term and so amounts to an inequality of arms regardless of whether actual or inevitable prejudice was suffered. This is acutely dignitarian and offers the accused a much greater level of protection than the above interpretation, without being an unfeasible standard to uphold in most cases, and should, it is submitted, be preferred wherever possible.

Irrespective of the aforementioned interpretations, a 'disadvantage' is not generally registered at Strasbourg if prosecution and defence are jointly deprived of the procedural right at issue. However, this can still advantage the prosecution if the right is more important to the defence, a consequence the Court should take into account. Nevertheless, a practicable solution for applicants is to pray in aid that the deprivation is inconsistent with another fair trial right.

The insight into the concept of equality of arms offered herein should be kept in mind throughout Chapters 3–5. These chapters rely on Articles 6(3)(b)–(d) to illustrate and assess the Court's approach to the concept in various procedural situations. This approach is predominated by a requirement that there be actual or inevitable prejudice arising from a procedural inequality in order for a breach to occur. Article 6(3)(d) is the first discussed hereafter.

CHAPTER 3

EQUALITY OF ARMS AND THE RIGHT TO CHALLENGE AND CALL WITNESS EVIDENCE

1. INTRODUCTION

A failure to challenge adverse witness evidence is tantamount to tacit acceptance of such evidence as truth. It is imperative, therefore, that opportunities exist for such evidence to be tested and for favourable witness evidence to be admitted. To this effect, Article 6(3)(d) grants the accused in criminal proceedings the right 'to examine or have examined witnesses against him and to obtain the attendance and examination of witnesses on his behalf under the same conditions as witnesses against him.'

This chapter considers the Court's approach to equality of arms in the light of Article 6(3)(d). The requirement in the latter of equal conditions is one of several aspects evidencing a strong nexus with the concept of equality of arms and this relationship is explained in section 2. Identified in sections 3 and 4 are those who fall into the category of witness or of examiner respectively as Article 6(3)(d) provides no express definition thereof. With such terms defined, analysis of the right to question adverse witnesses predominates the remainder of the chapter, for this component of Article 6(3)(d) engages the foremost attention of the Court. This analysis begins in section 5 by outlining an examination model that is a benchmark of compliance with Article 6(3)(d) and serves as a point of reference for the subsequent discussion on derogations therefrom. The Court accepts that this model may be legitimately derogated from in exceptional cases without occasioning a violation. It has done so principally out of concern for the safety and well-being of victims and witnesses and their ability to testify freely,[1] an interest now acknowledged widely as one of those to be accommodated in criminal proceedings.[2] The Court must, therefore, balance a 'triangulation of

1 Derogation can be legitimate also on purely practical grounds such as, for example, when the witness is deceased or untraceable at the time of trial but has provided a statement beforehand.

2 Eg Convention against Torture and Other Cruel, Inhuman or Degrading Treatment or Punishment (adopted 10 December 1984, entered into force 26 June 1987) 1465 UNTS 85 Art 13: 'Each State Party shall ensure that ... the complainant and witnesses are protected

interests' between the accused, the prosecution (representing the societal interest in the administration of justice), and victims and witnesses.[3] Whereas victims and adverse witnesses are not opponents as defined in the concept of equality of

---

against all ill-treatment or intimidation as a consequence of his complaint or any evidence given.'

Declaration of Basic Principles of Justice for Victims of Crime and Abuse of Power (adopted 29 November 1985) UNGA Res 40/34 Annex 40 GAOR Supp (No 53) 214 UN Doc A/40/53 (1985) Principle 6(d): 'The responsiveness of judicial and administrative processes to the needs of victims should be facilitated by: Taking measures to minimize inconvenience to victims, protect their privacy, when necessary, and ensure their safety, as well as that of their families and witnesses on their behalf, from intimidation and retaliation'.

Statute of the International Criminal Tribunal for the former Yugoslavia (adopted and entered into force 25 May 1993, as amended 7 July 2009) <www.icty.org/sid/135> Arts 20(1) ('The Trial Chambers shall ensure that ... proceedings are conducted ... with ... due regard for the protection of victims and witnesses'), 22.

International Criminal Tribunal for Rwanda Rules of Procedure and Evidence (adopted 29 June 1995, as amended 13 May 2015) <http://unictr.unmict.org/en/documents/rules-procedure-and-evidence> r 69(A): 'either of the parties may apply to a Trial Chamber to order the non-disclosure of the identity of a victim or witness who may be in danger or at risk'.

Rome Statute of the International Criminal Court (adopted 17 July 1998, entered into force 1 July 2002) 2187 UNTS 90 Art 68; Rules of Procedure and Evidence of the International Criminal Court (adopted and entered into force 9 September 2002) <www.icc-cpi.int/resource-library/Documents/RulesProcedureEvidenceEng.pdf> rr 86 ('A Chamber in making any direction or order ... shall take into account the needs of all victims and witnesses'), 87–88.

R v DJX (1990) 91 Cr App R 36 (CA) 40 (Lord Lane CJ): 'The learned judge has the duty ... to see that the system operates fairly: fairly not only to the defendants but also to the prosecution and also to the witnesses'; *Prosecutor v Tadić* (Decision on the Prosecutor's Motion Requesting Protective Measures for Victims and Witnesses) (Trial Chamber) ICTY-94-1 (10 August 1995) [55]: 'A fair trial means not only fair treatment to the defendant but also to the prosecution and to the witnesses.'

Recommendation No R (85) 11 on the Position of the Victim in the Framework of Criminal Law and Procedure (adopted by Committee of Ministers 28 June 1985) (Council of Europe, Strasbourg 1985) [8] ('At all stages of the procedure, the victim should be questioned in a manner which gives due consideration to his personal situation, his rights and his dignity'), [16] ('especially when organised crime is involved, the victim and his family should be given effective protection against intimidation and the risk of retaliation by the offender'); Recommendation No R (97) 13 Concerning Intimidation of Witnesses and the Rights of the Defence (adopted by Committee of Ministers 10 September 1997) (Council of Europe, Strasbourg 1998) Explanatory Memorandum [49] refers to the '[s]tate's duty to provide effective measures to protect the witness, with a view to ensuring that he can testify in security.'

L Ellison, *The Adversarial Process and the Vulnerable Witness* (OUP, Oxford 2001) 65: 'Traditionally, the interests of witnesses have not been balanced against the rights of defendants to a fair trial but have been marginalized, the relationship between the state and the offender dominating all aspects of the criminal process. The proposition that the scope of fair trial rights can be assessed without reference to the rights and legitimate expectations of those who testify as witnesses ... is, however, no longer tenable'; J Doak, 'The Victim and the Criminal Process: An Analysis of Recent Trends in Regional and International Tribunals' (2003) 23 Legal Stud 1, 2–3, 6–10.

3 *R v A (No 2)* [2001] UKHL 25; [2002] 1 AC 45 [38] (Lord Steyn); *Attorney-General's Reference (No 3 of 1999)* [2001] 2 AC 91 (HL) 118 (Lord Steyn).

arms,[4] the accommodation of their interests can place the prosecution, which relies upon their testimony, in a position of procedural advantage over the accused. Section 6, accordingly, discusses the Court's approach to the concept of equality of arms within the context of derogations from the benchmark examination model. Therein, witnesses for whom derogations have been made are separated into three categories: absent, anonymous and vulnerable (child victims in sexual offence prosecutions). Having considered the first component of Article 6(3)(d), section 7 focuses thereafter on the accompanying but less jurisprudentially prominent right to call witness evidence under the same conditions as the prosecution.

2. THE NEXUS BETWEEN EQUALITY OF ARMS AND ARTICLE 6(3)(D)

Article 6(3)(d) is a specific manifestation of the concept of equality of arms. Amongst the individual guarantees of Article 6(3), it is the language of sub-paragraph (d), granting the accused a right to summon and examine witnesses 'under the same conditions' as the prosecution, which bears the closest resemblance to the Court's definition of equality of arms. Aside from this particular resemblance, the nexus can be discerned at a legal and a conceptual level.

2.1. LEGAL NEXUS

Authoritative statements establish that the link between Article 6(3)(d) and the concept of equality of arms is accepted in law. The article was first linked to procedural equality by the architects of the Convention in its drafting stages: 'The purpose of this [article] is to place the accused on a footing of equality with the public prosecutor, as regards the hearing of witnesses.'[5] This connection was reaffirmed by the former Commission[6] and has been consistently reflected in the Court's jurisprudence: 'Its essential aim, as is indicated by the words "under the same conditions", is a full "equality of arms" in the matter.'[7] Similarly, the

---

4 Ch 2 text to n 91.

5 'Text of the Report Submitted by the Conference to the Committee of Ministers' (16 March 1950) Doc CM/WP 4 (50) 19; CM/WP 4 (50) 16 rev; A 1431 reprinted in Council of Europe, *Collected Edition of the "Travaux Préparatoires" of the European Convention on Human Rights* (Martinus Nijhoff, The Hague 1977) vol 4, 242, 262.

6 Eg *Austria v Italy* (App 788/60) (1961) 4 Yearbook 116 (EComHR) 172; *X v Belgium* (App 1134/61) (1961) 4 Yearbook 378 (EComHR) 382; *Wiechert v Germany* (App 1404/62) (1964) 7 Yearbook 104 (EComHR) 110, 112; *X v Austria* (App 4428/70) (1972) 40 CD 1, 8.

7 *Engel and others v the Netherlands* (App 5100/71 et seq) (1976) Series A no 22 [91]. See also eg *Bönisch v Austria* (App 8658/79) (1985) Series A no 92 [32]: 'principle of equality of arms ... exemplified in paragraph (3)(d) of Article 6'; *Vidal v Belgium* (App 12351/86) (1992) Series A

Human Rights Committee has advanced that the concept of equality of arms lies at the heart of the ICCPR's equivalent Article 14(3)(e): 'As an application of the principle of equality of arms, this guarantee … guarantees the accused the same legal powers of compelling the attendance of witnesses and of examining or cross-examining any witnesses as are available to the prosecution.'[8]

The nexus between Article 6(3)(d) and procedural equality is made possible in the law of the Convention because both are aspects of the Article 6(1) fair hearing requirement. Accordingly, in its assessment of cases concerning Article 6(3)(d), the Court conjointly considers Article 6(1).[9] However, despite the close nature of the relationship between the concept of equality of arms and Article 6(3)(d), it does not necessarily follow that the former is expressly referred to in the Court's every application of the latter. Such is sometimes the case both because the presence of the equality of arms principle is readily implied and because the principle does not exhaust the content of Article 6(3)(d).[10]

2.2. CONCEPTUAL NEXUS

Further demonstrative of the nexus is that the exercise of Article 6(3)(d) serves the values reflected in the concept of equality of arms. It should be recalled that Chapter 2 established two principal values – instrumental (correct outcome) and intrinsic (dignitarian) – and a secondary value arising thereof: good governance.[11]

The Article 6(3)(d) right of the defence to call witnesses on equal terms with the prosecution contributes to the realisation of a correct trial outcome. The purpose of calling a witness is to elicit evidence establishing the defence case or a relevant part thereof. Doing so under the same procedural conditions as

---

no 235-B [33]; *Solakov v the former Yugoslav Republic of Macedonia* (App 47023/99) ECHR 2001-X [57]; *Popov v Russia* (App 26853/04) ECHR 13 July 2006 [176]; *Pello v Estonia* (App 11423/03) ECHR 12 April 2007 [26]; *Dorokhov v Russia* (App 66802/01) ECHR 14 February 2008 [65].

With the exception of *Bönisch*, it is interesting to note that the word 'full' attached to the 'equality of arms' reference in *Engel and others* also finds itself repeated in the other cited judgements. Its inclusion, when compared to judgements in which it is absent, is superfluous and appears not to have impacted upon the Strasbourg interpretation of the concept of equality of arms.

8 Human Rights Committee (HRC), 'General Comment No 32: Article 14: Right to Equality before Courts and Tribunals and to Fair Trial' (2007) UN Doc CCPR/C/GC/32 [39].

9 Eg *Lüdi v Switzerland* (App 12433/86) (1992) Series A no 238 [43]; *Lucà v Italy* (App 33354/96) ECHR 2001-II [37]; *SN v Sweden* (App 34209/96) ECHR 2002-V [43]; *Bocos-Cuesta v the Netherlands* (App 54789/00) ECHR 10 November 2005 [64]; *Kovač v Croatia* (App 503/05) ECHR 12 July 2007 [23]; *Balčiūnas v Lithuania* (App 17095/02) ECHR 20 July 2010 [101]. *Engel and others* (n 7) [91] is an exception.

10 *Vidal* (n 7) [33]; *Solakov* (n 7) [57]; *Popov* (n 7) [178].

11 Ch 2 s 2.

the prosecution ensures that prosecution witnesses cannot exert a one-sided influence on the court to the detriment of a correct outcome.

Also reflecting the instrumental value of the concept of equality of arms is the right to challenge witnesses under the same conditions as the prosecution. The aim of examining or having examined an adverse witness is to elicit favourable testimony and compromise the prosecution case. The latter requires exposing the factual limitations of the evidence and/or its unreliability, and/or impeaching witness credibility. Testing prosecution witnesses in this manner, under conditions of equality, ensures that the impact of their testimony on case outcome is proportionate to its actual evidential value, rather than to the value purported by the prosecution, hence is more conducive to a correct outcome. Also contributive to this aim is that the prosecution is restricted to the same opportunities to challenge witnesses as the defence. Were this not the case, an undue impression would be created for the court, misrepresenting the strength and quality of the evidence favourable to the accused.

Within trial hearings of the accusatorial mould, of course, challenging witness evidence through cross-examination by the parties is the preferred means of contributing to a correct outcome. It is a practice that has been lauded as highly effective for testing the veracity and accuracy of witness evidence,[12] and looked upon famously by Wigmore as being 'beyond any doubt the greatest legal engine ever invented for the discovery of truth.'[13] Accepting that cross-examination is a component of the Sixth Amendment confrontation clause of the US Constitution,[14] the underlying purpose of the provision being 'to augment accuracy in the factfinding process by ensuring the defendant an effective means to test adverse evidence',[15] the US Supreme Court has oft-recited Wigmore's description in agreement.[16] It is submitted, however, that the contribution of cross-examination towards a correct outcome is certainly

---

12 Eg *Mechanical & General Inventions Co Ltd and Lehwess v Austin and the Austin Motor Co Ltd* [1935] AC 346 (HL) 359; A Denning, *Freedom Under the Law* (Stevens & Sons, London 1949) 62.

13 JH Wigmore, *A Treatise on the Anglo-American System of Evidence in Trials at Common Law* (3rd edn Little, Brown and Co, Boston 1940) vol 5, 29.

Compare RC Park, 'Adversarial Influences on the Interrogation of Trial Witnesses' in PJ van Koppen and SD Penrod (eds), *Adversarial Versus Inquisitorial Justice: Psychological Perspectives on Criminal Justice Systems* (Kluwer Academic/Plenum, New York 2003) 166 who extensively evaluates Wigmore's assertion and concludes that '[i]t seems likely that the greatest legal engine for discovering the truth is discovery and investigation, not trial cross-examination.'

14 'In all criminal prosecutions, the accused shall enjoy the right … to be confronted with the witnesses against him'. See eg *Mattox v United States* 156 US 237, 242–243 (1895); *Pointer v Texas* 380 US 400, 406–407 (1965); *Douglas v Alabama* 380 US 415, 418 (1965); *Barber v Page* 390 US 719, 725 (1968); *Coy v Iowa* 487 US 1012, 1019–1020 (1988).

15 *Ohio v Roberts* 448 US 56, 65 (1980) (Blackmun J). See also *Kentucky v Stincer* 482 US 730, 736–737 (1987); *Maryland v Craig* 497 US 836, 845 (1990).

16 Eg *California v Green* 399 US 149, 158 (1970); *White v Illinois* 502 US 346, 356 (1992); *Lilly v Virginia* 527 US 116, 124 (1999).

less than Wigmore suggests: 'because cross-examination allows so much latitude for bullying and other truth-defeating stratagems, it is frequently the source of fresh distortion when brought to bear against truthful testimony.'[17] Indeed, research indicates that the consequence of direct and leading questions in cross-examination is answers that are less accurate than when witnesses are encouraged to give 'a free narrative',[18] the latter being a more prominent feature of inquisitorial judge-led examinations. Nevertheless, the value of cross-examination to correctness of outcome is still significant, thus it justifiably continues to remain the primary means of challenging witness evidence in accusatorial style trials.

Accompanying its instrumental value is the contribution Article 6(3)(d) also makes to the practical realisation of the intrinsic dignitarian value of the concept of equality of arms. Not only does it afford the accused an opportunity to put his own witness evidence before the court, but it also ensures that prosecution witness evidence is not merely accepted against him without an opportunity for challenge. He can thus engage the court in a participatory capacity and have his dignity respected.[19] In doing so, he can meaningfully influence the outcome of the case against him and thereby influence his own fate. Further preserving his dignity is that Article 6(3)(d) entails that his participation in matters of witness evidence is under conditions of equality with the prosecution.

The collateral effect of this dignitarian value and the above-mentioned instrumental value is that it indicates that some form of good governance by the state is being exercised, a secondary value of equality of arms. Adherence to Article 6(3)(d) demonstrates to the public that the court will take account of the witness evidence of both parties and such evidence will be adequately tested, hence bolstering its confidence that a correct verdict was reached. Additionally, as this evidence is to be treated under the same conditions as afforded the prosecution, society is reassured that the dignity of its members will be respected when opposed by the state in criminal proceedings.

---

17 JH Langbein, 'The German Advantage in Civil Procedure' (1985) 52 U Chi L Rev 823, 833. See also eg R Vouin, 'The Protection of the Accused in French Criminal Procedure' (1956) 5 ICLQ 157, 168: 'it does not ensure free and frank testimony from the witness'; Australian Law Reform Commission, 'Manner of Giving Evidence' Research Paper No 8 (Sydney 1982) ch 10 [5]: 'So far as obtaining accurate testimony is concerned, it is arguably the poorest of the techniques employed at present in the common law courts'; DJ Birch, 'The Criminal Justice Act 1988 – Part 2: Documentary Evidence' [1989] Crim LR 15, 17: Cross-examination demonstrates 'the power of a skilful cross-examiner to make an honest witness appear at best confused and at worst a liar.'

18 Law Commission, 'Evidence in Criminal Proceedings: Hearsay and Related Topics' Consultation Paper No 138 (HMSO, London 1995) [6.45].

19 TM Massaro, 'The Dignity Value of Face-to-Face Confrontations' (1988) 40 U Fla L Rev 863, 902–907.

Nevertheless, the conceptual nexus between Article 6(3)(d) and the principle of equality of arms is not founded solely on shared values. Article 6(3)(d) consists of a procedural right that is feasibly reciprocal and essential to case preparation and presentation, all of which are features identified in Chapter 2 that bring the provision within the remit of the equality of arms concept.[20] Also adduced in that chapter was that this remit encompasses the adversarial principle.[21] The Court invariably associates Article 6(3)(d) with the requirement upon states to ensure that evidence in criminal proceedings is produced 'with a view to adversarial argument.'[22] This association, accordingly, serves to strengthen the connection between this article and the concept of equality of arms.

3. WITNESS DEFINED

Given that 'witnesses' fall within the scope of Article 6(3)(d) but are without express definition therein, it is a term necessitating elaboration.

3.1. WITNESS

At a most basic level, a witness is one who renders testimony. To bear testimony is to attest to a personal observation which can be taken into account by a court in order to establish or prove a relevant fact. The most readily recognisable testimony is that delivered orally by a witness present in court under questioning. One must also recognise, however, that testimony can take the form of a solemn pre-trial written statement, such as a verbatim transcription of a police interrogation, a witness statement, a deposition, an affidavit or a transcript record of oral testimony tendered at a previous hearing.[23] It is to such formal statements made to state investigative, prosecutorial and judicial bodies that the attention of the Court is principally directed.[24]

---

20 Ch 2 ss 4.2–4.3.1, 4.3.3–4.3.4.

21 Ibid s 4.3.2.

22 Eg *Barberà, Messegué and Jabardo v Spain* (App 10590/83) (1988) Series A no 146 [78]; *AM v Italy* (App 37019/97) ECHR 1999-IX [25]; *SN* (n 9) [44]; *WS v Poland* (App 21508/02) ECHR 19 June 2007 [55].

23 Whilst the US Supreme Court did not conclusively define a 'testimonial statement' in *Crawford v Washington* 541 US 36, 51–52 (2004), it did provide some guidance therein, referring, inter alia, to '"pretrial statements that declarants would reasonably expect to be used prosecutorially"' (fn omitted). It also gave examples of statements which are not testimonial in character: 'a casual remark to an acquaintance'; '[a]n off-hand, overheard remark'; 'business records or statements in furtherance of a conspiracy.'

24 *R v Owen (Martin James)* [2001] EWCA Crim 1018 [18] (Keene LJ): 'there is no case where the European Court found a breach [of Article 6(3)(d)] in situations where the court had not been concerned with what might be called in English terms a "witness statement" i.e. a statement made by a potential witness to the police or the prosecuting authorities.'

For the purposes of Article 6(3)(d), the Court has opted to give the term 'witnesses' an autonomous meaning.[25] This ensures that its interpretation is not restricted to the narrow definitions implemented in some domestic legal systems, which may unduly circumvent Convention applicability, and that a universal approach is forged to secure parity of treatment between states. Such autonomy is, however, limited to the extent that it does not involve reclassifying those types of persons already classified as witnesses in domestic law.[26] By adopting this autonomous approach, the Court has not restricted the applicability of the term 'witnesses' to those simply bearing oral testimony at a hearing in person. The crucial criterion for bestowing witness status upon an individual appears to be whether he authored at any time a statement that was taken into account by the national court in its appraisal of the case.[27] Whether or not this statement was read out at trial has no bearing on the determination of the issue.[28] Neither is it a bar to acquiring witness status that the statement was made by a co-accused. Under the autonomous approach, 'where a statement may serve to a material degree as the basis for a conviction, then, irrespective of whether it was made by a witness in the strict sense or by a co-accused, it constitutes evidence for the prosecution to which the [Articles 6(1) and 6(3)(d)] guarantees ... apply.'[29] Accordingly, a co-accused can occupy the position of both party to proceedings and witness.

3.2. STATUS OF EXPERTS

Remaining to be addressed herein is the issue of whether witness status can also be extended to include experts. Experts can be court-appointed or engaged by the parties to provide admissible opinion evidence by report and/or in person on matters calling for, inter alia, technical, scientific or medical expertise. The function of this expertise is to assist decision-makers, presumed to be without the requisite special knowledge, skill and experience, to comprehend the nature

---

25 Eg *Windisch v Austria* (App 12489/86) (1990) Series A no 186 [23]; *Delta v France* (App 11444/85) (1990) Series A no 191-A [34]; *Solakov* (n 7) [57]; *Mild and Virtanen v Finland* (Apps 39481/98; 40227/98) ECHR 26 July 2005 [43].

26 S Maffei, *The European Right to Confrontation in Criminal Proceedings: Absent, Anonymous and Vulnerable Witnesses* (Europa Law, Groningen 2006) 73: 'the autonomy of the interpretation is a one-way autonomy'.

27 Eg *Isgrò v Italy* (App 11339/85) (1991) Series A no 194-A [33]; *Asch v Austria* (App 12398/86) (1991) Series A no 203 [25]; *Artner v Austria* (App 13161/87) (1992) Series A no 242-A [19]; *Pullar v UK* (App 22399/93) ECHR 1996-III [45]; *Andandonskiy v Russia* (App 24015/02) ECHR 28 September 2006 [50].

28 *Kostovski v the Netherlands* (App 11454/85) (1989) Series A no 166 [40].

29 *Gossa v Poland* (App 47986/99) ECHR 9 January 2007 [56]. See also eg *Lucà* (n 9) [41]; *Kaste and Mathisen v Norway* (Apps 18885/04; 21166/04) ECHR 9 November 2006 [53]; *Melnikov v Russia* (App 23610/03) ECHR 14 January 2010 [66].

and significance of the evidence presented before them.[30] In providing this assistance, the expert is obliged to be objective and impartial, his paramount duty being to the court rather than to the instructing party. Whereas the weight attached to expert opinion evidence in each case will vary, there is ever-present potential for an expert to have a significant bearing on the trial outcome. It is, therefore, crucial that the rights of the defence are respected in the presence of evidence of this type.

Amongst the rights of the defence, it was equality of arms in particular and the status of the court-appointed expert that were in issue before the Court in *Bönisch v Austria*.[31] The applicant had been convicted on two occasions because his business employed a meat smoking technique that contravened food regulations. The Director of the Food Control Institute had been responsible for drafting the adverse reports that initiated both proceedings. He was also the sole court-appointed expert in both prosecutions, whereas the expert instructed by the applicant in the first proceeding was heard as a mere witness. The Court was of the view that, read literally, Article 6(3)(d) applies to witnesses, not experts.[32] On this basis, it may be conceded that an independent court-appointed expert is not intrinsically a witness.

This is not, however, to be construed as excluding him from acquiring witness status in all circumstances. The Court found that any doubts as to the neutrality of this expert were understandable given that the prosecutions against the applicant were consequent upon the reports he drafted. It thereby accepted that, on 'appearances', the expert 'was more like a witness against the accused.'[33] Recourse to appearances was, of course, also an approach highlighted in the previous chapter as used to identify opponents for the purposes of equality of arms.[34] It seems, therefore, that a court-appointed expert should not be regarded as an 'expert' but as an 'expert witness' if he appears to align himself with a party, such as the prosecution in this case, albeit informally. It was, accordingly, appropriate for the Court to refer to the defence expert as an 'expert witness'.[35]

In these circumstances, it is essential under the concept of equality of arms that opposing expert witnesses be treated on an equal footing. The absence

---

30 See further *Davie v Magistrates of Edinburgh* 1953 SC 34, 40 (Lord President Cooper): The duty of experts 'is to furnish the Judge or jury with the necessary scientific criteria for testing the accuracy of their conclusions, so as to enable the Judge or jury to form their own independent judgment by the application of these criteria to the facts proved in evidence.'

31 *Bönisch* (n 7).

32 Ibid [29]. See also eg *Brandstetter v Austria* (Apps 11170/84; 12876/87; 13468/87) (1991) Series A no 211 [42]; *Eskelinen and others v Finland* (App 43803/98) ECHR 8 August 2006 [30]. Contrast the equivalent provision in American Convention on Human Rights Art 8(2)(f) (emphasis added): 'right of the defense to examine witnesses present in the court and to obtain the appearance, *as witnesses, of experts* or other persons who may throw light on the facts'.

33 *Bönisch* (n 7) [32].

34 Ch 2 s 4.1.2.

35 *Bönisch* (n 7) [33].

of equal treatment in this case was 'particularly striking': the Director had been heard unduly as an official expert, 'formally invested with the function of neutral and impartial auxiliary of the court', thereby naturally giving his statements greater weight than those of the defence expert witness; and, unlike the latter, the Director was permitted to attend the hearings in full, examine the accused and witnesses, and comment upon their testimony.[36] These prejudicial inequalities placed the defence at a disadvantage vis-à-vis the prosecution, the Court consequently holding that Article 6(1) had been violated.[37]

The status of experts with regard to the concept of equality of arms again came to the fore in *Brandstetter v Austria*.[38] Of the two relevant proceedings against the applicant, the first concerned the quality of wine that he sold. He complained of an inequality of arms because the court appointed as official expert an employee of the institute which had set in motion his prosecution and refused to hear any other experts. Building on *Bönisch*, the European Court also took into account doubts raised by 'appearances' but made it express that such doubts must be 'objectively justified.'[39] It observed that the expert could not be regarded as a prosecution witness because his employment with the institute was not of itself sufficient to objectively justify fears that he would act without proper neutrality.[40] This is understandable given that, unlike the official expert in *Bönisch*, he was not involved in the initiation of the prosecution and to 'hold otherwise would in many cases place unacceptable limits on the possibility for courts to obtain expert advice.'[41] As prosecution witness status was not afforded to the official expert, the rejection of the defence request to appoint other experts could not constitute a procedural inequality, thus avoiding a violation of Articles 6(1) and 6(3)(d).[42]

The second proceeding centred on the applicant's conviction for tampering with evidence in relation to the first proceeding. The applicant complained that the official court expert was an employee of the institute and that the initial criminal suspicion emanated from him, whilst the defence expert was heard under the less privileged status of witness. The Court observed that doubts as to the official expert's neutrality could be held justified, in effect assimilating him to a witness for the prosecution, hence the defence witness should also have been examined under the same conditions.[43] Yet, it did not find an inequality of arms.[44] It distinguished the official expert from the Director in *Bönisch*

36 Ibid.
37 Ibid [35]. It forwent a separate ruling on Article 6(3)(d).
38 *Brandstetter* (n 32).
39 Ibid [44].
40 Ibid [44]–[45].
41 Ibid [44].
42 Ibid [45], [47].
43 Ibid [61].
44 Ibid [62]–[63].

because he did not pose questions or comment on the evidence of the defence witness and thereby assume a dominant position.[45] It also considered that the results of the defence witness's analysis were relevant only if it could be proved that the evidence could not have been tampered with. As the domestic court established that tampering could not be excluded, the ground for the request to appoint the defence witness as a second official expert became obsolete.[46] It appears, therefore, that the Court relied upon as decisive the absence of actual prejudice to override its recognition of the unequal treatment of prosecution and defence.

4. EXAMINER DEFINED

Having defined the term 'witness', it falls logically to also identify briefly those who can occupy the position of examiner in the conduct of witness examinations.

In allowing the accused the opportunity 'to examine or have examined' witnesses, the language of Article 6(3)(d) is indicative of a deliberate sensitivity towards accommodating the differences in the accusatorial and inquisitorial trial models adopted by Contracting States. In the tradition of the latter model, the examination of witnesses is conducted predominantly by the presiding judge on behalf of the parties ('to have examined'), though supplementary questions may be put by the parties to witnesses either directly or through the intermediary of the judge.[47] The accusatorial tradition, on the other hand, relies on the direct examination of witnesses by the parties ('to examine'), and the judge is tasked with ensuring that it is carried out in a fair manner. Although this is not such as to preclude the judge from questioning a witness altogether,[48] any intervention must be temperate,[49] such as that exercised merely for clarification of a particular point.

Where leave is granted for a party to question a witness, it is conventional practice in both trial models that the examination is undertaken by a qualified lawyer. An accused is to be identified with his legal representative for the purposes of Article 6(3)(d).[50] It is thus consistent with this provision for counsel to conduct an examination in the absence of his client in exceptional

---

45 Ibid [62].

46 Ibid.

47 Eg in France: Code of Criminal Procedure 1958 (as amended) Arts 312, 332. Translated in JR Spencer (tr), 'Code of Criminal Procedure' (Legifrance, 2006) <https://www.legifrance.gouv.fr/Traductions/en-English/Legifrance-translations>.

48 Eg *R v Remnant* (1807) Russ & Ry 136, 137–138; *R v Wilson* (1924) 18 Cr App Rep 108 (CCA) 109.

49 Eg *R v Hulusi (Kolliari Mehmet)* (1974) 58 Cr App R 378 (CA) 382, 385; *R v Marsh* The Times 6 July 1993 (CA).

50 *Kamasinski v Austria* (App 9783/82) (1989) Series A no 168 [91].

circumstances,[51] though it is from a dignitarian standpoint always preferable for the latter to be present to observe testimony influential to his fate. A competent counsel has the training and experience necessary for a forensic examination designed to test witness evidence effectively and to put his client's case to the witness, whilst remaining tactically astute and compliant with rules of criminal procedure. The accused, as a layperson, cannot be expected to have such qualities, the likely consequence of which is that his position will suffer detrimentally without professional representation.[52]

In this light, the Court in *Isgrò v Italy*[53] seems to have reached an unfortunate conclusion. During the investigation phase, the applicant was confronted with a crucial witness without the assistance of counsel. The Court concluded that Article 6(3)(d) had been satisfied sufficiently as 'the purpose of the confrontation did not render the presence of Mr Isgrò's lawyer indispensable; since it was open to the applicant to put questions and to make comments himself'.[54] It had not considered the absence of representation to have caused actual prejudice. This view appears misguided. It dismisses the significant disparity of competence and experience between lawyer and client in challenging and questioning a witness.[55] Though counsel was present at trial, a further opportunity to examine the witness was not available. Furthermore, the pre-trial investigation phase carries a particularly decisive weight in the inquisitorial tradition and, in fact, the witness's statements were relied upon in convicting the accused. It is submitted, therefore, that one cannot but describe the circumstances herein as prejudicial.

Nevertheless, the situation may arise in which an accused waives his right to representation and wishes to examine a witness in person. Whilst representation in the material confrontation in *Isgrò* was not permitted in law rather than waived, the judgement confirms that an unrepresented accused may conduct the examination himself. If, however, representation is available, domestic restrictions on examinations by a pro se accused in certain situations will be

51 Eg to prevent possible witness intimidation: *X v Denmark* (App 8395/78) (1981) 27 DR 50, 54–55; *Kurup v Denmark* (App 11219/84) (1985) 42 DR 287, 291–293.

52 Eg *Artico v Italy* (App 6694/74) (1980) Series A no 37 [34], [36]; New South Wales Law Reform Commission, 'Questioning of Complainants by Unrepresented Accused in Sexual Offence Trials' Report 101 (Sydney 2003) [5.8]: 'an experienced criminal advocate is in the best position to protect the interests of the accused as well as the public interest in ensuring that the evidence is appropriately tested. If cross-examination was to be conducted by someone other than a legal practitioner, the complainant's evidence is unlikely to be tested effectively.'

53 *Isgrò* (n 27).

54 Ibid [36].

55 See further SJ Summers, *Fair Trials: The European Criminal Procedural Tradition and the European Court of Human Rights* (Hart, Oxford 2007) 151 who remarks that the argument of the Court 'seems completely to ignore the reason for the existence of lawyers in the criminal process and casts doubt on the need for a lawyer at trial, if it is sufficient that the judge or the prosecutor can ask the questions for the accused or that he or she can ask them him- or herself. This is a spurious argument at odds with the Court's own definition of fairness and its arguments justifying the right to counsel.'

compatible with Article 6(3)(d). Such situations may include examinations of vulnerable witnesses such as sexual offence complainants and children[56] because of the risk of intimidation or further distress.

5. A BENCHMARK MODEL FOR THE CONDUCT OF EXAMINATIONS

It is useful to outline the benchmark examination model reflected in Article 6(3)(d)[57] to serve as a point of reference against which legitimate and illegitimate derogations therefrom can be discerned and measured. A benchmark model is, of course, intended to uphold the highest standard of protection for the dignity of the accused. Given that it is the trial hearing at which all admissible evidence is presented in its final form and the verdict is reached, as well as Article 6 having been designed predominantly to apply to the trial *stricto sensu*, it is natural that the benchmark model focuses on this stage of the proceedings. In its regard for Article 6(3)(d), the Court makes known consistently that 'evidence must normally be produced at a public hearing, in the presence of the accused, with a view to adversarial argument.'[58] The Commission also opined that 'the requirements of a fair trial and equality of arms generally make it necessary for all prosecution witnesses to be heard before the trial courts and during adversarial proceedings.'[59] On this basis and that of the language of Article 6(3)(d) itself, a model may be derived wherein live oral testimony[60] is elicited from a witness in a court accessible to public scrutiny, and the witness is physically confronted[61] by an accused exercising his right to question him, either pro se or indirectly through counsel or the judge, under a condition of equality of arms. This model may be extended to include two further elements identified

---

56 See further Youth Justice and Criminal Evidence Act 1999 (UK) (YJCEA) ss 34–35. In cases not covered by these sections, s 36 allows the court to prevent an examination by an accused in person if the quality of evidence provided by any witness is likely to be diminished and it is not contrary to the interests of justice.

57 See further the 'model of full compliance with the guarantee' in S Trechsel, *Human Rights in Criminal Proceedings* (OUP, Oxford 2005) 299.

58 Eg *Van Mechelen and others v the Netherlands* (App 21363/93 et seq) ECHR 1997-III [51]; *Sadak and others v Turkey (No 1)* (App 29900/96 et seq) ECHR 2001-VIII [64]; *B v Finland* (App 17122/02) ECHR 24 April 2007 [41]; *Zhoglo v Ukraine* (App 17988/02) ECHR 24 April 2008 [38].

59 *Cardot v France* (App 11069/84) EComHR Report 3 April 1990 [50].

60 In contrast to the heavy reliance upon written evidence in inquisitorial style trial hearings, the accusatorial trial model champions the superiority of live oral testimony: JR Spencer, 'Orality and the Evidence of Absent Witnesses' [1994] Crim LR 628, 628; L Ellison, 'The Protection of Vulnerable Witnesses in Court: An Anglo-Dutch Comparison' (1999) 3 Int'l J Evidence & Proof 29, 34, 38–39.

61 See also *X* (n 51) 54: 'in principle ... it is essential and indeed often indispensable that an accused be present when witnesses are being heard in a case against him'; *Kurup* (n 51) 292.

by Maffei in his 'confrontational paradigm': the requirement that evidence be sworn and that the real identity of the witness be disclosed to the defence.[62] Evidence that is sworn invites criminal penalties if it is knowingly false, thereby rendering more likely the appearance of procedural legitimacy. The realisation of adversarial argument requires, inter alia, the defence to have knowledge of all evidence adduced intended to influence the decision-maker. As disclosure of witness identity has an evidential value when assessing credibility, it is a feature that certainly accords with ensuring adversarialism. Article 6(3)(d) cases before the Court, however, concern by their very nature testimonial evidence obtained in derogation of this benchmark examination model.

6. DEROGATIONS FROM THE BENCHMARK MODEL

It is accepted in Convention jurisprudence that the aforementioned benchmark model is open to legitimate derogation without violating Article 6(3)(d). Derogation in this context refers to the absence of one or more features of the model in the conduct of the trial hearing. The replacement of live oral testimony at trial with a previously given written statement is the most prominent example of that. Acceptance of derogation measures demonstrates an acknowledgement by the Court that there exist exceptional cases in which a concessionary and practicable solution is required to reconcile the competing triangulation of interests between the defence, the prosecution and witnesses. The interest of the witness is to protect his life or well-being, especially if he is a victim of serious crime and/or vulnerable. If, however, the witness is deceased or untraceable at the time of trial, only the prosecution and defence interests remain relevant. The prosecution interest lies in putting all relevant testimonial evidence before the court, even if it is not live and oral but is merely in the form of written statements, with a view to influencing the trial outcome. Favourable to this interest is that rules governing the conduct of examinations be flexible, for the stricter the rules, the greater the likelihood that prosecutions are stifled and criminals remain at large. The interest of the accused, however, is in challenging the adverse testimonial evidence in accordance with the benchmark model, thereby exposing the witness to the best possible scrutiny.

It is possible to render derogation measures legitimate because the Court evaluates procedural fairness on the basis of the trial in its entirety rather than considering Article 6(3)(d) in isolation. This provision and Article 6(1) are thus conjointly assessed. The trial as a whole approach is a procedural appraisal and not an evidential one. The Court has firmly adopted the general rule that

62 Maffei (n 26) 23, 26–28.

the admissibility and assessment of evidence are primarily matters for the competence of domestic courts.[63] It is not, therefore, in principle the nature of the evidence itself but the use made of it that is the concern of the Court.[64] Engaging in an overall assessment of the trial also ensures that the Court will take account of state measures employed to offset the effect of derogations involving a procedural inequality. This offsetting can be such as to avoid a joint violation of Articles 6(1) and 6(3)(d).

The subsequent discussion considers the approach of the Court to the concept of equality of arms when derogations from the benchmark model have occurred. It is instructive to group judgements into separate categories of witness because the corresponding extent and rationale of the derogations differ.

6.1. ABSENT WITNESSES

6.1.1. *Introduction*

On several occasions, the Court has been called upon to determine the legitimacy of derogations from the benchmark model when the prosecution has failed to secure for examination the attendance of the witness at trial. Central to its jurisprudence in this area has been the impact of untested witness statements on the outcome of the case. More specifically, the following analysis demonstrates that, for most of the Court's jurisprudence, a conviction based solely or decisively on the statement of an absent witness (actual prejudice), never at any previous stage examined by the defence, was generally found incompatible with Article 6. More recently, however, the Court has been willing to accept that prejudice to the defence can be overcome if appropriate counterbalancing measures are present. Witness absence may be explained by reason of failure to comply with a summons, untraceability, illness, fear of reprisals, death, or the exercise of a right of exemption by the witness himself.

6.1.2. *Case-Law*

A right of exemption was indeed exercised in *Unterpertinger v Austria*.[65] The applicant had been convicted of causing criminal injury to his ex-wife and stepdaughter, both of whom had made statements to the police but refused to give evidence at trial by virtue of their entitlement as close relatives. The statements

---

63 Eg *Edwards v UK* (App 13071/87) (1992) Series A no 247-B [34]; *Doorson v the Netherlands* (App 20524/92) ECHR 1996-II [67]; *PS v Germany* (App 33900/96) ECHR 20 December 2001 [19]; *Borisova v Bulgaria* (App 56891/00) ECHR 21 December 2006 [46]; *Muttilainen v Finland* (App 18358/02) ECHR 22 May 2007 [21].

64 *Unterpertinger v Austria* (App 9120/80) (1986) Series A no 110 [31].

65 Ibid [30].

were read out at the hearing. The applicant complained that he had been convicted exclusively on the basis of these statements without being offered an opportunity to examine the witnesses at any stage of the proceedings. The Court ruled that neither the witness exemption, legitimately designed to avoid a moral dilemma, nor the reading out of the statements were in themselves incompatible with Articles 6(1) and 6(3)(d).[66] Nevertheless, what was incompatible with these articles was that, whilst other evidence was put before the courts, the conviction had been based 'mainly' on statements authored by witnesses the applicant had never been able to examine.[67] The extent of the prejudicial effect of these untested statements was, therefore, crucial in the Court's assessment.

Whereas the Court did not refer expressly to the concept of equality of arms in its reasoning, the finding of a violation was an implicit acknowledgement that the applicant had suffered disadvantage, despite the prosecution also having been prevented from orally examining the witnesses at trial. Given that the police are part of the wider prosecution team,[68] their questioning of a witness constitutes an out-of-court examination conducted on behalf of the prosecutor. It was in this case procedurally advantageous for the prosecutor to be allowed to admit adverse testimony already examined on his behalf and incapable of being adequately tested by the defence at any stage. Indeed, the testimony was treated 'as proof of the truth of the accusations'.[69] Though the finding of a violation was in itself correct, the absence of equality of arms was a procedural defect deserving of express rather than implied prominence in the judgement.

Inequality of this nature also underlies the *Delta v France*[70] judgement in which two material witnesses failed to attend trial despite being summoned. Their statements provided in the police investigation were put before the trial court, which made no effort to compel attendance, and resulted in the applicant's conviction. The Court considered this incompatible with Articles 6(1) and 6(3)(d) because at no stage in the proceedings had the defence an adequate and proper opportunity to examine these witnesses and the conviction was based decisively on their statements.[71]

This conclusion and rationale was echoed in *Lucà v Italy* where the sole basis of conviction was a pre-trial statement made by the co-accused witness to the public prosecutor.[72] The statement was read out at trial because of the

---

66 Ibid [30]–[31].

67 Ibid [30]–[33].

68 Eg the Crown Prosecution Service (CPS) lists 'working with the police from the outset of a case to its disposal' as part of its role: CPS, 'Annual Report 2004–2005' (12 July 2005) <www.cps.gov.uk/publications/docs/annualreport05.pdf> 5. See also *Van Mechelen* (n 58) [56]: 'the police … usually have links with the prosecution'.

69 *Unterpertinger* (n 64) [33].

70 *Delta* (n 25).

71 Ibid [37].

72 *Lucà* (n 9) [43]–[45].

co-accused's refusal under his statutory right to remain silent to be present for examination. The applicant had clearly been placed in a position of procedural disadvantage. Given the decisively prejudicial nature of the statement, it was appropriate that the conflict between the co-accused's privilege against self-incrimination and the applicant's right to procedural equality was resolved in favour of the latter.

It was not statutory privilege but the death of a witness before trial that prevented the accused in *Ferrantelli and Santangelo v Italy*[73] from conducting an examination. The witness's previous incriminatory written evidence was presented at trial. The Court found the written evidence admissible because the death was not attributable to the state[74] and there was a lack of actual prejudice: the testimony was corroborated and did not constitute the sole or main item of incriminatory evidence.[75] Generally, there will not be a violation if the evidence of the absent witness was not the sole or decisive evidence against the accused.[76]

In circumstances where the witness is absent through illness, *Bricmont v Belgium*[77] provides relevant guidance. The criminal proceedings brought against the applicants were based on the accusations of a witness unable to testify in person at trial because of poor health. A comprehensive confrontation with the witness had not taken place at any stage of the proceedings. In respect of Mr Bricmont, the Court found that the domestic court relied heavily upon the evidence of the witness to justify conviction.[78] It added that an examination should have been conducted at the home of the witness.[79] Consequently, it is clear that where a conventional examination is not possible due to illness, the Court requires that a suitable alternative arrangement for examination be made.[80] This serves to restrict the extent of the departure from the benchmark model. It is only if alternative arrangements are not feasible that written statements may replace oral testimony. In view of these circumstances, Mr Bricmont was placed in a disadvantageous position wherein actual prejudice occurred, the consequence of which was a violation of Article 6.[81] On the other hand, the Court did not consider the witness's evidence to have caused actual prejudice

---

73 (App 19874/92) ECHR 1996-III.

74 Ibid [52]–[53].

75 Ibid [30], [52].

76 *Mirilashvili v Russia* (App 6293/04) ECHR 11 December 2008 [164].

77 (App 10857/84) (1989) Series A no 158.

78 Ibid [83]–[84].

79 Ibid [81].

80 See further M Strange, 'Evidence' in K Starmer and others, *Criminal Justice, Police Powers and Human Rights* (Blackstone, London 2001) [16.5.1.3]: 'Where witnesses are ill … the case law needs to be considered in the light of advances in technology, which may allow for cross-examination via live video links, if necessary in the witnesses' home or in hospital.'

81 *Bricmont* (n 77) [85].

to Mrs Bricmont because the domestic court did not refer to such evidence in convicting her, hence avoiding a violation in her case.[82]

The suggestion by the Court that the examination could have been conducted at the home of the witness is a particularly apt example of the diligence demanded of states in the realisation of Article 6(3)(d). Where the statement of an absent witness is integral to the conviction, the Court has consistently demonstrated that a violation will occur if the state did not initially make a genuinely sincere and sustained effort to ensure that an examination would take place.[83] It may be submitted that it is only through taking such positive steps that the state can be viewed as not exploiting the opportunity offered by the absent witness to create an undue procedural advantage for the prosecution. If a material witness remains untraceable through no fault of the accused and despite positive efforts by the state, only a postponement of proceedings consistent with the fair trial 'within a reasonable time' requirement of Article 6(1) or an acquittal seems proper.

Criticism may be directed towards the judgement in *Asch v Austria*,[84] the facts of which are similar to *Unterpertinger*. The applicant had been convicted of causing actual bodily harm to a witness whose statements were read out at trial because she had availed herself of her right to refuse to give live testimony. The applicant did not have an opportunity to examine her at any stage. In finding that a violation did not occur, the Court reasoned that the statements did not constitute the only item of evidence on which the conviction was based as corroboration was provided by medical evidence and the personal assessment of the police officer who had interviewed the witness.[85] The implication is, of course, that a violation will occur if the statement forms the sole basis of the conviction, a stricter test than that merely requiring that the statement be the main reason for the conviction. Despite the corroborative evidence, the value of which was insufficient in itself to raise guilt beyond reasonable doubt, it was the witness evidence that formed the main item of proof for the conviction, a fact recognised only in the associated dissenting judgement which viewed the case as essentially the same as *Unterpertinger*.[86] The Court failed to give due regard to the actual weight attached by the domestic court to the effectively untested statements of the witness.[87] Moreover, the corroborative evidence and the

---

82 Ibid [86].

83 Eg *Sadak and others* (n 58) [66]–[67]; *Hulki Güneş v Turkey* (App 28490/95) ECHR 2003-VII [93], [95]; *Mild and Virtanen* (n 25) [45]–[47]; *Kostecki v Poland* (App 14932/09) ECHR 4 June 2013 [65]–[66].

84 *Asch* (n 27).

85 Ibid [30]–[31].

86 Ibid Diss Op Judges Vincent Evans and Bernhardt [1], [5]. See also C Osborne, 'Hearsay and the European Court of Human Rights' [1993] Crim LR 255, 265: 'There is no logical or consistent basis for a distinction between the *Asch* case and the *Unterpertinger* case'.

87 S Stavros, *The Guarantees for Accused Persons Under Article 6 of the European Convention on Human Rights: An Analysis of the Application of the Convention and a Comparison with Other Instruments* (Martinus Nijhoff, Dordrecht 1993) 235.

applicant's opportunity to comment on the witness's statements constitute a poor counterbalance to the actual prejudice arising from the prosecution advantage of putting forward evidence of a witness never examined by the defence. Thus, in accordance with the reasoning in *Unterpertinger*, a violation should have been found.[88]

The approach in *Asch* was, unfortunately, followed in *Artner v Austria*[89] where the pre-trial statements of the untraceable main witness were read out at trial. Despite the applicant not having an opportunity to examine the witness, the Court considered that a violation did not occur because the conviction had also been based on corroboratory evidence.[90] As with *Asch*, the testimony of the witness was the fundamental basis for the conviction, thereby occasioning severe and actual prejudice. This was an improper restriction of the rights of the applicants which was acknowledged by the four dissenting judges.[91] It appears, therefore, that the Court in *Asch* and *Artner* considered the use of corroboratory evidence to be a means of counterbalancing a procedural defect that had given rise to a prosecutorial advantage. However, the defect and prejudice arising therefrom was simply too great to be cured in this manner. Put simply, the applicants in both cases would not have been convicted had it not been for the untested statements. Fortunately, the strictness of the approach taken in *Asch* and *Artner* was not generally repeated in other relevant jurisprudence.[92] As indicated in the analysis preceding *Asch* and *Artner*, the conventional approach adopted by the Court was that Article 6 is breached when a 'conviction is based solely or to a decisive degree' on statements of a witness the defence has not had an opportunity to examine or have examined.[93]

However, more recently, counterbalancing has again featured in the jurisprudence on absent witnesses, resulting in a reduction of the level of protection available to the defence. The Grand Chamber case of *Al-Khawaja and Tahery v UK*[94] concerned two applicants. Al-Khawaja had been convicted of indecent assault on two female patients. One of these patients had committed suicide before the trial and her police statement was read to the jury. Tahery had been convicted for a stabbing. The key witness was too fearful to attend trial but his statement was also read to the jury. Both applicants complained about the admission of these statements as evidence in the absence of cross-examination. Admitting that some derogation is permitted from the rule that the accused

---

88 Trechsel (n 57) 295 marks the case as 'an exceptionally weak point in the Court's jurisprudence' to 'be regarded as an unfortunate mistake.'

89 *Artner* (n 27).

90 Ibid [22]–[24].

91 Ibid Diss Op Judge Thór Vilhjálmsson; Diss Op Judges Walsh, Macdonald and Palm [1]–[2].

92 Strange (n 80) [16.4].

93 See also eg *Hulki Güneş* (n 83) [86], [89], [96]; *Bonev v Bulgaria* (App 60018/00) ECHR 8 June 2006 [43]–[45]; *Zhoglo* (n 58) [39], [41], [43].

94 (Apps 26766/05; 22228/06) ECHR 2011.

should be given an adequate and proper opportunity to challenge and question a witness against him,[95] the Court set out three issues that must be examined in this regard.

First, there must be a good reason for a witness's non-attendance.[96] Whereas the Court considered that the death of the witness in Al-Khawaja's case satisfied this requirement,[97] absence owing to fear required a distinction to be drawn between fear caused directly by threats made by the accused or his agents, and a more general fear of what will happen if oral evidence is given at trial.[98] The Court will treat the accused as having waived his right to question the witness if fear is attributable directly to him or his agents.[99] For general fear, the trial court must inquire into whether there are objective grounds for the fear, which are supported by evidence.[100] It must also be satisfied that the admission of a statement in lieu of oral testimony is a last resort measure, having discounted as inappropriate or impracticable all available special measures, including witness anonymity.[101] In Tahery's case, the Court found that the good reason requirement was satisfied after relying on the trial judge's enquiry based conclusion that the witness had a genuine fear of testifying and that special measures would be inadequate.[102] Although the Grand Chamber seemed to suggest that a lack of a good reason for non-attendance entails by itself a breach of Article 6(3)(d), it clarified its position subsequently in *Schatschaschwili v Germany*, finding that the absence of good reason is a very important factor to be taken into account but 'cannot of itself be conclusive of the unfairness of a trial'.[103]

Second, it must be assessed whether the evidence of the absent witness was the sole or decisive basis for the conviction.[104] The Court found that the statements of the absent witnesses were the decisive evidence against both Al-Khawaja and Tahery.[105] However, it held that even if a hearsay statement constitutes the sole or decisive basis of the conviction, its admission will not automatically violate the right to a fair trial.[106] To do so, it reasoned, would be to accept an inflexible approach that 'runs counter to the traditional way in which the Court approaches the issue of the overall fairness of the proceedings,

95 Ibid [118].
96 Ibid [119].
97 Ibid [121], [153].
98 Ibid [122]. General fear includes, for example, 'fear ... attributable to the notoriety of a defendant or his associates' and 'fear of death or injury of another person or of financial loss' ([124]).
99 Ibid [123].
100 Ibid [124].
101 Ibid [125].
102 Ibid [159].
103 Ibid [120]; (App 9154/10) ECHR 2015 [113].
104 *Al-Khawaja and Tahery* (n 94) [119], [152].
105 Ibid [154], [160].
106 Ibid [147].

namely to weigh in the balance the competing interests of the defence, the victim, and witnesses, and the public interest in the effective administration of justice.'[107]

Third, it must be examined, with 'the most searching scrutiny', whether there were sufficient counterbalancing factors to compensate for the handicap suffered by the defence and to ensure that the trial as a whole was fair.[108] *Schatschaschwili* has clarified that sufficient counterbalancing factors are still necessary if the untested witness evidence was neither the sole nor decisive basis for the conviction, but nevertheless carried significant weight; '[t]he more important that evidence, the more weight the counterbalancing factors will have to carry in order for the proceedings as a whole to be considered fair.'[109] It also discloses a counterbalancing factor that may carry significant weight when a key witness is absent at trial: the provision to the defence of an opportunity to have the witness questioned at least during the pre-trial stage.[110] Such an opportunity was not possible in *Al-Khawaja and Tahery*, which did not concern proceedings of the inquisitorial tradition. In Al-Khawaja's case, the counterbalancing factors were that the witness's statement was corroborated by the two friends she had promptly confided in, both of whom gave evidence at trial; the other complainant gave a similar description of the alleged assault; and the judge had directed the jury that the untested statement should be given less weight.[111] These factors, the Court held, were sufficient to ensure that there was no breach of Articles 6(1) and 6(3)(d).[112] However, it reached the opposite conclusion in respect of Tahery.[113] Neither the ability of the applicant to cross-examine other witnesses present at the scene of the stabbing, none of whom had seen the applicant stab the victim, nor the judge's warning to the jury about untested evidence were sufficient counterbalancing factors to compensate for the difficulties caused to the defence by the admission of the untested statement of the only eyewitness.[114] Thus, the key distinction between both cases was the lack of any strong corroborative evidence in Tahery's case.

The value the Court placed on counterbalancing as a means to avert a violation of Article 6(3)(d) when dealing with absent witnesses diminished the level of protection for the accused that was established in most of its previous case-law. Previously, the Court generally treated as unfair convictions resting solely or decisively on untested witness statements. This is a safeguard to ensure that the defence ought to be able, at least, to examine key or crucial witnesses.

107 Ibid [146].
108 Ibid [147], [152].
109 *Schatschaschwili* (n 103) [116].
110 Ibid [162].
111 *Al-Khawaja and Tahery* (n 94) [156]–[157].
112 Ibid [158].
113 Ibid [165].
114 Ibid [162]–[165].

In the absence of any opportunity to examine such witnesses in *Al-Khawaja and Tahery*, the applicants suffered a prejudicial handicap – the untested evidence was decisive – which the Court considered was surmountable through counterbalancing. In other words, the Court accepted that it was possible even for key or crucial witnesses to put their statements into evidence without having been subjected to any form of defence questioning at any stage of the proceedings, provided there was strong corroborating evidence, an approach which undermines the essence of Article 6(3)(d). Indeed, it is submitted that the disadvantage to the defence of not being able to challenge effectively highly prejudicial witness evidence is of such a degree that it cannot be effectively counterbalanced.

6.2. ANONYMOUS WITNESSES

6.2.1. Introduction

Another species of derogation from the benchmark model has presented itself in a series of cases involving serious crime where use at trial is made of the testimony of prosecution witnesses whose identities and addresses are withheld intentionally from the defence. Special measures preserving anonymity can also involve use of screens,[115] disguise and voice distortion. Prosecutors tend to seek anonymity for their witnesses in two particular scenarios. The first of these involves the desire to avoid a state asset being compromised so that the asset may continue to provide valuable covert information in the future. Such assets include security service operatives, undercover police and customs officers, and informants. The second scenario concerns the witness whose life or safety is, or is reasonably expected to be, at serious threat from the accused or his affiliates (witness intimidation). This is especially the case where the accused is involved in organised crime or domestic violence. The Court has certainly acknowledged the valuable contribution made by anonymous witnesses to the investigation of crime.[116] Indeed, it has often professed that the use of anonymous evidence 'is not under all circumstances incompatible with the Convention.'[117] The justification for this has been expressed as follows:

---

115 Eg Criminal Code of Canada RSC 1985 c C-46 s 486.2(1)–(2). Reproduced in Government of Canada Justice Laws Website (2016) <http://laws.justice.gc.ca/eng/acts/C-46/index.html>; YJCEA s 23(1).

116 *Windisch* (n 25) [30]: 'The collaboration of the public is undoubtedly of great importance for the police in their struggle against crime. In this connection the Court notes that the Convention does not preclude reliance, at the investigation stage, on sources such as anonymous informants.' See also eg *Kostovski* (n 28) [44]; *Doorson* (n 63) [69]; *Ramanauskas v Lithuania* (App 74420/01) ECHR 5 February 2008 [53].

117 Eg *Doorson* (n 63) [69]; *Van Mechelen* (n 58) [52]; *Birutis and others v Lithuania* (Apps 47698/99; 48115/99) ECHR 28 March 2002 [29]; *Taal v Estonia* (App 13249/02) ECHR

> It is true that Article 6 ... does not explicitly require the interests of witnesses ... called upon to testify ... to be taken into consideration. However, their life, liberty or security of person may be at stake, as may interests coming generally within the ambit of Article 8 ... of the Convention. Such interests ... are in principle protected by other, substantive provisions of the Convention, which imply that Contracting States should organise their criminal proceedings in such a way that those interests are not unjustifiably imperilled. Against this background, principles of fair trial also require that in appropriate cases the interests of the defence are balanced against those of witnesses ... called upon to testify.[118]

The legitimacy of using anonymous evidence is, therefore, dependent upon a fair balance being struck between the competing rights of witnesses and the accused. Neither conflicting right is to be forfeited for the preservation of the other. Instead, and in the same manner as Hesse's constitutional law concept of *praktische Konkordanz* (practical concordance), both rights are limited by proportionate concessions so that each can be preserved to the optimal extent possible.[119] This case-specific balancing exercise does not detract from the absolute nature of the overall right to a fair trial.

The realisation of a fair balance is, however, particularly difficult to attain in view of the inherent risk associated with the use of anonymous testimony. The ability of the accused to test effectively the accuracy and credibility of a witness account is severely restricted when he is oblivious to the identifying particulars of the latter.[120] The accused is simply denied the opportunity to exploit the evidential value attached to the identity of the author of an adverse statement.

---

22 November 2005 [31]; *Krasniki v the Czech Republic* (App 51277/99) ECHR 28 February 2006 [76].

118 *Doorson* (n 63) [70]; *Van Mechelen* (n 58) [53]; *Marcello Viola v Italy* (App 45106/04) ECHR 2006-XI [51].

119 K Hesse, *Grundzüge des Verfassungsrechts der Bundesrepublik Deutschland* (16th edn CF Müller, Heidelberg 1988) 27 cited in DP Kommers, 'German Constitutionalism: A Prolegomenon' (1991) 40 Emory LJ 837, 851; E Brems, 'Conflicting Human Rights: An Exploration in the Context of the Right to a Fair Trial in the European Convention for the Protection of Human Rights and Fundamental Freedoms' (2005) 27 HRQ 294, 303, 317.

120 See further *Smith v Illinois* 390 US 129, 131–132 (1968) (Stewart J) (fns omitted): 'when the credibility of a witness is in issue, the very starting point in "exposing falsehood and bringing out the truth" through cross-examination must necessarily be to ask the witness who he is and where he lives. ... To forbid this most rudimentary inquiry at the threshold is effectively to emasculate the right of cross-examination itself. ... "Prejudice ensues from a denial of the opportunity to place the witness in his proper setting and put the weight of his testimony and his credibility to a test"'.

S v Leepile and others (5) (1986) (4) SA 187 (W) 189 (Ackerman J): The consequences of anonymous testimony are: '(a) No investigation could be conducted by the accused's legal representatives into the witness' background to ascertain whether he has a general reputation for untruthfulness, whether he has made previous inconsistent statements nor to investigate other matters which might be relevant to his credibility in general. (b) It would make it more difficult to make enquiries to establish that the witness was not at places on the occasions mentioned by him. (c) It would further heighten the witness' sense of impregnability and increase the temptation to falsify or exaggerate.'

It appears an affront to the pursuit of adversarialism. The difficulty facing the defence has been acknowledged by the Court:

> If the defence is unaware of the identity of the person it seeks to question, it may be deprived of the very particulars enabling it to demonstrate that he or she is prejudiced, hostile or unreliable. Testimony or other declarations inculpating an accused may well be designedly untruthful or simply erroneous and the defence will scarcely be able to bring this to light if it lacks the information permitting it to test the author's reliability or cast doubt on his credibility.[121]

Accordingly, the use of incriminatory anonymous evidence at trial can be a highly prejudicial handicap, which by the Court's own admission is for the accused 'almost insurmountable',[122] and can serve to place the prosecution in a position of undue advantage.

Whereas sufficient counterbalancing measures ensuring that the rights of the defence are restricted to the least extent possible are prescribed by the Court as an essential mitigating tool of the state in anonymous evidence cases, such measures are not in themselves enough to prevent an Article 6 violation. The jurisprudence below reveals that the Court will also consider two other crucial factors: the extent to which the evidence in issue influenced the conviction (sole or decisive basis: prejudice), a factor transplanted from its rulings on absent witnesses; and, since *Doorson v the Netherlands*,[123] whether anonymity was reasonably justified in the first place.

6.2.2. Case-Law

Kostovski v the Netherlands[124] provides the earliest example of the Court's treatment of anonymous evidence. The applicant's conviction for armed robbery involved the use of statements of two anonymous witnesses, neither of whom were present at trial. Both had been interviewed by the police and one had also

---

Recommendation No R (97) 13 (n 2) Explanatory Memorandum [37]: 'allowing a witness to give evidence anonymously always entails a risk ...: i. the anonymous witness could be unreliable for subjective reasons associated with his personal history, for instance former mental disorders, hallucinations, or simply former episodes of regular lying, which could not be brought to light without the defence knowing his identity and verifying his personal history; ii. the anonymous witness might have had in the past some undisclosed relationship or contact or indirect connection with the defendant which, on the contrary, ought to be known and taken into consideration in order to verify whether it might be the source of a prejudiced attitude towards the defendant; iii. the anonymous witness could be plotting against the defendant.'

121 *Kostovski* (n 28) [42]. See also *Van Mechelen* (n 58) [54]: 'if the anonymity of prosecution witnesses is maintained, the defence will be faced with difficulties which criminal proceedings should not normally involve'; *Doorson* (n 63) [72]; *Krasniki* (n 117) [76].

122 *Windisch* (n 25) [28].

123 *Doorson* (n 63) [71].

124 *Kostovski* (n 28).

been heard by examining magistrates who were not aware of the individual's identity, the defence being absent in each case.

Included in the general principles applied by the Court and repeated identically or similarly in subsequent judgements on Article 6(3)(d) was the following:

> to use as evidence ... statements obtained at the pre-trial stage is not in itself inconsistent with paragraphs (3)(d) and 1 of Article 6 ... provided the rights of the defence have been respected.
>
> As a rule, these rights require that an accused should be given an adequate and proper opportunity to challenge and question a witness against him, either at the time the witness was making his statement or at some later stage of the proceedings.[125]

Accordingly, a defence examination of live oral testimony at trial is not essential to the realisation of Article 6. Pre-trial statements are admissible in the alternative and the requirement to provide an opportunity for examination is satisfied if an adequate and proper defence examination occurs at any point in the proceedings,[126] thus including the judicial investigation and police inquiry stages. This approach is unfortunate given that it does not encourage compliance with the benchmark model where, significantly, witness evidence is tested before to the eyes of those actually reaching the verdict.

Nevertheless, at no stage in the instant case was an opportunity afforded to the defence to directly question the witnesses. Instead, the defence were able to submit written questions to one of the witnesses indirectly through the second examining magistrate. The nature and scope of these questions was considerably restricted so as not to compromise anonymity. The defence were also able to examine both magistrates and, in regard to the other witness, an interviewing police officer but the same questioning restrictions applied.

In view of the almost ineffectual measures adopted by the judicial authorities, it is appropriate that the Court did not consider the constraints on the defence to have been counterbalanced.[127] Without direct defence examinations, the anonymous evidence effectively remained untested throughout the proceedings. The Court also criticised the absence of the anonymous witnesses as precluding the trial judges from observing their demeanour under examination in order

125 Ibid [41]. See also eg *Saïdi v France* (App 14647/89) (1993) Series A no 261-C [43]; *Birutis* (n 117) [28]; *Bocos-Cuesta* (n 9) [68]; *Vladimir Romanov v Russia* (App 41461/02) ECHR 24 July 2008 [100].

126 An adequate and proper opportunity for examination does not include questioning a witness solely during the pre-trial investigation stage if his material evidence subsequently is significantly amended and is of decisive importance to the conviction: *Vladimir Romanov* (n 125) [105]–[106].

127 *Kostovski* (n 28) [43]. *Windisch* (n 25) [28] followed suit in reaffirming that putting restricted questions to third parties in relation to anonymous statements is not a counterbalance capable of replacing direct examination of material prosecution witnesses at trial.

to gain a direct impression of their reliability.[128] Whereas the reliability of demeanour evidence as a significant gauge of credibility has been denied by the Law Commission of England and Wales[129] and consistently in psychological studies,[130] the Court herein and in subsequent jurisprudence clearly regards it as a valuable aspect of procedural fairness.[131] Furthermore, the Court found it irreconcilable with Article 6 that the conviction had been based to a decisive extent on the anonymous evidence.[132] In these circumstances, the prosecution had been placed in an unduly advantageous position leading to actual prejudice for the applicant, hence a breach of Articles 6(1) and 6(3)(d).[133]

Whilst *Kostovski* concerned civilian witnesses, *Lüdi v Switzerland*[134] provides guidance on the use of anonymous evidence from those serving the state in a covert capacity. The written statements of an undercover policeman played a part in securing the conviction of the applicant for drug trafficking. On the ground of preserving anonymity, the operative was absent at trial and, significantly, at no stage in the proceedings had the defence had the opportunity to question him. Though the untested evidence of the operative was influential in the conviction, it did not constitute the sole or decisive basis for it.[135] The Court, therefore, focussed upon the extent of the restriction on the defence. Unlike *Kostovski* where the witnesses were anonymous *stricto sensu*, the operative in the present case was known to the accused, albeit not by real identity but by physical appearance because of their several meetings. In this light, the Court considered that it would have been possible for the operative to be examined by the defence in a manner that did not disclose his identifying particulars.[136] Thus, the prosecution had essentially placed itself in an unduly advantaged position

128 *Kostovski* (n 28) [43].

129 Law Commission (n 18) [6.21]–[6.30].

130 Eg OG Wellborn, 'Demeanor' (1991) 76 Cornell L Rev 1075, 1075: It 'diminishes rather than enhances the accuracy of credibility judgements'; M Stone, 'Instant Lie Detection? Demeanour and Credibility in Criminal Trials' [1991] Crim LR 821, 829: 'There is no sound basis for assessing credibility from demeanour'; JA Blumenthal, 'A Wipe of the Hands, A Lick of the Lips: The Validity of Demeanor Evidence in Assessing Witness Credibility' (1993) 72 Neb L Rev 1157, 1189: It 'promotes faulty judgements and greatly disserves the truth-seeking process.'

131 Eg *Windisch* (n 25) [29]; *Van Mechelen* (n 58) [59], [62]; *Hulki Güneş* (n 83) [95]; *Bocos-Cuesta* (n 9) [71]; *Kovač* (n 9) [30]; *Vladimir Romanov* (n 125) [105].

See further *R v Collins* (1938) 26 Cr App R 177 (CA) 182 (Humphreys J): The opportunity to observe demeanour is an 'inestimable advantage'; *Government of the Virgin Islands v Aquino* 378 F2d 540, 548 (3rd Cir 1967) (Judge Freedman): 'Demeanor is of the utmost importance in the determination of the credibility of a witness'; Osborne (n 86) 266–267: Demeanour is 'a useful, if not infallible guide to credibility'.

132 *Kostovski* (n 28) [44].

133 Ibid [45]. This outcome was mirrored in *Windisch* (n 25) [31]–[32] where anonymous statements were of decisive importance to the conviction and *Saïdi* (n 125) [44] where the 'sole basis' for the conviction was anonymous evidence.

134 *Lüdi* (n 9).

135 Ibid [46]–[47].

136 Ibid [49].

when a less restrictive measure would have sufficed for its purposes; strict necessity had not been observed. Indeed, there was a complete absence of any effective attempt to counterbalance the handicap arising from the anonymity. Accordingly, a finding of violation was appropriate.[137] Clearly, the decision demonstrates that a violation is possible even if anonymous evidence is neither the sole nor decisive basis for the conviction.[138] Counterbalancing measures are required even if the anonymous witness is not a key witness.[139]

In contrast to the above cases, the judicial authorities in *Doorson* avoided a breach of Articles 6(1) and 6(3)(d) despite the handicap imposed on the defence by the use of anonymous testimony.[140] The applicant had been convicted for drug trafficking in part on the evidence of two anonymous witnesses whom he had not been able to confront.

The Court for the first time devoted more than just cursory attention to whether or not anonymity was justified. It referred to two grounds upon which regard must be had: it was an established fact that drug dealers often used intimidation measures against prosecution witnesses; previously, one of the witnesses had been injured by a drug dealer after testifying against him and the other had been threatened by dealers to deter him from testifying. The Court viewed these grounds as reasonably justifying the witnesses' fears of possible reprisals by the applicant, thus justifying anonymity.[141] This appears to be an unsound rationale. The applicant had neither threatened the witnesses nor was he known to have ever resorted to violence or threats, or to have illegally carried or handled weapons. Anonymity should only have been contemplated had this not been the case. The Court relied unreasonably on a generalisation as a justification for the restriction of defence rights.

The Court also determined that sufficient measures had been implemented to counterbalance the disadvantage to the accused: the anonymous witnesses were questioned during the appeal stage by an investigating judge who was aware of their identities; the judge submitted a record of her findings regarding the witnesses' reliability; defence counsel was present at the examination and able to put questions to the witnesses, except those designed to reveal identity, and

137 Ibid [50].

138 See *Birutis* (n 117) [30]–[35] for evidence of the same. The case is unique to the extent that the decision concerning two of the applicants turned on the failure of the courts to conduct an inquiry into the *manner in which the anonymous evidence was obtained* (obtained allegedly under conditions of improper pressure and incentives) and on the absence of an opportunity for the defence to question the witnesses. Accordingly, the handicaps faced by the applicants were not counterbalanced. A violation was also found in respect of the third applicant because, although anonymity was justified, his conviction rested solely upon anonymous evidence.

139 *Sarkizov and others v Bulgaria* (App 37981/06 et seq) ECHR 17 April 2012 [57]–[58].

140 *Doorson* (n 63) [83].

141 Ibid [71].

all were answered.[142] These measures are certainly superior to those applied in *Kostovski* and this was the first time that the Court found the counterbalancing measures to have offered satisfactory compensation. It would, however, have been more satisfactory had the additional measure of screening been implemented so as to allow the accused to at least be present at the examination whilst still preserving anonymity.

Nevertheless, the Court declared that 'even when "counterbalancing" procedures are found to compensate sufficiently the handicaps under which the defence labours, a conviction should not be based either solely or to a decisive extent on anonymous statements.'[143] Accordingly, it treated counterbalancing practices as a subordinate consideration to the actual extent of prejudice arising from the anonymous evidence. It clearly considered that when such evidence constitutes the sole or decisive basis of the conviction, the degree of prejudice is too great and ought to be sufficient in itself to justify a violation. It did not consider, however, that the anonymous evidence in the case met the 'sole or decisive' threshold in view of other available evidence.[144]

This conclusion is, however, highly questionable. The national court based its conviction principally on the evidence of the anonymous witnesses and two identified witnesses, N and R.[145] N had made a statement to the police incriminating the accused but retracted it when questioned in open court both at first instance and on appeal. R's evidence was effectively untested as he had only been heard by the police. Given the fundamental flaws in N and R's evidence, it is particularly unconvincing not to assert that the conviction was based to a decisive extent on the anonymous evidence. It is thus, in addition to the aforementioned unsound basis for anonymity, another ground upon which a violation should have been found. The impact of the anonymous testimony unduly tilted the balance between defence and prosecution in favour of the latter.

It is also notable that the Court observed without meaningful elaboration that witness evidence obtained under conditions in which the rights of the defence are not 'secured to the extent normally required by the Convention should be treated with extreme care.'[146] The Dutch authorities had apparently adhered to this requirement.[147] The Court seems to be suggesting that a cautionary approach to the assessment of evidence is a special measure. However, evidence in any context carries an implicit condition that it be treated with caution and circumspection. Accordingly, treatment of evidence in this manner by a state

142 Ibid [72]–[73], [75].
143 Ibid [76].
144 Ibid.
145 Ibid [34].
146 Ibid [76]. See also *Visser v the Netherlands* (App 26668/95) ECHR 14 February 2002 [44]; *SN* (n 9) [53]; *Krasniki* (n 117) [77]; *Gossa* (n 29) [55]; *Zhoglo* (n 58) [40].
147 *Doorson* (n 63) [76].

should not be included in the evaluation of any catalogue of positive measures applied by the state to mitigate a handicap to the accused.

Doorson was subsequently distinguished in *Van Mechelen and others v the Netherlands* where the Court did find the rights of the defence unacceptably restricted.[148] The applicants were convicted for attempted murder and robbery in circumstances wherein the only positive identification evidence was provided by police officers who wished to remain anonymous principally for the protection of their families from reprisals.

The Court distinguished the position of police officers from that of the ordinary witness as found in *Doorson*. It specified that the role of a policeman inherently involves testifying in open court, thus anonymity should only be implemented in exceptional circumstances.[149] It is also right that police officers be treated differently from civilian witnesses for the reason mentioned in the above analysis of *Unterpertinger*: the police are part of the wider prosecution team. The danger of this relationship is that anonymity could be used for prosecution self-interest rather than for actual witness protection. Unlike *Doorson*, the Court was not convinced that the national authorities had made sufficient inquiry into whether or not there was an actual threat of reprisals justifying anonymity. Indeed, a named civilian witness had made statements identifying one of the applicants and was never threatened.[150]

A further distinction is apparent between the two cases in respect of the counterbalancing measures adopted by the judicial authorities. In *Doorson*, the anonymous witnesses were questioned crucially in the presence of defence counsel. By contrast, in *Van Mechelen*, the officers were questioned by an investigating judge, who was aware of their identity and provided an opinion as to their reliability in his official report, whilst the defence and prosecution were listening and could ask questions from a separate room by sound-link. Thus, not only were the identities withheld from the defence, but this separation ensured that, unlike in *Doorson*, demeanour could not be observed by it either which, according to the Court, resulted in untested testimony.[151] The measures did not satisfactorily offset the disadvantage to the accused.[152] The Court had thus taken the view that anonymous witnesses should be present before the defence during questioning.

Expressly applying a test of strict necessity,[153] the Court also held that the national authorities had failed to justify the necessity for the measures adopted or explain why less restrictive measures, such as disguise or prevention of eye

148 *Van Mechelen* (n 58) [66].
149 Ibid [56].
150 Ibid [61], [64].
151 Ibid [59], [64].
152 Ibid [62].
153 Ibid [58]: 'any measures restricting the rights of the defence should be strictly necessary. If a less restrictive measure can suffice then that measure should be applied.'

contact, were not considered.[154] Trechsel suggests that the use of disguise is not realistically conducive to reliable observation of demeanour and risks creating a carnivalesque atmosphere.[155] Whilst this may be the case, there is a feasible alternative measure. Providing that the accused and the public were present at hearing and could listen to the live testimony, the witnesses could be screened off to ensure that only the decision-makers and prosecution and defence counsels could observe their demeanour during questioning. In such circumstances, the in-court identification of the accused by the witnesses could be conducted by live video feed (the screened witness can view the accused on his monitor) or by a clear photograph taken at the beginning of the hearing.

The final feature distinguishing the present case from *Doorson* is the actual prejudicial impact of the anonymous evidence as perceived by the Court. The convictions in *Van Mechelen* were based to a decisive extent on the identification evidence provided by anonymous witnesses.[156] Consequently, the domestic procedure allowing this occurrence placed the prosecution at an advantage vis-à-vis the defence.

The same conclusion was reached in *Visser v the Netherlands* which is of particular interest because the Court in finding a violation did not consider it necessary to examine the adequacy of the counterbalancing measures adopted therein.[157] It simply bypassed this aspect and grounded the violation on two other concerns, the first of which was the justification for witness anonymity. Anonymity had been sought for fear of reprisals since the applicant's co-accused carried a violent reputation and the offence for which the applicant was tried was revenge kidnapping. The Court, however, ruled anonymity unjustified because the judicial authorities had not demonstrated adequately that they had at any stage carried out a proper assessment of whether the fear of reprisals was well-founded.[158] In refusing to accept at face value the grounds for anonymity, the Court again exhibited a reassuring stance so as to ensure that the prosecution could not use non-essential anonymity to the detriment of the defence. The second concern was the prejudicial effect of the anonymous testimony. The Court viewed the conviction as having been based to a decisive extent on this evidence.[159]

It is evident from the approach taken by the Court that whilst it regarded counterbalancing measures as important, they were clearly a subordinate concern to both the adequacy of the grounds for anonymity and, as already indicated in the *Doorson* analysis, the impact of the associated evidence on the accused. If the judicial authorities fail to adequately substantiate their rationale

154 Ibid [60].
155 Trechsel (n 57) 319.
156 *Van Mechelen* (n 58) [63]–[64].
157 *Visser* (n 146) [51]–[52].
158 Ibid [47]–[48].
159 Ibid [50].

for anonymity, there is no legitimate ground upon which to derogate from the benchmark model and it is a logical consequence that measures designed to counterbalance the anonymity are rendered irrelevant. Furthermore, if actual prejudice arises from the evidence of the witness inappropriately awarded anonymity, the Court will generally find a violation.[160]

Also meriting discussion in the present analysis is the admissibility decision in *Kok v the Netherlands*[161] because it was inconsistent with the majority of Strasbourg judgements concerning derogations from the benchmark model.

This inconsistency stems from a principle therein which was also recited subsequently in two judgements on the merits, *Visser* and *Krasniki v the Czech Republic*:

> in assessing whether the procedures involved in the questioning of the anonymous witness were sufficient to counterbalance the difficulties caused to the defence due weight must be given to the above conclusion that the anonymous testimony was not in any respect decisive for the conviction of the applicant. The defence was thus handicapped to a much lesser degree.[162]

The relationship between the two variables – counterbalancing measures and the impact of the anonymous evidence – presented in this proposition is one of correlation. It seems to indicate that even where anonymous evidence forms to a decisive extent the basis of a conviction, this is a disadvantage capable of being offset by sufficient procedural countermeasures. In other words, the Court did not view it as an absolute condition of procedural fairness that the conviction not be based to a decisive extent on such evidence. Also providing authority to this effect is *SN v Sweden*,[163] though it concerned a vulnerable rather than anonymous witness. Despite observing that the statements of a child witness who never testified in court were virtually the sole evidence upon which the accused's conviction was based, the Court concluded, nevertheless, that the counterbalancing measures applied were sufficient to avoid a violation.[164]

This approach appeared inconsistent with the opinion held by the Court for most of its jurisprudence not only in respect of anonymous witnesses, but also of those within the absent and vulnerable categories. The following principle in *AM v Italy* reflected this majority view:

> the rights of the defence are restricted to an extent that is incompatible with the requirements of Article 6 if the conviction is based solely, or in a decisive manner, on

160 The approach and outcome in *Visser* was subsequently mirrored in *Krasniki* (n 117) [80]–[86].
161 (App 43149/98) ECHR 2000-VI.
162 Ibid [1] ('The Law'); *Visser* (n 146) [46]; *Krasniki* (n 117) [79].
163 *SN* (n 9).
164 Ibid [46]–[47], [49]–[54].

> the depositions of a witness whom the accused has had no opportunity to examine or to have examined either during the investigation or at trial.[165]

On this contrary view, therefore, it was in principle an absolute condition that a conviction should not be founded solely or to a decisive degree on anonymous testimony. *Visser* and *Krasniki* also made reference to this absolute requirement to accompany their citation of the *Kok* principle.[166] Neither case is, however, particularly useful authority for *Kok* outside of reciting the relevant principle in the latter. The convictions in these cases were based solely or to a decisive extent on anonymous testimony and violations were found without any examination of counterbalancing measures.[167]

The contradiction between the *Kok* and *AM* principles demonstrated a failure by the Court to create necessary legal certainty. A natural repercussion of this was uncertainty in the former House of Lords in *R v Davis*:

> It is considerably less certain ... that there is an absolute requirement that anonymous testimony should not be the sole or decisive evidence, or whether the extent to which such testimony is decisive may be no more than a very important factor to balance in the scales. I doubt whether the Strasbourg court has said the last word about this.[168]

A possible means of resolving this uncertainty would be to dismiss the *Kok* principle and rely on as authoritative the *AM* principle simply because it was consistently cited in most judgements. However, authoritative status for a principle should not be assumed without regard to the actual practice of the Court. All the cases cited concerning anonymous evidence reveal that the Court did not seem inclined to settle at finding a violation with regard exclusively to the fact that the conviction was based solely or to a decisive extent on anonymous evidence. It also reflected on the justification for anonymity and, with the exception of *Visser* and *Krasniki*, the applied counterbalancing measures. Counterbalancing measures were treated as a subordinate concern. Regard for factors additional to the importance of the evidence to the conviction evidences an attempt to comply with the examination of the trial as a whole approach. In these circumstances, therefore, one could not assert with absolute certainty that, in practice, the *AM* principle was in itself sufficient to justify a finding of violation. Nevertheless, it is undeniable that it has for the Court been a particularly useful indicator of actual prejudice.

---

165 *AM* (n 22) [25] (vulnerable). See also eg *Doorson* (n 63) [76] (anonymous); *Van Mechelen* (n 58) [55] (anonymous); *Lucà* (n 9) [40] (absent); *PS* (n 63) [24] (vulnerable); *Vladimir Romanov* (n 125) [100] (absent).

166 *Visser* (n 146) [45]; *Krasniki* (n 117) [78].

167 Ibid respectively [50]–[52]; [84]–[86].

168 [2008] UKHL 36; [2008] 3 WLR 125 [89] (Lord Mance). See also [95]: 'the Strasbourg case law may itself prove to have a greater flexibility than some of the dicta used in them would suggest.'

The admissibility decision of *Ellis, Simms and Martin v UK*[169] illustrates the position the Court has taken more recently. The Court relied on the three-step approach to absent witnesses in *Al-Khawaja and Tahery* and applied it to the context of an anonymous witness in a case concerning gang-related murders.[170] First, it examined whether there were good reasons to keep secret the identity of the witness: it accepted that there were because the witness genuinely feared retribution given the backdrop of ongoing gang violence.[171] Second, the Court considered whether the evidence of the anonymous witness was the sole or decisive basis for each applicant's conviction: it accepted that his evidence may have been decisive.[172] Third, the Court examined whether there were sufficient counterbalancing factors to ensure that the trial as a whole was fair. It had regard to the following: the judge, the jury, the prosecution, and defence counsel could see and hear the witness give evidence in court (the witness was cross-examined by defence counsel), thus were able to observe his demeanour; the judge handed down three rulings on the witness's anonymity in which he considered carefully the support for the witness's evidence, the extent of the disclosure in the case and the need to protect the right to a fair trial; the judge kept his anonymity ruling under review and refused to permit anonymous evidence from another witness; the jury were given careful directions on how to approach the evidence of the witness, which included them being advised to take into account the considerable limitations on the defence and the need for independent evidence implicating the accused; and the substantial disclosure in the case, including information relevant to credibility, permitted extensive and effective cross-examination of the witness.[173] The Court concluded that these counterbalancing factors were sufficient and dismissed the complaint as manifestly ill-founded.[174] Clearly, the Court took the view that the prejudicial effect of an anonymous witness giving decisive evidence against the accused can be compensated for if sufficient counterbalancing factors exist. Counterbalancing factors are, therefore, no longer treated as a subordinate consideration.

6.2.3. Alternative Approach

The analysis of the jurisprudence on anonymous witnesses illustrates incontrovertibly that the Court has engaged deliberately in a balancing exercise between the rights of the witness and the accused. It has already been stated with reference to the concept of *praktische Konkordanz* that this balancing exercise involves restricting the rights of both actors through proportionate concessions.

169 (Apps 46099/06; 46699/06) ECHR 10 April 2012.
170 Ibid [76]–[79].
171 Ibid [80].
172 Ibid [81].
173 Ibid [82]–[87].
174 Ibid [89].

In *Doorson*, for example, the identities of the witnesses were disclosed to the investigating judge, defence counsel was present at the examination and could pose questions (protection afforded to the witnesses limited); questions potentially revealing identity, however, could not be asked and the accused could not attend the examination (limitation on the accused). A balancing of interests is undertaken because the Court accepts that use of anonymous testimony from the public and covert state agents is necessary in exceptional circumstances. It is submitted, however, that the extent of this acceptance is misguided. Lusty's observation is pertinent: 'There is now emerging a general consensus amongst the international community that witness anonymity is a cure worse than the disease.'[175]

There are numerous measures available to states that offer a feasible alternative to anonymity. These measures are capable of providing effective protection for lay and expert witnesses without restricting the rights of the defence, hence derogation from the benchmark model and the accompanying inequality between the parties is avoidable. The following measures are proposed as examples:[176]

a) The creation and strict enforcement of a specific offence of intimidation of witnesses to deter acts not already addressed under other legislation.
b) Withholding bail and remanding the accused in custody.
c) Revealing the identity of the witness at the latest possible stage in the proceedings, but in such time as is reasonable to allow the defence to sufficiently prepare its examination.
d) Exclusion of the public and media but only during the live testimony of the witness in issue (requires limited derogation from the benchmark model but is permissible under Article 6(1)). If the press are to be present during the testimony, reporting restrictions may be implemented.
e) The provision of overt or covert protective surveillance and/or alternative accommodation for the witness and relatives under threat until the conclusion of trial.
f) The use of a short- or long-term protection scheme for the witness and relatives under threat after trial involving one or more of the following steps: domestic or international relocation (including employment assistance), identity change and protective surveillance.

It is unfortunate that the Court provides criteria to be satisfied if anonymous evidence is to be admitted rather than using the opportunity afforded it to

175 D Lusty, 'Anonymous Accusers: An Historical & Comparative Analysis of Secret Witnesses in Criminal Trials' (2002) 24 Sydney L Rev 361, 424.

176 Ibid 424 fn 377; Recommendation No R (97) 13 (n 2) Appendix [3], [9], [15] and Explanatory Memorandum [65], [80]–[81], [83]–[89].

reject witness anonymity and encourage states to pursue innovate and effective alternative measures where procedural equality is not endangered.

Though the above measures may also be deployed where the life or safety of a covert state agent is under specific threat, agents are faced with a unique obstacle as compared to the lay or expert witness. A possible consequence of the identification of an agent at trial is that his ability to ever continue in an undercover operational capacity may be irreparably compromised. It is submitted that the realisation of this possibility is unlikely in most scenarios and anonymity is thereby unwarranted. These scenarios involve for the most part short-term undercover assignments that are highly localised and involve suspects linked to either a closely or loosely associated group or small network. It is not unreasonable to consider that the agent could continue to operate undercover effectively in either the same or surrounding areas and target those outside the aforementioned network. Delaying the agent's next assignment is a further strategy that may lessen the likelihood of recognition when undercover status is re-established. It cannot be ignored, however, that there will be operations conducted on occasion against the most serious of organisations within the criminal fraternity which retain a widespread network of members. It may be possible for agents who have subsequently testified without anonymity to undertake undercover investigations of individuals or groups unaffiliated with the prior target organisation. The onus must be on the state to prove on a case-by-case basis that this is not possible.

If the same is proved, this will constitute an exceptional circumstance in which practical realities ensure that anonymity cannot be ruled out as a solution of last resort. It is likely in such an exceptional circumstance that effective anonymity would require the additional use of screening. If anonymity is sought, strict conditions must be attached to the proceedings. The Committee of Ministers of the Council of Europe have recommended 'the establishment of an independent verification mechanism capable of providing an effective substitutive form for the defendant and his counsel in the research of any doubtful circumstance that might seriously affect the reliability … of the anonymous witness.'[177] This pre-trial counterbalancing mechanism should include an investigation concerning the personal history of the witness carried out by an independent magistrate to ensure that the witness is not plotting against the accused; a subsequent report by the magistrate detailing the reliability and genuineness of the witness; an opportunity for the defence to comment and ask questions on the personal history of the witness; and a right of the defence to object to the application for anonymity.[178] Anonymity must,

177 Recommendation No R (97) 13 (n 2) Explanatory Memorandum [38]. See also [66], [75] and Appendix [10].

178 Ibid Explanatory Memorandum [76].

of course, be justified and the evidence of the witness need be significant.[179] In regard to trial, the Committee also suggested that a conviction should not solely or to a decisive extent be based on anonymous evidence.[180] Additionally, it is paramount that the defence be able to examine or have examined the witness. If screening measures are employed, defence counsel should be in a position to observe demeanour. The application of such conditions in the above exceptional circumstance must be accompanied by caution so as not to encourage the remit of an 'exceptional circumstance' from becoming unduly inclusive. It is the absence of caution that breeds the normalisation of witness anonymity,[181] the natural consequence of which is to place the accused in a disadvantaged position.

6.3. VULNERABLE WITNESSES: CHILD VICTIMS IN SEXUAL OFFENCE PROSECUTIONS

6.3.1. Introduction

The final category of witness in which states harbour a tendency to derogate from the benchmark model encompasses those considered vulnerable. Though a condition of vulnerability is also suffered by mentally disabled victims and rape complainants,[182] the few cases considered thus far by the Court in this category relate specifically to children.

Accordingly, those vulnerable for present purposes are child victims of sexual offences whose traumatic experiences 'present the prosecuting authorities and the courts with serious evidential difficulties in the course of the proceedings.'[183] Children are often acutely susceptible to serious emotional distress occasioned by face-to-face confrontation with the alleged perpetrator of the traumatic event.[184] Recounting the intimate particulars of the event before the accused

179 Ibid [77].

180 Ibid Appendix [13] and Explanatory Memorandum [38], [79].

181 R Costigan and PA Thomas, 'Anonymous Witnesses' (2000) 51 NILQ 326, 343–348; Lusty (n 175) 425.

182 See further *A* (n 3) especially [34]–[35], [38]–[40], [43], [45] (Lord Steyn) concerning the interpretation of YJCEA s 41 which prevented the accused from examining a rape complainant on her previous sexual behaviour, including with the former, except in particularly narrow circumstances. The House of Lords held the provision to be, on ordinary principles of statutory construction, a 'prima facie excessive inroad on the right to a fair trial' as it denied the accused the opportunity of putting forward relevant evidence for 'a full and complete defence', hence was incompatible with Art 6. It is, however, questionable whether the same would be found in Strasbourg given that rules on the admissibility of evidence are primarily a matter within the broad margin of appreciation afforded to states.

183 *Mattoccia v Italy* (App 23969/94) ECHR 2000-IX [71].

184 JR Spencer, 'Children's Evidence in Legal Proceedings in England' in JR Spencer and others (eds), *Children's Evidence in Legal Proceedings: An International Perspective* (Cambridge

may bring about negative and revived feelings of helplessness, hurt, shame, guilt and, if the abuser was in a position of trust, betrayal.[185] Such feelings may jeopardise the quality of the evidence elicited or prove to be an insurmountable obstacle to obtaining any testimony at all. These possible negative effects assume even greater significance because the nature of sexual offences is such that the testimony of the child is often the foremost basis for the prosecution. Though an adverse emotional impact is particularly prominent in cases involving children, sexual offence prosecutions are, of course, also capable of becoming a painful ordeal for adult victims facing their perceived offenders.

It is in view of these circumstances that the Court recognises the welfare of the victim-witness in sexual offence proceedings as a legitimate interest in the application of Article 6:

> In the assessment of ... whether or not ... an accused received a fair trial, account must be taken of the right to respect for the private life of the perceived victim. Therefore, the Court accepts that in criminal proceedings concerning sexual abuse certain measures may be taken for the purpose of protecting the victim, provided that such measures can be reconciled with an adequate and effective exercise of the rights of the defence. In securing the rights of the defence, the judicial authorities may be required to take measures which counterbalance the handicaps under which the defence labours.[186]

Lawful derogation from the benchmark model to accommodate a vulnerable witness is, therefore, possible but contingent once again on a fair balancing of interests. The threat underlying derogation in the present context is, of course, that the vulnerable witness may be protected to the extent that the defence is unable to properly test important evidence and is thereby unduly disadvantaged vis-à-vis the prosecution.

In its analysis of whether or not a fair balance was achieved, the jurisprudence below indicates that the Court adopts the key factors to be taken into account that were given prominence in cases concerning absent and anonymous witnesses. Thus, as indicated in the above quotation, the Court

---

University Law Faculty, Cambridge 1990) 117; GS Goodman and others, 'Testifying in Criminal Court: Emotional Effects on Child Sexual Assault Victims' (1992) 57 Monogr Soc Res Child Dev 1, 100–101, 120–121; J McEwan, *Evidence and the Adversarial Process: The Modern Law* (Blackwell, Oxford 1992) 112; LC Brannon, 'The Trauma of Testifying in Court for Child Victims of Sexual Assault v The Accused's Right to Confrontation' (1994) 18 Law & Psychol Rev 439, 440, 442, 459.

See further M Wąsek-Wiaderek, *The Principle of "Equality of Arms" in Criminal Procedure Under Article 6 of the European Convention on Human Rights and its Functions in Criminal Justice of Selected European Countries: A Comparative View* (Leuven UP, Leuven 2000) 33 who suggests that such distress is tantamount to secondary victimisation.

185 Goodman and others (n 184) 120; Brannon (n 184) 442–443.

186 *SN* (n 9) [47]. See also *PS* (n 63) [22]–[23]; *Bocos-Cuesta* (n 9) [69]; *WS* (n 22) [47], [57]; *Kovač* (n 9) [27].

will consider whether measures implemented by the judicial authorities were sufficient to counterbalance the unconventional burden on the defence. It will also assess the reasonableness of the justification for the derogation and whether the conviction was based to a sole or decisive extent (prejudice) on the evidence of the vulnerable witness.

6.3.2. Case-Law

These factors featured in *PS v Germany*,[187] a case where the applicant was convicted of sexually abusing an eight-year-old girl. The trial court relied on statements made by the girl, her mother and the police officer who questioned her after the offence.

The girl was never heard before the courts because she had repressed her recollection of the event and reminding her thereof would be detrimental to her personal development. The Court opined, however, that such a rationale was irrelevant for it was 'rather vague and speculative'.[188] Quite rightly, therefore, the Court is not prepared to accept as given a condition of vulnerability in all child sexual abuse prosecutions. Accordingly, in the subsequent case of *Bocos-Cuesta v the Netherlands*, it criticised the failure of the judicial authorities to base the derogation on 'concrete evidence' and it also highlighted in *Kovač v Croatia* the 'absence of any explanation' for refusing the applicant the opportunity to question the child victim-witness.[189] In the light of the consequences for the accused, it is essential that derogation from the benchmark model grounded on the vulnerability of the witness is, like anonymity, adequately justified.

The Court also noted in the case that at no stage in the proceedings had the girl been questioned by a judge and the applicant been able to observe her demeanour as an indicator of reliability.[190] Though the appeal court had at its disposal an expert opinion on the girl's credibility, the European Court considered its value as a countermeasure highly compromised since it had been prepared 18 months after the alleged offence.[191] This is understandable because a significantly delayed opinion does not necessarily reflect accurately the actual credibility of a witness at the time the incriminating statements were made. Additionally, the countermeasure was certainly outweighed by the fact that the conviction was based to a decisive extent on the girl's evidence.[192]

In these circumstances, the prosecution gained a prejudicial advantage from the opportunity to use evidence that the defence could not effectively test. It was

187 *PS* (n 63).
188 Ibid [28].
189 *Bocos-Cuesta* (n 9) [72]; *Kovač* (n 9) [31]. Breach of Arts 6(1) and 6(3)(d) found in both cases: [74], [33] respectively.
190 *PS* (n 63) [26].
191 Ibid [29]. Contrast Trechsel (n 57) 321 who finds this view unconvincing.
192 *PS* (n 63) [30].

determined, accordingly, that the rights of the defence had been restricted to an unacceptable extent in breach of Articles 6(1) and 6(3)(d).[193]

No such breach was found in *SN* where the conviction of the accused was for the sexual abuse of a child of 10 who did not appear before the courts.[194]

The Court did not, unfortunately, require the same standard of evidential substantiation for the derogation from the benchmark model as that apparent in *PS*, *Bocos-Cuesta* and *Kovač*. It seemed to accept the derogation as justified merely on the status of the witness as a child victim of sexual abuse.[195] Such a stance risks an unnecessary restriction of defence rights given that it is not inevitable that a confrontation with the accused in all such cases will be to the severe emotional short- and/or long-term detriment of the child.

It has already been referred to in the above analysis on anonymous witnesses that the Court acted against the trend that had been set in most of its jurisprudence by not finding a violation despite observing that the child's evidence constituted virtually the sole basis for the conviction. The fundamental basis for its decision was that the applied counterbalancing measures were sufficient to have enabled the defence to challenge the child's statements and credibility.[196] The videotape of the first police interview with the child was shown at trial and on appeal. The transcript of the second interview was read out at trial and the defence listened to the audiotape of the same at the appeal stage. This evidence was disclosed to the defence pre-trial. Defence counsel had consented to not being present at the second interview and failed to request that it be videotaped, though he was able to have his questions put to the child by the interviewer. Accordingly, he had not availed himself of the opportunities to view directly or indirectly both the child's response under questioning, which may have provided evidence to undermine the child's credibility, and the conduct of the interview. Despite this failure on the part of the defence, the procedure applied remains subject to criticism: it did not allow for anyone independent of the prosecution to question directly the child at any stage.[197] A possible remedy to this defect is the suggestion of Judges Türmen and Maruste that an expert in child forensic psychology could have been engaged to assess the child's evidence.[198] It was in view of the defect that these judges considered in their dissenting opinion that the judicial authorities had failed in their duty to implement all feasible counterbalancing measures.[199]

When this criticism is combined with the highly prejudicial impact of the child's evidence, which significantly was not corroborated by an independent

193 Ibid [31]–[32].
194 *SN* (n 9) [54].
195 Ibid [47].
196 Ibid [52].
197 Ibid Concurring Op Judges Thomassen and Casadevall.
198 Ibid Diss Op Judges Türmen and Maruste.
199 Ibid.

witness, and the absence of adequate substantiation for the derogation, the accused was placed in an unduly disadvantaged position irrespective of the failings of his counsel. Accordingly, contrary to the Court's actual decision, a finding of violation was a warranted response.

A violation was found to have occurred subsequently in *WS v Poland*, a case concerning the conviction of the applicant for the repeated sexual abuse of his daughter between the ages of two and four.[200] The child was never at any stage questioned by the defence, prosecutor, police or courts.

An expert, however, twice conducted a psychological examination of the child, the findings of which were of decisive importance to the conviction.[201] Accordingly, the information gleaned from the girl was particularly prejudicial to the accused. Having noted that the soundness of the methodology used by the expert psychologist was confirmed, the Court declared that her opinion that it would be harmful to the well-being and development of the child to be heard (rationale for the derogation) was sufficiently motivated and not disproved.[202] However, the Court did highlight that the absence of video recordings of the examinations denied the parties and courts a necessary opportunity to observe the child's demeanour under questioning.[203] A video record is also a particularly prudent safeguard in view of the suggestibility of children and the ever-present threat of distortions by the adult interviewer.[204] Additionally, the Court observed that the judicial authorities failed to make any attempts during the proceedings to enable the defence to test the reliability of the child in a manner alternative to direct questioning.[205] It suggested, as examples, an interview in the presence of a psychologist with written questions from the defence or an interview in a studio wherein the accused or his counsel could be present indirectly through the use of a one-way mirror or video-link.[206] In these circumstances, the Court concluded that the restrictions on the defence right of examination were not counterbalanced.[207] Furthermore, the Government could not rely on as a defence the fact that the prosecutor had also not questioned the child, for the Court held that it was 'not sufficient for a finding that the applicant was not put in a disadvantageous position *vis-à-vis* the other party.'[208]

---

200 *WS* (n 22) [64]. The child was aged four at the initiation of the investigation and seven at the time of trial.

201 Ibid [58].

202 Ibid [58]–[59].

203 Ibid [59], [63]. This was also a ground of criticism expressed, mutatis mutandis, in *Bocos-Cuesta* (n 9) [71] and *Kovač* (n 9) [30].

204 LS McGough, 'Good Enough for Government Work: The Constitutional Duty to Preserve Forensic Interviews of Child Victims' (2002) 65 Law & Contemp Probs 179, 184.

205 *WS* (n 22) [61].

206 Ibid. Video-links are also encompassed within the suggested example by the Court in *Bocos-Cuesta* (n 9) [71] and *Kovač* (n 9) [30] that the accused be able to observe children under questioning from 'another room via technical devices'.

207 *WS* (n 22) [63].

208 Ibid [49], [63].

Such a finding has particular merit in its approach to the concept of equality of arms. The procedure implemented by the judicial authorities, the most notable aspect of which were the interviews by the psychologist, proved to be particularly advantageous to the prosecution. Whereas the formal opinion of the psychologist was susceptible admittedly to challenge, the defence could only mount an 'effective' challenge thereto if a proper and adequate opportunity to test its evidential source – the child – had been provided. Given that such an opportunity was not granted and the evidence of the child occasioned actual prejudice, the prosecutor was unduly advantaged by the process despite not questioning the child himself.

6.3.3. *Acceptable Level of Derogation from Benchmark Model*

Vulnerability sufficiently justified merits protection. Court preparation programmes customised to the needs of each child are propounded as a means of enhancing communication skills to deal with examinations and of empowering the child with stress management techniques and essential information on court procedure to reduce anxiety and fear.[209] Though such preparation is not without value, it is insufficient to overcome for the vulnerable child the trauma arising from an actual face-to-face confrontation with his perceived abuser. One can accept, therefore, that where the state has, through expert opinion, adequately substantiated that a severe adverse impact on the well-being and development of the child is highly likely if a confrontation with the accused were to occur, derogation from the benchmark model will be necessary.

In order to restrict the extent of this derogation and the possible disadvantage to the accused, whilst accommodating simultaneously the interests of the vulnerable witness, the Court has in the above jurisprudence formulated feasible measures that are worth expanding upon. An audio-visual record of the initial interview of the child should be made as evidence-in-chief and subsequently disclosed to the defence to enable preparation of its lines of inquiry. Thereafter, in accusatorial style systems, defence counsel could question with delicacy the child at trial through the medium of video-link, the latter giving evidence from a separate child-friendly room. Alternatively, in inquisitorial style systems, a further and final pre-trial interview should be conducted in a child-friendly location by an investigating judge and/or an expert in child psychology. From a separate room, audio and video devices will allow the accused and his representative to observe the propriety of the interview and to feed the interviewer questions to be put to the child. As in the case of the initial interview, this interview should also be recorded for transmission at trial. It is, of course, an option for procedures of the inquisitorial tradition to make use of

209 Recommendation No R (97) 13 (n 2) Explanatory Memorandum [107]; IM Cordon, GS Goodman and SJ Anderson, 'Children in Court' in van Koppen and Penrod (n 13) 182–183.

audio-visual techniques for an examination of the child at the trial hearing in lieu of or in addition to this second pre-trial interview. It is through the adoption of such solutions that the child is both adequately protected but subject still to effective challenge by the defence.

7. THE RIGHT TO CALL WITNESSES

Whereas the predominant focus of the analysis hitherto has been the examination of adverse witnesses, the accompanying right of the accused to call fact and expert witnesses on an equal footing with the prosecution remains to be considered.

Contrary to the conclusion drawn by Maffei,[210] the right of the accused to call a witness 'on his behalf' as articulated in Article 6(3)(d) is not restricted merely to those considered favourable to the defence. This was exemplified in *Cardot v France* where the onus was placed by the Court on the defence to call the prosecution witnesses it wished to examine, the prosecutor having deemed their attendance at trial unnecessary.[211] A prosecution witness is, accordingly, capable of incorporation into the category of witness on behalf of the defence. The remit of this category has been defined most accurately by Trechsel as including any witness 'called upon the initiative of the defence', hence extending its reach to even the neutral witness.[212] In the adversarial tradition, it is on the initiative of the parties that witnesses are called. On the other hand, courts of the inquisitorial tradition assume primary responsibility for selecting witnesses to be summoned, though the accused may make a request for additional witnesses. There is an expectation that he employ all lawful means at his disposal (reasonable effort) to communicate that request to the court.[213] The same is applicable in adversarial systems if the accused seeks to rely on a court issued summons when the witness indicates that he is unwilling to appear voluntarily. Whenever a court is relied upon to secure the attendance of a witness, it must make every reasonable effort to do so.[214]

The exercise of the right to call witnesses is, however, subject to a particularly potent discretion on the part of the domestic courts, it having been settled as a general rule that Article 6(3)(d) entrusts them with the assessment of whether the calling of a particular witness is appropriate.[215] It is in the light of this vested discretion that the courts are not required to facilitate the attendance and

---

210 Maffei (n 26) 75.
211 (App 11069/84) (1991) Series A no 200 [35]–[36].
212 Trechsel (n 57) 323.
213 *Dorokhov* (n 7) [67], [70]–[71].
214 *Pello* (n 7) [34]–[35].
215 Eg *Vidal* (n 7) [33]; *Perna v Italy* (App 48898/99) ECHR 6 May 2003 [29]; *Dorokhov* (n 7) [65]; *Rumyana Ivanova v Bulgaria* (App 36207/03) ECHR 14 February 2008 [42].

examination of every witness demanded by the accused.[216] Indeed, the Court has stipulated that only in exceptional circumstances will it conclude that a refusal to hear such a witness is incompatible with Article 6.[217] The provision of this discretion and the reticence of the Court to intervene are consistent with the broader principle that the admissibility and assessment of evidence is primarily the responsibility of national courts. It is a reaffirmation of the Court's position as a subsidiary body of oversight rather than a court of fourth instance. In this capacity, the Court will seek to ensure that state discretion is exercised in a manner compatible with the concept of equality of arms: the conditions for calling witnesses must be equal between the parties.

Complaints grounded on the second limb of Article 6(3)(d) arise because the competent authorities are alleged to have exercised their discretion to an unfair extent in refusing to admit the evidence of a witness the defence sought to introduce. It is a condition of substantiating this allegation that the accused prove that he was unable, upon his request, to call the proposed witness and that he establish that the evidence anticipated therefrom was relevant:

> It is ... not sufficient for a defendant to complain that he has not been allowed to question certain witnesses; he must, in addition, support his request by explaining why it is important for the witnesses concerned to be heard and their evidence must be necessary for the establishment of the truth.[218]

The qualification of relevance is an appropriate obstruction to proposals for witnesses that are from the outset without merit.[219] It is not a standard that presents an affront to the reasonable level of protection an accused should expect. The judicial authorities bear a corresponding duty of giving adequate consideration to whether the accused's assertion of the relevance of the proposed witness is sound. If a court is not convinced sufficiently of the accused's argument towards relevance, adequate consideration entails that its decision must be expressly reasoned, particularly in the light of *Vidal v Belgium*.[220] It is only right that the court explain itself if arbitrary decisions are to be avoided. The fact that a rejection is reasoned, however, should not of itself satisfy the requirement of adequate consideration, for the reasons given in some cases will

---

216 Eg *Engel and others* (n 7) [91]; *Vidal* (n 7) [33]; *Popov* (n 7) [176]; *Polufakin and Chernyshev v Russia* (App 30997/02) ECHR 25 September 2008 [205]. See also 'Text of the Report' (n 5) 262: 'It is obviously not a question of giving the accused the right to summon witnesses without any restriction.'

217 *Bricmont* (n 77) [89]; *Popov* (n 7) [179]; *Pello* (n 7) [27].

218 *Perna* (n 215) [29], [32]. See also *Bocos-Cuesta* (n 9) [67]; *Koval v Ukraine* (App 65550/01) ECHR 19 October 2006 [116]; *Borisova* (n 63) [46]; *Pello* (n 7) [26]; *Muttilainen* (n 63) [21].

219 See further Osborne (n 86) 260: 'attempts to prolong trials or abuse the process of the court, e.g. by summoning Government Ministers or foreign nationals, would certainly fail.'

220 *Vidal* (n 7) [34]–[35]: It was especially the absence of reasons for the appellate court's refusal to admit a proposed witness that gave rise to an Art 6 violation.

be especially unreasonable. The European Court should, accordingly, define the scope of adequate consideration to include a condition that the grounds for rejection not be manifestly unreasonable. To do so would be another means of reaffirming to national courts that their discretion is not unlimited.

Only through adequate consideration of relevance can a court's refusal to admit a proposed witness constitute a responsible and reliable exercise of its discretion and avert a violation. Such consideration was acknowledged as absent in *Popov v Russia*: 'the domestic courts' refusal to examine the defence witnesses without any regard to the relevance of their statements led to a limitation of the defence rights incompatible with the guarantees of a fair trial enshrined in Article 6.'[221] To deny the admission of a proposed witness without first confirming irrelevance through adequate consideration amounts, essentially, to unduly limiting the opportunity of the accused to put relevant evidence before the court. Meanwhile, the prosecution would be entitled to admit all its relevant evidence, for the charge relies upon it. The accused, accordingly, would be subject to a prejudicial inequality in the opportunity to have admitted relevant witnesses, hence contravening the concept of equality of arms.

It is in the light of this analysis that *Dorokhov v Russia*[222] should be viewed as an out of place decision not to be followed. The Court considered 'regrettable' the failure of the domestic courts to duly examine the defence request to call two witnesses who were, in its view, 'clearly relevant'.[223] The prosecution had secured the attendance of its witnesses. Unexpectedly, however, the Court maintained that Articles 6(1) and 6(3)(d) had not been violated.[224] The rationale was that there was a solid evidentiary basis for the conviction and the probative value of the anticipated witness evidence was sufficiently low so as to render an acquittal unlikely.[225] The Court certainly exceeded its competence. The possible probative value of evidence from witnesses the accused had sought to call is an issue primarily for the competence of the national courts but was used unduly by the Court, after having made its own assessment, to effectively offset a prejudicial procedural inequality. The Court must retain a principally procedural focus if it is to avoid assuming a fourth instance role. A violation should, therefore, have been found on the basis of the inequality associated with the failure to give adequate consideration to the accused's request.[226]

---

221 *Popov* (n 7) [188]. See also eg *Pello* (n 7) [35]: A failure to 'examine adequately' a witness admission request was held to contravene Arts 6(1) and 6(3)(d); *Jorgic v Germany* (App 74613/01) ECHR 12 July 2007 [86], [88]: The refusal to call certain proposed witnesses on grounds of irrelevance was held legitimate given that the applicant's request had been duly examined and detailed reasons for the refusal were provided.

222 *Dorokhov* (n 7).

223 Ibid [72]–[74].

224 Ibid [75].

225 Ibid [74].

226 See also ibid Partly Diss Op Judges Lorenzen and Tsatsa-Nikolovska.

The courts must not, however, focus their efforts exclusively on duly examining a witness request if they are to successfully avert procedural inequalities. Even in cases where a request to call witnesses is granted, a procedural inequality ensues if the court fails to take effective measures to secure the witnesses' presence because relevant witnesses are in practice still being excluded to the advantage of the prosecution, whose witnesses are in attendance.[227]

Also impacting on the effective exercise of the right to call witnesses under conditions of equality from the outset may be circumstances where the accused is denied adequate time and facilities to prepare a defence. The provision of an adequate opportunity for case preparation is necessary to effectively enable the accused to be in a position to propose witnesses. In *Borisova v Bulgaria*,[228] the accused was party to an expedited procedure without prior notice in which she was unable to call defence witnesses and was convicted within three hours of being detained. The Court considered it reasonable that she failed to provide the trial court with the names of witnesses she wished to call as she lacked the time and facilities to prepare an effective defence.[229] As prosecution witnesses had been secured, the Court concluded correctly that the prosecution was advantaged unfairly in its opportunity to prepare its case and find supporting witnesses, thereby infringing, inter alia, Articles 6(1) and 6(3)(d).[230] The case illustrates an instance in which a violation was easily avoidable. The burden imposed by the Court of placing the accused in a position to propose witnesses was certainly not an onerous one. Indeed, neither is it particularly onerous for national courts to adequately examine a witness request, given their broad discretion, and to make reasonable efforts to obtain the attendance of a witness upon approval of that request. Whereas the realisation of procedural equality in the opportunity to call witnesses is, therefore, a relatively undemanding endeavour for judicial authorities, the demands that are imposed generally protect the accused to an acceptable degree.

8. CONCLUSION

The object of this discussion was to consider the Court's approach to equality of arms within the context of the Article 6(3)(d) right to challenge and call witness evidence.

A strong nexus exists between equality of arms and this provision. This is authoritatively recognised in law by the Court, the Commission and the Human Rights Committee, and made possible in the ECHR because both are

227 *Polufakin and Chernyshev* (n 216) [207].
228 *Borisova* (n 63).
229 Ibid [47].
230 Ibid [48]–[50].

components of the right to a fair hearing in Article 6(1). At a conceptual level, the nexus is evident in the contribution that observance of Article 6(3)(d) makes to furthering the instrumental, intrinsic and secondary (collateral) values of procedural equality. The right to challenge and call witness evidence is also feasibly reciprocal, essential to case preparation and presentation, and associated with the adversarial principle, all of which are features placing it within the remit of equality of arms.

The discussion identified those who can assume witness or examiner status. The Court has rightly adopted an autonomous interpretation of 'witness' to prevent states unduly avoiding Article 6(3)(d) applicability through formal labels. A witness is one who authored at any time a statement taken into account by the domestic court. This can include co-defendants and experts engaged by the parties. An independent court-appointed expert is not intrinsically a witness. He can, however, assume witness status if doubts as to his neutrality, raised by appearances, are objectively justified (expert witness). Recourse to appearances, as is done when identifying an 'opponent', is a manifestation of the autonomous interpretation approach. Examiner status can apply to a judge, a legal representative and a pro se accused, though in the latter case it is not unreasonable for him to be restricted from examining a demonstrably vulnerable witness when representation is available.

A benchmark model, reflected in Article 6(3)(d), for the conduct of examinations was presented in the chapter to serve as a reference point by which to discern and measure legitimate and illegitimate derogations therefrom. The model features live oral testimony before an open trial court; face-to-face contact between witness and accused; and questioning conducted under a condition of procedural equality. A requirement that evidence is sworn and the real identity of the witness is revealed is a worthwhile addition.

In exceptional cases, the Court accepts that this model can be legitimately derogated from without violating Article 6(3)(d). This is grounded on a need to reconcile the competing interests of the accused, the prosecution and adverse witnesses. The danger in accommodating the interests of adverse witnesses is that prosecutors, who rely on the evidence of these witnesses, can find themselves procedurally advantaged over a defence which is unable to properly test this evidence. Derogations are considered in the light of the trial as a whole, a procedural rather than an evidential assessment. They are implemented in relation to three categories of witness and the response of the Court thereto reveals its approach to equality of arms.

This approach was first discussed regarding absent witnesses. The Court has considered consistently that a procedural advantage will result to the prosecution if actual prejudice occurs. For most of its jurisprudence, the Court generally found Article 6 infringed if a conviction was based solely or to a decisive degree on the statement of an absent witness the defence had not had an opportunity to examine or have examined. *Al-Khawaja and Tahery*, however, signalled a reduction in the level of protection for the accused: it demonstrates that the Court is willing to accept that substantial prejudice to the defence can still be overcome if sufficient counterbalancing measures exist, even when the key witness has never been subjected to any form of defence questioning at any stage of the proceedings. The prejudice arising from the absence of any such examination is such that it should be treated as incapable of being effectively counterbalanced. A dignitarian approach is possible and preferable: it should be an inequality of arms for statements of absent witnesses to be admitted, regardless of prejudice (unequivocal inequality). The state must provide sufficient other evidence to maintain the prosecution.

Anonymous witnesses were the second category of witness discussed. The Court again only considers the accused procedurally disadvantaged upon the occurrence of actual prejudice. It thus takes account of state measures intended to counterbalance the handicap arising from anonymous evidence, an indicator also of whether the rights of the defence were restricted to the least extent possible. A strong indicator of prejudice is that the anonymous evidence is the sole or decisive basis for the conviction. For much of the Court's jurisprudence, this factor was in principle sufficient in itself to cause a violation, with counterbalancing being a subordinate concern. However, in practice, the Court was inclined to only find a violation once counterbalancing measures and the justification for anonymity had also been taken into account. More recently, the Court has relied on the approach in *Al-Khawaja and Tahery* and adopted the position that even the prejudice arising from the decisive evidence of an anonymous witness is capable of being counterbalanced, thus avoiding a violation. It is submitted, however, that an alternative approach which better protects the accused is necessary. The Court should generally reject witness anonymity and thus avoid the accused being disadvantaged altogether. The discussion provided several examples of measures capable of protecting witnesses without derogation from the benchmark model. Only in exceptional cases of where a state can adequately demonstrate that the capacity of its agent to ever carry out another undercover operation would be irreparably compromised should anonymity be possible. The strict conditions suggested in the discussion to accompany this anonymity should be implemented as a safeguard. An actual prejudice approach would be necessary in this instance.

The third category of witness discussed concerned those considered vulnerable: child victims in sexual offence prosecutions. The extent of the counterbalancing measures implemented and the impact of the evidence on the conviction are considerations also applied to these witnesses to identify actual prejudice and thereby establish an inequality of arms. Also assessed is the reasonableness of the justification for derogating from the benchmark model. Whereas in the absent and anonymous witness categories an actual prejudice approach should be avoided, it is submitted that it is called for when vulnerability is adequately substantiated as a certain level of derogation will be necessary. The extent of this derogation should be restricted in line with the suggestions in the discussion, which will still allow effective defence challenge of evidence, to prevent prejudicial disadvantage.

Cases on all three categories of witnesses are consistent in equating procedural disadvantage with actual prejudice, albeit certain cases were wrongly decided in not registering an inequality of arms. Only in the case of vulnerable witnesses, and perhaps of a minority of covert agents, is this approach warranted; otherwise, departures from the benchmark model should not be permitted, thus maintaining procedural equality as far as the parties' roles permit.

The final part of the discussion considered the right to call witnesses. The defence is entitled to request the calling of any witness, favourable or otherwise. Adopting a non-interventionist stance consistent with the fourth instance doctrine, the Court has allowed states a broad discretion to assess the appropriateness of acceding to each request. The accused must demonstrate the relevance of witnesses requested and national courts must give adequate consideration thereto, though the European Court should make express a condition that the grounds for rejecting a request not be manifestly unreasonable. These burdens are intended to unearth actual prejudice: rejection of proposed witnesses without first confirming irrelevance through adequate consideration renders unequal the defence with the prosecution who can call all their relevant witnesses; this inequality gives rise to actual prejudice because the accused has been unduly restricted in his opportunity to put relevant evidence before the court. This approach to procedural equality is acceptable because the qualification of relevance is an appropriate bar to abuse of process and does not offend the dignity of the accused.

The link between equality of arms and actual prejudice is not exclusive to the context of examining and calling witnesses. It also features strongly in cases on adequacy of time and facilities for case preparation, which are discussed next.

CHAPTER 4

EQUALITY OF ARMS AND THE RIGHT TO ADEQUATE TIME AND FACILITIES

1. INTRODUCTION

An opportunity for adequate defence preparation is essential if an effective response to the charge is to be mounted at hearing. The realisation of such an opportunity requires crucially that the accused be afforded 'adequate time and facilities' as guaranteed in Article 6(3)(b). One may infer from the standard of 'adequate' an acknowledgement that the time and facilities reasonably required in each particular case are variable by context. The degree of time and facilities provided in one case will not be enough necessarily to mount an effective defence in another which differs in seriousness of offence, complexity and difficulty. The inherent nature of time and facilities is such that Article 6(3)(b) is the most far-reaching and flexible provision of the Article 6(3) catalogue. Its non-observance is capable of placing the accused in a position of procedural disadvantage vis-à-vis the prosecution, which has access to considerable state resources to aid its preparation.

Article 6(3)(b) is, accordingly, a facet of concern for the concept of equality of arms, section 2 of this chapter defining the nexus between them. The concern of the discussion thereafter is the Strasbourg approach to this concept in determinations on adequacy of time and facilities. It begins in section 3 by examining the right to adequate time with a particular emphasis on the key matters taken into account when it is applied at Strasbourg. It is not, however, complaints of inadequate time that predominate Article 6(3)(b) jurisprudence. Attracting greater regard is the right to adequate facilities, which is dealt with in section 4. Though it briefly provides examples of several facilities considered necessary for securing equality of arms, the facility of disclosure is the most prominent in the case-law and thus predominates the discussion in the section. The character of disclosure is outlined, which addresses questions of what must be disclosed, the timing of disclosure and who disclosure must be made to. This serves as a useful prelude to discussing the Court's approach to the concept of equality of arms as applied to issues of disclosure. Its approach is explained with reference to cases of non-disclosure both of evidence on grounds of public interest immunity and of written observations of legal officers joined to the proceedings.

2. THE NEXUS BETWEEN EQUALITY OF ARMS AND ARTICLE 6(3)(B)

Article 6(3)(b) issues from the concept of equality of arms. The nexus between them can be identified from both a legal and a conceptual perspective.

2.1. LEGAL NEXUS

Authoritative weight has been given to the existence of a nexus in law. The former Commission expressed that Article 6(3)(b) 'was designed, in particular, to help establish between the prosecuting authority and the defendant the equality necessary for a fair trial'.[1] The Court has also affirmed that a failure to respect this provision undermines the requirement of procedural equality.[2] Similarly, the Human Rights Committee has oft-professed that the ICCPR's equivalent Article 14(3)(b) is an aspect of the equality of arms principle.[3] The legal foundation for the nexus at Strasbourg lies in the right to a fair hearing in Article 6(1), of which the concept of equality of arms and Article 6(3)(b) are constituent parts. It is for such reason that Articles 6(1) and 6(3)(b) are sometimes expressly assessed in conjunction with each other when determining whether the latter has been violated.[4] In cases where Article 6(3)(b) is applied without express reference to Article 6(1), the concept of equality of arms remains present as an underlying doctrine.

---

1 *Jespers v Belgium* (App 8403/78) (1981) 27 DR 61 [70].

2 *Moiseyev v Russia* (App 62936/00) ECHR 9 October 2008 [223].

3 Eg *Paul Kelly v Jamaica* (Comm 253/1987) UN Doc CCPR/C/41/D/253/1987 60 (1991) [5.9]; *Michael Sawyers, Michael and Desmond McLean v Jamaica* (Comm 256/1987) UN Doc CCPR/C/41/D/256/1987 (1991) [13.6]; *Little v Jamaica* (Comm 283/1988) UN Doc CCPR/C/43/D/283/1988 (1991) [8.3]; *Smith v Jamaica* (Comm 282/1988) UN Doc CCPR/C/47/D/282/1988 (1993) [10.4]; Human Rights Committee, 'General Comment No 32: Article 14: Right to Equality before Courts and Tribunals and to Fair Trial' (2007) UN Doc CCPR/C/GC/32 [32].

4 Eg *Hadjianastassiou v Greece* (App 12945/87) (1992) Series A no 252 [37]; *Kremzow v Austria* (App 12350/86) (1993) Series A no 268-B [50]; *GB v France* (App 44069/98) ECHR 2001-X [57], [63], [70]; *Galstyan v Armenia* (App 26986/03) ECHR 15 November 2007 [84], [88]; *Ashughyan v Armenia* (App 33268/03) ECHR 17 July 2008 [66]–[67].

2.2. CONCEPTUAL NEXUS

The existence of the nexus is also discernible at a conceptual level. Chapter 2 maintained that procedural rights characterised as feasibly reciprocal and essential for case preparation and/or presentation fell within the equality of arms remit.[5] Article 6(3)(b) guarantees a right that is self-evidently of this nature. That chapter also identified the adversarial principle as encompassed within the scope of the concept of equality of arms.[6] Disclosure, a facility within the meaning of Article 6(3)(b), is an application of the adversarial principle, for it enables the accused to inform himself of the observations and evidence of the other side. This relationship thus reinforces the nexus between Article 6(3)(b) and the principle of equality of arms.

This nexus is even closer because the instrumental, intrinsic and collateral values of the latter, also established in Chapter 2,[7] are served by the realisation of Article 6(3)(b).

The provision of adequate time and facilities for case preparation encourages a correct trial outcome (reflects the instrumental value of equality of arms). The prosecution is acknowledged as having considerable state resources at its disposal to prepare its case.[8] The facilitation of case preparation gives the defence a real opportunity at hearing to counter effectively the prosecution position and to deliver its best case possible in the circumstances to influence the court. Essentially, therefore, preparation potentially influences the strength of the case presented at trial and its consequential impact upon those determining the outcome.[9] The Court, accordingly, recognises that Article 6(3)(b) affords the accused 'the opportunity to organise his defence in an appropriate way and without restriction as to the possibility to put all relevant defence arguments before the trial court, and thus to influence the outcome of the proceedings.'[10] It is thus partially through preparation that the opportunity to influence the court becomes equal between the parties and a correct verdict becomes more likely to be reached.

This instrumental value sits alongside the contribution Article 6(3)(b) makes towards preserving the dignity of the accused (reflects the intrinsic value of

5 Ch 2 ss 4.2–4.3.1, 4.3.3–4.3.4.

6 Ibid s 4.3.2.

7 Ibid s 2.

8 *Jespers* (n 1) [55]: 'the prosecution has at its disposal, to back the accusation, facilities deriving from its powers of investigation supported by judicial and police machinery with considerable technical resources and means of coercion.'

9 See further T Bakken, 'International Law and Human Rights for Defendants in Criminal Trials' (1985) 25 Indian J Int'l L 411, 414: 'A trial ... without adequate planning and strategy is a sterile procedure devoid of probing inquiry'.

10 *Mayzit v Russia* (App 63378/00) ECHR 20 January 2005 [78]; *Galstyan* (n 4) [84]; *Moiseyev* (n 2) [220]. See further *McLean and another v Buchanan and another* [2001] UKPC D3; [2001] 1 WLR 2425 [56] (Lord Clyde): Art 6(3)(b) 'is principally directed to the securing for an accused person the opportunity and the services necessary for the preparation of his defence. It strikes at the imposition of restraints on his freedom to organise the preparation of his defence.'

equality of arms). Article 6(3)(b) expresses to the accused that the state considers him deserving of a meaningful opportunity to prepare for the hearing that will decide his fate. This opportunity is also conducive to the accused feeling that he is a participant of the trial process equal to the prosecution, as far his role inherently permits, and his defence will be a considered and effective one.

It is a collateral consequence of the aforementioned instrumental and dignitarian values that a perception that some form of good governance by the state is present is rendered more likely (reflects the secondary value of equality of arms). Observance of Article 6(3)(b) makes apparent to the public that the accused was not placed at a disadvantage vis-à-vis the prosecution in his ability to prepare his case effectively. Not only does this suggest to the public that his dignity was being safeguarded, but also that greater confidence can be had in the safety of an outcome influenced by a meaningfully prepared defence.

3. ADEQUATE TIME

Unduly hastened proceedings present an affront to Article 6(3)(b).[11] To preclude for the accused the availability of adequate time for effective case preparation is to place him in a position of disadvantage vis-à-vis the prosecution, which is presumed to have such time. Given that the latter is responsible for prosecuting criminal cases, its case preparation will begin naturally at an earlier stage than that of the defence. The concept of equality of arms does not imply that adequate time is synonymous with time equal to that of the prosecution; it merely refers to the condition that both parties be afforded preparatory time adequate to their respective needs. If, however, the inequality in the time available to the prosecution and the defence is overwhelmingly unreasonable, it is unlikely that the time will be accepted as adequate for defence purposes.[12] The defence, nevertheless, is only entitled to reasonably expect such preparatory time as would be adequate for counsel of average competence[13] to deal with the issues raised in the case. The right to adequate time is applicable even if the accused opts to defend himself in person.[14] This time is not restricted to one fixed allocation as criminal proceedings comprise a series of stages which all necessitate a defence response, hence require periods of preparation time. Accordingly, the Commission asserted that '[t]he time necessary to prepare a defence must ... be estimated on a different basis at the various stages of the proceedings.'[15]

11 *Bonzi v Switzerland* (App 7854/77) (1978) 12 DR 188, 190; *Kröcher and Möller v Switzerland* (App 8463/78) (1981) 26 DR 24, 53.
12 *U v Luxembourg* (App 10142/82) (1985) 42 DR 86, 96.
13 S Trechsel, *Human Rights in Criminal Proceedings* (OUP, Oxford 2005) 216.
14 *Galstyan* (n 4) [86].
15 *Herbert Huber v Austria* (App 5523/72) (1974) 46 CD 99, 107.

3.1. ASSESSING ADEQUATE TIME

In determining whether the period of time in issue is adequate, hence does not disadvantage the accused vis-à-vis the prosecution, one must consider the circumstances of the case rather than the period in isolation.[16]

Amongst the relevant circumstances is whether the available preparation time is proportionate to both the complexity of the case[17] and the importance of the unrealised preparatory act. The application of these factors is evident, for example, with respect to case documentation. The volume of documentation is a contributor to complexity and perusal thereof is important for the identification of relevant defence arguments. The Court has held that 21 days for an applicant to examine and formulate his response to a 49-page Attorney-General's position paper was proportionate, thus adequate.[18] In contrast, 20 days in which to peruse a case-file of some 17,000 pages was not.[19]

The situation of defence counsel must also be taken into account. He cannot be expected to devote all his time exclusively to a particular case, given the usual workload commitments of practitioners, though there is an expectation that he make special provision for cases requiring urgent action.[20] It is important to compare the date of his actual appointment with the date of the hearing requiring preparation.[21] A late appointment attributable to the accused cannot substantiate a complaint of inadequate time.[22] Cases where a change of counsel is necessary require that the initial time available to the defence be extended to reflect the preparatory needs of new counsel.[23]

Also to be reflected in the amount of available time is the extent to which the defence is expected to be already familiar with the case material required to formulate the response at the next procedural stage. Thus, for example, it is legitimate for the preparatory time available for lodging an appeal or a plea of nullity to reflect the fact that, following the trial, the defence will be familiar with the case-file, supporting evidence and nature of the charges.[24] Accordingly, in most cases, the appellate stage will justify a shorter preparatory period. It is also at this stage that a deficiency in the amount of preparation time at first

---

16 *X and Y v Austria* (App 7909/74) (1978) 15 DR 160, 162.

17 *Albert and Le Compte v Belgium* (Apps 7299/75; 7496/76) (1983) Series A no 58 [41]; *S v UK* (App 11821/85) EComHR 12 December 1987 [1] ('The Law').

18 *Kremzow* (n 4) [48], [50].

19 *Öcalan v Turkey* (App 46221/99) ECHR 2005-IV [142]–[144], [148].

20 *X and Y* (n 16) 163.

21 Ibid 162; *Perez Mahia v Spain* (App 11022/84) (1985) 9 EHRR 145, 146.

22 *X v Austria* (App 8251/78) (1979) 17 DR 168, 169–170.

23 *Goddi v Italy* (App 8966/80) (1984) Series A no 76 [31].

24 *Herbert Huber* (n 15) 107; *Hilden v Finland* (App 32523/96) ECHR 14 September 1999 [3] ('The Law').

instance may be capable of remedy, though the accused should endeavour to alert the appeal court of such a shortcoming.[25]

Of further relevance is whether any attempt was made by the defence to remedy its position at the time it perceived its preparatory period as inadequate. It is not unreasonable that remedial action be required of the defence to the extent that it request a postponement (before the hearing) or an adjournment (during the hearing) of proceedings for an adequate period of time. Not to do so is to fail to comply with the Article 35(1) requirement to exhaust all available and effective domestic remedies, for the state must have an opportunity to correct its wrongdoing within the domestic fora.[26] It is necessary for the state, however, to demonstrate that the accused unequivocally enjoyed, both in law and in practice, a right of adjournment and that an adjournment may have been granted upon request.[27] If it is impracticable for the accused to request a postponement or an adjournment, the domestic court should consider suspending the proceedings on its own initiative for a time sufficient to compensate for the manifest inadequacy.[28] Diligence is thus also demanded of states in such circumstances to avert a disadvantage accruing to the accused.

Further to all the factors mentioned hitherto, limited additional guidance may be found from preparatory periods of time assessed in the case-law. The following periods are examples of those found adequate: four days to examine witness statements, the substance of which was already known;[29] five days for a prison disciplinary hearing;[30] over 15 days for a medical disciplinary hearing;[31] 10[32] and 17[33] days for trial; five weeks pre-trial and an interval (over two months) between trial sessions;[34] over a year pre-trial;[35] 14 days to formulate and submit a plea of nullity;[36] and 30 days to prepare an appeal, 10 of which were to examine the first instance judgement.[37] Given that the adequacy of

25 *Twalib v Greece* (App 24294/94) ECHR 1998-IV [40]–[43]. The reasoning of the Court leaves much to be desired: Partly Diss Op of Judges van Dijk, Makarczyk and Jambrek.

26 *Murphy v UK* (App 4681/70) (1972) 43 CD 1, 12–13 where a complaint that official counsel had been appointed only 10 minutes before the hearing was declared inadmissible because the accused failed to request an adjournment.

27 *Galstyan* (n 4) [85].

28 *Goddi* (n 23) [31]. Neither the applicant (in custody for another matter) nor his counsel (not notified of hearing) were present at the appeal sitting. The court appointed on the day of the hearing a new lawyer who was not acquainted with the case and rendered a conviction.

29 *S* (n 17) [1] ('The Law').

30 *Campbell and Fell v UK* (Apps 7819/77; 7878/77) (1984) Series A no 80 [98].

31 *Albert and Le Compte* (n 17) [41]–[42].

32 *Perez Mahia* (n 21) 146.

33 *X and Y* (n 16) 162–163.

34 *Svinarenkov v Estonia* (App 42551/98) ECHR 15 February 2000 [3(d)] ('The Law').

35 *Harward v Norway* (App 14170/88) EComHR 12 March 1990 [1] ('The Law').

36 *Herbert Huber* (n 15) 107.

37 *Hilden* (n 24) [3] ('The Law'). See also eg *Erdem v Germany* (App 38321/97) ECHR 9 December 1999 [3(d)] ('The Law'): One month for submitting a statement of appeal.

these periods was determined heavily by the surrounding circumstances of the cases, it is difficult to conceive of them as a particularly reliable indicator of the preparatory time an accused is entitled to expect.

Each period was accepted at Strasbourg because it did not occasion a prejudicial disadvantage for the accused as compared to the prosecution. The role of prejudice is, therefore, decisive in assessing an alleged inequality of arms. Accordingly, in a case where counsel was appointed shortly before the hearing, the preparatory period was still considered adequate because the applicant 'failed to show that as a result of inadequate time to instruct his lawyer on a particular point, he suffered a prejudice in the proceedings'.[38] If this approach is to be used, it is submitted that when the time permitted appears prima facie inadequate, the state should bear a burden of proving prejudice did not occur, thus lowering the extent of the challenge of proof the applicant must overcome for a successful claim.[39] Applicants should only bear the reverse burden when the time appears prima facie adequate for purpose.

The presence of prejudice resulting from inadequate time vis-à-vis the prosecution has been acknowledged predominantly in two scenarios.

The first concerns accelerated procedures reserved for the efficient prosecution of minor offences. The existence of such procedures is recognised as legitimate, provided the guarantees of Article 6 remain observed.[40] The applicant was the subject of an accelerated proceeding in *Borisova v Bulgaria*[41] where the preparation period for trial was no more than two hours, during which time she was either being transferred to court or was being held in police custody and unable to consult counsel. The right to adequate preparation time could clearly not be exercised effectively. This was such as to place the applicant at a considerable procedural disadvantage, hence effecting an infringement of Articles 6(1) and 6(3)(b).[42] Similarly, in *Galstyan v Armenia*,[43] the applicant was also either in transit to court or in police custody without outside contact during

---

38 *X v Austria* (App 2370/64) (1967) 22 CD 96, 100. See also eg *X v UK* (App 4042/69) (1970) 13 Yearbook 690 (EComHR) 696: Despite meeting counsel for only 10 minutes on the actual day of trial, the applicant 'failed to show that, as a result, he suffered any prejudice in his representation during the proceedings'; *Kremzow* (n 4) [50]: 'although the applicant may have been to some extent disadvantaged in the preparation of his defence, he nevertheless had "adequate time ..." to formulate his response to the croquis.'

See further D Harris and others, *Harris, O'Boyle and Warbrick: Law of the European Convention on Human Rights* (3rd edn OUP, Oxford 2014) 471 who submit that the Court should not apply an actual prejudice requirement.

39 S Stavros, *The Guarantees for Accused Persons Under Article 6 of the European Convention on Human Rights: An Analysis of the Application of the Convention and a Comparison with Other Instruments* (Martinus Nijhoff, Dordrecht 1993) 176–177. See also Ch 2 text to n 128.

40 *Borisova v Bulgaria* (App 56891/00) ECHR 21 December 2006 [40]; *Galstyan* (n 4) [85].

41 *Borisova* (n 40).

42 Ibid [45], [50].

43 *Galstyan* (n 4).

the pre-trial period of only a few hours. A prejudicial disadvantage was suffered because he had not been afforded adequate time to familiarise himself properly with the charge, assess prosecution evidence and formulate a defence strategy.[44]

The second scenario in which the accused is particularly susceptible to suffering procedural inequality is when there is significant and late alteration of the characterisation of the charge with inadequate time to respond effectively thereto. Such was the case in *Pélissier and Sassi v France*,[45] for example, where the appeal court decided during deliberations to convict the applicants not of the offence charged of criminal bankruptcy, to which all arguments had been confined, but of aiding and abetting criminal bankruptcy. Where the defence is aware of or should have foreseen a change in a material aspect of a case, it is expected to adapt its position if time permits or request an adjournment. In this case, however, the Court considered that it had not been established that the applicants were either aware or ought to have been aware of the possibility that the alternative verdict may be returned.[46] It was noted as plausible that the applicants would have relied on different arguments had the alternative charge been known beforehand, particularly as aiding and abetting was not an element intrinsic to the initial accusation.[47] Notification of the new charge was clearly too late as it denied the applicants any time to prepare an alternative defence.[48] In such circumstances, the defence suffered a prejudicial disadvantage, hence there was a breach of Articles 6(1) and 6(3)(b).[49] It is possible to cure such a defect with a procedural and substantive review of the case at an oral hearing in the superior courts where the accused, having been given adequate opportunity to prepare, can present his defence to the reformulated charge.[50] Preparatory time, therefore, must be adequate to the extent that it allows the accused the opportunity at some stage in the proceedings to adapt his case in response to alteration of the charge.[51] Indeed, preparation time must adequately reflect any fundamental change in circumstance requiring defence reply.

---

44 Ibid [87]–[88]. See *Ashughyan* (n 4) [66]–[67] for a further example of the same.

45 (App 25444/94) ECHR 1999-II.

46 Ibid [56]–[60].

47 Ibid [60]–[61].

48 Ibid [62].

49 Ibid [63]. For a finding of the same, see eg *Sadak and others v Turkey (No 1)* (App 29900/96 et seq) ECHR 2001-VIII [51]–[59]; *Abramyan v Russia* (App 10709/02) ECHR 9 October 2008 [36], [38]–[40].

50 Eg *Dallos v Hungary* (App 29082/95) ECHR 2001-II [48]–[53]; *Sipavičius v Lithuania* (App 49093/99) ECHR 21 February 2002 [29]–[34].

51 See further *Mattoccia v Italy* (App 23969/94) ECHR 2000-IX [61].

4. ADEQUATE FACILITIES

'Facilities' are those procedural conditions or measures that assist or may assist a party in the adequate performance of its case preparation.[52] Given this inherently broad scope, it is not extraordinary that neither a precise definition nor exhaustive catalogue of facilities exists. The facilities available to the prosecution are presumed adequate for case preparation and capable of placing the accused at a distinct disadvantage. Accordingly, the accused must also be afforded facilities for case preparation if procedural equality is to be preserved. In the same vain as 'adequate time', however, it is not equal facilities that are required but facilities that accommodate adequately the needs of the defence. Such needs vary between defendants and adequacy of facility can be determined only within the context of the particular case in issue. States must cater to these needs in two respects: the provision of adequate facilities (positive obligation) and non-interference with available facilities (negative obligation). A failure to meet these obligations can cause undue prejudice to the accused as compared to the prosecution. The presence of prejudice is a decisive determinant of adequacy of facility.[53] It is for the applicant to prove the existence of actual prejudice,[54] though Stavros's suggestion that the state should be required to prove the absence thereof when a particular facility seems, prima facie on the facts, necessary in the interests of procedural fairness[55] warrants approval for strengthening the position of applicants. Consistent with the above suggestion on the burden of proof for claims of inadequate time, it is submitted that, if an actual prejudice approach is applied, applicants should only be required to prove prejudice if the facility appears prima facie dispensable.

---

52 *Jespers* (n 1) [57]; *Ross v UK* (App 11396/85) (1986) 50 DR 179, 183; *Mayzit* (n 10) [79]; *Mironov v Russia* (App 22625/02) ECHR 5 October 2006 [5(d)(2)] ('The Law').

53 Contrast prima facie *Korellis v Cyprus* (App 54528/00) ECHR 7 January 2003 [35]–[36], a case decided under Art 6(1) though still pertinent to Art 6(3)(b). The defence were denied an opportunity to conduct their own expert tests on a piece of evidence and the Court noted that prejudice need not be demonstrated. However, the Court's subsequent rationale for finding that Art 6(1) was not infringed appears inconsistent with this and does take account of whether prejudice occurred. Factors relevant thereto were that: an examination by a defence expert would have been manifestly ineffective in the circumstances; the defence were supplied a forensic expert report on the evidence; the defence cross-examined this expert; the defence failed to produce any evidence to contradict or create doubt about the key part of the expert's adverse opinion; the defence did not complain at trial of unfairness arising from the non-discovery; the applicant's conviction was mainly based on the testimony of a 'completely credible' complainant, and this testimony was further corroborated by two credible witnesses. The Court concluded that the evidence the defence sought to examine 'did not in fact play a decisive role' in the case outcome. In other words, the denial of this examination did not irretrievably prejudice the defence.

54 Trechsel (n 13) 211.

55 Stavros (n 39) 184, 186. See also Ch 2 text to n 128.

4.1. EXAMPLES OF FACILITIES

It is useful at this stage to briefly highlight examples of particular facilities deemed necessary for placing accused persons on an equal footing with the prosecution.

The defence cannot rely entirely upon the investigative thoroughness of the prosecuting authorities. Accordingly, states must facilitate and not unduly hinder the capacity of the defence to conduct its own non-coercive investigations. Such investigations may include an examination of the crime scene; searches for documentary or real evidence; conducting interviews with a view to finding additional witnesses; and carrying out relevant and practicable[56] expert tests, under conditions of procedural equality, on objects that may be relied upon by the prosecution.[57] If, however, a coercive measure is required and reasonable justification is provided, the defence must be able to request the prosecuting authorities to carry out the measure on its behalf, with the possibility for judicial determination of the matter in case of refusal.[58]

When a person is detained pending trial, the Court has also interpreted 'facilities' as possibly including 'such conditions of detention that permit the person to read and write with a reasonable degree of concentration.'[59] In *Moiseyev v Russia*, for example, the conditions of the applicant's detention on remand, transport to and from the courthouse and confinement therein amounted to inhuman and degrading treatment contrary to Article 3.[60] The Court considered that the consequential suffering and frustration felt by the applicant was prejudicial, for it 'undoubtedly impaired his faculty for concentration and intense mental application in the hours immediately preceding the court hearings.'[61] It concluded that the applicant was not afforded adequate facilities for the advance preparation of his defence.[62]

It is also possible that access to law reference works for case preparation is a required facility when requested by a self-represented accused detained before

56 'If this is impossible then arrangements must be made by the prosecution so that the experts of the accused will be enabled to follow effectively the tests carried out by the prosecution experts and make their own observations': LG Loucaides, 'Questions of Fair Trial Under the European Convention on Human Rights' (2003) 3 Hum Rts L Rev 27, 39.

57 *Korellis v Cyprus* (App 60804/00) ECHR 3 December 2002 ('The Law').

58 Trechsel (n 13) 227.

59 *Mayzit* (n 10) [81]; *Moiseyev* (n 2) [221].

60 *Moiseyev* (n 2) [127], [136], [143].

61 Ibid [222].

62 Ibid [222]–[225]. Contrast *Mayzit* (n 10) [42]–[43], [81], [84]: Despite accepting that the conditions of the applicant's detention on remand violated Art 3, thus did not favour intense mental work, the Court noted that appropriate facilities were, nevertheless, available because access to the case-file and to legal assistance was unrestricted. In *Moiseyev*, however, access to the case-file and to counsel was severely restricted ([207], [218]).

appeal, though account must be taken of the practical limits to the steps which prison authorities could reasonably be expected to take to find such materials.[63]

Irrespective of whether or not an accused is detained pending hearing, diligence is required of the state with respect to the facility of notification. States must ensure that the defence is effectively notified of the date of the hearing[64] and of time-limits for filing a pleading.[65]

At the end of the trial, a particularly important facility is the provision of a reasoned judgement, for it 'makes it possible for the accused to exercise usefully the rights of appeal available to him.'[66] An appeal is bound to fail, and the prosecution is placed at an advantage, if the accused is unable to address the reasons for his conviction in his preparation (actual prejudice). The reasoning requirement, however, must be qualified to the extent that it allow for jury trials.[67] The Court has found non-prejudicial a reasoned judgement in abridged form that addressed the issues concerning the defence, though did not enumerate the items of evidence grounding the conviction.[68] Despite the entitlement to a reasoned judgement, if a copy is not supplied to the defence, it is required to exercise a certain diligence and either procure a copy of it itself or take advantage of any opportunities for inspection.[69]

---

63 *Ross* (n 52) 184. The prison purchased two textbooks requested by the applicant and made unsuccessful attempts to acquire his other materials by contacting local libraries, the Procurator Fiscal and the Justiciary Office. Given these efforts and the fact that the self-represented applicant was still able at the appeal hearing to argue his points of appeal and raise the issue of the possible nullity of proceedings, it was not established that he was given inadequate facilities to prepare for it.

64 *Goddi* (n 23) [30].

65 *Vacher v France* (App 20368/92) ECHR 1996-VI [27], [28] ('Putting the onus on convicted appellants to find out when an allotted period of time starts to run or expires is not compatible with the "diligence" which the Contracting States must exercise to ensure that the rights guaranteed by Article 6 are enjoyed in an effective manner').

66 *Hadjianastassiou* (n 4) [33]. See also within a civil context *Van de Hurk v the Netherlands* (App 16034/90) (1994) Series A no 288 [61]; *Hiro Balani v Spain* (App 18064/91) (1994) Series A no 303-B [27]; *Hirvisaari v Finland* (App 49684/99) ECHR 27 September 2001 [30].

67 *R v Belgium* (App 15957/90) (1992) 72 DR 195, 198.

68 *Zoon v the Netherlands* (App 29202/95) ECHR 2000-XII [46]–[48], [50]–[51].

69 Eg ibid [36]–[38], [51]: The applicant complained that he did not have available a copy of the first instance judgment before expiry of the time-limit for lodging an appeal. A violation of Arts 6(1) and 6(3)(b) was not found because the operative part of the judgement was read out to the defence at first instance and was available for inspection in abridged form at the court registry well before expiry of the time-limit, and a copy could also have been supplied on request; *Melin v France* (App 12914/87) (1993) Series A no 261-A [24]–[25]: The self-represented applicant (lawyer) complained that, despite his request, he had not been supplied a copy of the Court of Appeal's judgement before the subsequent Court of Cassation hearing. The European Court opined that he could have consulted the judgement at the appeal court registry; repeated his request for it; or made enquiries at the Court of Cassation's registry as to the date on which the court was to give judgment and sought an adjournment. Art 6 was held not to have been infringed. However, the view in the Joint Diss Op of Judge Bernhardt and others that the extent of the diligence required was excessive appears reasonable in the light of the full facts of the case.

4.2. DISCLOSURE

Whereas the aforementioned facilities are important in their own right for maintaining equality of arms, the facility of disclosure is the most prominent in the Court's jurisprudence, hence the remaining discussion is devoted entirely thereto.

4.2.1. *Character of Disclosure*

A brief sketch of the character of disclosure can serve as a useful prelude to the subsequent analysis of the Court's approach to the concept of equality of arms as applied to issues of disclosure.

4.2.1.1. Content of Disclosure

Within the remit of 'facilities' in Article 6(3)(b), the state bears the burden of disclosing to the defence 'all material evidence' (adequate disclosure): information and objects that incriminate or exculpate the accused.[70] The test of what should be disclosed is, therefore, based on materiality rather than relevance, the latter including all information and objects associated with the case. Accordingly, the materiality standard requires a lesser degree of disclosure than the relevance standard and thus accords with the minimum standard setting mandate of the Court under Article 6. It also accords with the Court's consistent application of the prejudice proviso as material information and objects will influence the position of the defence and, in turn, the trial outcome. It is perhaps an appropriate standard given that implementation of a test of relevance is likely

---

70 Eg *Edwards v UK* (App 13071/87) (1992) Series A no 247-B [36]; *Fitt v UK* (App 29777/96) ECHR 2000-II [44]; *Dowsett v UK* (App 39482/98) ECHR 2003-VII [41]; *V v Finland* (App 40412/98) ECHR 24 April 2007 [74].

For examples of exculpatory material, see Attorney General's Office, 'Attorney General's Guidelines on Disclosure (2005)' (Gov.UK) <https://www.gov.uk/guidance/attorney-general-s-guidelines-on-disclosure-2005-and-2011> [12]: '(i) Any material casting doubt upon the accuracy of any prosecution evidence. (ii) Any material which may point to another person, whether charged or not … having involvement in the commission of the offence. (iii) Any material which may cast doubt upon the reliability of a confession. (iv) Any material that might go to the credibility of a prosecution witness. (v) Any material that might support a defence that is either raised by the defence or apparent from the prosecution papers. (vi) Any material which may have a bearing on the admissibility of any prosecution evidence.'

Specific examples of disclosable material include tape recordings, transcripts, notes, first drafts of statements, documentation of interviews with the accused, results of expert tests and experiments, crime reports and custody records: J Niblett, *Disclosure in Criminal Proceedings* (Blackstone, London 1997) 98.

See further *Hardiman v UK* (App 25935/94) EComHR 28 February 1996 [2] ('The Law'): Prison psychiatric reports on defendants, obtained for the judge to determine fitness to plead and stand trial and, in murder cases, issues of insanity and diminished responsibility, need not be disclosed to co-defendants as they are designed to protect their subjects.

to cause proliferation of disclosure of material which is negligible in value. This could impair the effective functioning of disclosure regimes and provide a readily available opportunity for strategic misuse of disclosure requests by the accused. Alternatively, dignitarian concerns could be met by lowering the disclosure threshold from materiality to relevance in cases where reasonable suspicion of suppression of material evidence by the prosecution exists.[71] It is worth noting that the Court is prone to employing interchangeably the terms 'material evidence' and 'relevant evidence' despite its application in practice of the materiality standard.[72] This standard was applied in *Jespers v Belgium* where it was pronounced that, for the purposes of exonerating oneself or securing a reduced sentence, both of which require material evidence, Article 6(3)(b) grants a right of access to 'the results of investigations carried out throughout the proceedings' and 'all relevant elements that have been or could be collected by the competent authorities.'[73] The reference to elements that 'could be collected' exists to render unlawful the deliberate suppression of material evidence. Access to material evidence in proceedings of the inquisitorial tradition includes access to the official case-file because its content is evidential and integral to the conduct of such proceedings.[74] Disclosure may only reasonably be expected of evidence the prosecution is aware or ought to have been aware of. There may be occasion when the prosecution is aware of but elects not to rely upon a particular piece of evidence (unused material). If that evidence appears prima facie immaterial, the accused must briefly provide specific justification for requiring it.[75]

Material evidence is not the only object requiring disclosure. Cases have come before the European Court concerning final appeals in civil law systems where a legal officer joined to the proceedings has submitted written observations to the national court.[76] These observations are material because they allow the author to express his position on the appeal with a view to influencing the court, thus merit a defence reaction. It should be recalled from section 2.2 above that, under the adversarial principle, it is not just evidence but also 'observations' that the defence is entitled to be informed of. It is on the basis of this principle and that of equality of arms, and Article 6(3)(b), that material observations are relevant to disclosure requirements.

---

71 Stavros (n 39) 179: 'Should not the standard of proof be significantly lowered in cases where the general behaviour of the prosecution warrants legitimate suspicions as to its willingness to comply with the rules of disclosure?'

72 Eg *Jasper v UK* (App 27052/95) ECHR 16 February 2000 [51]–[52]; *Rowe and Davis v UK* (App 28901/95) ECHR 2000-II [60]–[61]; *PG and JH v UK* (App 44787/98) ECHR 2001-IX [67]–[68]; *Botmeh and Alami v UK* (App 15187/03) ECHR 7 June 2007 [37], [39]–[41].

73 *Jespers* (n 1) [56], [58]. See also eg *Galstyan* (n 4) [84].

74 See further *Foucher v France* (App 22209/93) ECHR 1997-II [36].

75 *Bendenoun v France* (App 12547/86) (1994) Series A no 284 [52]–[53]. The applicant failed to provide such justification and was aware of most of the content of the non-disclosed evidence. On this basis, the Court held the equality of arms principle not to have been infringed.

76 Ch 4 s 4.2.2.2.

4.2.1.2. Timing of Disclosure

It is not only what must be disclosed that is important, but also the timing of disclosure. It is, of course, in the interests of the accused that all material evidence collected before charge be disclosed as soon as the actual charges are lodged, thereby maximising his time to react thereto. This is not, however, the standard applied by the Court. Instead, the Article 6(3)(b) right to adequate time implies that disclosure need only be made in time sufficient to afford the defence a reasonable opportunity to acquaint itself with the nature and weight of the material and address it effectively in its preparations.[77] Disclosure within adequate time should not necessarily be construed as a one-off act. There is a continuing duty on the state to disclose the material findings of all investigations associated with the case[78] and any written observations submitted to the court. Thus, disclosure can be required at several points from the pre-trial stage to final appeal, depending on the content of the material involved.

4.2.1.3. Recipient of Disclosure

It naturally follows from the above that one must also address who precisely disclosure should be made to. Conventionally, disclosed material comes into the possession of counsel, and his client is able to consult or have a copy of it. According to *Kamasinski v Austria* and *Kremzow v Austria*, however, a procedural disadvantage does not occur when access to the court file is restricted to defence counsel,[79] the rationale being to prevent misuse by the accused[80] and that Article 6(3)(b) is a provision for the defence in general.[81] The same is

---

77 See further *Krčmář and others v the Czech Republic* (App 35376/97) ECHR 3 March 2000 [42]: 'A party to the proceedings must have the possibility to familiarise itself with the evidence before the court, as well as the possibility to comment on its existence, contents and authenticity in an appropriate form and within an appropriate time, if need be, in a written form and in advance.'

Basic Principles on the Role of Lawyers (Eighth UN Congress on the Prevention of Crime and the Treatment of Offenders, Havana 27 August to 7 September 1990) UN Doc A/CONF.144/28/Rev.1 118 (1990) principle 21: 'It is the duty of the competent authorities to ensure lawyers access to appropriate information, files and documents in their possession or control in sufficient time to enable lawyers to provide effective legal assistance to their clients. Such access should be provided at the earliest appropriate time.'

78 *Jespers* (n 1) [56]: 'results of investigations carried out throughout the proceedings'; 'the Commission cannot restrict the scope of the term "facilities" to acts carried out during certain specified phases of the proceedings, e.g. the preliminary investigation. ... Any investigations [the prosecuting authority] causes to be carried out ... and the findings thereof consequently form part of the "facilities" within the meaning of Article 6, paragraph 3(b)'.

79 *Kamasinski v Austria* (App 9783/82) (1989) Series A no 168 [87]–[88]; *Kremzow* (n 4) [51]–[52]. See also eg *Svinarenkov* (n 34) [3(d)] ('The Law').

80 *Kitov v Denmark* (App 29759/96) ECHR 16 March 1999 [2(d)] ('The Law').

81 *Ofner v Austria* (App 524/59) (1960) 3 Yearbook 322 (EComHR) 352. See further Stavros (n 39) 184–185 who argues that, as a legally aided accused may lack effective controlling power over appointed counsel, a right for the defence in general does not provide adequate

applicable to disclosed material within common law systems. Under a restricted access approach, the accused may be denied a full opportunity to highlight particular evidential weaknesses and inaccuracies in the disclosed material that only his unique knowledge can. To avert such a shortcoming, it is submitted that there should be an additional specific right for the accused himself to access the disclosed material, whether by inspection or by obtaining a copy thereof. This would be a dignitarian measure, for it affords the accused a feeling of greater participation in the preparation of his defence and in the proceedings overall. If he is not entitled access to the case-file but remains unrepresented, the Court, unsurprisingly, considers this to be an inequality of arms.[82]

4.2.2. Disclosure and Equality of Arms

The right of the accused to fair and proper disclosure is an integral attribute of fair trial.[83] It is intended to serve the concept of equality of arms. The accused is vulnerable to the unrivalled resources of his opponent. This is reflected aptly by Fitzpatrick: 'massive differentials in information access ... pertain between State and individual, in a forum in which the nexus of knowledge and power is at its most pronounced.'[84] In view of this disparity, it was pronounced in *Jespers* that '[i]t is in order to establish equality, as far as possible, between the prosecution and the defence that national legislation in most countries ... instructs the ... [prosecuting authority] to gather evidence in favour of the accused as well as evidence against him.'[85] Disclosure also serves the adversarial principle – which section 2.2 above reaffirmed is encompassed within the equality of arms concept – for it affords the defence an opportunity to be aware of and comment on the observations and evidence submitted by the other side.[86] Adequate awareness of all material evidence and observations in advance is fundamental to preparing an effective defence response to the issues before the court.[87] Consequently, non-disclosure is capable of placing the accused at a disadvantage

protection unless appropriate national mechanisms are in place to ensure that counsel exercises his duties adequately.

82 *Foucher* (n 74) [35]–[36].

83 An observation echoed in *R v Brown (Winston)* [1994] 1 WLR 1599 (CA) 1606; *R v Brown (Winston)* [1998] AC 367 (HL) 374; Attorney General's Office (n 70) [1].

84 B Fitzpatrick, 'Disclosure: Principles, Processes and Politics' in C Walker and K Starmer (eds), *Miscarriages of Justice: A Review of Justice in Error* (Blackstone, London 1999) 151.

85 *Jespers* (n 1) [55].

86 For cases where non-disclosure was held to infringe both the adversarial and equality of arms principles, see eg *Borgers v Belgium* (App 12005/86) (1991) Series A no 214-B [27]–[29]; *Bulut v Austria* (App 17358/90) ECHR 1996-II [49]–[50]; *Werner v Austria* (App 21835/93) ECHR 1997-VII [67] (civil); *Reinhardt and Slimane-Kaïd v France* (Apps 23043/93; 22921/93) ECHR 1998-II [103], [105]–[107]; *Kuopila v Finland* (App 27752/95) ECHR 27 April 2000 [38]; *Lanz v Austria* (App 24430/94) ECHR 31 January 2002 [62]–[64].

87 For further elaboration of the role of disclosure, see JA Epp, *Building on the Decade of Disclosure in Criminal Procedure* (Cavendish, London 2007) 29, 31–32, 254.

with the state, hence creating an inequality of arms.[88] It also runs contrary to the principle of open justice, the 'internal openness' aspect of which refers to the right of the defence to have access to material pertaining to the case.[89]

Case-law on equality of arms within the context of complaints of non-disclosure splits into two categories: non-disclosure of material evidence and non-disclosure of material observations.

4.2.2.1. Non-Disclosure of Material Evidence

The defence right to disclosure of all material evidence is not an absolute requirement of procedural fairness.[90] The Court accepts that circumstances may arise where departure from the disclosure norm is legitimate:

> In any criminal proceedings there may be competing interests, such as national security or the need to protect witnesses at risk of reprisals or keep secret police methods of investigation of crime, which must be weighed against the rights of the accused. In some cases it may be necessary to withhold certain evidence from the defence so as to preserve the fundamental rights of another individual or to safeguard an important public interest.[91]

It must be emphasised that it is not within the competence of the Court to determine whether non-disclosure was strictly necessary, for that is an evidential matter for domestic courts.[92] Crucially, its mandate is to assess whether the

---

88 The same is recognised by the International Criminal Tribunal for the former Yugoslavia (ICTY): *Prosecutor v Krajišnik & Plavšić* (Decision on Prosecution Motion for Clarification in Respect of Application of Rules 65 *ter*, 66(B) and 67(C)) (Trial Chamber) ICTY-00-39 & 40-PT (1 August 2001) [7]: 'The only way in which the Defence can properly prepare for trial is by having notice in advance of the material on which the Prosecution intends to rely, including exhibits. The Prosecution, by not disclosing the documents prior to trial, places the Defence in a position in which it will not be able to prepare properly; and it is this fact that is likely to lead to a violation of the principle of equality of arms.'

For an in-depth account of equality of arms and disclosure at the ICTY, see G McIntyre, 'Equality of Arms – Defining Human Rights in the Jurisprudence of the International Criminal Tribunal for the former Yugoslavia' (2003) 16 LJIL 269, 271–320.

89 M Malsch, 'Victims on View: Are Victims Served by the Principle of Open Justice?' in H Kaptein and M Malsch (eds), *Crime, Victims and Justice: Essays on Principles and Practice* (Aldershot, Ashgate 2004) 115. See also *Brown* 1998 (n 83) 374 (Lord Hope): 'It would be contrary to that principle [of open justice] for the prosecution to withhold from the defendant material which might undermine their case against him or which might assist his defence.'

90 *Jasper* (n 72) [52]; *Rowe and Davis* (n 72) [61]; *Fitt* (n 70) [45]; *Edwards and Lewis v UK* (Apps 39647/98; 40461/98) ECHR 2004-X [46]; *V* (n 70) [75].

91 Ibid. See further *Klass and others v Germany* (App 5029/71) (1978) Series A no 28 [48] for an earlier indication of the Court's acceptance that secretive methods of investigation may be 'necessary in a democratic society in the interests of national security and/or for the prevention of disorder or crime.'

92 *Jasper* (n 72) [53]; *Rowe and Davis* (n 72) [62]; *Fitt* (n 70) [46]; *Atlan v UK* (App 36533/97) ECHR 19 June 2001 [41]; *PG and JH* (n 72) [69]; *Dowsett* (n 70) [43]; *Edwards and Lewis* (n 90) [46].

decision to withhold disclosure was reached in a fair procedure compliant with the concept of equality of arms and the adversarial principle encompassed therein.[93] If the procedure applied involves a restriction of defence rights, the Court requires that it must only be to an extent strictly necessary and, to prevent actual prejudice, must involve sufficient counterbalancing measures.[94] This is a reapplication of principles derived from the right to challenge witness evidence.[95] In some cases, the Court has also had regard, as an influential indicator of prejudice, to whether the non-disclosed material at issue formed any part of the prosecution case and was put to the tribunal of fact.[96]

The most marked jurisprudence in this area concerns evidence withheld by the UK on grounds of public interest immunity (PII). A successful application for PII 'enables the prosecution to withhold disclosure of material where, in the court's view, the public's interest in non-disclosure outweighs the defendant's interest in having full access to all relevant material.'[97] The case-law may be grouped into two broad categories: cases where undisclosed material was not put before the trial judge and cases where it was. Whereas Article 6(3)(b) is often invoked within both categories, the Court is inclined to refer to the guarantee therein as one subsumed by Article 6(1) and thus deal with PII non-disclosure matters under the latter.[98]

(A) Undisclosed evidence not examined by trial judge

Cases have arisen wherein certain material evidence has been withheld from the defence at trial on public interest grounds solely on the initiative of the prosecuting authorities. This unilateral manner of making a non-disclosure decision was considered inconsistent with Article 6(1) in *Rowe and Davis v UK*, *Atlan v UK* and *Dowsett v UK*.[99] It was an acknowledgement that such a procedure cannot satisfy a test of strict necessity. It was also a recognition of the disadvantage created for the applicants by the prosecution acting as judge in their own cause on the disclosure issue and precluding arguments being put on behalf of the defence.

This disadvantage gives rise to the issue of whether it may be sufficiently counterbalanced through an appeal procedure.

---

93 Ibid.

94 *Jasper* (n 72) [52]; *Rowe and Davis* (n 72) [61]; *Fitt* (n 70) [45]; *Atlan* (n 92) [40]; *PG and JH* (n 72) [68]; *Dowsett* (n 70) [42]; *Edwards and Lewis* (n 90) [46]; *V* (n 70) [75].

95 Ch 3 ss 6.1–6.3.

96 *Jasper* (n 72) [55]; *Fitt* (n 70) [48]; *PG and JH* (n 72) [71]; *Edwards and Lewis* (n 90) [46].

97 Auld LJ, 'Review of the Criminal Courts of England and Wales' (HMSO, London 2001) 476.

98 Eg *Jasper* (n 72) [50]; *Rowe and Davis* (n 72) [59]; *Fitt* (n 70) [43]; *IJL and others v UK* (Apps 29522/95; 30056/96; 30574/96) ECHR 2000-IX [77]; *V* (n 70) [73]; *Botmeh and Alami* (n 72) [36]. The Court in *Dowsett* (n 70) [40], [52] appeared so inclined but referred expressly to finding a violation of Art 6(1) taken in conjunction with Art 6(3)(b).

99 *Rowe and Davis* (n 72) [63]; *Atlan* (n 92) [44]; *Dowsett* (n 70) [44].

Both *Rowe and Davis* and *Atlan* featured hearings in the absence of the defence (ex parte) where the appeal court reviewed the material and ruled non-disclosure justified. The Strasbourg Court considered that, rather than the appeal judges, 'the trial judge is best placed to decide whether or not the non-disclosure of public interest immunity evidence would be unfairly prejudicial to the defence.'[100] This is because the appeal judges were reliant upon prosecution counsel and trial transcripts for their understanding of the possible relevance of the undisclosed material, whereas the trial judge observed witness testimony and was fully acquainted with all the issues and evidence.[101] Furthermore, the appeal court carried out its assessment *ex post facto*, and may have been unconsciously influenced by the jury's verdict into underestimating the significance of the undisclosed material, whereas the trial judge would have been in a position to review its importance throughout the trial.[102] The Court also added in *Atlan* that 'had the trial judge seen the evidence he might have chosen a very different form of words for his summing up to the jury.'[103] The conclusion reached in both cases was that the appeal court review was not sufficient to counterbalance the disadvantage at trial created by bypassing the scrutiny of the trial judge.[104] Rather than relying almost entirely on this missed scrutiny, it is submitted that the Court should also have placed greater emphasis on the lack of adversarialism in the appeal procedure, for there was no opportunity to put arguments on behalf of the defence. Its silence on this ex parte aspect of the procedure suggests, by implication, that it is an aspect not in itself incompatible with procedural fairness. Nevertheless, as the significant disadvantage of the trial disclosure procedure remained uncured, the applicants suffered prejudice vis-à-vis the prosecution in contravention of the concept of equality of arms.

Rowe and Davis and *Atlan* should not, however, be understood as demonstrating that disadvantage to the defence arising from excluding the trial judge from the disclosure process can never be remedied at appeal.

---

100 *Atlan* (n 92) [45] on the authority of *Rowe and Davis* (n 72) [65].

101 Ibid.

102 Ibid. Of course, the judge must be made aware of the content of the material to be in a position to adequately monitor its importance: *V* (n 70) [78].

103 *Atlan* (n 92) [45].

104 Ibid [45]–[46]; *Rowe and Davis* (n 72) [65]–[67]. In *Dowsett* (n 70) [49], the Court commented that if an ex parte review procedure at the appeal court had taken place, it 'could not be regarded as an adequate safeguard for the defence.'

See further T Owen, 'Disclosure' in K Starmer and others, *Criminal Justice, Police Powers and Human Rights* (Blackstone, London 2001) 150–151: 'No doubt the prospect of having no choice but to quash a conviction and order a retrial whenever public interest immunity material emerges after conviction is an unpalatable one to both the prosecuting authorities and courts. But this seems an inevitable consequence of a procedure whose somewhat fragile integrity crucially depends on the role of the first instance judge in conducting a scrupulous and continuing review of the disclosure issue.'

In *Botmeh and Alami v UK*,[105] the prosecution sought PII from the appeal court for material not put before the trial judge. Following an ex parte hearing, a summary of the undisclosed material and the reasons for non-disclosure at trial were supplied to the applicants. Thereafter, before a differently constituted appeal court, the applicants were afforded an opportunity to make submissions on the summary and its significance to the case. Having regard to these submissions, the court concluded that non-disclosure had not created injustice as the material added nothing of significance to that already disclosed at trial. Taking this into account with the extent of the disclosure at appeal, and the consideration given to the impact of the new material on the safety of the convictions after detailed defence arguments, the European Court did not regard the exclusion of the trial judge from the disclosure process as prejudicial; the defect was remedied on appeal.[106]

The case can be distinguished from *Rowe and Davis* and *Atlan* to justify the difference in outcome. Crucially, the adversarial argument missing from these cases was present in *Botmeh and Alami* because an inter partes appeal hearing on disclosure took place and, having been given a summary of the undisclosed material, the defence submissions were informed as far as possible without revealing the material in full. The appeal judges considered the material in the light of these submissions. Adversarialism at appeal, therefore, counterbalanced the procedural disadvantage for the defence in the trial disclosure procedure. This conclusion is even more likely when adversarial argument is informed by material withheld at trial but disclosed in full before the appeal hearing.[107]

It appears, therefore, that a failure to lay material evidence before the trial judge is capable of being cured so as not to occasion actual prejudice to the accused vis-à-vis the prosecution and thus an inequality of arms. This can be achieved through an inter partes appeal hearing on the possible prejudice the non-disclosure might have had on the trial, in advance of which the material should be disclosed either in full or to an extent allowing defence submissions to be informed as far as possible without revealing it in full. The approach is consistent with the Article 35(1) exhaustion of all domestic remedies rule, which affords states the opportunity to put right the alleged procedural shortcoming through their own courts before the matter can be referred to the Strasbourg Court, the latter being of subsidiary character.[108]

---

105 *Botmeh and Alami* (n 72).

106 Ibid [44].

107 *Edwards* (n 70) [36]–[37], [39] (PII claim not made); *IJL and others* (n 98) [114], [117]–[119].

108 *Selmouni v France* (App 25803/94) ECHR 1999-V [74]; *Kudła v Poland* (App 30210/96) ECHR 2000-XI [152]; *Cocchiarella v Italy* (App 64886/01) ECHR 2006-V [38]–[39]; *Orlova v Russia* (App 21088/06) ECHR 9 October 2008 [22]–[23].

(b) Undisclosed evidence examined by trial judge

Cases have also been referred to the Court when PII has been applied to material evidence upon assessment by the trial judge.

Most have not resulted in the Court registering an inequality of arms, one such case being *Jasper v UK*.[109] The prosecution were successful in their ex parte application to the trial judge for PII for material evidence. Beforehand, the defence were notified that an application was to be made and were permitted to outline their case to the judge and request disclosure of material relevant thereto. This satisfied the Court that the defence were kept informed and were able to make representations and participate in the disclosure decision-making process as far as was possible without revealing to them the withheld material.[110] It also noted that this material formed no part of the prosecution case and was never put to the jury, and attached importance to the safeguard of the judge assessing continuously, before and during trial, whether the material need be disclosed.[111] Furthermore, the appeal court's consideration of whether such disclosure was needed was viewed as an additional safeguard.[112] The Court concluded that the disclosure decision-making process satisfied Article 6(1) in that it adequately safeguarded the interests of the defence and complied with the requirements of adversarial proceedings and equality of arms.[113] The reasoning and conclusion herein were mirrored in *Fitt v UK* for an ex parte procedure held under the same conditions.[114]

It is submitted, however, that *Jasper* was decided incorrectly. This is reflected in the considerable dissent therein, the decision having been made on a bare majority of nine votes to eight. The dissent relied upon four key arguments, which were also reproduced in the dissent in *Fitt*.[115]

First, the non-adversarial character of the disclosure procedure at first instance placed the parties on an unequal footing. Argument is adversarial only if it is informed. When outlining their case to the judge, the defence were unaware of any particulars of the withheld material, including even the category thereof, thus it was purely a matter of chance whether they made any relevant points. They were also uninformed of the reasons for the non-disclosure decision, hence could not respond adequately thereto. Additionally, the ex parte aspect of the procedure afforded the prosecution an opportunity to influence the judge in the absence of the defence. The absence and uninformed position

---

109 *Jasper* (n 72).
110 Ibid [55].
111 Ibid [55]–[56].
112 Ibid [56].
113 Ibid [58].
114 *Fitt* (n 70) [47]–[50].
115 *Jasper* (n 72) Diss Op Judge Palm and others; Diss Op Judge Hedigan; *Fitt* (n 70) Diss Op Judge Palm and others; Diss Op Judge Hedigan.

of the defence evidences a lack of adversarialism in the disclosure procedure. Without adversarial argument, the prosecution is better placed than the defence to influence the disclosure decision in their own favour.

Second, the monitoring by the judge of the need for disclosure throughout the trial was insufficient to counterbalance the defence's absence from the ex parte procedure. Proper fulfilment of his role requires that he be informed by the opinions of both parties, not just those of the prosecution.

Third, the appeal proceedings were inadequate to remedy the inequality at first instance because the inability of the defence to make informed submissions continued there also.

Fourth, the Government failed to demonstrate that the PII procedure placed restrictions on the defence which were strictly necessary. A less restrictive measure, already applied by the Government to other contexts, would have been to instruct special independent counsel[116] to represent the interests of the accused in the ex parte proceedings. This would introduce an adversarial element to counterbalance the defence's absence therefrom. The independence of special counsel would also ensure that he could consult the material in issue but keep confidential any information which cannot be disclosed. The defence could brief him before he viewed the material and communication thereafter would be only with the leave of the court. Furthermore, it was not demonstrated by the Government that the practical difficulties in adapting an existing system of special counsel to criminal cases were insurmountable. Use of special counsel was thus an example of a viable alternative measure which would place a lesser restriction on the defence, hence undermining the claim of strict necessity for the PII procedure actually applied.

To add to these arguments, one must also address the account taken by the Court of the fact that the withheld material formed no part of the prosecution case and was never put to the jury. The implication is that this fact was viewed as strengthening the case that the PII procedure did not result in actual prejudice to the defence. The above arguments demonstrate that this procedure lacked adversarial argument and sufficient counterbalancing measures to compensate for the defence's absence, thereby placing the parties on an unequal footing. Furthermore, the restrictions on the defence were not strictly necessary, for an alternative less restrictive measure was available and adaptable. Special counsel would have introduced an adversarial element to make sufficiently equal between

116 Special counsel, unlike traditional counsel, is not responsible to the instructing party. His position is contrasted with the classic lawyer–client relationship in Constitutional Affairs Select Committee, 'The Operation of the Special Immigration Appeals Commission (SIAC) and the Use of Special Advocates' HC (2004–2005) 323-I [62]. For an example of a UK special counsel scheme, see Special Immigration Appeals Commission Act 1997 s 6(1); Special Immigration Appeals Commission (Procedure) Rules 2003 SI 2003/1034 (as amended) rr 9A–10A, 34–38, 44, 47. On the origins, expansion and effectiveness of special counsel in the UK, see J Ip, 'The Rise and Spread of the Special Advocate' [2008] PL 717, 718–737.

the parties the opportunity to influence the disclosure decision. It is submitted, therefore, that PII was not attached to the evidence under a condition of procedural fairness. Evidence withheld as a result of an unfair procedure should not be withheld; its relevance or possible relevance to the defence cannot be viewed as having been properly assessed. This should be considered prejudicial to the defence, which is unduly denied the use of this evidence, irrespective of the fact that it was not used by the prosecution and never put to the jury.

In the light of the arguments discussed herein, one can submit that the defence were placed at a disadvantage vis-à-vis the prosecution, contrary to the concept of equality of arms, and an Article 6(1) violation should have been registered. The same can be said of *Fitt*.

Relying on much of the same reasoning as *Jasper* and *Fitt*, the Court reached the same conclusion as in those cases in *PG and JH v UK*[117] where the non-disclosure on PII grounds included both oral and documentary evidence. The trial judge decided in a *voir dire* (legal submissions made in the absence of the jury) that part of the documentary evidence relating to the authorisation of a surveillance listening device could be withheld. Additionally, during a defence cross-examination therein, a witness refused to answer certain questions related to the background of the surveillance for fear of divulging sensitive material. The judge proceeded to put those unanswered questions to the witness alone in chambers and concluded that the answers need not be divulged to the defence. The Court was satisfied that the defence were kept informed and permitted to participate in the PII process as far as was possible without revealing to them the sensitive oral and documentary evidence.[118] It also took into account that this evidence formed no part of the prosecution case and was never put to the jury, and that the judge monitored the need for disclosure throughout the trial.[119] Finally, it pointed out that the applicants failed to include non-disclosure as a ground of appeal, hence denying themselves the additional safeguard of an appellate review of the disclosure issue as undertaken in *Jasper* and *Fitt*.[120] In these circumstances, the Court did not consider the disclosure decision-making procedure to have been prejudicial to the defence, hence equality of arms was secured and no violation of Article 6(1) resulted.[121]

It certainly had greater justification for reaching this conclusion than had been the case in *Jasper* and *Fitt*. The defence were more engaged in the disclosure decision-making process. They were aware of the category into which the documentary material fell and its non-disclosure was decided on the basis of an inter partes hearing. The decision to withhold this material was thus informed by adversarial argument. The same may be said of the oral evidence. The defence

117 *PG and JH* (n 72).
118 Ibid [71].
119 Ibid.
120 Ibid [72].
121 Ibid [73].

were able to put their own unanswered questions to the witness through the judge, ensuring that a degree of adversarialism was maintained. There is no reason to suspect that an independent and impartial judge will not adequately press the witness and elicit a full response. Additionally, the questions were adequately informed, for the defence again knew the category into which the evidence fell. Given the adversarial elements of the disclosure procedure, the judge was informed by the opinions of both parties when monitoring the need for disclosure throughout the trial, a feature missing in *Jasper* and *Fitt*. The Court may also be viewed as having responded appropriately to the absence of an appellate review of the non-disclosure. It is reasonable to expect a certain diligence from the defence to the effect that non-disclosure be cited as a ground of appeal before a review can be undertaken.

In contrast to the three cases mentioned hitherto, an inequality of arms was registered in *Edwards and Lewis v UK*[122] when the Court considered the procedure used to determine the issues of disclosure and police entrapment. The issue of whether entrapment occurred was of 'determinative importance' because, had impropriety been established, the prosecution would have to be discontinued.[123] It was for the trial judge in each case to decide this issue. Following ex parte hearings, the judges ruled that certain evidence related, or potentially related, to the issue could be withheld from the defence on PII grounds. The Court viewed this non-disclosure as having prevented the defence in both cases from subsequently arguing the case on entrapment in full before the judge.[124] It also observed that the trial judges had already seen the withheld evidence in their rejection of the defence submissions on entrapment.[125] These circumstances infringed Article 6(1):[126] 'the Court does not consider that the procedure employed to determine the issues of disclosure of evidence and entrapment complied with the requirements to provide adversarial proceedings and equality of arms and incorporated adequate safeguards to protect the interests of the accused.'[127]

This conclusion merits approval. The judges were the tribunal of fact on the entrapment issue and also they reviewed the PII material in a procedure without adversarial argument, for only the prosecution were represented therein. No measures were implemented to counterbalance this inequality such as, for example, appointing special counsel to represent defence interests.[128] The material

122 *Edwards and Lewis* (n 90).
123 Ibid [46].
124 Ibid.
125 Ibid.
126 Ibid [48].
127 Ibid [46].
128 Subsequently, the former House of Lords in *R v H and others* [2004] UKHL 3; [2004] 2 AC 134 [22] (Lord Bingham) accepted that there could possibly be a place for special counsel in criminal PII matters but only as 'a course of last and never first resort.'

may have influenced, albeit unconsciously, the judges' decision on entrapment, which was an issue of decisive importance to the outcome of the proceedings. Accordingly, the disclosure decision-making procedure was prejudicial to the defence vis-à-vis the prosecution. An influential factor for the Court's opposite conclusion in *Jasper*, *Fitt* and *PG and JH* was that the PII procedures in those cases did not concern material put before the tribunal of fact (jury).[129]

4.2.2.2. Non-Disclosure of Material Observations

Aside from cases of non-disclosure of material evidence, there exists a series of cases arising from appeal proceedings in civil law systems on non-disclosure of written observations made by legal officers joined to the proceedings. Chapter 2 identified these officers as capable of attracting opponent status within the definition of the concept of equality of arms,[130] their intention being to influence the outcome of the proceedings. Unlike in the case of non-disclosure of evidence, there is no legitimate justification for departure from the disclosure norm for material observations. The Court thus adopts a stricter approach towards states in determining whether or not equality of arms was upset. Whereas cases on observations were decided under Article 6(1), the consideration in them of the issue of disclosure renders them relevant to Article 6(3)(b), which is a specific aspect of the former.

Bulut v Austria[131] provides a useful illustration of the Court's application of the concept of equality of arms when observations are involved. The Attorney-General submitted observations on the applicant's appeal to the Supreme Court which were not served on the defence. The Court considered that the opinion of the Attorney-General could not be regarded as neutral, particularly as his office was charged with the prosecution.[132] It thereafter held it inconsistent with the principle of equality of arms for an opponent to make submissions to a court without the knowledge of the defence, thus finding an Article 6(1) violation.[133] This conclusion was reached notwithstanding the observations being purely procedural in nature, for '[i]t is a matter for the defence to assess whether a submission deserves a reaction.'[134] The element of prejudice in the inequality of arms thus did not stem from the content of the observations. Rather, prejudice arose because the Attorney-General was afforded an additional opportunity

129 *Jasper* (n 72) [55]; *Fitt* (n 70) [48]; *PG and JH* (n 72) [71].
130 Ch 2 s 4.1.2.
131 *Bulut* (n 86).
132 Ibid [48].
133 Ibid [49]–[50].
134 Ibid [49]. This principle is repeated in eg *Kuopila* (n 86) [28]; *Josef Fischer v Austria* (App 33382/96) ECHR 17 January 2002 [19]; *Lanz* (n 86) [58]; *Sharomov v Russia* (App 8927/02) ECHR 15 January 2009 [44]; *Nasteska v the former Yugoslav Republic of Macedonia* (App 23152/05) ECHR 27 May 2010 [28]; *Zahirović v Croatia* (App 58590/11) ECHR 25 April 2013 [43].

to assert his position and influence the appeal outcome without the possibility of a response from the accused that may have been material.[135] The approach herein, which derives from *Borgers v Belgium*,[136] has also been reflected in other cases to confirm an inequality of arms on account of the non-disclosure of observations.[137]

Yet, in *JJ v the Netherlands*,[138] *Meftah and others v France*[139] and *Şahin Çağdaş v Turkey*,[140] the Court did not refer to the concept of equality of arms but only to the adversarial principle as the basis for finding Article 6(1) infringed, an approach applied particularly in civil cases.[141] The adversarial principle entitles the accused to have knowledge of and comment on all observations filed, even by an independent member of the national legal service.[142] The approach allowed the Court to avoid addressing whether or not the legal officer could be regarded as an 'opponent', a status necessary for the equality of arms doctrine to be applicable, but it also created an inconsistency with its approach in *Bulut* and other cases. Though the facts of *Meftah and others* do not reveal the content of the observations of the legal officer therein, the observations in *JJ* and *Şahin Çağdaş* were manifestly not neutral.[143] Accordingly, in the latter two cases at least, there would have been adequate justification for affording opponent status to the legal officers and dealing with the non-disclosure also as an inequality of arms, thereby fostering greater consistency in the case-law. Consistency would, of course, further encourage the Court to use the concept of equality of arms for resolving future similar cases.

In resolving complaints of inequality of arms, the Court has encountered the argument that indirect disclosure of observations is sufficient. This argument

---

135 *Bulut* (n 86) [49]; Ch 2 s 4.4.4.

136 *Borgers* (n 86) [26]–[27], [29]; Ch 2 s 4.1.2.

137 *APEH Üldözötteinek Szövetsége and others v Hungary* (App 32367/96) ECHR 2000-X [42]–[44] (civil); *Josef Fischer* (n 134) [21]–[22]; *Lanz* (n 86) [60], [64]. See also *Reinhardt and Slimane-Kaïd* (n 86): The EComHR expressly followed this approach, declaring that an inequality of arms (reporting judge's file only made available to advocate-general) had been accentuated by non-disclosure of the advocate-general's observations ([103]). The Court, however, implied that the advocate-general was an opponent ([105]) but seems to have relied solely on the adversarial principle to declare the non-disclosure unfair ([106]–[107]).

138 (App 21351/93) ECHR 1998-II [42]–[43].

139 (Apps 32911/96; 35237/97; 34595/97) ECHR 2002-VII [51]–[52].

140 (App 28137/02) ECHR 11 April 2006 [28]–[30].

141 Ch 2 n 106.

142 *Lobo Machado v Portugal* (App 15764/89) ECHR 1996-I [31] (civil); *JJ* (n 138) [43]; *Kress v France* (App 39594/98) ECHR 2001-VI [65] (civil); *Meftah and others* (n 139) [51].

143 *JJ* (n 138) [14]: The Advocate-General expressed the view that the decision of the Court of Appeal had been correct and gave extensive reasons why the applicant's alternative submission should be rejected; *Şahin Çağdaş* (n 140) [15], [20]: The Principal Public Prosecutors advised that the applicant should not be granted compensation for non-pecuniary damage, that the appeal be rejected and that the first instance judgment be approved. See further *Borgers* (n 86) [26]: 'By recommending that an accused's appeal be allowed or dismissed, the official of the procureur général's department becomes objectively speaking his ally or his opponent.'

was raised in *Brandstetter v Austria*.[144] The Commission considered that, as the observations of the Senior Public Prosecutor were 'reproduced almost literally' in the appeal judgement, the applicant had the opportunity to deal with them in the second set of proceedings.[145] Disagreeing, the Court held that Article 6(1) was violated: 'An indirect and purely hypothetical possibility for an accused to comment on prosecution arguments included in the text of a judgment can scarcely be regarded as a proper substitute for the right to examine and reply directly to submissions made by the prosecution.'[146] The same approach was evident in *Lanz v Austria*[147] where the Government argued that it was unnecessary to serve the Senior Public Prosecutor's written observations on the applicant as they were essentially repeated at an oral hearing. Relying on *Brandstetter*, the Court attached no weight to this indirect disclosure: 'where a court … has at its disposal in addition to oral statements made at a hearing written statements filed beforehand, a party which is not informed about written submissions of the opposing party and thus deprived from reacting thereto is put at a substantial disadvantage vis-à-vis its opponent.'[148] Indirect disclosure of observations is thus not adequate disclosure and, accordingly, remains prejudicial to the defence.

Whenever observations have not been served on an applicant, it is also tempting for states to argue that his counsel could have consulted or obtained a copy of such material, at or from the court registry, had counsel made efforts to that effect. The Court was unpersuaded by this argument in the civil case of *Göç v Turkey*, considering it incumbent on the registry, as a matter of fairness, to have informed the applicant that the Principal Public Prosecutor's observations had been filed and a response could be submitted.[149] Additionally, requiring counsel to take the initiative and inform himself periodically on whether new additions had been made to the case-file was viewed as a disproportionate burden on him, and would not necessarily have guaranteed a real opportunity to comment on the observations.[150] Citing *Göç*, the Court did not depart from these findings in the subsequent criminal case of *Şahin Çağdaş*.[151] The onus, therefore and rightly, is on the state to take measures to ensure that the defence will be aware that observations have been filed and will enjoy a real opportunity to comment thereon[152] if it is to avoid placing the accused at a disadvantage.

144 (Apps 11170/84; 12876/87; 13468/87) (1991) Series A no 211.
145 Ibid [68].
146 Ibid [68]–[69].
147 *Lanz* (n 86).
148 Ibid [62].
149 (App 36590/97) ECHR 2002-V [57].
150 Ibid.
151 *Şahin Çağdaş* (n 140) [28]–[29].
152 *Brandstetter* (n 144) [67].

5. CONCLUSION

This discussion was concerned with the Strasbourg approach to equality of arms in cases about adequacy of time and facilities.

It first established a nexus between equality of arms and Article 6(3)(b). As with Article 6(3)(d), the nexus is acknowledged in law by the Court, the Commission and the Human Rights Committee, and derives at Convention level from both elements being part of the Article 6(1) fair hearing right. A conceptual nexus derives from the instrumental, intrinsic and collateral values of equality of arms being served by the realisation of Article 6(3)(b). This article also falls conceptually into the equality of arms remit as it specifies a right that is feasibly reciprocal and essential for case preparation, and linked to the adversarial principle.

Equality of arms does not imply that the accused be afforded time and facilities equal to that of the prosecution; he need only be afforded time and facilities adequate to his preparatory needs so as to prevent disadvantage. As preparatory needs vary between accused persons, adequacy of time and facilities is determined not in a vacuum but by reference to the demands of the specific circumstances of each case. When such circumstances are assessed at Strasbourg, it is decisive to a finding of inadequate time or facilities, and thus to confirming an inequality of arms, that actual prejudice was suffered. On this approach, it was suggested in the discussion that the state should bear a burden of proving the absence of prejudice if the preparatory time or facilities appear prima facie inadequate for purpose; if such time or facilities seem prima facie adequate, the applicant should be required to prove prejudice. Nevertheless, an alternative approach is preferred to strengthen the concept of equality of arms: if, on the circumstances of the case, the time or facilities are inadequate, an inequality of arms should be registered, irrespective of whether actual prejudice occurred (unequivocal inequality).

Whereas several examples of facilities important to securing equality of arms were highlighted in the discussion, the facility of disclosure is the most prominent in the case-law. Three elements elucidate the character of disclosure: i) its content is comprised of all material evidence and observations; ii) it need only be made in time adequate to afford the defence a reasonable opportunity to familiarise itself with and comment on the material; iii) disclosed material is accessible conventionally to counsel and his client (through counsel) but access can be restricted to the former. This restriction, it was submitted, may reduce unduly the accused's unique input into the defence case, thus the provision of an additional specific right for the accused himself to access the disclosed material would be a worthwhile dignitarian measure.

The discussion explored equality of arms within the context of complaints of non-disclosure both of material evidence and of observations of legal officers joined to the proceedings.

The Court accepts that non-disclosure of material evidence can be legitimate on PII grounds. It is not within the Court's remit to decide on whether non-disclosure was strictly necessary; it must determine whether the decision was made in a procedure that maintained equality of arms.

The actual prejudice proviso underpins cases where evidence was withheld on PII grounds without first being put before the trial judge. Though admitting that the trial judge is best placed to decide on non-disclosure, the Court accepts that the disadvantage to the defence of the prosecution bypassing his real-time scrutiny can be counterbalanced at appeal. This is possible through an inter partes, thus adversarial, appeal hearing on the possible prejudice at trial of the non-disclosure, in advance of which the material should be disclosed fully or to a degree enabling the defence to be informed as far as possible without full revelation. Informed adversarialism can thus counterbalance a disadvantage so as to avoid actual prejudice and an inequality of arms. A dignitarian approach would entail that the disadvantage to the defence at trial from the prosecution bypassing the scrutiny of the best placed decision-maker on disclosure/non-disclosure, and avoiding entering into adversarial argument for disclosure/non-disclosure, represents an inequality of arms, irrespective of subsequent counterbalancing measures – measures which cannot compensate for the extent of the infringement of dignity at trial. This higher level of protection should be preferred.

Yet, if potential PII material is placed before the trial judge, the Court is willing to accept ex parte procedures on disclosure as not upsetting equality of arms. Reliance upon the actual prejudice proviso to this effect is evident in two respects. First, account is taken of whether the defence's absence from the ex parte procedure was counterbalanced through adequate safeguards. In *Jasper*, for example, the following were considered sufficient: the defence could outline their case to the judge before the ex parte hearing; the judge monitored the need for disclosure throughout the trial; and the appeal court assessed the disclosure issue. The discussion argued, however, that the value of such measures is undermined by an uninformed defence and by the trial and appeal judges not being informed by adversarial argument. Without adversarial argument, informed as far as possible, the prosecution are better placed than the defence to influence the disclosure decision in their own favour. Thus, if counterbalancing measures are to be applied, it is submitted that they should involve informed adversarialism, a condition not always upheld by the Court. The second indicator of actual prejudice applied is whether the material formed part of the prosecution case or was ever put to the tribunal of fact. It was suggested in the discussion, however, that the relevance or possible relevance to the defence of evidence withheld as a result of a procedure lacking in adversarial argument cannot be considered as having undergone proper evaluation. This should be viewed as prejudicial, for the defence are unduly denied the use of this evidence, even if it was not part of the prosecution case or put to the tribunal of fact. The Court's approach to and application of the actual prejudice proviso is thus an unsatisfactory means of safeguarding equality of arms.

A more dignitarian approach would prove a stronger safeguard. PII hearings in which the defence is not represented should be seen as involving an inequality of arms and as never strictly necessary, irrespective of whether any prejudice arises therefrom. The decision to withhold disclosure must be informed by adversarial argument. Accordingly, in most cases, the defence should be notified of at least the category of material for which PII is sought and an inter partes hearing held. If, in rare cases, revealing the category of material would defeat the purpose of the PII application, adversarialism could be maintained through measures such as the engagement of special counsel to represent the interests of the accused, the practical difficulties of which are not insurmountable. Any procedural restrictions imposed upon the defence in the inter partes hearing, or upon special counsel, that are not strictly necessary should be viewed as an inequality of arms, even in the absence of prejudice.

A stricter approach to that applied by the Court to PII cases is taken in respect of non-disclosure in civil law jurisdictions of written observations of legal officers joined to the proceedings. Opponent status can attach to these officers, bringing them within the applicability remit of the concept of equality of arms. The Court does not recognise any legitimate grounds on which such observations can be exempt from disclosure. Indirect disclosure is not adequate, the onus rightly being on the state to ensure that the defence are informed directly that observations have been filed and to provide an adequate opportunity to comment thereon. The discussion established that it is not non-disclosure in itself but the prejudice arising therefrom that grounds the Court's findings of inequality of arms. It is submitted, however, that non-disclosure of observations put by an opponent to the court should in itself be viewed as a procedural inequality, regardless of prejudice (unequivocal inequality). The discussion also argued that in cases where the Court dealt with non-disclosure of observations solely under the adversarial principle, there would have been adequate justification for relying on the concept of equality of arms instead. The latter should be relied on in resolving similar cases to ensure consistency of approach.

The regard had to prejudice in confirming an inequality of arms from inadequate time or facilities continues also in respect of Article 6(3)(c), though the Court's approach to the latter, which is discussed hereafter, takes account not only of actual but also of inevitable prejudice.

CHAPTER 5

EQUALITY OF ARMS AND THE RIGHT TO LEGAL ASSISTANCE

1. INTRODUCTION

Article 6(3)(c) essentially secures for the accused a right to a defence. It encompasses three guarantees for this purpose: a right to defend himself in person (pro se accused); a right to defend himself through legal assistance of his own choosing (privately retained counsel); and, in certain cases, an entitlement to state-funded legal assistance (legal aid). Each right is linked in the English text by 'or', implying that they are alternatives and that state discretion determines which right is conferred upon the accused, whereas the French text employs *'et'* ('and') between the second and third guarantees. The Court views the French version as authoritative given that it is more consistent with ensuring effective protection of the rights of the defence, hence an accused cannot be compelled to mount a pro se defence.[1] The pro se accused, who assumes a burden of diligence,[2] is not of particular concern to this chapter, except insofar as he raises the issue of whether counsel can be imposed upon him, for his condition is self-prescribed.[3] The concept of equality of arms is at issue only when a disadvantageous procedural condition is the fault of the state and, within the context of Article 6(3)(c), this occurs most often in respect of the article's legal assistance provisions. It is these provisions that occupy the substance of the discussion herein.

The provision of an opportunity for legal assistance is a manifestation of the concept of equality of arms, hence the absence thereof may disadvantage

---

1 *Pakelli v Germany* (App 8398/78) (1983) Series A no 64 [31].

2 *Melin v France* (App 12914/87) (1993) Series A no 261-A [25]. See further DJ Harris, M O'Boyle and C Warbrick, *Law of the European Convention on Human Rights* (Butterworths, London 1995) 258: 'The duty to show diligence does not mean that any accused who defends himself should be held to the standards of a professional lawyer; account must be taken of the particular accused's capabilities and the knowledge and expertise that can be expected of them.'

3 See further *R v Brown and others* [2001] EWCA Crim 1771; [2001] All ER (D) 392 (Jul): A defendant who chooses to exercise his right under Art 6(3)(c) to a pro se defence cannot ordinarily pray in aid his own incompetence in conducting the defence in support of an argument that an inequality of arms had occurred to render his conviction unsafe.

the accused vis-à-vis the significant prosecutorial expertise of the state. Indeed, the value of the rights to challenge witness evidence and to adequate time and facilities – rights discussed in Chapters 3 and 4 respectively – is reliant heavily upon the right to engage legal assistance.[4] The essence of this assistance for the purposes of criminal proceedings, and steps preliminary or incidental thereto, is the delivery of legal advice, the taking of relevant practical measures on behalf of the accused, and representation before any court. The norm in practice is that the provider of effective legal assistance will be a qualified lawyer, all references to counsel in this chapter being to this effect, though others may also be considered competent for this purpose where domestic rights to give legal advice and of audience permit.[5] Whoever is instructed in this regard, the state cannot suppress him from defending a client merely on account of the latter's absence at hearing.[6] The interest in achieving equality of arms must prevail.

The interest of this discussion is to examine the Strasbourg approach to equality of arms in the application of the Article 6(3)(c) right to legal assistance. It begins in section 2 by establishing a nexus between these two requirements of a fair trial. Section 3 thereafter concentrates specifically on the right to privately retained counsel, the predominant focus being the Strasbourg response to domestic restrictions thereupon. It is not a right, however, that impacts upon the majority of accused persons, for their indigence renders more relevant the right to legally aided assistance. Section 4, accordingly, gives greater consideration to the latter to reflect its importance. The grant of legal aid is, nevertheless, subject to an accused fulfilling financial and interests of justice criterions. The Court's interpretation of these eligibility criterions is assessed. Once an accused is eligible for legal aid, the issue of whether he is entitled to influence the selection of appointed counsel also becomes relevant and is addressed. Even if an accused

4 See further WV Schaefer, 'Federalism and State Criminal Procedure' (1956) 70 Harv L Rev 1, 8: 'Of all of the rights that an accused person has, the right to be represented by counsel is by far the most pervasive, for it affects his ability to assert any other rights he may have.'

5 Eg *X v Germany* (App 509/59) (1960) 3 Yearbook 174 (EComHR) 180, 182 where adequate legal assistance was held to include that provided by a probationary legal trainee (*Gerichtsreferendar*); *Ofner v Austria* (App 524/59) (1960) 3 Yearbook 322 (EComHR) 352 where 'defending counsel' was interpreted as meaning 'the legal representative of the accused or simply a person acting on his behalf'; *Engel and others v the Netherlands* (App 5100/71 et seq) (1976) Series A no 22 [91] concerning legal assistance in military disciplinary proceedings supplied by 'a fellow conscript who was a lawyer in civil life'; *F v Switzerland* (App 12152/86) (1989) 61 DR 171, 175 in which a pupil advocate was held to have conducted an effective defence.

6 *Poitrimol v France* (App 14032/88) (1993) Series A no 277-A [34]–[35] (suppression of legal assistance is a disproportionate response to an absent accused); *Lala v the Netherlands* (App 14861/89) (1994) Series A no 297-A [33]; *Pelladoah v the Netherlands* (App 16737/90) (1994) Series A no 297-B [40]; *Van Geyseghem v Belgium* (App 26103/95) ECHR 1999-I [33]–[35]; *Krombach v France* (App 29731/96) ECHR 2001-II [89]–[90]; *Sejdovic v Italy* (App 56581/00) ECHR 2006-II [91].

is so eligible, or is capable of privately retaining counsel, he may wish instead to conduct his case pro se. Section 5 examines whether a state can set aside this preference and insist that counsel be instructed. Whatever the manner in which counsel is instructed, the procedural conditions under which his assistance is rendered in the pre-trial phase of proceedings can be of crucial importance to the effectiveness of the defence presented at trial. Section 6 considers the Court's approach to pre-trial legal assistance when issues of access to and private communication with counsel have arisen. Legal assistance at this or any stage of the proceedings can make a useful contribution to securing equality of arms only insofar as it is effective in practice. Section 7 reveals the circumstances in which a state can be held responsible when faced with a complaint of ineffective assistance.

2. THE NEXUS BETWEEN EQUALITY OF ARMS AND ARTICLE 6(3)(C)

The right to legal assistance in Article 6(3)(c) is an application of the concept of equality of arms. A legal and a conceptual based nexus can be established.

2.1. LEGAL NEXUS

A nexus between Article 6(3)(c) and the principle of procedural equality has been recognised readily in law by the Strasbourg organs. The former Commission pronounced that the aim of the article 'is primarily to place the accused in a position to put his case to the court in such a way that he is not at a disadvantage *vis-à-vis* the prosecution'.[7] The same is also expressed in the Court's acknowledgement that undue restrictions on the right to legal assistance undermine the equality of arms concept.[8] A legal nexus is made possible because both elements are encompassed within the wider fair hearing provision of

7 *Goddi v Italy* (App 8966/80) EComHR Report 14 July 1982 [55]; *X v Germany* (App 10098/82) (1984) 8 EHRR 214, 225. See also *Glaser and others v Austria* (App 834/60 et seq) EComHR Report 17 December 1963, 66: 'the denial to an accused person of legal assistance on appeal or the exclusion of his lawyer from the hearing of that appeal raise the … issue of "equality of arms"'; *X v UK* (App 8295/78) (1978) 15 DR 242, 244: 'In examining questions under Article 6(3)(c) the Commission takes … "particular regard to the principle of equality of arms …".'

8 *Moiseyev v Russia* (App 62936/00) ECHR 9 October 2008 [207]. See also *Salduz v Turkey* (App 36391/02) ECHR 27 November 2008 [53]: Legal assistance 'contribute[s] to the prevention of miscarriages of justice and the fulfilment of the aims of Article 6, notably equality of arms between the investigating or prosecuting authorities and the accused.'

Article 6(1). Articles 6(1) and 6(3)(c) are thus sometimes considered conjointly.[9] Whereas the application of Article 6(3)(c) will not always be accompanied by an express reference to the concept of equality of arms, the latter still remains relevant for it assumes an implied presence.

2.2. CONCEPTUAL NEXUS

The nexus is also appreciable from a sound conceptual standpoint. Chapter 2 made known that feasibly reciprocal procedural rights useful for case preparation and/or presentation live within the ambit of the equality of arms concept.[10] The right of legal representation belongs self-evidently to this category of rights. Additionally, the proper exercise of this right serves the fundamental values highlighted in the same chapter that are represented in the concept.[11]

The opportunity to engage counsel contributes to furthering the instrumental value of procedural equality: enhancement of the likelihood of a correct trial outcome. The investigation and subsequent trial process exposes the accused, who is not expected to have legal acumen and skills,[12] to the vast resources of the state and the considerable legal, evidential and procedural expertise and experience of its prosecuting authorities. The danger, therefore, is that the prosecution, to whom a right of representation is always available, may be in a position to exert a disproportionate influence over the decision-maker(s) when establishing the case against the accused and thereby compromise the accuracy of the verdict. To counterbalance this threat is the right of the accused to instruct counsel, which 'guarantees ... that the proceedings against him will not take place without an adequate representation of the case for the defence'.[13]

9 Eg *Granger v UK* (App 11932/86) (1990) Series A no 174 [43]; *Twalib v Greece* (App 24294/94) ECHR 1998-IV [57]; *Öcalan v Turkey* (App 46221/99) ECHR 2005-IV [148]; *Popov v Russia* (App 26853/04) ECHR 13 July 2006 [174]; *Klimentyev v Russia* (App 46503/99) ECHR 16 November 2006 [113]; *Moiseyev* (n 8) [225].

10 Ch 2 ss 4.2–4.3.1, 4.3.3–4.3.4.

11 Ibid s 2.

12 See further S Rogers, 'The Ethics of Advocacy' (1899) 15 LQR 259, 261: 'The natural man when inquiring into anything knows nothing of the inadmissibility of evidence. He admits everything, hearsay or otherwise, and concerns himself solely with its credibility'; *Powell v Alabama* 287 US 45, 69 (1932) (Sutherland J): 'Even the intelligent and educated layman has small and sometimes no skill in the science of law. If charged with crime, he is incapable, generally, of determining for himself whether the indictment is good or bad. He is unfamiliar with the rules of evidence. ... [H]e may be put on trial without a proper charge, and convicted upon incompetent evidence, or evidence irrelevant to the issue or otherwise inadmissible. He lacks both the skill and knowledge adequately to prepare his defense, even though he have a perfect one.'

13 *X v Austria* (App 2676/65) (1967) 23 CD 31, 35; *Pakelli v Germany* (App 8398/78) (1981) 24 DR 112, 119–120. See also *Ensslin, Baader and Raspe v Germany* (Apps 7572/76; 7586/76; 7587/76) (1978) 14 DR 91, 114: 'the purpose of ... [Article 6(3)(c)] is to ensure that both sides of the

To allow adequate representation of the defence case is to promote equality of opportunity with the prosecution to influence the court, which renders a correct outcome more probable.

Counsel, for whom it is incumbent to 'fearlessly and by all proper and lawful means'[14] obtain an acquittal or the most lenient outcome possible, is better placed than the accused to adequately counter prosecutorial influence because of his understanding of relevant legal, evidential and factual issues and capacity to guard against any inaccuracies arising therefrom; his strategically sound judgement[15] based on experience and an objective eye;[16] his expertise in testing witness evidence, especially if practising within an accusatorial style legal system; and his proficiency in the preparation and presentation of skilled argument. Additionally, counsel is competent to observe whether procedural integrity has been maintained throughout the proceedings[17] and to acquaint the accused with his procedural and substantive rights. These attributes are acknowledged by the US Supreme Court as being of such fundamental importance that '[t]he right to be heard would be, in many cases, of little avail if it did not comprehend the right to be heard by counsel.'[18] This observation was essentially shared by the European Court in *Pakelli v Germany* when it pronounced that the accused could not have made a useful contribution to his appeal on a point of law without the services of counsel.[19] It was held, therefore, that the refusal to appoint defence counsel during the oral stage of the proceedings deprived the accused of the opportunity to influence the case outcome.[20] Without this opportunity of real influence and the balancing effect thereof on the decision-maker(s), the

case are actually heard by giving the accused, as necessary, the assistance of an independent professional.'

14 Bar Standards Board, *Handbook* (2nd edn, London 2015) rC15.1 (Code of Conduct). Improper conduct can include counsel, for example, knowingly or recklessly misleading the court (rC3.1). See also *Re G Mayor Cooke* (1889) 5 TLR 407, 408 (Lord Esher MR): An advocate is 'bound to use his utmost skill for his client, but ... [not] to degrade himself for the purpose of winning his client's case.'

15 See further *Pishchalnikov v Russia* (App 7025/04) ECHR 24 September 2009 [84]: 'criminal law ... and ... proceedings are a rather complex and technical matter which is often incomprehensible to laypersons ... Moreover, practically at every stage of criminal proceedings decisions have to be taken, the wrong decision being able to cause irreparable damage. Reliable knowledge of law and practice is usually required in order to assess the consequences of such decisions.'

16 The pro se accused risks compromising his objectivity because of his deep personal attachment to the case, hence the familiar proverb 'whosoever is his own counsel has a fool for his client'.

17 In *Ensslin, Baader and Raspe* (n 13) 114, counsel was described as '"the watchdog of procedural regularity".'

18 *Powell* (n 12) 68–69 (Sutherland J).

19 *Pakelli* (n 1) [38]. See also *Granger* (n 9) [47]: 'free legal assistance ... would ... have served the interests of justice and fairness by enabling the applicant to make an effective contribution to the proceedings.'

20 *Pakelli* (n 1) [39]. See also *Shulepov v Russia* (App 15435/03) ECHR 26 June 2008 [34]: 'the Court considers that the assistance of a legal-aid lawyer ... was essential for the applicant, as

correctness of the case outcome may be jeopardised. Thus, the provision of an opportunity to rely on counsel can make the right to be heard effective, hence conducive to a correct outcome.

It also contributes to the practical realisation of the intrinsic value of the concept of equality of arms: preservation of the dignity of the accused. The counsel–client relationship is a manifestation of the maxim *qui facit per alium, facit per se* (he who acts through another, acts for himself). The adequate representation and protection of the accused's interests through this relationship ensures that the accused is an empowered and meaningful participant in the proceedings against him. Greater value is added to his right, drawn from the adversarial principle inherent in the concept of equality of arms,[21] to comment on the observations filed and evidence adduced by the prosecution. As his participation in the process becomes effective,[22] he will feel that the opportunity of influencing the outcome of his case is a real one.[23] Therefore, the accused becomes conceptually a meaningful participant equal sufficiently to his opponent in legal knowledge and skill, and opportunity of influence. His dignity is preserved.[24] The dignitarian value of the right to legal assistance is evidenced further in the accompanying power of choice granted to the accused in the second clause of Article 6(3)(c). Respect is afforded to his capacity to choose through independent will and reason his own counsel in the determination of his fate.

The collateral repercussion of this dignitarian value and of the contribution legal assistance makes to correctness of outcome serves the secondary value of equality of arms: it contributes to achieving a perception that the state is exercising some form of good governance. An opportunity to procure adequate legal advice and representation contributes to creating a public perception that the accused was not disadvantaged by his lack of legal knowledge and skill vis-à-vis the expertise of the prosecuting authorities. Legal assistance instils confidence in society that the defence case was adequately impressed upon the court and procedural irregularities were guarded against, increasing its

---

the former could effectively draw the appeal court's attention to any substantial argument in the applicant's favour, which might influence the court's decision.'

21 On the relationship between the adversarial and equality of arms principles, see Ch 2 s 4.3.2.

22 *Granger* (n 9) [47]; *Lagerblom v Sweden* (App 26891/95) ECHR 14 January 2003 [49]; *Popov* (n 9) [170]; *Vozhigov v Russia* (App 5953/02) ECHR 26 April 2007 [40].

23 *Pakelli* (n 1) [39].

24 See further DJ Galligan, *Due Process and Fair Procedures: A Study of Administrative Procedures* (Clarendon, Oxford 1996) 364: 'For those who value a hearing for its own sake, legal representation might be seen as a way of making it more meaningful and, in that way, enhancing dignitarian values.'

S Trechsel, *Human Rights in Criminal Proceedings* (OUP, Oxford 2005) 246 offers a valid different dignitarian perspective, though it is not associated with procedural equality: 'The assistance of counsel … also serves the humanitarian aim of providing the defendant with a human companion, to lessen the feeling that he … has been abandoned by the world only to be "processed" by the judicial machinery which can be perceived as distant and cold, if not downright hostile.'

perception that a correct trial outcome was reached and the dignity of one of its members was rightly respected by the state conducting a prosecution on its behalf. Defence counsel, therefore, not only serves the accused, but also exercises a public function by infusing greater legitimacy into criminal proceedings.

3. LEGAL ASSISTANCE BY PRIVATELY RETAINED COUNSEL

The Article 6(3)(c) right of the accused to 'legal assistance of his own choosing' refers to his entitlement, provided his means are sufficient to pay representation fees, ordinarily to retain counsel of his choice for the purposes of his defence.[25] If the financial assets of the accused are seized by the state, the motive thereof must not be to prevent him from securing such counsel.[26] A legitimate purpose of seizure would be to preserve the proceeds of an alleged crime, the collateral effect of which may require an application for legal aid. An accused who has sufficient legitimate means cannot be denied an opportunity to retain private counsel and compelled instead to accept ex officio appointed counsel.[27] No distinction is made in the aforementioned article between privately retained and court assigned counsel in respect of their competence to conduct an effective defence,[28] hence both are capable of counterbalancing adequately prosecutorial expertise to secure equality of arms. Nevertheless, the element of choice in one's counsel gives legal assistance a greater dignitarian value and is more conducive to creating from the outset a counsel–client relationship of trust and confidence.

It is in view of the importance of this relationship that 'as a general rule an accused must not be deprived, against his will or without his knowledge, of

---

25 *X v Germany* (App 646/59) (1960) 3 Yearbook 272 (EComHR) 276, 278; *X v Austria* (App 4338/69) (1970) 36 CD 79, 82. More specifically, the right entails representation by a lawyer of one's own 'informed' choice. In *Dvorski v Croatia* (App 25703/11) ECHR 2015 [92]–[93], [111]–[113], although the applicant had formally chosen a lawyer to represent him during police interrogation, the Court considered that his choice was not an informed one because the police failed to inform him that another lawyer had been hired by his parents and had attended the police station with a view to representing him. Also, this inability, as a result of the police's conduct, to make an informed choice of lawyer was prejudicial since the applicant's confession during interrogation was admitted in evidence at trial. Consequently, a violation of Articles 6(1) and 6(3)(c) was found.

26 *X* 1970 (n 25) 82.

27 *Goddi* (n 7) [64]: The Convention 'gives a defence lawyer assigned by the court a subsidiary role in so far as such a lawyer is called upon only in the absence of one chosen by the accused.'

See also infringements found by the Human Rights Committee (HRC) of ICCPR Art 14(3)(d) (right to legal assistance of own choosing) following the undue imposition of ex officio counsel in Uruguay: eg *Miguel Angel Estrella v Uruguay* (Comm 74/1980) UN Doc Supp No 40 (A/38/40) 150 (1983) [1.8], [8.6], [10]; *Delia Saldias de Lopez v Uruguay* (Comm 52/1979) UN Doc CCPR/C/OP/1 88 (1984) [2.3], [11.5], [13]; *Antonio Viana Acosta v Uruguay* (Comm 110/1981) UN Doc Supp No 40 (A/39/40) 169 (1984) [13.2], [15].

28 *Goddi* (n 7) [64].

the assistance of ... counsel he has appointed.'[29] This dignitarian rule is not, however, absolute and states are recognised as entitled to place reasonable restrictions on the right to privately retained counsel,[30] the exclusion of certain counsel outright or during the proceedings being the consequence thereof. Exclusion is an especially serious measure:

> It ... may intimidate other potential defence counsel or cast discredit on the defence in general; further, a succession of defence lawyers may be damaging to the presentation of the case and introduce greater uncertainty into the barrister's role as "the watchdog of procedural regularity".[31]

Reasonableness implies that the restriction must be appropriate to its intended purpose. Reasonable restrictions are acceptable because the exigencies of justice and securing the adequate defence of the accused may so require. Where such restrictions result in the exclusion of particular counsel,[32] a real opportunity to choose suitable alternative counsel should be made available within ample time to maintain a fair procedural equilibrium between the parties. Where the choice of counsel is interfered with on the basis of an undue restriction, the environment created is not conducive to the right to privately retained counsel being practical and effective, thus the position of the accused reliant upon the right is compromised unreasonably. The reasonableness of a particular domestic restriction is not the sole criterion for Convention compliance. The Convention organs have also considered critical whether the exclusion of counsel was prejudicial to the presentation of an effective defence and undermined an essential safeguard against procedural irregularity, hence placed the accused at a disadvantage vis-à-vis the prosecution. The prejudice proviso is thus consistent with that applied to the principle of equality of arms within the context of the rights to test witness evidence and to adequate time and facilities, which were discussed in Chapters 3 and 4 respectively.

Several examples of the application of the aforementioned prejudice and reasonableness criteria in response to domestic restrictions on the right to privately retained counsel merit attention as a point of guidance.

---

29 Ibid.

30 Eg *X* 1978 (n 7) 244; *Popov* (n 9) [171]; *Klimentyev* (n 9) [116]; *Rozhkov v Russia* (App 64140/00) ECHR 5 February 2007 [6(b)(b)] ('The Law'). Contrast *X v Germany* (App 722/60) (1962) 5 Yearbook 104 (EComHR) 106 where, though the Commission also confirmed the non-absolute nature of the right to privately retained counsel, it did not refer expressly to reasonableness and seemed to award states an excessive margin of appreciation in their restrictive powers, namely 'full discretion to exclude lawyers from appearing before the courts'.

31 *Ensslin, Baader and Raspe* (n 13) 114.

32 See further S Stavros, *The Guarantees for Accused Persons Under Article 6 of the European Convention on Human Rights: An Analysis of the Application of the Convention and a Comparison with Other Instruments* (Martinus Nijhoff, Dordrecht 1993) 206 for a suggestion that the threshold of reasonableness should be such that the exclusion of counsel on behavioural grounds should be considered reasonable only when the behaviour has an essentially criminal character.

It is conventional and uncontroversial for rights of audience to be restricted to qualified persons – those who have complied with all applicable practising requirements imposed by the state of jurisdiction.[33] This includes restricting rights of audience to an additional extent in the supreme courts to specialist advocates[34] and precluding representation by lawyers qualified exclusively in a foreign jurisdiction.[35] Such regulations on the qualification of those providing legal assistance are overwhelmingly in the interests of justice and of the accused, for they establish a minimum standard of competence in representation, hence are reasonable and non-prejudicial to an adequate defence.

Reasonable regulations are also permissible concerning the conduct of counsel in court in order to preserve procedural order and the integrity of the proceedings. It was thus considered in *Ensslin, Baader and Raspe v Germany* that the right to privately retained counsel is limited by the obligation on counsel not to infringe rules on professional ethics.[36] Certain lawyers therein were excluded from the defence because they were strongly suspected of supporting the criminal organisation affiliated with the accused. The Commission held that this measure was reasonable to maintain procedural order, especially given the prosecution of the lawyers themselves, and non-prejudicial since the accused were still adequately represented by other counsel, some of whom were chosen.[37] Also based on a rationale of professional ethics was the exclusion in another case of counsel who was representing his accused father.[38] The Commission viewed the exclusion as reasonable not because of the filial relationship itself, but the fact that counsel was involved intimately in the subject matter of the charge.[39] Furthermore, it was found non-prejudicial as the accused had ample opportunity to choose another advocate but made no effort in this regard.[40] Also considered reasonable was the exclusion of defence counsel in an earlier case for refusing to wear robes.[41] Though the accused was requested to choose alternative counsel and given adequate time to do so, he failed to act and the court appointed ex officio another counsel. The reasonable exclusion was thus considered not prejudicial to the right of the accused to an adequate defence or

---

33 See further *Mayzit v Russia* (App 63378/00) ECHR 20 January 2005 [25], [68]–[71]: The Court considered that the applicant's wish to have his lay mother and sister act as counsel was rejected reasonably as, inter alia, 'they would not be able to ensure the applicant's efficient defence in compliance with the procedure' ([68]). Prejudice did not arise consequently as the court appointed effective defence counsel in the absence of any effort by the applicant to choose alternative representation.

34 Eg *Meftah and others v France* (Apps 32911/96; 35237/97; 34595/97) ECHR 2002-VII [30]–[32], [47].

35 *V v UK* (App 11465/85) EComHR 3 March 1986 ('The Law').

36 *Ensslin, Baader and Raspe* (n 13) 114.

37 Ibid.

38 *X* 1978 (n 7).

39 Ibid 243–244.

40 Ibid 244.

41 *X and Y v Germany* (Apps 5217/71; 5367/72) (1972) 42 CD 139, 139.

to choose counsel.[42] The same was held when a defence counsel was excluded for disrespect to the court and the accused was provided the opportunity to choose alternative representation.[43] It is submitted that reliance upon this ground to effect exclusion should only be considered reasonable and proportionate if the level of disrespect is gross.

Aside from the acceptable regulation of the conduct of counsel in court, limits are also permissible on the number of defence counsel chosen in a case.[44] Such limits are reasonable to ensure against unnecessary practical and logistical difficulties that prevent the proceedings from progressing with the requisite expediency. Additionally, the limitation does not occasion prejudice provided that the number of counsel is sufficient to counterbalance the prosecution. It was thus that the restriction to a maximum of three chosen defence lawyers in *Ensslin, Baader and Raspe* was held acceptable.[45]

It is evident from all the above examples that the Strasbourg approach has been consistently to ensure that the accused has representation of his own choosing to guard against disadvantage vis-à-vis the prosecution, though states need not always accommodate his initial choice of counsel or every individual in a group of counsel he wishes to retain.

A further issue arising is that of the extent to which a court should accommodate private counsel when he is unavailable for a particular hearing date. In *Hanževački v Croatia*,[46] private counsel had suddenly fallen ill a day before the concluding hearing and duly informed the trial court on the morning of the hearing of his inability to attend. The court denied a request for an adjournment and the accused was compelled to proceed without representation. The European Court considered this prejudicial as counsel was required, and hence there would have been good cause for an adjournment, given the significance of the final hearing, which was an opportunity to present influential closing arguments and the defence view of the entire case.[47] The case should not be regarded as providing support for the proposition that observance of equality of arms requires an adjournment in every instance private counsel is unable to attend. Where adequate preparatory time is available, the engagement of another private counsel in the alternative will be sufficient to comply with Article 6(3)(c), rendering an adjournment unnecessary. An adjournment is, nevertheless, the dignitarian option as it evidences respect for and secures continuity of the accused's first choice of counsel, though it is good practice for

42 Ibid.
43 *X v UK* (App 6298/73) (1975) 2 Digest 831.
44 *Ensslin, Baader and Raspe* (n 13) 114.
45 Ibid. See also *Popov* (n 9) [172]–[174] where the refusal to admit the accused's uncle as his additional representative was held permissible as the accused was represented by an advocate of his choosing which was sufficient to secure equality of arms.
46 (App 17182/07) ECHR 16 April 2009.
47 Ibid [25]–[26], [29].

domestic courts to take account of the availability of first choice counsel as far as practicable when scheduling hearing dates.

An occasion may arise wherein the accused is unable to secure acceptable or any private counsel because those approached are unwilling to represent him. Article 6(3)(c), nonetheless, operates on the flawed presumption that the accused will always be able to secure private counsel provided he is of sufficient financial means. It is a common and legitimate practice for counsel to refuse any instructions that would cause professional embarrassment.[48] However, the accused may find that counsel's refusal is rooted unduly in the political unpopularity of the case.[49] Given that the Convention remedies acts attributable to the state rather than to private individuals, the refusal of private counsel to accept instructions can compel the accused, who is not entitled to legal aid, to mount a pro se defence and may create an inequality of arms for which the state is not liable. As a remedial measure at domestic level, Bar regulatory bodies should, if not already in existence, enforce through professional disciplinary measures a regulation to the effect of that applied to a barrister in England and Wales, who must not withhold his services 'on the ground that the nature of the case is objectionable to [him] or to any section of the public; on the ground that the conduct, opinions or beliefs of the prospective client are unacceptable to [him] or to any section of the public'.[50] At Convention level, provision should be made requiring the assignment of legal assistance by competent national authorities in cases where the accused has made all reasonable efforts to secure private counsel but has failed to do so. Article 14(3)(d) of the ICCPR offers such a solution, the accused being entitled 'to have legal assistance assigned to him, in any case where the interests of justice so require',[51] though a proviso allowing him to select one of the possible appointees should be added to ensure retention of the choice element in ECHR Article 6(3)(c). Article 6(3)(c) does, nevertheless, invoke state responsibility for procedural inequality when the refusal of private counsel 'is really due to pressure or manoeuvres by the public authority'.[52] Such pressure or manoeuvres may be manifested, for example, as the threatened or actual intimidation, harassment, maltreatment, detention, exile, disappearance

---

48 Bar Standards Board (n 14) rC21 (Code of Conduct) provides useful examples of circumstances in which professional embarrassment may arise, including where counsel lacks adequate experience or competence to handle the matter; counsel is unable to adequately prepare the case given his other professional commitments; the accused's instructions require counsel to act illegally or contrary to professional regulations; and a conflict of interest arises between the accused and other clients.

49 See the US based discussion of M Alexander, 'The Right to Counsel for the Politically Unpopular' (1962) 22 Law in Transition 19 who refers to the difficulties of retaining counsel for those associated, inter alia, with Communism in the 1940s and 1950s.

50 Bar Standards Board (n 14) rC28.1–2 (Code of Conduct).

51 See further D Harris, 'The Right to a Fair Trial in Criminal Proceedings as a Human Right' (1967) 16 ICLQ 352, 365 who suggests that ECHR Art 6(3)(c) is perhaps somewhat deficient in its failure to include such protection.

52 *X and Y v Belgium* (Apps 1420/62; 1477/62; 1478/62) (1963) 6 Yearbook 590 (EComHR) 628.

or murder of lawyers representing the politically unpopular, conditions which have in the past been acutely present in states within the jurisdiction of the Inter-American Commission on Human Rights.[53]

4. LEGALLY AIDED ASSISTANCE

The right to legal assistance should not in practice merely be the preserve of those with sufficient financial means. Not only would it create an inequality of arms between those lacking such means and the prosecution, with all its expertise and experience, but it would also render unequal the treatment between the indigent and non-indigent accused. The legal aid guarantee of Article 6(3)(c) is designed to ensure that such inequalities are not suffered for reason of financial insufficiency.[54] It establishes for the indigent accused a right to free legal assistance when the interests of justice so require. States are thus obliged positively to implement a system of legal assistance[55] in which the defence is funded from the public purse. The existence of this funding is in itself dignitarian: society is

---

53 Eg Cuba: Case 2286 in Inter-American Commission on Human Rights (IACHR), 'Sixth Report on the Situation of Political Prisoners in Cuba' OEA/Ser.L/V/II.48 doc 24 (1979) ch 3 s C [1]: Representation refused by counsel as he risked imprisonment; IACHR, 'Seventh Report on the Situation of Human Rights in Cuba' OEA/Ser.L/V/II.61 doc 29 rev 1 (1983) ch 4 s D [21]–[23]: 'Testimony from several detainees affirmed that their attorneys had been intimidated about defending them from fear of being "sanctioned"' ([23]).

Paraguay: IACHR, 'Report on the Situation of Human Rights in Paraguay' OEA/Ser.L/V/II.43 doc 13 corr 1 (1978) ch 5 [8]–[13]: 'The Commission has specific denunciations by attorneys who have been victims of every kind of violence due only to their active participation in the defense of detainees for reasons of state security or for assumed violations against the public order' ([13]).

Suriname: IACHR, 'Second Report on the Human Rights Situation in Suriname' OEA/Ser.L/V/II.66 doc 21 rev 1 (1985) ch 3 s C [2]: 'Since December of 1982 when four prominent attorneys ... were murdered, not surprisingly private lawyers have been loath to represent persons accused of crimes against state security.'

Uruguay: IACHR 'Report on the Situation of Human Rights in Uruguay' OEA/Ser.L/V/II.43 doc 19 corr 1 (1978) ch 6 [36], [39]–[41]: 'Intimidation, harassment and imprisonment of defense lawyers have the effect that more and more prisoners are reduced to having *defensores de oficio* (court-appointed counsel), and not lawyers of their own choice as defense counsel' ([39]).

Argentina: IACHR, 'Report on the Situation of Human Rights in Argentina' OEA/Ser.L/V/II.49 doc 19 corr 1 (1980) ch 6 s G [1]–[3], referring to 'complaints ... alleging the death, disappearance, detention or maltreatment of defense lawyers' ([1]).

Guatemala: IACHR, 'Report on the Situation of Human Rights in the Republic of Guatemala' OEA/Ser.L/V/II.53 doc 21 rev 2 (1981) ch 5 s E [1]–[2]: Lawyers murdered.

54 Concerning inequality between prosecution and indigent accused, see *Pakelli v Germany* (App 8398/78) EComHR Report 12 December 1981 [92]: 'This legal aid clause constitutes a specific application of the principle of "equality of arms"'. Concerning inequality between indigent and non-indigent accused, see *Luedicke, Belkacem and Koç v Germany* (Apps 6210/73; 6877/75; 7132/75) EComHR Report 18 May 1977 [35]: Art 6(3)(c) is intended 'to avoid any inequality between accused persons'.

55 *Artico v Italy* (App 6694/74) (1979) 2 Digest 836–837.

prepared to delve into its own purse to confer legal assistance upon those whose indigence would otherwise preclude it in order to counterbalance state power applied on its behalf. Whereas several well-established models for the delivery of this assistance exist,[56] states must strive in their chosen model to achieve cost[57] and systemic efficiency without compromising to an extent incompatible with Article 6(3)(c) the availability and quality of legal service provision for those most in need. Though adults can be expected to inform themselves of the possible availability of legal aid for hearings, no such presumption applies to young persons, who must be informed by states of the right to apply for it and given the opportunity to do so.[58] If the accused accepts legal aid, he cannot instruct counsel to not heed basic principles of his professional duty when presenting the defence.[59] Where the result of such instruction is the accused having necessarily to conduct a pro se defence, 'any consequent "inequality of arms" can only be attributable to his own behaviour.'[60] An accused thus seeking to benefit from legal aid and the concept of equality of arms must be willing to act in conformity with legitimate requirements designed to preserve the integrity of the proceedings.

4.1. ELIGIBILITY FOR LEGAL AID

The Article 6(3)(c) entitlement to access state-funded legal services to secure equality of arms is confined to accused persons able to fulfil financial and interests of justice criterions, the Strasbourg interpretations of which thus hold crucial importance.

---

56 Three models predominate: i) judicare model: delivery by private practitioners paid by the case; ii) staff model: delivery by salaried practitioners employed directly by the legal aid authority; iii) contract model: delivery by individual practitioners or firms/organisations under contract with the legal aid authority. These models may also be applied in combination to create a model involving both state salaried and private practitioners.

The advantages and disadvantages of each model are considered in Scottish Office Home Department, 'A Literature Review of Public Defender or Staff Lawyer Schemes' (Legal Studies Research Findings No 19, 1998) <http://www.gov.scot/Publications/1998/12/39b894a7-b729-4715-901f-033fc34767a6>; MJ Trebilcock and RJ Daniels, *Rule of Law Reform and Development: Charting the Fragile Path of Progress* (Edward Elgar, Cheltenham 2008) 243–246.

57 See further *M v UK* (App 9728/82) (1983) 36 DR 155, 158: 'financial restraints may be necessary to ensure the most cost-effective use of the funds available for legal aid'.

58 *Lloyd and others v UK* (App 29798/96 et seq) ECHR 1 March 2005 [141]–[142]. Two applicants therein were under 21.

59 *X v UK* (App 8386/78) (1980) 21 DR 126, 130. Neither can one insist that counsel act without regard for his professional opinion: *X v Switzerland* (App 9127/80) (1981) 26 DR 238, 240: 'the Convention does not entitle the accused to require his lawyer to adopt a particular defence strategy which the latter regards as impossible to maintain especially if the accused is given the opportunity to address the court himself.'

60 *X* 1980 (n 59) 130. The Commission considered that the accused was, nevertheless, offered every assistance and advice for the conduct of his own defence after the withdrawal of counsel (131).

4.1.1. *Financial Criterion*

The grant of legal aid is first dependent upon whether the accused is at the material time of insufficient means to retain counsel.[61] The issue is not one that has encountered extensive deliberation by the Court, which has left 'sufficient means' undefined and avoided ruling on the resources and thresholds pertaining to means testing, hence affording states a wide margin of appreciation.

The Court has, nevertheless, provided some useful guidance on the matter. It is discernible from *Pakelli* that the applicant bears the burden of proving indigence,[62] though the standard of proof is not one of 'beyond all doubt' but that of 'some indications' that such is the case.[63] The indications of indigence therein that satisfied the financial criterion were that the applicant had been in custody for two years preceding the case; he supplied the Commission with an uncontested and officially confirmed declaration of means, for which it granted legal aid; and he offered to prove his indigence before the Federal Court.[64] Reliance upon indications as adequate confirmation of indigence was also evidenced in *Twalib v Greece* where the Court referred to the fact that the applicant was represented in trial and appeal proceedings by lawyers who were either court-appointed or supplied by a humanitarian organisation; he had been in prison for over three years at the time of lodging his appeal; he had made enquiries about the availability of legal aid; and the Commission granted him legal aid in the proceedings before it.[65] The approach is further consistent with *RD v Poland* where the indications of an undue denial of legal aid for an intended cassation appeal were that legal aid was earlier granted in the appellate proceedings and there was no improvement thereafter in the applicant's financial situation.[66]

Pragmatism appears to underpin the Court's resort to indications of indigence in these cases. This is a reasonable response having regard to state failure to conduct a proper and reasoned assessment of means, and considering that conclusive proof of indigence at the material time cannot be expected of the applicant when significant time has transpired between the domestic and Strasbourg proceedings.[67] States should thus carry out a proper and reasoned

---

61 See further S Duke, 'The Right to Appointed Counsel: *Argersinger* and Beyond' (1975) 12 Am Crim L Rev 601, 626 for an argument, on the basis of principle (but not in the context and on the basis of the ECHR), that all accused persons should possibly be offered free defence counsel.

62 See further *Croissant v Germany* (App 13611/88) (1992) Series A no 237-B [37]: 'the burden of proving a lack of sufficient means should be borne by the person who pleads it.'

63 *Pakelli* (n 1) [34].

64 Ibid.

65 *Twalib* (n 9) [49], [51].

66 (Apps 29692/96; 34612/97) ECHR 18 December 2001 [46].

67 Ibid; *Pakelli* (n 1) [33]–[34]; *Twalib* (n 9) [51], [56].

assessment whenever the accused's financial situation is at issue. The same was reinforced in the civil context of *Kreuz v Poland* where the applicant's financial standing was relevant to his Article 6(1) right of access to a court and the fact that he had been subject to an assumption rather than evidence based means assessment contributed to a breach thereof.[68]

Official confirmation of indigence raises the accompanying issue of whether the 'free' aspect of legal assistance affords the accused a definitive or merely provisional or partial exemption from liability for the costs incurred in his defence. The term 'free' is also employed in Article 6(3)(e) in relation to interpreter assistance. Within the context of this provision, the Court in *Luedicke, Belkacem and Koç v Germany* interpreted the term to denote 'a once and for all exemption or exoneration.'[69] However, it emphasised that its intention was not to establish such an interpretation for Article 6(3)(c), a provision it was not called upon to evaluate.[70] Crucially, this article is distinguishable from Article 6(3)(e) because its grant of legal aid is conditional upon the accused being of insufficient means, hence exposing itself to an alternative textually valid interpretation. The Commission thus held it compatible with Article 6(3)(c) to interpret 'free' to mean 'a mere temporary exemption from costs' which could after final and binding conviction be withdrawn, and an order for reimbursement issued, if the accused no longer remains of insufficient financial standing.[71] It is not only provisional but also partial exemptions from costs that are compatible with the same. Partial exemptions require the legally aided accused to contribute as far as his means reasonably allow towards the anticipated or incurred defence costs. The Court in *Morris v UK* accordingly considered that an offer of legal aid subject to a down-payment commensurate with the accused's income was neither arbitrary nor unreasonable.[72]

The Strasbourg authorities' interpretation of 'free' as non-definitive has attracted the criticism that an indigent accused may be inappropriately inclined to limit or forgo the use of counsel in order to mitigate or avoid potential liability for legal aid expenses.[73] It is difficult to lend significant weight to this criticism. The accused understands that he will bear the burden of compliance with contribution or reimbursement orders only if he is or becomes on proper and reasoned assessment capable financially of doing so, hence the burden is not in principle unreasonable, unsustainable or disproportionate. He would also wish

---

68 (App 28249/95) ECHR 2001-VI [63]–[64], [67].

69 (Apps 6210/73; 6877/75; 7132/75) (1978) Series A no 29 [40], [46].

70 Ibid [44].

71 *X v Germany* (App 9365/81) (1982) 28 DR 229, 231; *Croissant v Germany* (App 13611/88) EComHR Report 7 March 1991 [36], [38].

72 (App 38784/97) ECHR 2002-I [89], [93].

73 Eg *Croissant* (n 71) [32]; D Harris and others, *Harris, O'Boyle and Warbrick: Law of the European Convention on Human Rights* (3rd edn OUP, Oxford 2014) 479. The same concern was raised within the context of interpreters and costs in *Luedicke, Belkacem and Koç* (n 69) [42].

for his case to be represented in the most effective manner possible and for the integrity of the proceedings to be protected. These factors render it unlikely that an indigent accused aspiring to the full benefit of legal aid provision would in practice feel discouraged sufficiently from exercising his entitlement thereto and jeopardise his defence. Costs orders imposed with proper regard to the financial situation of the accused thus in principle themselves neither deprive the accused of a practicable opportunity for legal assistance nor in turn impact negatively on equality of arms. Orders such issued are indeed a prudent measure for their capacity to ensure that those who are subject to them both benefit from and replace legal aid funds. Such funds are limited and their replacement contributes to the delivery of sustainable legal aid schemes.

4.1.2. Interests of Justice Criterion

Upon satisfaction of the means criterion, the grant of legal aid is subject to whether the circumstances of the case are such that it is required in the interests of justice. This merits criterion is to be applied without regard for instances of public disapproval of their funds benefiting an unpopular accused, who remains entitled to 'a realistic chance to defend himself throughout the entire trial.'[74] Since the purpose for which legal aid is given is to help effect equality of arms, the Court's application of the interests of justice criterion amounts essentially to an assessment of the underlying question of whether the absence of legal assistance, having regard to the entirety of the proceedings, occasioned an inequality of arms. The accused will not, in principle, be placed necessarily in a position of disadvantage vis-à-vis the prosecution if an adequate representation of the defence case can be achieved without counsel.

Consideration of the role of prejudice for the purpose of the aforementioned assessment was provided in *Artico v Italy*.[75] The indigent applicant therein was unrepresented before the Court of Cassation but the Government contended that this did not contravene the interests of justice as prejudice had not arisen. The European Court was of the view that requiring proof of prejudice arising from a lack of assistance was impracticable.[76] It could not, for instance, be proven indubitably that a defence counsel would have pleaded statutory limitation – a crucial issue hardly touched upon by the applicant in his submissions to the Court of Cassation – and been successful.[77] Consequently, the Court considered that the interests of justice criterion could be met merely by demonstrating that it appears 'plausible' in the circumstances that the assistance of a lawyer would have added to the effectiveness of the accused's defence, which had

74 *RD* (n 66) [49].
75 (App 6694/74) (1980) Series A no 37.
76 Ibid [35].
77 Ibid [34]–[35].

been demonstrated in the case and resulted in a finding of a breach of Article 6(3)(c).[78] In effect, therefore, prejudice is intrinsic to the absence of legal aid when it appears plausible on the facts that counsel was required in the interests of justice (inevitable prejudice). This progressive approach deserves merit for its contribution to creating a real opportunity for an indigent accused to fulfil the interests of justice criterion; an opportunity which would otherwise be illusory were it susceptible to frustration by an impracticable requirement of proving prejudice. Indeed, rather than requiring proof, it is a self-evident truth that the non-provision to the accused of necessary legal assistance will create a disadvantage vis-à-vis the prosecution pervading all aspects of the proceedings. The absence of this assistance in *Artico* deprived the accused of an opportunity, which was available to the prosecution, to put his case adequately to the court because an adequate representation of the defence would have required certain acts[79] only a lawyer would or could plausibly have done. Accordingly, in holding that legal assistance was required in the interests of justice, the Court was simultaneously but implicitly declaring an inequality of arms without attaching a requirement of proving prejudice; inevitable prejudice was sufficient.

4.1.2.1. Key Assessment Factors

Certain key factors are to be taken into consideration in deciding whether the interests of justice 'plausibly' necessitated free legal assistance in a particular case. The Court has certainly been more inclined than the former Commission, which relied heavily upon state discretion,[80] to conduct its own effective assessment of the issue.[81] States would thus be wise in cases where doubt arises as to whether counsel is required to ensure that it falls to be resolved in favour of the accused. They certainly cannot rely upon appointing counsel at appeal to cure the lack thereof at first instance where the scope of review at appeal precludes a redetermination of all disputed questions of

78 Ibid [34]–[35], [37]. This approach is also evident in *Biondo v Italy* (App 8821/79) (1983) 64 DR 5 [46], [49], [51].

79 *Artico* (n 75) [34]: 'A qualified lawyer would have been able to … give the requisite emphasis to the crucial issue of statutory limitation which had hardly been touched on … In addition, only a lawyer could have countered the pleadings of the public prosecutor's department by causing the Court of Cassation to hold a public hearing devoted … to a thorough discussion of this issue.'

80 Eg *X v Germany* (App 599/59) (1961) 8 CD 12, 18; *X v UK* (App 5871/72) (1974) 1 DR 54, 54–55; *Bell v UK* (App 12322/86) EComHR 13 October 1987 [1] ('The Law'): 'The evaluation of the requirements of the interests of justice under Article 6 para. 3(c) … lies in the first place with the domestic courts'; *Drummond v UK* (App 12917/87) EComHR 9 December 1987 [1] ('The Law').

81 An especially apt example of which is *Quaranta v Switzerland* (App 12744/87) (1991) Series A no 205 [31]–[38]: Though the Court viewed the factors relied upon by the Government to refuse legal aid as relevant, it applied them with its own assessment on the facts and found Art 6(3)(c) to have been infringed.

fact and law.[82] Whereas a Strasbourg presumption in favour of the grant of legal aid would be desirable in view of the positive contribution professional expertise can offer towards securing equality of arms,[83] it does not exist. The Court has principal regard to three factors: the severity of the sentence risked; case complexity; and the competence of the accused to defend himself.[84] It is submitted that the Court has rightly focussed on these particular factors, for they have the capacity to provide the most persuasive arguments for granting legal assistance in the interest of preserving equality of arms. After all, 'it will not be sufficient to argue that equality is automatically absent where … the state is legally represented and the accused is not'.[85] Each factor is in itself capable of revealing an imbalance between the capacities of the unrepresented accused and the prosecution to present adequately their cases and thus rendering unjustified the refusal of legal assistance.[86] Nevertheless, the Court will reinforce its conclusion drawn from one factor that legal assistance was necessary with additional reference to the remaining factors whenever the facts of the case allow.[87] Alternatively, it will confirm that the interests of justice called for legal aid only once all applicable factors have been referred to.[88]

(A) Severity of potential punishment

Marked account is taken of the severity of the possible penalty at stake for the accused,[89] which corresponds naturally to the seriousness of the offence. A defence is adequate only if the quality of its presentation reflects appropriately

82 Ibid [37].

83 Stavros (n 32) 214.

84 Whereas these factors relate principally to the interests of the accused, it has been suggested that an additional factor may be whether the case raises a wider issue of public interest: JES Fawcett, *The Application of the European Convention on Human Rights* (Clarendon, Oxford 1987) 192; P van Dijk and M Viering, 'Right to a Fair and Public Hearing (Article 6)' in P van Dijk and others (eds), *Theory and Practice of the European Convention on Human Rights* (4th edn Intersentia, Antwerp 2006) 643; D Harris and others, *Harris, O'Boyle and Warbrick: Law of the European Convention on Human Rights* (2nd edn OUP, Oxford 2009) 318 fn 1134 cite *Pakelli* (n 1) [37] in support as regard was had by the Court to the value of the case 'for the development of case-law.'

85 P Plowden and K Kerrigan, *Advocacy and Human Rights: Using the Convention in Courts and Tribunals* (Cavendish, London 2002) 259.

86 Eg *Quaranta* (n 81) [33]; *Boner v UK* (App 18711/91) (1994) Series A no 300-B [41]; *Twalib* (n 9) [52]; *Shulepov* (n 20) [34]; *Shilbergs v Russia* (App 20075/03) ECHR 17 December 2009 [122].

87 Eg *Quaranta* (n 81) [33]–[36], [38]; *Twalib* (n 9) [52]–[54]; *Shilbergs* (n 86) [122].

88 Eg *Granger* (n 9) [47]–[48]; *Benham v UK* (App 19380/92) ECHR 1996-III [61]–[62], [64]; *Perks and others v UK* (App 25277/94 et seq) ECHR 12 October 1999 [76]; *Gutfreund v France* (App 45681/99) ECHR 2003-VII [33]–[34], [40].

89 Eg *Quaranta* (n 81) [33]; *Boner* (n 86) [41], [44]; *Maxwell v UK* (App 18949/91) (1994) Series A no 300-C [38], [41]; *Benham* (n 88) [61], [64]; *Twalib* (n 9) [52]; *Perks and others* (n 88) [76]; *Gutfreund* (n 88) [33]–[34], [40]; *Lloyd and others* (n 58) [138]; *Shulepov* (n 20) [34].

the seriousness of the charge and the severity of the potential punishment. An adequate defence to a modest charge and possible penalty is achievable without counsel.[90] However, the more serious the offence and severe the possible repercussions, the greater the need for professional expertise and experience capable of counterbalancing the prosecution effort and securing equality of arms. When assessing severity of penalty, the Court evidenced in *Quaranta v Switzerland* that it will rely upon the maximum sentence imposable theoretically (three years' imprisonment) rather than upon a subjective state assessment of the likely sentence on the facts (imprisonment not exceeding 18 months).[91] Legal assistance was held warranted.[92] The approach is essentially one of disregard for state discretion in favour of protecting the accused from possible misjudgement as to likely penalty and consequent denial of legal assistance. Though the approach is favourable from a dignitarian stance, it is difficult not to be sympathetic to Trechsel's view that it is unduly strict on states: 'The Convention rights are meant to be practical, not theoretical; this does not only work for the applicant but also for the domestic authorities.'[93] It is, of course, the severity of the imposed rather than possible sentence that is to be considered where appeals are concerned.[94] Significantly, it was asserted in *Benham v UK* and thereafter consistently that 'where deprivation of liberty is at stake, the interests of justice in principle call for legal representation.'[95] Deprivation of liberty, for the purposes of this general principle, refers to real imprisonment and not to other penalties restricting liberty, such as community service or curfew orders,

---

90 See further *Hinds v Attorney-General of Barbados* [2001] UKPC 56; [2002] 1 AC 854 [17] (Lord Bingham): 'There will be very many cases ... which may be fairly heard without representation of the defendant. The less serious the charge, the more straightforward the facts and the more modest the potential penalty, the likelier this is to be true.'

91 *Quaranta* (n 81) [33].

92 Ibid [33], [38].

93 Trechsel (n 24) 274.

94 Eg *Boner* (n 86) [41]; *Maxwell* (n 89) [38]; *Shilbergs* (n 86) [122].

95 *Benham* (n 88) [61]. See eg *Hooper v UK* (App 42317/98) ECHR 16 November 2004 [20]; *Lloyd and others* (n 58) [134]; *Beet and others v UK* (App 47676/99 et seq) ECHR 1 March 2005 [38]; *Shabelnik v Ukraine* (App 16404/03) ECHR 19 February 2009 [58]; *Mikhaylova v Russia* (App 46998/08) ECHR 19 November 2015 [82].

The HRC also applies this approach to ICCPR Art 14(3)(d) cases involving capital sentences: eg *Frank Robinson v Jamaica* (Comm 223/1987) UN Doc CCPR/C/35/D/223/1987 (1989) [10.3]; *Carlton Reid v Jamaica* (Comm 250/1987) UN Doc CCPR/C/39/D/250/1987 (1990) [11.4]; *Henry v Jamaica* (Comm 230/1987) UN Doc CCPR/C/43/D/230/1987 (1991) [8.3]; *Campbell v Jamaica* (Comm 248/1987) UN Doc CCPR/C/44/D/248/1987 (1992) [6.6]; *Wright v Jamaica* (Comm 459/1991) UN Doc CCPR/C/55/D/459/1991 (1995) [10.2]; *Robinson LaVende v Trinidad and Tobago* (Comm 554/1993) UN Doc CCPR/C/61/D/554/1993 (1997) [5.8]; *Abdool Saleem Yasseen and Noel Thomas v Republic of Guyana* (Comm 676/1996) UN Doc CCPR/C/62/D/676/1996 (1998) [7.8]; *Devon Simpson v Jamaica* (Comm 695/1996) UN Doc CCPR/C/73/D/695/1996 (2001) [7.3]; *Oral Hendricks v Guyana* (Comm 838/1998) UN Doc CCPR/C/76/D/838/1998 (2002) [6.4]. See also HRC, 'General Comment No 32: Article 14: Right to Equality before Courts and Tribunals and to Fair Trial' (2007) UN Doc CCPR/C/GC/32 [38].

or to a suspended sentence of imprisonment. Legal aid is not just called for only in cases where actual imprisonment is possible. In *Pham Hoang v France*, it was the imposition of a substantial financial penalty (joint and several liability for FRF 5,670,000) that contributed to the conclusion that counsel was required in the interests of justice.[96] In contrast, the same was not found in *Y v Germany* and *Gutfreund v France*, for they involved minor offences and small fines of DM 160 and FRF 5,000 respectively.[97] As 'severity' of possible punishment is crucial, it is submitted that the Court would do well to be mindful of whether such punishment is also likely to lead to loss of livelihood or serious damage to reputation, both of which could be regarded as of sufficient severity to justify legal assistance.[98]

(b) Case complexity

The Court is, nonetheless, minded to consider the degree of factual, legal and evidential complexity in a particular case during its evaluation of whether legal aid was called for.[99] The appropriate handling of a case demands a level of competence commensurate with its complexity. Unrepresented accused persons facing simple and accessible procedures will not be much cause for concern.[100] The more complex the case, however, the less competent the accused is reasonably expected to be in handling it in a manner conducive to an effective defence. Accordingly, an accused involved in a case entailing complexities beyond his competence requires legal assistance to prevent an advantage being afforded to the prosecution, which has a right of representation, and to thus preserve equality of arms. The Court observed in *Benham* that the applicant ought to have benefited from legal assistance as the applicable legal test had proven difficult to understand and operate.[101] It also viewed such assistance as necessary in *Shilbergs v Russia* given that the applicant could not competently address several legal issues of 'particular complexity' arising therein, involving, for example, determination of the constituent elements of several aggravated offences and assessment of the degree of individual liability

96 (App 13191/87) (1992) Series A no 243 [40]–[41].

97 (App 11777/85) EComHR 13 October 1986 ('The Law'); *Gutfreund* (n 88) [33]–[34], [40]. See further an example of the same before the HRC: *Lindon v Australia* (Comm 646/1995) UN Doc CCPR/C/64/D/646/1995 (1998) [6.5].

98 These elements are considered relevant to the interests of justice in Legal Aid, Sentencing and Punishment of Offenders Act 2012 (UK) (LASPO) s 17(2)(a).

99 Eg *Granger* (n 9) [47]; *Quaranta* (n 81) [34]–[35]; *Pham Hoang* (n 96) [40]; *Benham* (n 88) [62], [64]; *Twalib* (n 9) [53]; *Perks and others* (n 88) [76]; *Gutfreund* (n 88) [33]–[34], [40]; *Shilbergs* (n 86) [122]. See further *X* 1980 (n 59) 130: 'the right to counsel, especially in a complex criminal trial, must normally be considered an essential ingredient of a fair trial.'

100 Eg *Gutfreund* (n 88) [33].

101 *Benham* (n 88) [62], [64].

of several co-defendants, hence he was unable to defend himself effectively.[102] Even when a legal issue is not particularly complex, but is complex enough to render an accused unable competently to address it, *Boner v UK* and *Maxwell v UK* make evident that legal aid is still warranted.[103] Interestingly, these cases also indicate that it should not be a concern of the legal aid decision that the accused's prospects of success at appeal are little or none.[104] The decision must rest simply on whether the preservation of equality of arms in the particular case requires legal assistance.

Further guidance can also be offered. Cases raising human rights arguments are generally of sufficient complexity to merit legal assistance.[105] In *Pham Hoang*, the accused sought to challenge before the Court of Cassation the compatibility of customs legislation with Articles 6(1) and 6(2). In the eyes of the European Court, the presentation and development of arguments on such a complex matter could only be undertaken by experienced counsel, the absence of whom thus infringed Article 6(3)(c).[106] The accused in *Twalib* similarly sought to challenge at cassation level the fairness of earlier proceedings and the Court observed that the preparation of a notice of appeal required the knowledge, skills and experience of a legal practitioner.[107] It noted, additionally, that the domestic requirement that parties be represented in cassation proceedings also confirmed the complexity of the case.[108] A case could further be considered complex to a degree beyond the competence of the accused where it requires the tracing of witnesses or the expert handling of witnesses in court.[109] Occasion may also arise where a case reveals itself at a later stage to be more complicated than reasonably anticipated at the time of the legal aid refusal decision. If such a situation were permitted to stand, the unassisted accused could be placed in a disadvantageous position. Fortunately, in such circumstances, the Court maintained in *Granger v UK* that states must make available a mechanism to have the refusal reconsidered.[110] This review requirement must be applicable equally to any relevant change in the circumstances under which legal aid was refused.

---

102 *Shilbergs* (n 86) [122]–[124].

103 *Boner* (n 86) [41], [44]; *Maxwell* (n 89) [38], [41].

104 Ibid respectively [40]–[41]; [37]–[38].

105 Plowden and Kerrigan (n 85) 261.

106 *Pham Hoang* (n 96) [40]–[41].

107 *Twalib* (n 9) [53]–[54].

108 Ibid [53].

109 See further LASPO s 17(2)(d) in which the interests of justice require account to be taken of 'whether the proceedings may involve the tracing, interviewing or expert cross-examination of witnesses'.

110 *Granger* (n 9) [47].

(c) Competence of accused to defend himself

Cognisance is further taken of the contribution the accused was capable of making without counsel to the presentation of his defence, a factor that sometimes overlaps with that of case complexity.[111] An accused capable of providing an adequate representation of his case will not require counsel in order to be placed on an equal footing with the prosecution.[112] However, the personal circumstances of an accused may provide cogent reason to believe that were he unrepresented, he would be incapable of mounting an effective defence, and the expertise and representation of the prosecution would deny equality of arms between the parties. Personal circumstances of relevance include mental or physical impairment. It was thus held in *Timergaliyev v Russia* that as the accused's hearing impairment undermined his capacity for effective participation in the proceedings, the interests of justice called for legal representation before the appeal court.[113] Legal assistance was also held warranted at the trial stage in *Prežec v Croatia*, in which the accused suffered from a severe mental illness.[114] In the absence of mental or physical impairment, it may simply be that the accused requires legal assistance because he lacks the aptitude to understand sufficiently the proceedings or state his case. The Court in *Twalib*, for instance, had regard to the accused being a foreigner unfamiliar with the Greek language and legal system who was unable to indicate any grounds of appeal in his written appeal notice.[115] In *Quaranta*, the Court appeared to indicate that it could not expect an underprivileged young adult of foreign origin, with repeated involvement in criminality and drug use, and lacking real occupational training, to present an adequate defence to the serious charge faced.[116] Even when submissions are prepared on behalf of an accused, he may lack the aptitude to develop the arguments raised therein when acting alone.[117] Such was the case in *Granger* where a solicitor without rights of audience prepared for the accused statements to read out concerning his grounds of appeal. The Court considered that the accused was unable to comprehend fully these statements or the opposing arguments and would not, had occasion arisen, have been capable of responding to such arguments or to judicial questioning.[118]

---

111 Eg ibid; *Quaranta* (n 81) [35]; *Pham Hoang* (n 96) [40]; *Twalib* (n 9) [53]; *Vaudelle v France* (App 35683/97) ECHR 2001-I [58], [60]–[61]; *Timergaliyev v Russia* (App 40631/02) ECHR 14 October 2008 [59]; *Prežec v Croatia* (App 48185/07) ECHR 15 October 2009 [29]; *Shilbergs* (n 86) [122].

112 Eg *X v Germany* (App 7300/75) (1976) 2 Digest 857; *X v Norway* (App 8202/78) (1979) 2 Digest 857.

113 *Timergaliyev* (n 111) [59]–[60].

114 *Prežec* (n 111) [29], [32]. See also the relevance of mental condition in *Vaudelle* (n 111) [58], [60]–[61].

115 *Twalib* (n 9) [53]–[54].

116 *Quaranta* (n 81) [35], [38].

117 Eg *Pham Hoang* (n 96) [40]–[41]; *Shilbergs* (n 86) [122], [124].

118 *Granger* (n 9) [47]–[48].

4.2. CHOICE AND CONSULTATION IN THE APPOINTMENT OF COUNSEL

The state obligation to deliver legally aided assistance to an eligible accused does not include a condition that he be entitled to exercise the same power of choice in the appointment of counsel as that attached to the right to privately retained counsel. The Court was unequivocal in its view in *Franquesa Freixas v Spain* that Article 6(3)(c) 'does not guarantee the right to choose an official defence counsel who is appointed by the court, nor does it guarantee a right to be consulted with regard to the choice of an official defence counsel.'[119] This is consistent with the settled view of the Commission.[120] There exist three cases, however, that prima facie invite an alternative interpretation of the article, the Court pronouncing in each one that the accused 'must be able to have recourse to legal assistance of his own choosing; if he does not have sufficient means to pay for such assistance, he is entitled ... to be given it free when the interests of justice so require.'[121] The legal aid limb herein could on one textual interpretation be viewed as sharing the choice element of the previous limb ('such assistance'), thus conferring a right to choose counsel upon the legally aided.[122] Nevertheless, these cases lend no further weight to this interpretation in their subsequent legal and factual analysis as choice in the selection of legal aid counsel was never at issue. In the absence of the Court making a clear and direct connection in each case between choice and legal aid, a right of choice for the indigent accused remains insufficiently substantiated.[123]

---

119 (App 53590/99) ECHR 2000-XI [1] ('The Law').

120 Eg *X v Germany* (App 6946/75) (1976) 6 DR 114, 116–117; *F* (n 5) 175; *Bazil v UK* (App 14385/88) EComHR 10 March 1989 [1] ('The Law'). Other cases also deny the existence of a right to choose but without an accompanying comment concerning a right of consultation: eg *X* 1960 (n 25) 276, 278; *X* 1970 (n 25) 82; *M* (n 57) 158; *K v Denmark* (App 19524/92) EComHR 5 May 1993 [2] ('The Law').

121 *Pakelli* (n 1) [31]; *Frommelt v Liechtenstein* (App 49158/99) ECHR 2003-VII [2] ('The Law') (slight difference in wording); *Balliu v Albania* (App 74727/01) ECHR 16 June 2005 [32].

122 P van Dijk and GJH van Hoof, *Theory and Practice of the European Convention on Human Rights* (3rd edn Kluwer Law International, The Hague 1998) 468, 471; Trechsel (n 24) 277.

123 See further the rejection of a right to choose legal aid counsel at a broader international level: eg HRC: *Wright* (n 95) [10.5]: 'article 14, paragraph 3(d), does not entitle the accused to choose counsel provided to him free of charge'; *Hezekiah Price v Jamaica* (Comm 572/1994) UN Doc CCPR/C/58/D/572/1994 (1996) [9.2].

Amnesty International, 'International Criminal Tribunal for Rwanda: Trials and Tribulations' (Report) (31 March 1998) AI-Index IOR 40/003/1998 38: 'international law does not guarantee the accused the right to choose defence counsel where they are indigent'.

International Criminal Tribunal for Rwanda: *Prosecutor v Kambanda* (Judgement) (Appeals Chamber) ICTR-97-23-A (19 October 2000) [33]; *Prosecutor v Akayesu* (Judgement) (Appeals Chamber) ICTR-96-4-A (1 June 2001) [61]: 'in principle, the right to free legal assistance of counsel does not confer the right to counsel of one's own choosing. The right to choose counsel applies only to those accused who can financially bear the costs of counsel.'

The reading of this right into Article 6(3)(c) would, nonetheless, be desirable on two levels. First, the values of the concept of equality of arms would be better reinforced. The dignitarian quality of a right to choose is evidenced in its respect for the independent will and reason of the accused. Additionally, accuracy of outcome is more achievable when defence representation is effective. The prospect of effective representation is increased when a relationship of trust exists between client and counsel; a relationship that is more probable when counsel is actually chosen by his client. In view of this context, the legitimacy of counsel appointment processes, as an issue of good governance, could be strengthened in the eyes of the public were choice a feature thereof. On a second level, a right of choice would create greater parity between those retaining private counsel, for whom choice is available, and the indigent. This right could be conferred upon indigent defendants through a less restrictive, though still textually valid, interpretation of Article 6(3)(c) in the manner proffered by Stavros: 'the word "it" in the third clause could be read as referring to "legal assistance of his own choosing", as guaranteed in the second clause ..., and not to "legal assistance" ... mentioned in the clause setting the conditions for the third right.'[124] A proposed right of choice for indigent defendants should necessarily be capable of reasonable restriction to overcome justifiable qualification, availability, number of counsel and ethical concerns – concerns which featured in the above discussion on privately retained counsel. Where the accused is detained in custody without a particular counsel in mind, he should be offered an opportunity to choose counsel from a supplied list of those who have expressed their availability to attend detainees. Irrespective of whether the accused is in custody or at liberty, if he is incapable manifestly of making a meaningful choice of counsel, perhaps by reason of insufficient age or mental competence, or simply fails to make a choice within proper time constraints, the selection decision should be one for the legal aid authority.

Whereas a right of choice has evaded the indigent accused, states do not appear to be entitled arbitrarily to exclude him altogether from the process of selecting counsel. The Court seems to recognise that securing a relationship of confidence between client and counsel requires that the accused be allowed at least to exercise a qualified influence over the appointment of his representative. With the exception of *Franquesa Freixas* above, the Court has asserted recurrently that '[w]hen appointing defence counsel the national courts must certainly have regard to the defendant's wishes ... However, they can override those wishes when there are relevant and sufficient grounds for holding that this is necessary in the interests of justice.'[125] 'Interests of

124 Stavros (n 32) 215 fn 678.

125 *Croissant* (n 62) [29]. See also *Kitov v Denmark* (App 29759/96) ECHR 16 March 1999 [2(c)] ('The Law'); *Lagerblom* (n 22) [54]; *Mayzit* (n 33) [66]; *Mironov v Russia* (App 22625/02) ECHR 5 October 2006 [5(b)(2)] ('The Law'); *Vozhigov* (n 22) [41].

justice' in this context can encompass, inter alia, concerns over the availability of proposed counsel, the adequacy of his experience and qualifications to handle the matter, and the financial[126] or ethical[127] repercussions of such an appointment. Where the necessity of the appointment of more than one counsel is at issue, 'a court should pay heed to the accused's views as to the number needed', but those views are also capable of being overridden by 'relevant and sufficient justification.'[128] These statements of respect for the views and wishes of the accused attest to a requirement of consultation in the appointment of counsel.

Whilst this requirement contributes to strengthening the values of the concept of equality of arms if one follows, *mutatis mutandis*, the same reasoning applied to the above-mentioned link between this concept and a right of choice, it does so to a lesser extent than would the latter. This is because choice, in principle, curtails the capacity of the appointing authority to interfere with the will of the accused to a stronger extent than consultation. An accused permitted to choose counsel bears greater individual responsibility for the appointment than one who is merely consulted. Considering that individual autonomy and responsibility are conditions of human dignity,[129] a right of choice is more dignitarian in design than being consulted. It also follows that the broader scope for interference with the will of the accused in the requirement of consultation creates a lesser likelihood of his preferred counsel being appointed than would be the case had a right of choice instead been available. The latter right is consequently more conducive to ensuring a relationship of full confidence between client and counsel for effective representation, which in turn contributes to achieving an accurate outcome. Confidence in the relationship is additionally important because once counsel is appointed, Article 6(3)(c) does not secure a right to have him replaced.[130] Given the value attributed herein to a right of choice over a requirement of consultation, a counsel selection process involving the former could raise the overall legitimacy of the trial procedure to a higher standard than the latter. A right of choice should, therefore, be preferred to consultation having regard to its superior contribution to furthering the fundamental values of the concept of equality of arms.

---

126 *Lagerblom* (n 22) [59]: 'the general desirability of limiting the total costs of legal aid'.

127 Eg *Croissant* (n 62) [30]: 'a possible conflict of interests'.

128 Ibid [27]–[28], [30]. The appointment of a third counsel against the wishes of the accused was held justified on the grounds of ensuring that his trial proceeded without interruptions or adjournments, and that he would be adequately represented throughout the trial, considering its anticipated length and the size and complexity of the case.

129 O Schachter, 'Human Dignity as a Normative Concept' (1983) 77 AJIL 848, 851.

130 *Östergren v Sweden* (App 13572/88) (1991) 69 DR 198, 204; *Lagerblom* (n 22) [55].

5. IMPOSED LEGAL ASSISTANCE

Some accused wish to forgo available legal assistance in favour of appearing pro se.[131] An issue arising therefrom is whether states are permitted to dismiss such a preference in certain cases and insist instead on the engagement of counsel on the ground that it is in the interests of the accused. The issue may be viewed from two dignitarian standpoints. Non-interference with the desire of the accused for self-representation is dignitarian in its respect for the individual's autonomy of choice in the method by which he makes his defence. Yet, a mandatory requirement of counsel is also dignitarian, for the interests of the accused are represented and protected with a professional level of competence. Without assistance, the ability of the accused to participate effectively in the proceedings may be compromised to such an extent that he finds himself in a position of inequality of arms.

It appears that the position adopted at Strasbourg is that the Article 6(3)(c) right to a pro se defence is not absolute and the wishes of the accused can consequently be overridden.[132] The Commission ruled on a number of occasions that the accused does not under this provision have 'the right to decide himself in what manner his defence should be assured.'[133] It thus follows that 'a requirement to be represented by a lawyer in proceedings before a higher court is not incompatible with Article 6'.[134] The Court has held the same for first instance proceedings[135] and formulated the following general principle: 'A legal requirement that an accused be assisted by counsel in criminal proceedings cannot be deemed incompatible with the Convention.'[136]

---

131 Several possible rationales exist: eg an accused ineligible for legal aid may be unwilling to instruct private counsel as he wishes to avoid representation fees either in themselves or because of little or negligible prospects of acquittal; he may seek to establish a strong personal rapport with a jury and appeal to their natural sympathy; JF Decker, 'The Sixth Amendment Right to Shoot Oneself in the Foot: An Assessment of the Guarantee of Self-Representation Twenty Years after *Faretta*' (1996) 6 Seton Hall Const LJ 483, 485–487: 'Some defendants may proceed pro se to symbolize their lack of respect for any kind of authority, such as that of the courts, or because they are unable to get their way and so represent themselves as an act of defiance … Other criminal defendants may be cleverly manipulating the criminal justice system for their own secret agenda … On the other hand, while some pro se defendants may not harbor a hidden motive behind the request, … they believe they can do it all themselves'; EJ Hashimoto, 'Defending the Right of Self-Representation: An Empirical Look at the Pro Se Felony Defendant' (2007) 85 NC L Rev 423, 463: 'dissatisfaction with, or distrust of, lawyers.'

132 The same approach has been applied to ICCPR Art 14(3)(d): HRC (n 95) [37].

133 Eg *X* (n 13) 35; *X v Norway* (App 5923/72) (1975) 3 DR 43, 44; *X v Austria* (App 7138/75) (1977) 9 DR 50, 52; *X* 1978 (n 7) 244.

134 *Philis v Greece* (App 16598/90) EComHR 11 December 1990 [1] ('The Law').

135 *Croissant* (n 62) [27].

136 *Lagerblom* (n 22) [50]. The accused may be liable to pay the fees of imposed counsel: eg *Croissant* (n 62) [28], [36]; *Pfister v Germany* (App 19512/92) EComHR 7 September 1993 ('The Law').

The Court's position was elaborated further in *Correia de Matos v Portugal*.[137] It viewed states as enjoying a margin of appreciation in their determination of whether to allow self-representation or impose legal assistance in a particular case.[138] It considered that the legitimate imposition of legal assistance at certain stages of the proceedings requires states to invoke sufficient and relevant reasons to justify the measure as being in the interests of justice.[139] The accused is thus rightly safeguarded from arbitrary interference with his right to self-representation. The interests of justice in the case included ensuring the proper defence of the interests of the accused, who, despite being a lawyer himself, was not necessarily in a position to assess the interests at stake properly and thus defend himself effectively.[140]

The Court has taken the right position. It is essential that representation be imposable when a case requires it for the realisation of equality of arms. The benefit a position of equality of arms offers to the presentation of an effective defence outweighs the benefit of allowing an accused complete freedom to choose self-representation. Such freedom of choice is indeed susceptible in some cases to uninformed or frivolous decision-making even when professional expertise is needed most. Though the focus hitherto has been on the imposition of counsel to protect defence interests, it is submitted that one should also regard such a measure as acceptable in the interests of justice on two other grounds: to prevent further obstruction, where it has already been substantial and persistent, of the proper and expeditious conduct of the case;[141] and to prevent vulnerable witnesses suffering further distress or intimidation if the accused were to question them directly.[142] Mandatory and effective representation in such circumstances is a reasonable and proportionate response.

6. PRE-TRIAL ACCESS TO AND PRIVATE COMMUNICATION WITH COUNSEL

The pre-trial phase of proceedings is often highlighted as being of crucial importance because the evidence obtained therein determines the framework in which the charge will be assessed at trial.[143] Article 6(3)(c) is applicable at this

---

137 (App 48188/99) ECHR 2001-XII.

138 Ibid s C ('The Law').

139 Ibid.

140 Ibid.

141 *Prosecutor v Slobodan Milošević* (Decision on Interlocutory Appeal of the Trial Chamber's Decision on the Assignment of Defense Counsel) (Appeals Chamber) ICTY-02-54-AR73.7 (1 November 2004) [13]; *Prosecutor v Šešelj* (Decision on Appeal Against the Trial Chamber's Decision (No 2) on Assignment of Counsel) (Appeals Chamber) ICTY-03-67-AR73.4 (8 December 2006) [19].

142 HRC (n 95) [37].

143 Eg *Can v Austria* (App 9300/81) EComHR Report 12 July 1984 [50]; *Salduz* (n 8) [54]; *Pishchalnikov* (n 15) [69]; *Eraslan and others v Turkey* (App 59653/00) ECHR 6 October

stage if and insofar as the fairness of the trial in a particular case is likely to be seriously prejudiced by an initial failure to comply therewith.[144] It is also at the pre-trial stage that the natural imbalance of power and resources between the accused and the prosecutorial machinery of the state is most pronounced. Legal assistance is intended to contribute towards mitigating this imbalance and allowing for the competent undertaking of all preparatory activities conducive to an effective defence at trial. The absence or undue restriction of such assistance is capable of occasioning a pre-trial disadvantage for the accused that bears adversely on the quality of defence presented in the ensuing proceedings and, in turn, on the correctness of the case outcome. The Strasbourg approach to pre-trial legal assistance is thus of profound importance to whether or not the defence case was presented at trial under a condition of equality of arms. The focus of the approach is directed towards the capacity of a detained accused to access counsel throughout the pre-trial stage, including during periods of questioning in particular, and confer with him in private.[145]

6.1. ACCESS TO COUNSEL AT INTERROGATION

Counsel is of great importance to an accused thrust into the psychologically intimidating atmosphere of a pre-trial interrogation into his suspected criminality. Interrogation can 'subjugate the individual to the will of his examiner'[146] and lead even the innocent to undermine their own credibility irreparably or incriminate themselves. Indeed, interrogation is 'the central investigative strategy',[147] generating evidence that is highly influential or decisive to the trial outcome, and thus is 'regarded by most informed observers

2009 [12]; *Fatma Tunç v Turkey (No 2)* (App 18532/05) ECHR 13 October 2009 [14]; *Diallo v Sweden* (App 13205/07) ECHR 5 January 2010 [24]; *Melnikov v Russia* (App 23610/03) ECHR 14 January 2010 [79]; *Pavlenko v Russia* (App 42371/02) ECHR 1 April 2010 [101].

See further JH Langbein, 'The Historical Origins of the Privilege Against Self-Incrimination at Common Law' (1994) 92 Mich L Rev 1047, 1059: 'the everyday reality is that pretrial is vastly more important than trial. The evidence gathered determines many more outcomes than how it is subsequently presented. The trial is mostly a pageant that confirms the results of the pretrial investigation'.

144 *Imbrioscia v Switzerland* (App 13972/88) (1993) Series A no 275 [36]; *John Murray v UK* (App 18731/91) ECHR 1996-I [62]; *Magee v UK* (App 28135/95) ECHR 2000-VI [41]; *Brennan v UK* (App 39846/98) ECHR 2001-X [45]; *Öcalan* (n 9) [131]; *Salduz* (n 8) [50]; *Pishchalnikov* (n 15) [65].

145 Save for the issue of representation during periods of questioning, matters of counsel visits and of privacy during consultations have sometimes been considered conjointly under Art 6(3)(c) and the 'facilities' component of Art 6(3)(b): eg *Bonzi v Switzerland* (App 7854/77) (1978) 12 DR 188, 190; *Schertenleib v Switzerland* (App 8339/78) (1979) 17 DR 205, 225–226; *Kröcher and Möller v Switzerland* (App 8463/78) (1981) 26 DR 24, 52–53; *Campbell and Fell v UK* (Apps 7819/77; 7878/77) (1984) Series A no 80 [99]; *Lanz v Austria* (App 24430/94) ECHR 31 January 2002 [46]–[47].

146 *Miranda v Arizona* 384 US 436, 457 (1966) (Warren CJ).

147 M McConville, A Sanders and R Leng, *The Case for the Prosecution* (Routledge, London 1991) 57.

as a critical – perhaps the most critical – stage in the processing of almost all criminal cases.'[148] The interposition of counsel at this critical questioning stage is capable of redressing the power imbalance between the examiner and the accused, the latter being presumed to have little or no legal knowledge or skills. Counsel can protect his client from the application of improper interrogation techniques; make him aware of his rights; advise on whether or not to remain silent; ensure that his client's version of events is fully presented; keep faithful account of the proceedings; and provide moral support at a time of distress. It is thus a rule of the Court that 'Article 6 will normally require that the accused be allowed to benefit from the assistance of a lawyer already at the initial stages of police interrogation.'[149] The onus is on the authorities to inform the accused sufficiently of his right to consult counsel before being questioned.[150]

The requirement of counsel at interrogation is, however, capable of restriction for 'good cause',[151] a term the Court has failed to define. Such qualification presents an affront to the importance of establishing a just balance between the examiner and the accused as soon as possible. The latter, it is submitted, should not be questioned without access, as soon as practicably possible, to counsel upon being detained in custody. A comment made without legal advice and in the presence of the investigating authorities can influence their handling of the case to the prejudice of the accused even when the comment is inadmissible at trial.[152] Nevertheless, the Court has at least limited the effect of the qualification to the extent that it accepts that even a justified restriction of access to counsel is capable of depriving the accused of a fair hearing when proceedings are viewed in their entirety.[153]

It is when such a restriction during pre-trial questioning raises prejudice for the accused in the ensuing proceedings that an inequality of arms will be effected. Such is evidenced both in cases where the accused responded to questioning and in cases where he exercised his right to silence. The accused in *John Murray v UK* was denied access to counsel for a 48-hour period at the interrogation stage and his decision to maintain silence resulted in adverse inferences being drawn legitimately[154] at trial. The Court maintained that such a significant and difficult

---

148 J Baldwin, 'Police Interrogation: What are the Rules of the Game?' in D Morgan and GM Stephenson (eds), *Suspicion and Silence: The Right to Silence in Criminal Investigations* (Blackstone, London 1994) 66.

149 Eg *John Murray* (n 144) [63]; *Magee* (n 144) [41]; *Brennan* (n 144) [45]; *Öcalan* (n 9) [131]; *Galstyan v Armenia* (App 26986/03) ECHR 15 November 2007 [89]; *Salduz* (n 8) [52]; *Pishchalnikov* (n 15) [67].

150 *Panovits v Cyprus* (App 4268/04) ECHR 11 December 2008 [72]–[73].

151 Eg *John Murray* (n 144) [63]; *Brennan* (n 144) [45]; *Öcalan* (n 9) [131]; *Salduz* (n 8) [52]; *Pishchalnikov* (n 15) [67].

152 See further Trechsel (n 24) 283: 'the behaviour of the suspect immediately after the arrest will *always* have consequences.'

153 Eg *John Murray* (n 144) [63], [65]–[66]; *Salduz* (n 8) [52]; *Pishchalnikov* (n 15) [67].

154 *John Murray* (n 144) [54], [56]–[58].

decision[155] should have been informed by legal advice in view of the prejudice arising therefrom at trial, irrespective of the justification for the restriction.[156] In effect, the restriction was unduly advantageous to the prosecution. This undue advantage was present also in *Magee v UK*[157] where the accused was questioned without counsel for the same period but he decided not to remain silent. The Court has a certain regard to the particulars of the environment in which such decisions are made. The conditions of the accused's detention and his incommunicado status created an 'intimidating atmosphere specifically devised to sap his will and make him confess to his interrogators.'[158] Counsel was held to have been required as a 'counterweight' to this atmosphere.[159] Indeed, his absence was prejudicial as statements made without legal advice formed the basis of the conviction.[160] It appears crucial to finding Article 6(3)(c) infringed that a statement given during an interrogation in which access to counsel was denied be prejudicial to the defence. The Court has acknowledged consistently that a statement made under this restriction will be prejudicial where it is used for a conviction.[161] The statement need not be the sole basis for the conviction, but need merely have a significant bearing upon it.[162] Such prejudice is confirmation

155 Ibid [66]: 'If he chooses to remain silent, adverse inferences may be drawn against him … On the other hand, if the accused opts to break his silence …, he runs the risk of prejudicing his defence without necessarily removing the possibility of inferences being drawn against him.'

156 Ibid [63] ('National laws may attach consequences to the attitude of an accused at the initial stages of police interrogation which are decisive for the prospects of the defence in any subsequent criminal proceedings'), [65]–[66], [68] ('the applicant was undoubtedly directly affected by the denial of access and the ensuing interference with the rights of the defence'), [70]. The same was held in *Averill v UK* (App 36408/97) ECHR 2000-VI [59]–[61] after the accused was denied access to counsel for a 24-hour period of interrogation and his silence was used to his prejudice at trial.

157 *Magee* (n 144).

158 Ibid [43].

159 Ibid [43], [46].

160 Ibid [45].

161 Eg *Öcalan* (n 9) [131], [148]; *Salduz* (n 8) [55] ('The rights of the defence will in principle be irretrievably prejudiced when incriminating statements made during police interrogation without access to a lawyer are used for a conviction'), [57]–[58], [63]; *Shabelnik* (n 95) [53], [59]–[60]; *Płonka v Poland* (App 20310/02) ECHR 31 March 2009 [35], [39], [40]–[42]; *Pishchalnikov* (n 15) [70], [90]–[92]; *Oleg Kolesnik v Ukraine* (App 17551/02) ECHR 19 November 2009 [35], [37]–[38]; *Musa Karataş v Turkey* (App 63315/00) ECHR 5 January 2010 [90]–[91], [97]. In *Titarenko v Ukraine* (App 31720/02) ECHR 20 September 2012 [87], where the accused had confessed during police questioning without legal assistance, the Court did not consider the fact that he repeated his confession with his lawyer present to undermine its conclusion that his defence rights were irretrievably prejudiced at the outset; his initial statements should have been excluded from the evidential basis for his conviction.

See also *Brennan* (n 144) [46], [48] where prejudice did not result from a 24-hour deferral of access to counsel during interrogation, applied in good faith and on reasonable grounds, as no incriminating admissions were made or adverse inferences subsequently drawn.

162 *Panovits* (n 150) [76]; *Płonka* (n 161) [39]; *Pishchalnikov* (n 15) [90]. See also *Öcalan* (n 9) [131] ('major contributing factor'); *Salduz* (n 8) [55] ('main evidence'); *Shabelnik* (n 95) [59] ('decisive extent'); *Oleg Kolesnik* (n 161) [37] ('crucial element'); *Musa Karataş* (n 161) [91] ('relied on it in convicting the applicant').

of the occurrence of an inequality of arms.[163] This inequality will be even more marked when the statement is made by a minor because of his vulnerability and capacities.[164] A state is not, of course, liable for an inequality of arms if the prejudicial statement is made when counsel is absent through no measure imposed by the authorities.[165]

6.2. VISITATION BY AND PRIVATE COMMUNICATION WITH COUNSEL

Not only is effective representation of the accused's interests important for equality of arms in interrogations, but also throughout the entire pre-trial stage. Counsel is entitled during this stage to visit his detained client with a view to the client's defence.[166] To find otherwise would be to limit his capabilities for effective case preparation to the advantage of the prosecution and thus upset equality of arms. It is during these custodial client conferences that discussions will occur concerning the factual and evidential aspects of the case, and defence activities and strategy. These discussions must be full and frank if counsel is to represent his client's interests effectively. Full and frank communication will be interfered with or made impossible if conducted within earshot, either direct or indirect, of the prosecutorial authorities because of a legitimate fear of them becoming better informed against the accused to his prejudice. Such an affront to confidentiality not only limits the effectiveness of legal assistance,[167] but also undermines the counsel-client relationship of trust and confidence. Supervised conferences

---

163 *Pishchalnikov* (n 15) [91].

164 *Salduz* (n 8) [57]–[58], [60] ('the Court stresses the fundamental importance of providing access to a lawyer where the person in custody is a minor'), [63]; *Panovits* (n 150) [67], [71]–[77].

See further *T v UK* (App 24724/94) ECHR 16 December 1999 [84]: 'it is essential that a child charged with an offence is dealt with in a manner which takes full account of his age, level of maturity and intellectual and emotional capacities, and that steps are taken to promote his ability to understand and participate in the proceedings.'

165 *Brennan* (n 144) [47]–[48].

166 *Bonzi* (n 145) 190: 'the opportunity for the accused to confer with his defence counsel is fundamental to the preparation of his defence'; *Schertenleib* (n 145) 226; *Kröcher and Möller* (n 145) 53; *Campbell and Fell* (n 145) [99]: 'a lawyer could scarcely "assist" his client … unless there had been some previous consultation between them.' A violation of Arts 6(3)(b) and (c) was found therein because no provision was made for consultations with counsel before the hearing; *Can* (n 143) [54]: 'Art 6(3)(c) … gives the accused a … right to assistance and support by a lawyer throughout the whole proceedings.'

167 *S v Switzerland* (Apps 12629/87; 13965/88) (1991) Series A no 220 [48]: 'If a lawyer were unable to confer with his client and receive confidential instructions from him without … surveillance, his assistance would lose much of its usefulness, whereas the Convention is intended to guarantee rights that are practical and effective'; *Brennan* (n 144) [58]; *Lanz* (n 145) [50]; *Öcalan* (n 9) [133]; *Marcello Viola v Italy* (App 45106/04) ECHR 2006-XI [61]; *Moiseyev* (n 8) [209]; *Rybacki v Poland* (App 52479/99) ECHR 13 January 2009 [56].

are thus capable of placing the prosecution in an unduly advantageous position in contravention of the concept of equality of arms. The Court consequently recognises in Article 6(3)(c) a right of the accused to communicate with his advocate out of the hearing of third parties.[168] The Court does not necessarily require third parties to actually hear defence discussions before free discussion is inhibited and the right to be effectively defended is hampered; a genuine belief held on reasonable grounds that such discussions were not confidential may suffice.[169] It may be during these discussions that documents are exchanged between counsel and client. The routine reading of these documents by the prosecuting authorities can reveal defence strategy and has been held to offend against equality of arms.[170]

Nevertheless, the entitlement to both receive visits from counsel and confer with him in private is susceptible of restriction where cogent justification exists.[171] Cases indicate that cogent justification could relate, for example, to a risk of collusion with or through counsel,[172] to the professional ethics of counsel or the lawfulness of his conduct being called into question at any time in the case,[173] or to security considerations.[174] Regard seems to be had to two particular factors when cogency of justification is assessed. Account is taken of the duration of the restriction as a measure of proportionality. Violations have been found where the restriction was imposed for periods of two,[175] three,[176] over five,[177] or over seven[178] months, or was imposed throughout and beyond the entire pre-trial stage.[179] Yet, more critical to finding these violations was consideration of whether or not the restrictions were necessary on the facts. An unnecessary restriction can infringe Article 6(3)(c) even if it is of very limited duration.[180] It is quite straightforward for

168 Eg ibid. The EComHR recognised the same earlier in *Can* (n 143) [57].

169 *Oferta Plus SRL v Moldova* (App 14385/04) ECHR 19 December 2006 [147]; *Castravet v Moldova* (App 23393/05) ECHR 13 March 2007 [51]; *Istratii and others v Moldova* (Apps 8721/05; 8705/05; 8742/05) ECHR 27 March 2007 [91]; *Modarca v Moldova* (App 14437/05) ECHR 10 May 2007 [89]; *Cebotari v Moldova* (App 35615/06) ECHR 13 November 2007 [60].

170 *Moiseyev* (n 8) [211]–[212]. In specific respect of interference with 'correspondence' between counsel and client, the matter is treated usually as an ECHR Art 8 concern: eg *Campbell and Fell* (n 145) [108]–[110]; *Schönenberger and Durmaz v Switzerland* (App 11368/85) (1988) Series A no 137 [23]–[30]; *Campbell v UK* (App 13590/88) (1992) Series A no 233 [33]–[54]; *Erdem v Germany* (App 38321/97) ECHR 2001-VII [53]–[70].

171 Eg *Campbell and Fell* (n 145) [113]; *Can* (n 143) [52], [57]; *S* (n 167) [49]; *Brennan* (n 144) [58]; *Lanz* (n 145) [52]; *Öcalan* (n 9) [133], [135]; *Marcello Viola* (n 167) [61]; *Rybacki* (n 167) [56].

172 *Can* (n 143) [59]; *S* (n 167) [49].

173 *S* (n 167) [49]; *Rybacki* (n 167) [59].

174 *Campbell and Fell* (n 145) [113]. Security considerations could include, for example, when a detained accused exhibits a demonstrable propensity to escape or the presence of counsel at certain times would interfere with essential security protocols.

175 Ibid [111], [113]; *Lanz* (n 145) [51], [53].

176 *Can* (n 143) [59]–[61].

177 *Rybacki* (n 167) [60], [62].

178 *S* (n 167) [49], [51].

179 *Öcalan* (n 9) [133], [148]; *Moiseyev* (n 8) [204], [207], [224]–[225].

180 Eg *Brennan* (n 144) [59]–[60], [63]. A police officer was present at only one client–counsel interview, the unnecessary restriction being applicable for a 48-hour period.

the Court to find the supervision of client-counsel conferences, and limitations upon the number and length thereof, unnecessary when a state fails to adduce the grounds, even of a general nature, for the restriction.[181] Even when grounds are provided, a restriction cannot be considered necessary if a less restrictive measure can suffice.[182] Thus, it was held unnecessary in *Öcalan v Turkey* that counsel-client meetings were conducted within the hearing of the authorities to ensure the applicant's security because visual surveillance, accompanied by other measures, would have been adequate.[183] Justified visual surveillance is tolerable[184] from an equality of arms standpoint, for the interference with privacy is not of an extent to really restrict effective defence discussions.

States often rely on the risk of collusion to justify the necessity of listening in on discussions. Merely assuming a danger of collusion cannot necessitate a restriction; compelling arguments must be made.[185] Collusion does not include several defence counsel collaborating in order to coordinate their defence strategy, a practice that is not unusual.[186] It refers instead to the accused using counsel to, for example, influence witnesses and/or tamper with or remove incriminating documents or other evidence not yet seized. Even if an argument based on collusion or the questionable legal or ethical conduct of counsel at any time during the case is compelling in its justification for holding consultations within the hearing of third parties, or for placing limitations upon necessary counsel visits, it is submitted that equality of arms remains undermined. Less restrictive alternatives to both measures that also avoid hampering state investigations must thus be proposed. A lawyer could be appointed, either officially or through the competent bar authority, to accompany defence counsel in consultations and act as intermediary in exchanges of documents

181 Eg *Campbell and Fell* (n 145) [113]; *Öcalan* (n 9) [135]: 'the Government have not explained why the authorities did not permit the lawyers to visit their client more often or why they failed to provide more adequate means of transport [to his location], thereby increasing the length of each individual visit'; *Rybacki* (n 167) [58]–[59].

182 *Van Mechelen and others v the Netherlands* (App 21363/93 et seq) ECHR 1997-III [58]; *Visser v the Netherlands* (App 26668/95) ECHR 14 February 2002 [43]; *Marcello Viola* (n 167) [62].

183 *Öcalan* (n 9) [133].

184 See further Basic Principles on the Role of Lawyers (Eighth UN Congress on the Prevention of Crime and the Treatment of Offenders, Havana 27 August to 7 September 1990) UN Doc A/CONF.144/28/Rev.1 118 (1990) principle 8: 'consultations may be within sight, but not within the hearing, of law enforcement officials'; Standard Minimum Rules for the Treatment of Prisoners (the Nelson Mandela Rules) (adopted 17 December 2015) UNGA Res 70/175 UN Doc A/Res/70/175 (2015) rr 61, 120(1).

185 *Can* (n 143) [59]–[60]; *Brennan* (n 144) [59]; *Lanz* (n 145) [51]–[52]. Contrast *Kempers v Austria* (App 21842/93) EComHR 27 February 1997 [1] ('The Law') where the EComHR considered that fear of collusion was justified, and thus surveillance of discussions was necessary, as several co-suspects were still at large. The decision is unconvincing. Collusion was possible only through counsel and neither his integrity was ever called into question nor was the risk of any sophisticated coded message being forwarded unwittingly through him adequately substantiated.

186 *S* (n 167) [49].

and correspondence.[187] A second alternative, though less preferable than the first, would be for an officially or bar authority appointed counsel to be the representative from the outset or the replacement counsel during the case depending on prevailing circumstances.[188] These alternative solutions would avoid the contradiction between allowing legal representation and limiting through restrictive measures the representative's capacity to perform his role effectively, and would thereby sufficiently secure equality of arms.

It was the need to secure equality of arms that weighed heavily on the Court's mind as it examined the restriction upon counsel visits in *Moiseyev v Russia*.[189] Counsel was required for the entire duration of the proceedings to apply for a permit from the prosecuting authority before each visit to the applicant. The imposition of this condition was viewed by the Court as unnecessary given that it was devoid of legal basis in domestic law; advocates were merely required to present proof of identity and status during visits.[190] It also considered that the 'excessively onerous' character of the condition must have detracted time and effort from substantive defence activity.[191] It seems in this respect that the defence did not have to establish prejudice because prejudice was assumed inevitable.[192] The essence of the restriction was that 'the prosecuting authority enjoyed unrestricted access to the applicant for its own purposes but exercised full and effective control over his contacts with … counsel'.[193] It was thus especially concerning to the Court that the defence were compelled to be dependent on, and subordinate to, prosecution discretion and it acknowledged, accordingly, an inequality of arms.[194] Whereas one must accept naturally that custodial contact with counsel requires state facilitation, unfettered discretion in this regard should never be a power bestowed upon the opponent of the accused if equality of arms is to be assured.

Not only does an assumption of inevitable prejudice feature in the inequality of arms in *Moiseyev*, but it also features in cases involving consultations within the hearing of the authorities where such inequality was implicit and Article 6(3)(c) was held violated. *S v Switzerland* made evident that proof of actual prejudice stemming from supervised consultations was unnecessary for finding Article 6(3)(c) infringed.[195] The same was evidenced in *Brennan v UK*

187 Trechsel (n 24) 282.

188 Stavros (n 32) 62 also advocates using officially appointed counsel as a less restrictive measure, citing *S* (n 167) [49] in support because the European Court therein considered the court-appointed status of counsel to be one of the factors negating a risk of collusion.

189 *Moiseyev* (n 8).

190 Ibid [206].

191 Ibid [205]–[206].

192 See further *Campbell and Fell* (n 145) [99] which implies that prejudice can be readily assumed when there is no opportunity for a lawyer to visit his client before a hearing.

193 *Moiseyev* (n 8) [205].

194 Ibid [205], [207].

195 *S* (n 167) [50]–[51]. The same was implied in *Can* (n 143) [60]–[61] and *Lanz* (n 145) [49]–[53].

but accompanied with an express requirement for the applicant to demonstrate that he was 'directly affected by the restriction in the exercise of the rights of the defence.'[196] In the case, the first consultation since arrest was supervised and the consequent impediment to free communication was acknowledged by the Court:

> the presence of the police officer would have inevitably prevented the applicant from speaking frankly to his solicitor and given him reason to hesitate before broaching questions of potential significance to the case against him. Both ... had been warned that no names should be mentioned and that the interview would be stopped if anything was said which was perceived as hindering the investigation.[197]

The applicant thus satisfied the aforementioned condition of being 'directly affected by the restriction' at a time he undeniably needed legal advice.[198] This was sufficient to constitute a joint infringement of Articles 6(3)(c) and 6(1).[199] The finding indicates that the Court was prepared to accept, upon taking account of the above manner in which supervision affected the applicant during the consultation, that such supervision would, as a natural and self-evident consequence, have been prejudicial to a fair hearing. This was essentially an assumption of inevitable prejudice. It is self-evident that significant hindrance of free communication can pervasively and negatively affect all or many activities of the defence to the prejudice of the trial outcome. Implicit in this assumed prejudice was an acknowledgement that the defence incurred an inequality of arms. The concept of equality of arms is indeed stronger when an applicant need not prove actual prejudice arising from an inequality. The Court's willingness to assume prejudice reflects the importance it attaches to meaningful counsel-client communication for ensuring equality of arms and procedural fairness generally, and signals an appreciation that proving actual prejudice from supervised consultations can be an impractical endeavour. Prejudice was also assumed in the similar circumstances of *Rybacki v Poland*: 'it cannot be said that the applicant's contacts with his lawyer were, in such a setting, capable of assisting him in the effective exercise of his defence rights.'[200] The Court considered this disadvantage vis-à-vis the prosecution to have been reinforced by the fact that the supervision lasted over five months.[201] The strength of an assumption of prejudice, therefore, will be greater the longer the restriction lasts. Given that the Court is content to assume inevitable prejudice, the thrust of its approach to counsel visits and private consultations is thus firmly fixed on

196 *Brennan* (n 144) [58].

197 Ibid [62]. A similar observation was made in *Öcalan* (n 9) [133]: 'the inevitable consequence of that restriction ... was to prevent the applicant from conversing openly with his lawyers and asking them questions that might prove important to the preparation of his defence.'

198 *Brennan* (n 144) [62].

199 Ibid [63].

200 *Rybacki* (n 167) [60], [62].

201 Ibid [61].

determining whether a particular restriction is necessary and is proportionate in duration.

7. EFFECTIVE LEGAL ASSISTANCE

The Court has observed recurrently that:

> the Convention is intended to guarantee not rights that are theoretical or illusory but rights that are practical and effective; this is particularly so of the rights of the defence in view of the prominent place held in a democratic society by the right to a fair trial, from which they derive.[202]

The accused is thus entitled under Article 6(3)(c) to legal assistance that is effective in practice. The mere pro forma appointment of counsel will consequently not suffice.[203] It is only through the effective performance of the essential functions of a legal representative that Article 6(3)(c) can pursue meaningfully its primary aim of redressing, in accordance with the principle of equality of arms, the inherent imbalance in the capacities and competencies of the state and the accused to present adequately their cases. The value of legal assistance to the realisation of equality of arms thus becomes illusory when such assistance is ineffective. Whereas the Court has opted not to define clearly the meaning of 'effective' in this context, one can infer from its minimum standard setting competence that an accused is only entitled to expect from his counsel no more than adequate representation of the defence case. Adequate representation requires counsel to at least use the ordinary level of skill and care appropriate to the circumstances of the case. The concept of equality of arms does not demand that he be of equal skill and experience to his prosecution counterpart,[204] but only that he be equal in procedural rights as far as the parties' different roles allow. The Court's reluctance to establish exacting rules defining effective assistance is explained by a wish to avoid inevitable interference, actual and perceived, with the independent decision-making of counsel on the conduct of the defence. It is essential that counsel enjoy a strong degree of professional independence to perform his duties, from both the Court and states, if he is to make a necessary contribution towards upholding the rule of law.

---

202 Eg *Artico* (n 75) [33]; *Coëme and others v Belgium* (App 32492/96 et seq) ECHR 2000-VII [98]; *Dolenec v Croatia* (App 25282/06) ECHR 26 November 2009 [215].

203 *Artico* (n 75) [33]; *Kamasinski v Austria* (App 9783/82) (1989) Series A no 168 [65]; *Imbrioscia* (n 144) [38]; *Daud v Portugal* (App 22600/93) ECHR 1998-II [38]; *Czekalla v Portugal* (App 38830/97) ECHR 2002-VIII [60]; *Prežec* (n 111) [31]; *Sabirov v Russia* (App 13465/04) ECHR 11 February 2010 [43]; *Pavlenko* (n 143) [99].

204 See further *Attorney-General's Reference (No 82a of 2000)* [2002] EWCA Crim 215; [2002] 2 Cr App R 24 [14] (Lord Woolf CJ): 'The principle of equality of arms ... does not necessarily entail representation by a Queen's Counsel merely because the Crown are represented by a Queen's Counsel.'

It is not, however, counsel but exclusively the state against whom complaints of ineffective assistance can be directed under Article 6(3)(c).[205] Counsel is not a state organ, even when officially appointed, for his professional independence affords him the status of private individual.[206] It follows from this independence that the conduct of the defence is essentially a matter between client and counsel, whether the latter is instructed privately or under a legal aid scheme, and states cannot be held responsible for every professional shortcoming of counsel.[207] Counsel is indeed presumed to render effective assistance. Nevertheless, his professional independence does not absolve states from all responsibility when such assistance is ineffective. There is an onus on the competent authorities to intervene whenever ineffective assistance is manifest or otherwise sufficiently brought to their attention.[208] In the case of manifest ineffectiveness, therefore, the accused is afforded the additional protection of the state being obliged to act on its own initiative. The duty of intervention is crucially important for safeguarding equality of arms which would otherwise suffer serious upset if states could remain passive in the face of a prosecution advantage arising from known inefficacious representation. Intervention may take the form of either replacing

---

205 At Strasbourg, a competence to admit applications directed against private individuals does not exist: *X v Germany* (App 2646/65) (1966) 19 CD 89, 92; *X* (n 13) 36; *X v UK* (App 3852/68) (1969) 32 CD 38, 39–40; *X and Z v Germany* (App 3897/68) (1970) 35 CD 75, 80–81.

206 *Jopkiewicz v Poland* (App 24248/94) EComHR 17 January 1997 [2(b)] ('The Law'); *Rutkowski v Poland* (App 45995/99) ECHR 2000-XI [2] ('The Law'); *Skrobol v Poland* (App 44165/98) ECHR 8 July 2003 [2] ('The Law'); *Bakalov and others v Bulgaria* (App 55796/00) ECHR 18 September 2007 [3] ('The Law'). The same is applicable even if counsel has the status of 'officer of the court': *X v UK* (App 6956/75) (1976) 8 DR 103, 104. See also *Alvarez Sanchez v Spain* (App 50720/99) ECHR 2001-XI [1] ('The Law') which refers to 'the independence of the attorneys' professional association from the State.'

207 *Kamasinski* (n 203) [65]; *Daud* (n 203) [38]; *Czekalla* (n 203) [60]; *Prežec* (n 111) [30]; *Sabirov* (n 203) [44]; *Pavlenko* (n 143) [99].

208 Ibid. Though these cases refer to the onus to intervene in relation to legal aid counsel, it does not follow that it is inapplicable when counsel is privately retained. In *Imbrioscia* (n 144) [41] and *Stanford v UK* (App 16757/90) (1994) Series A no 282-A [28], the onus to intervene was mentioned in relation simply to 'counsel' without distinction of status. Furthermore, in *Goddi v Italy* (App 8966/80) (1984) Series A no 76 [30]–[31], the Court considered that securing an effective defence required intervention as the accused's privately retained counsel was absent at hearing. *Güveç v Turkey* (App 70337/01) ECHR 2009 [131]–[133] and Trechsel (n 24) 287 provide additional support.

See further HRC: *Hervin Edwards v Jamaica* (Comm 529/1993) UN Doc CCPR/C/60/D/529/1993 (1997) [5.2]: States can be held accountable for the shortcomings of privately retained counsel when it should have been manifest to the competent authorities that his behaviour was incompatible with the interests of justice.

It is right that states are obliged to intervene upon becoming aware of ineffective assistance by privately retained counsel. No ground exists in the present context for distinguishing between him and his legal aid counterpart given that even the latter is not a state organ, and states are obliged to ensure a fair trial even if counsel is not state-appointed. Additionally, either counsel is capable of advantaging the prosecution through ineffective representation. It is also important for those retaining private counsel, on grounds of parity of treatment between accused persons and the general guarantee of practical and effective Convention rights, that there be an equal right to effective representation.

counsel or causing him to fulfil his duties.[209] It is the positive steps taken in either of these regards, or lack thereof, that attracts the focus of the Court. In the event that intervention was necessary but absent or weak, it will occasionally even suggest specific steps the authorities could possibly have applied to enable counsel to fulfil his obligations.[210] The Court essentially seeks to determine whether steps were taken by the state to correct the serious shortcomings of counsel to a degree that ensured the accused effective representation, and ultimately equality of arms, when proceedings are viewed in their entirety. In so doing, it does not require the applicant to prove that the ineffective legal assistance was prejudicial.[211] Prejudice can instead be readily assumed as inevitable, for ineffective assistance will pervasively and adversely affect many or all aspects of the proceedings, including frustrating equality of arms by undermining the representation of the defence case to the advantage of the prosecution.

It is the failure of the state to respond adequately to an inactive counsel, or one whose amount of defence activity falls well below that sufficient for purpose, that most often begets a finding of ineffective legal assistance, whereby inequality of arms is implied. Ineffectiveness in this particular context is not infrequently manifest,[212] requiring the competent authority to intervene *proprio motu*. It was not so in *Artico*, however, where it was the accused who drew the attention of the Court of Cassation to the inactivity, from the outset, of his legal aid counsel. Refusing to accede to a request for a substitute counsel, the Cassation Court remained passive and left the accused unrepresented. According to the Strasbourg Court, positive state action was called for and its absence left the applicant without effective legal assistance,[213] a condition advantaging the prosecutor at hearing. It observed the same in cases of counsel failing to attend a hearing[214] or several hearings.[215] It did so also in circumstances where counsel took some action but the amount thereof far from constituted an effective defence and the authorities failed to intervene. Such circumstances have included counsel making oral appeal submissions but on the basis of four-year-old grounds originally filed by the applicant, having not prepared any herself, and without ever having contacted the applicant;[216] counsel lodging an appeal but without acquainting himself with his client's version of the facts as he failed to contact the latter who

209 *Artico* (n 75) [33]; *Kemal Kahraman and Ali Kahraman v Turkey* (App 42104/02) ECHR 26 April 2007 [35]; *Ananyev v Russia* (App 20292/04) ECHR 30 July 2009 [52]; *Sabirov* (n 203) [43].

210 Eg *Goddi* (n 208) [31]; *Daud* (n 203) [42]; *Czekalla* (n 203) [68].

211 *Artico* (n 75) [35].

212 Eg *Goddi* (n 208) [30]–[31]; *Czekalla* (n 203) [68]; *Sannino v Italy* (App 30961/03) ECHR 2006-VI [51]; *Kemal Kahraman and Ali Kahraman* (n 209) [36]; *Ananyev* (n 209) [54]; *Sabirov* (n 203) [46].

213 *Artico* (n 75) [33], [36]–[37].

214 *Sabirov* (n 203) [46]–[48].

215 *Kemal Kahraman and Ali Kahraman* (n 209) [36]–[37].

216 *Ananyev* (n 209) [53]–[56].

remained silent at trial;[217] and counsel being present for some interrogations and a victim identification procedure, though failing to attend and advise at most of the interrogations and to undertake other pre-trial activity, such as arranging private consultations.[218] An obvious step towards possibly avoiding such ineffectiveness in the first place, thereby encouraging equality of arms, would be for states to remunerate legal aid counsel on a basis commensurate with the reality of the efforts and outlays required for adequate case preparation and presentation.

It is not sufficient to merely replace a counsel who is inactive or fulfils only some of his defence obligations, for the authorities must continue to take whatever measures necessary, if any, to effect equality of arms. Counsel in *Daud v Portugal*[219] was inactive and eventually withdrew from the case, whereas counsel in *Goddi v Italy*[220] failed to attend an appeal hearing. Replacements were appointed, three days before trial in *Daud* and on the day of the hearing in *Goddi*, though neither counsel adequately prepared their cases. In the eyes of the Court, the preparatory time was inadequate and the domestic courts should not have remained passive after the appointments,[221] for doing so was advantageous to the prosecution. Instead, positive measures were required to enable the new representatives to conduct an effective defence, such as ordering an adjournment or suspending a sitting for a sufficient period of time, irrespective of the representatives' failure to request such measures.[222] The need for such intervention to ensure equality of arms can be recurrent when different lawyers are appointed ad hoc at each hearing in a series of hearings, especially if each lawyer fails to seek an adjournment to familiarise himself with the case.[223]

It is not only the inadequate state response to the shortcomings of counsel mentioned hitherto that may occasion a deprivation of both effective legal assistance and equality of arms, but also the inadequate state response when the shortcoming concerns the failure to adhere to a formal procedural rule. Counsel in *Czekalla v Portugal*[224] failed to comply with such a rule when lodging an appeal, resulting in the appeal's inadmissibility. Adding to the seriousness of this procedural negligence was the fact highlighted by the Court that the applicant was a foreigner, unfamiliar with the language of the proceedings, facing a long prison sentence.[225] The Court viewed the shortcoming as manifest, requiring positive measures from the appeal court such as, for example, inviting counsel

217 *Prežec* (n 111) [31]–[32].
218 *Pavlenko* (n 143) [95], [109], [111]–[114].
219 *Daud* (n 203).
220 *Goddi* (n 208).
221 Ibid [31]; *Daud* (n 203) [39], [42].
222 Ibid respectively [31]; [42].
223 *Sannino* (n 212) [50]–[51]. See further *Köplinger v Austria* (App 1850/63) (1966) 9 Yearbook 240 (EComHR) 264, 266: Frequent changes in legal aid counsel do not in themselves deprive the accused of effective assistance.
224 *Czekalla* (n 203).
225 Ibid [65].

to add to or rectify her pleading instead of ruling the appeal inadmissible.[226] It considered that such an invitation would be 'a manifestation of the judge's power to direct the proceedings, exercised with a view to the proper administration of justice', and neither impinge upon the independence of the legal profession nor deny the prosecution equality of arms.[227] Without it, or some other intervening measure, the state denied the accused an effective defence,[228] the implication being that he was disadvantaged vis-à-vis the prosecution.

Whereas the foregoing discloses circumstances where the conduct of counsel required intervention to secure effective assistance and equality of arms, it remains for the purpose of contrast to outline particular conduct for which state liability was held not to have arisen. As already indicated, state liability is not engaged when a shortcoming in representation is neither manifest nor sufficiently brought to the attention of the competent authorities. Thus, since chosen counsel in *Imbrioscia v Switzerland* did not request to be present at interrogations and the period of her pre-trial inactivity was brief, and not met with a complaint from the accused, 'the relevant authorities could scarcely be expected to intervene.'[229]

This necessary sensitivity towards preserving the independence of legal professionals also explains the general exclusion of state liability for the conduct of counsel in matters of professional judgement and strategy. Of course, if state liability cannot attach to such matters, the state is not obliged to intervene. Intervention is not accordingly required when dissatisfaction with counsel stems from 'an injudicious line of defence or a mere defect of argumentation.'[230] Neither is intervention necessary when counsel takes adequate steps for the defence but acts, in some respects, contrary to what his client feels to be in his own best interests.[231] Even if the client seeks a particular remedy counsel is unwilling to pursue, it has been observed that it is not for a court to oblige counsel to lodge any remedy contrary to his opinion as to its prospects of success.[232] Such deference towards professional judgement and strategy was repeated when a counsel's tactical choice to remain silent about his client's hearing difficulties in court was not accompanied subsequently by state liability.[233] Neither did state responsibility arise for the misjudgement of a privately retained counsel who,

---

226 Ibid [68]. No such intervention was held to have been required in *Alvarez Sanchez* (n 206) [1] ('The Law') where an *amparo* appeal to the Constitutional Court was lodged by counsel but declared inadmissible as being out of time. The case is distinguishable from *Czekalla* as the task of the Constitutional Court was not to reconsider the validity of the accused's conviction or length of sentence imposed, which was reduced by the Supreme Court.

227 *Czekalla* (n 203) [70].

228 Ibid [66], [71].

229 *Imbrioscia* (n 144) [41]. Neither was the manifest ineffectiveness or sufficient notification of ineffectiveness condition satisfied in *Kamasinski* (n 203) [66], [68] and *Stanford* (n 208) [27]–[28].

230 *Czekalla* (n 203) [65].

231 *Kamasinski* (n 203) [66], [68]–[71].

232 *Rutkowski* (n 206) [2] ('The Law').

233 *Stanford* (n 208) [27]–[28], [32].

despite knowing in ample time that he would be unable to attend an essentially written appeal hearing, failed to engage a substitute counsel and relied instead on his request for an adjournment which was subsequently rejected, and the hearing was held in his absence.[234] The trend is clearly that there is little prospect of an applicant succeeding in a claim of ineffective assistance and implied inequality of arms when he feels that a professional misjudgement or strategic inadequacy occurred. If professional independence is to be upheld, an integral part of which is freedom of judgement and strategy, the Court inevitably finds itself constrained and unable to rely upon the principle of equality of arms to resolve the applicant's dissatisfaction.

8. CONCLUSION

This discussion sought to examine the approach taken at Strasbourg towards the concept of equality of arms in the application of the Article 6(3)(c) right to legal assistance.

A nexus between this provision and equality of arms was first identified. As is the case with Articles 6(3)(b) and (d), this nexus is accepted in law by the Court and former Commission, which have been able to do so because both elements constitute part of the Article 6(1) fair hearing guarantee. A conceptual nexus also exists because the proper observance of the right to legal assistance serves the instrumental, intrinsic and collateral values of equality of arms. This conceptual link is further evident because the right is feasibly reciprocal and useful for case preparation and presentation, characteristics bringing it within the equality of arms remit.

The discussion next fell on equality of arms and the right to legal assistance by privately retained counsel. Whereas generally the accused must not be deprived of the counsel he has instructed, states are entitled to place reasonable restrictions on the right, thus resulting in the exclusion of certain counsel outright or during the proceedings. Reasonableness implies that the restriction must be in the interests of securing justice and an adequate defence. It has also been considered crucial by the Strasbourg organs that the restriction not create actual prejudice and thus undermine equality of arms. Restrictions on the qualification, professional conduct and number of counsel have been accepted at Strasbourg as reasonable and not prejudicial if the accused is afforded adequate opportunity to instruct alternative counsel. Whilst these reasonable restrictions do not offend the dignity of the accused, it is submitted that if chosen counsel is excluded because of a restriction deemed unreasonable, this does offend against dignity and should be sufficient to constitute an inequality of arms

[234] *Tripodi v Italy* (App 13743/88) (1994) Series A no 281-B [29]–[31]. Counsel had, nevertheless, made written submissions.

(unequivocal inequality), even if actual prejudice was averted through the instruction of alternative counsel. The Court's regard for prejudice also entails that maintaining equality of arms does not require an adjournment in every instance private counsel is unable to attend a particular hearing date; adequate opportunity to engage alternative counsel can avert prejudice. An adjournment is the dignitarian option – preserving the accused's first choice of counsel – and should be preferred. State responsibility for procedural inequality can arise if private counsel refuses to act for his client because of undue state pressure. To protect an accused unable to secure private counsel through no fault of the state, it is suggested that provision be made at Convention level requiring the assignment of legal assistance by competent national authorities.

The assignment of state-funded legal assistance to secure equality of arms is restricted to accused persons who meet financial and interests of justice criterions.

The financial criterion requires that the accused be of insufficient means to retain counsel at a material time. 'Sufficient means' is undefined but the Court rightly resorts, as a pragmatic solution, to indications of indigence when the state has failed to conduct a proper and reasoned assessment of means. The 'free' aspect of the legal assistance does not guarantee the accused a definitive exemption from costs; a temporary or partial exemption can be sufficient. This, it was argued, would not in practice likely discourage sufficiently the accused from instructing counsel and does not in principle impact negatively on equality of arms, provided proper regard is had to his financial situation.

If the financial criterion is satisfied, the grant of legal aid is dependent upon whether it is required in the interests of justice. *Artico* established that this second criterion can be met by demonstrating that it is prima facie 'plausible' in the circumstances that legal assistance would have added to the effectiveness of the accused's defence. If this is demonstrated, prejudice is considered inevitable and need not be proven to establish an inequality of arms. This is a progressive approach which recognises that proving actual prejudice is simply impracticable in this context and that the disadvantage flowing from denial of necessary counsel will pervade all aspects of the proceedings. Even more progressive and preferable would be a dignitarian approach: if legal assistance is in the interests of justice but not provided, this is an inequality of arms in itself and not because it would inevitably have caused prejudice. To determine whether counsel was plausibly required in the interests of justice, and thus highlight whether an undue imbalance existed between the parties' capabilities to present their cases effectively, regard is rightly had to three key factors, all of which have been reasonably applied in the case-law: the severity of the sentence risked; case complexity; and the competence of the accused to defend himself. Though the Court accepts each factor as sufficient in itself to justify legal assistance as in the interests of justice, it refers to all three whenever the facts of the case permit.

In the event that legal aid is granted, the accused must be consulted in the selection of counsel but does not enjoy a specific right to choose counsel. The discussion argued, however, that a right of choice would be more desirable, with reasonable restrictions, because it reinforces to a superior extent the values of equality of arms and creates greater parity between those retaining private counsel, for whom choice is available, and the indigent. Only if the accused is incapable manifestly of making a meaningful choice of counsel or fails to make a choice within proper time limits should the legal aid authority make the selection decision.

Even if an accused qualifies for legal aid or is capable of retaining private counsel, he may wish to forgo legal assistance. The discussion established, however, that the Court allows states to insist upon the engagement of counsel if sufficient and relevant reasons justifying the measure as in the interests of justice – which include the interests of the accused – are provided. This, it was argued, is the appropriate response since the value, through counsel, of a position of equality of arms to presenting an effective defence outweighs the value of the freedom to choose self-representation; both are dignitarian. It was further suggested that the imposition of counsel is acceptable if the pro se accused frustrates, to a substantial and persistent extent, the proper and expeditious conduct of the case or will likely cause a vulnerable witness to experience further distress or intimidation during questioning.

The discussion moved to consider the Strasbourg approach to legal assistance at the pre-trial stage, to which Article 6(3)(c) remains applicable, and equality of arms. This approach was assessed with regard to the capacity of a detained accused to access counsel at interrogation, generally receive visits from him and confer in private.

Whereas the general rule is that the accused is entitled to an opportunity for legal assistance at interrogation, the Court accepts that this may be restricted for 'good cause' (undefined). It appears that it is only when a restriction in this context is prejudicial to the ensuing proceedings that an inequality of arms is recognised. Thus, in cases where access to counsel was denied, prejudice was acknowledged when adverse inferences from silence at interrogation were drawn at trial or a statement given during interrogation had a significant bearing upon the conviction. It is submitted that the accused should unequivocally not undergo questioning without access, as early as practicably possible, to counsel whilst detained in custody; a just balance must be preserved between him and the examiner at the influential interrogation stage. A failure to grant such early access creates an undue imbalance at interrogation that offends the dignity of the accused and should be treated as an inequality of arms without regard to prejudice.

Outside of interrogation, the entitlement of the accused to both receive visits from counsel and confer with him in private may also exceptionally be restricted for cogent justification. The case-law indicates that this justification can refer, for example, to a risk of collusion, to the questionable legal or ethical conduct of counsel, or to security concerns. Cogency of justification is assessed with regard to the duration of the restriction (proportionality) and to whether the restriction was strictly necessary. Whereas the analysis suggested that justified visual surveillance of counsel–client consultations is tolerable as it does not actually restrict effective discussions, the Court will not find acceptable generally consultations held within the hearing of third parties or accept excessive limitations on counsel visits since both can unduly limit the effectiveness of legal assistance and thus advantage the prosecution. Less restrictive alternatives to both measures were proposed in the discussion involving an officially or bar authority appointed lawyer which secure equality of arms whilst avoiding hampering state investigations. It is not actual but inevitable prejudice that confirms a procedural disadvantage, for undue restrictions on visitation and free communication can self-evidently affect in an adverse and pervasive manner all or many activities of the defence to the detriment of the trial outcome, and actual prejudice can be impracticable to prove. Nevertheless, the imbalance between the prosecuting authorities and the accused created by undue restrictions undermines dignity and should, it is submitted, be viewed as an inequality of arms in itself, irrespective of inevitable prejudice.

Also capable of disadvantaging the accused vis-à-vis the prosecution is the ineffective assistance of counsel. The discussion established that although the conduct of the defence is generally a matter for counsel and client, states are not entirely immune from responsibility for ineffective legal assistance. The Court places an onus on the competent authorities to intervene whenever ineffective assistance is manifest or otherwise sufficiently brought to their attention. The categories of shortcomings from which an inequality of arms is possible include when counsel is inactive, his amount of defence activity falls well below that adequate for purpose, or he fails to comply with a formal procedural rule. State liability is not generally incurred if the shortcoming relates to misjudgement or strategic inadequacy, for the Court seeks to preserve the essential professional independence of counsel. The Court assesses whether measures taken by the state, if any, to correct counsel's shortcomings were sufficient to ensure that the accused, in the light of the proceedings as a whole, enjoyed effective legal assistance and thus equality of arms. Prejudice is considered inevitable and need not be proven if legal assistance is ineffective. The dignitarian approach, which should be preferred, is that ineffective assistance is an inequality of arms in itself and not because prejudice therefrom is inevitable.

In the analysis presented herein, it appears that, under Article 6(3)(c), it is only in cases concerning interference with the right to privately retained counsel or concerning denial of access to counsel at interrogation that actual prejudice need be proven to confirm an inequality of arms. In other cases of shortcomings concerning observance of the right to legal assistance, proving prejudice can be impracticable but one cannot but conclude that prejudice must inevitably have arisen, hence prejudice need not be proven.

CONCLUDING OVERVIEW

States parties to the Convention recognise in their criminal justice systems that the control of crime is not an objective that should be pursued in disregard of the interests of accused persons. This recognition is manifested in their accepted obligation, which also reflects a commitment to the rule of law, to secure to everyone within their jurisdiction the right to a fair trial in Article 6.

The content of the right is a product of a gradual historical evolution in Western standards of procedural fairness. This evolution began with developments in trial rights in national laws designed to secure correct trial outcomes. Article 6 has benefited from the lessons gleaned from both progressive and regressive developments at national level. Its content was also influenced by procedural rights entrenched in instruments of constitutional significance, for procedural fairness evolved to become a contributor to securing some form of good governance. It was the emergence of a shared respect for the dignity of the individual in the aftermath of the Second World War that procedural fairness became an interest to be protected in international law, the fair trial provisions in the UDHR and in early drafts of the ICCPR becoming influential precursors to Article 6. The emergence and recurrence through different stages of Western procedural history of certain trial safeguards, in various formulations, which present some resemblance to those included in Article 6, demonstrates that attempts have always been made, to varying degrees, to lessen the extent to which accused persons suffer procedural disadvantage vis-à-vis the prosecution or accuser.

Article 6 does not exhaustively define the concept of a fair trial. It merely requires that the accused have adequate opportunity to exercise certain minimum procedural rights. These rights consist of those that are express and implied in the article. The concept of equality of arms has a legal basis as an implied element of the Article 6(1) fair hearing guarantee. Indeed, it is also a well-established aspect of a fair trial in international law.

The value of equality of arms derives principally from its instrumental and intrinsic values. It is instrumental to rendering more probable a correct trial outcome. Its intrinsic value – which it is submitted has theoretical primacy over its instrumental value – is one of respect for the dignity of the accused, enabling him to feel like an empowered and effective participant in the proceedings in which his fate will be determined. As a collateral consequence of these values, equality of arms also has a secondary value as an ingredient in securing some form of good governance, particularly because it reflects the state's respect for the rule of law and assists in securing a public perception of criminal process legitimacy.

Equality of arms calls for equality in the parties' procedural opportunities, as far as their naturally dissimilar roles permit, to prepare and present their cases. These procedural opportunities refer both to rights that can feasibly and desirably be reciprocal and those that are not logically required by the prosecution but are designed to remove disadvantage (non-reciprocal). In both cases, the rights must be those required for case preparation and/or presentation.

Equality of arms is a construct applicable only to opposing parties. Whilst the opponent of the accused is predominantly the conventional prosecutor, a party joined to the proceedings, such as an *avocat général* or similar quasi-judicial officer, whose position or observations cannot be regarded as neutral can also attract opponent status.

Article 6(3) contains rights designed to ensure procedural equality between prosecution and defence. Specific regard was had in the book to the nexus between the concept of equality of arms and Articles 6(3)(b)–(d). This nexus is authoritatively recognised in law by the Court and former Commission, and made possible in the Convention because both are elements of the right to a fair hearing in Article 6(1). A nexus also exists at a conceptual level because rights within Articles 6(3)(b)–(d) serve the instrumental, intrinsic and collateral values of equality of arms, and they are feasibly reciprocal and useful for case preparation and presentation, thus come within the equality of arms remit. Despite the strong nexus, the principle of equality of arms is not referred to expressly in all cases concerning these rights; it has an underlying presence.

The rights to challenge and call witness evidence, to adequate time and facilities, and to legal assistance in Articles 6(3)(b)–(d) were relied upon as the context in which the Court's approach to equality of arms was demonstrated and assessed. While the trial as a whole must be fair, the case-law of the Court reveals that these rights can in certain circumstances be limited by states for a proper public interest objective, but only insofar as is strictly necessary.

The predominant approach applied is that an inequality of arms is registered if the procedural inequality gave rise to actual prejudice (an adverse and material effect on the defence case, influencing the reliability of the outcome of the proceedings). This approach accords with the Court's emphasis on examining the trial as a whole and presents an opportunity for states to counterbalance the impact of inequalities, through additional procedural safeguards, to prevent them from becoming prejudicial and amounting to an inequality of arms. It confirms, therefore, that the Court is willing to accept some unequal treatment and the consequent impingement on the dignity of the accused. The burden on applicants of proving that an inequality was prejudicial can in some cases be an especially challenging one. It was submitted that, if an actual prejudice approach is applied, applicants should only bear this burden in cases where the Court does not reasonably expect prima facie that the inequality could have been prejudicial in the circumstances.[1]

Rather than requiring proof of prejudice, the Court has in finding inequality of arms been willing to accept that certain inequalities relevant to the right to legal assistance in Article 6(3)(c) are such that prejudice is manifestly inevitable. This progressive approach is, in other words, an acknowledgement by the Court that certain types of interference with this right or lack of effective legal representation will inevitably create a disadvantage for the accused that pervades many or all aspects of the proceedings to the detriment of the outcome. The approach also reflects an effort by the Court to ensure that the right is practical and effective since proving prejudice can in some instances be impracticable. From the jurisprudence on legal assistance, only in cases on interference with the right to retain private counsel or on denial of access to counsel at interrogation does it appear that resort is had to the actual prejudice approach.

An alternative and more progressive approach would be to treat a procedural inequality as sufficient in itself to constitute a disadvantage – thus it amounts to an inequality of arms – regardless of whether actual or inevitable prejudice arose. This is the approach that allows the concept of equality of arms to express in practice its intrinsic value to the greatest extent – that is, it offers the most protection to the dignity of the accused. It is submitted, nevertheless, that specifically in cases on the examination of vulnerable witnesses and some covert agents, and on the right to call witnesses, application of the actual prejudice proviso should, for good cause, be accepted as unavoidable.[2] In most cases, though, it would be feasible to apply a dignitarian approach to equality of arms and this should be preferred.

1 Ch 2 text to n 128.
2 Ch 3 ss 6.2.3, 6.3.3, 7–8.

BIBLIOGRAPHY

ADAMS CD (tr), *Aeschines: The Speeches* (Heinemann, London 1919)

ADAMS GB, *The Origin of the English Constitution* (2nd edn Yale UP, New Haven 1920)

ALEXANDER M, 'The Right to Counsel for the Politically Unpopular' (1962) 22 Law in Transition 19

ALLEN R, 'The Trial of Socrates: A Study in the Morality of the Criminal Process' in ML Friedland, *Courts and Trials: A Multidisciplinary Approach* (Toronto UP, Toronto 1975)

AMERICAN LAW INSTITUTE, *Restatement of the Law Third: The Foreign Relations Law of the United States* (American Law Institute, St Paul Minnesota 1987) vols 1 and 2

AMNESTY INTERNATIONAL, 'International Criminal Tribunal for Rwanda: Trials and Tribulations' (Report) (31 March 1998) AI-Index IOR 40/003/1998

ANDREWS RM, *Law, Magistracy, and Crime in Old Regime Paris 1735–1789* (CUP, Cambridge 1994) vol 1

ASHWORTH AJ, 'Concepts of Criminal Justice' [1979] Crim LR 412

ASHWORTH A and REDMAYNE M, *The Criminal Process* (4th edn OUP, Oxford 2010)

AULD LJ, 'Review of the Criminal Courts of England and Wales' (HMSO, London 2001)

AUSTRALIAN LAW REFORM COMMISSION, 'Manner of Giving Evidence' Research Paper No 8 (Sydney 1982)

BAKKEN T, 'International Law and Human Rights for Defendants in Criminal Trials' (1985) 25 Indian J Int'l L 411

BALDWIN J, 'Police Interrogation: What are the Rules of the Game?' in D Morgan and GM Stephenson (eds), *Suspicion and Silence: The Right to Silence in Criminal Investigations* (Blackstone, London 1994)

BANNING L, *Jefferson and Madison: Three Conversations from the Founding* (Madison House, Lanham 1995)

BAR STANDARDS BOARD, *Handbook* (2nd edn, London 2015)

BARTLETT R, *Trial by Fire and Water: The Medieval Judicial Ordeal* (Clarendon, Oxford 1986)

BASSIOUNI MC, 'A Functional Approach to "General Principles of International Law"' (1990) 11 Mich J Int'l L 768

BASSIOUNI MC, 'Human Rights in the Context of Criminal Justice: Identifying International Procedural Protections and Equivalent Protections in National Constitutions' (1993) 3 Duke J Comp & Int'l L 235

BATES E, *The Evolution of the European Convention on Human Rights: From its Inception to the Creation of a Permanent Court of Human Rights* (OUP, Oxford 2010)

BAYLES MD, *Procedural Justice: Allocating to Individuals* (Kluwer, Dordrecht 1990)

BEATTIE JM, *Crime and the Courts in England 1660–1800* (Princeton UP, Princeton 1986)

BENNETT A, *The Queen v Palmer: Verbatim Report of the Trial of William Palmer at the Central Criminal Court, Old Bailey, London, May 14, and Following Days, 1856* (J Allen, London 1856)

BENTHAM J, *Rationale of Judicial Evidence* (Hunt and Clarke, London 1827) vol 5

BÉVENOT M, 'The Inquisition and its Antecedents' (1966) 7 Heythrop J 257 (pt 1), 381 (pt 2); (1967) 8 Heythrop J 52 (pt 3), 152 (pt 4)

BIRCH DJ, 'The Criminal Justice Act 1988 – Part 2: Documentary Evidence' [1989] Crim LR 15

BLACKSTONE W, *Commentaries on the Laws of England* (13th edn A Strahan, London 1800) vols 3 and 4

BLAUSTEIN AP, 'Our Most Important Export: The Influence of the United States Constitution Abroad' (1987) 3 Conn J Int'l L 15

BLAUSTEIN AP, 'The Influence of the United States Constitution Abroad' (1987) 12 Okla City U L Rev 435

BLUMENTHAL JA, 'A Wipe of the Hands, A Lick of the Lips: The Validity of Demeanor Evidence in Assessing Witness Credibility' (1993) 72 Neb L Rev 1157

BOURNE HE, 'American Constitutional Precedents in the French National Assembly' (1903) 8 Am Hist Rev 466

BRANNON LC, 'The Trauma of Testifying in Court for Child Victims of Sexual Assault v The Accused's Right to Confrontation' (1994) 18 Law & Psychol Rev 439

BREMS E, 'Conflicting Human Rights: An Exploration in the Context of the Right to a Fair Trial in the European Convention for the Protection of Human Rights and Fundamental Freedoms' (2005) 27 HRQ 294

BROOKS CW, *Pettyfoggers and Vipers of the Commonwealth: The 'Lower Branch' of the Legal Profession in Early Modern England* (CUP, Cambridge 2004)

BRYCE J, *The American Commonwealth* (Macmillan, New York 1914) vol 1

BURDICK WL, *The Principles of Roman Law and their Relation to Modern Law* (Lawyers Co-Operative, Rochester New York 1938)

BURTT JO (tr), *Minor Attic Orators* (Heinemann, London 1962)

BYFIELD B, 'The Right to a Fair Trial: Article 6 of the European Convention' in AD Byre and BY Byfield (eds), *International Human Rights Law in the Commonwealth Caribbean* (Martinus Nijhoff, Dordrecht 1991)

CALVO-GOLLER KN, *The Trial Proceedings of the International Criminal Court: ICTY and ICTR Precedents* (Martinus Nijhoff, Leiden 2006)

CAPPELLETTI M and JOLOWICZ JA, *Public Interest Parties and the Active Role of the Judge in Civil Litigation* (Oceana, Dobbs Ferry New York 1975)

CASSESE A, *International Law* (OUP, Oxford 2001)

CASSESE A, 'The Influence of the European Court of Human Rights on International Criminal Tribunals – Some Methodological Remarks' in M Bergsmo (ed), *Human Rights and Criminal Justice for the Downtrodden* (Martinus Nijhoff, Leiden 2003)

CHENG B, *General Principles of Law as Applied by International Courts and Tribunals* (CUP, Cambridge 1993)

CHEYETTE FL, 'Inquest, Canonical and French' in JR Strayer (ed), *Dictionary of the Middle Ages* (Scribner, New York 1985) vol 6

CLARK W, 'Magna Carta and Trial by Jury' (1924) 58 Am L Rev 24

CLAYTON R and TOMLINSON H, *Fair Trial Rights* (2nd edn OUP, Oxford 2010)

COHN SA, 'International Adjudication of Human Rights: A Survey of its Procedural and Some of its Substantive Holdings' (1977) 7 Ga J Int'l & Comp L 315
COKE E, *The Third Part of the Institutes of the Laws of England* (6th edn W Rawlins, London 1680)
COKE E, *The Second Part of the Institutes of the Laws of England* (6th edn W Rawlins, London 1681)
COLE RJV, 'Validating the Normative Value and Legal Recognition of the Principle of Equality of Arms in Criminal Proceedings in Botswana' (2012) 56 JAL 68
COMMENTS, 'Human Rights – Equality of Arms – Presence of Attorney General at Deliberations of Belgian Court of Cassation Held Not Violative of Article 6(1) of the European Court of Human Rights: *Delcourt* Case' (1971) 4 NYU J Int'l L & Pol 124
CONSTITUTIONAL AFFAIRS SELECT COMMITTEE, 'The Operation of the Special Immigration Appeals Commission (SIAC) and the Use of Special Advocates' HC (2004–2005) 323-I
COPPEL J, *The Human Rights Act 1998: Enforcing the European Convention in the Domestic Courts* (J Wiley & Sons, Chichester 1999)
CORDON IM, GOODMAN GS and ANDERSON SJ, 'Children in Court' in PJ van Koppen and SD Penrod (eds), *Adversarial Versus Inquisitorial Justice: Psychological Perspectives on Criminal Justice Systems* (Kluwer Academic/Plenum, New York 2003)
CORNISH WR, *The Jury* (Penguin, Harmondsworth 1971)
COSTIGAN R and THOMAS PA, 'Anonymous Witnesses' (2000) 51 NILQ 326
COUNCIL OF EUROPE, *Collected Edition of the "Travaux Préparatoires" of the European Convention on Human Rights* (Martinus Nijhoff, The Hague 1975) vol 1
COUNCIL OF EUROPE, *Collected Edition of the "Travaux Préparatoires" of the European Convention on Human Rights* (Martinus Nijhoff, The Hague 1977) vol 4
CROOK JA, *Legal Advocacy in the Roman World* (Duckworth, London 1995)
CROWN PROSECUTION SERVICE, *The Code for Crown Prosecutors* (7th edn, London 2013)
DALBERG-ACTON JEE, FIGGIS JN and LAURENCE RV (eds), *Lectures on the French Revolution* (Macmillan, London 1910)
DAMAŠKA M, 'Evidentiary Barriers to Conviction and Two Models of Criminal Procedure: A Comparative Study' (1973) 121 U Pa L Rev 506
DAMAŠKA M, 'Structures of Authority and Comparative Criminal Procedure' (1975) 84 Yale LJ 480
DE GLANVILL R and HALL GDG (ed) (tr), *The Treatise on the Laws and Customs of the Realm of England* (Nelson, London 1965)
DE LA ROCHEFOUCAULD LA (tr), *Constitutions des Treize États-Unis de l'Amérique* (Pierres & Pissot, Paris 1783)
DECKER JF, 'The Sixth Amendment Right to Shoot Oneself in the Foot: An Assessment of the Guarantee of Self-Representation Twenty Years after *Faretta*' (1996) 6 Seton Hall Const LJ 483
DELMAS-MARTY M, 'Toward a European Model of the Criminal Trial' in M Delmas-Marty (ed), *The Criminal Process and Human Rights: Toward a European Consciousness* (Martinus Nijhoff, Dordrecht 1995)
DELMAS-MARTY M, *Towards a Truly Common Law: Europe as a Laboratory for Legal Pluralism* (CUP, Cambridge 2002)

DENNING A, *Freedom Under the Law* (Stevens & Sons, London 1949)

DEPARTMENT OF THE ARMY (ed), *Trials of War Criminals Before the Nuernberg Military Tribunals Under Control Council Law No 10* ('TWC') (Government Printing Office, Washington 1953) vol 15

DEVLIN P, *The Criminal Prosecution in England* (OUP, London 1960)

DOAK J, 'The Victim and the Criminal Process: An Analysis of Recent Trends in Regional and International Tribunals' (2003) 23 Legal Stud 1

DODD CH (ed), *The New English Bible: New Testament* (OUP, Oxford 1961)

DODD CH (ed), *The New English Bible: Old Testament* (OUP, Oxford 1970)

DONOVAN JM, *Juries and the Transformation of Criminal Justice in France in the Nineteenth and Twentieth Centuries* (North Carolina UP, Chapel Hill 2010)

DOSWALD-BECK L and KOLB R, *Judicial Process and Human Rights: United Nations, European, American and African Systems: Texts and Summaries of International Case Law* (NP Engel, Kehl 2004)

DUFF A and others, 'Introduction: Towards a Normative Theory of the Criminal Trial' in A Duff and others (eds), *The Trial on Trial (1): Truth and Due Process* (Hart, Oxford 2004)

DUFF A and others, 'Introduction: Judgement and Calling to Account' in A Duff and others (eds), *The Trial on Trial (2): Judgement and Calling to Account* (Hart, Oxford 2006)

DUFF A and others, *The Trial on Trial (3): Towards a Normative Theory of the Criminal Trial* (Hart, Oxford 2007) 95.

DUFF P, 'Changing Conceptions of the Scottish Criminal Trial: The Duty to Agree Uncontroversial Evidence' in A Duff and others (eds), *The Trial on Trial (1): Truth and Due Process* (Hart, Oxford 2004)

DUFF RA, *Trials and Punishments* (CUP, Cambridge 1986)

DUKE S, 'The Right to Appointed Counsel: *Argersinger* and Beyond' (1975) 12 Am Crim L Rev 601

DWORKIN R, *Taking Rights Seriously* (Duckworth, London 1977)

ELLISON L, 'The Protection of Vulnerable Witnesses in Court: An Anglo-Dutch Comparison' (1999) 3 Int'l J Evidence & Proof 29

ELLISON L, *The Adversarial Process and the Vulnerable Witness* (OUP, Oxford 2001)

EMMERSON B and others, *Human Rights and Criminal Justice* (3rd edn Sweet & Maxwell, London 2012)

EPP JA, *Building on the Decade of Disclosure in Criminal Procedure* (Cavendish, London 2007)

ESMEIN A, *A History of Continental Criminal Procedure* (J Murray, London 1914)

EVANS M and JACK RI, *Sources of English Legal and Constitutional History* (Butterworths, Sydney 1984)

FAWCETT JES, *The Application of the European Convention on Human Rights* (Clarendon, Oxford 1987)

FEDOROVA M, *The Principle of Equality of Arms in International Criminal Proceedings* (Intersentia, Cambridge 2012)

FELDMAN D, 'Human Dignity as a Legal Value: Part 1' [1999] PL 682

FERENCZ BB, 'Nurnberg Trial Procedure and the Rights of the Accused' (1948) 39 J Crim L & Criminology

FINDLAY M, 'Synthesis in Trial Procedures? The Experience of International Criminal Tribunals' (2001) 50 ICLQ 26

FITZPATRICK B, 'Disclosure: Principles, Processes and Politics' in C Walker and K Starmer (eds), *Miscarriages of Justice: A Review of Justice in Error* (Blackstone, London 1999)

FLETCHER GP, *The Grammar of Criminal Law: American, Comparative, and International* (OUP, New York 2007) vol 1

FORSYTH W, *Hortensius: or, The Advocate: An Historical Essay* (J Murray, London 1849)

FORSYTH W, *History of Trial by Jury* (JW Parker, London 1852)

FRAHER RM, 'The Theoretical Justification for the New Criminal Law of the High Middle Ages: "Rei Publicae Interest, Ne Crimina Remaneant Impunita"' [1984] U Ill L Rev 577

FRANK JP, 'Disqualification of Judges' (1947) 56 Yale LJ 605

FULLER LL, *The Morality of Law* (Yale UP, New Haven 1969)

GALLIGAN DJ, *Due Process and Fair Procedures: A Study of Administrative Procedures* (Clarendon, Oxford 1996)

GARNSEY P, *Social Status and Privilege in the Roman Empire* (Clarendon, Oxford 1970)

GEARTY C, *Principles of Human Rights Adjudication* (OUP, Oxford 2004)

GIVEN J, 'The Inquisitors of Languedoc and the Medieval Technology of Power' (1989) 94 Am Hist Rev 336

GOLDSTEIN AS, 'The State and the Accused: Balance of Advantage in Criminal Procedure' (1960) 69 Yale LJ 1149

GOLDWASSER K, 'Limiting a Criminal Defendant's Use of Peremptory Challenges: On Symmetry and the Jury in a Criminal Trial' (1989) 102 Harv L Rev 808

GÖNCZ Á, opening ceremony speech in Council of Europe, *8th International Colloquy on the European Convention on Human Rights* (Council of Europe, Strasbourg 1996)

GOODMAN GS and others, 'Testifying in Criminal Court: Emotional Effects on Child Sexual Assault Victims' (1992) 57 Monogr Soc Res Child Dev 1

GREY TC, 'Procedural Fairness and Substantive Rights' in JR Pennock and JW Chapman (eds), *Due Process* (New York UP, New York 1977)

HALE M and EMLYN S (ed), *The History of the Pleas of the Crown* (E and R Nutt and R Gosling, London 1736) vol 2

HAMILTON A, 'On Maintaining a Just Partition of Power Among the Necessary Departments' in A Hamilton, J Jay and J Madison, *The Federalist* (The Colonial Press, New York 1901)

HAMILTON B, *The Medieval Inquisition* (E Arnold, London 1981)

HANNUM H, 'The Status of the Universal Declaration of Human Rights in National and International Law' (1995–1996) 25 Ga J Int'l & Comp L 287

HANSON JA (ed) (tr), *Apuleius: Metamorphoses Books 7–11* (Harvard UP, Cambridge 1989) vol 2

HARRIES J, *Law and Empire in Late Antiquity* (CUP, Cambridge 1999)

HARRIS D, 'The Right to Fair Trial in Criminal Proceedings as a Human Right' (1967) 16 ICLQ 352

HARRIS D and others, *Harris, O'Boyle and Warbrick: Law of the European Convention on Human Rights* (2nd edn OUP, Oxford 2009)

HARRIS D and others, *Harris, O'Boyle and Warbrick: Law of the European Convention on Human Rights* (3rd edn OUP, Oxford 2014)
HARRIS D, O'BOYLE M and WARBRICK C, *Law of the European Convention on Human Rights* (Butterworths, London 1995)
HASHIMOTO EJ, 'Defending the Right of Self-Representation: An Empirical Look at the Pro Se Felony Defendant' (2007) 85 NC L Rev 423
HATCHARD J, HUBER B and VOGLER R (eds), *Comparative Criminal Procedure* (BIICL, London 1996)
HAYEK FA, *The Road to Serfdom* (Routledge, London 1944)
HAZELTINE HD, 'The Influence of Magna Carta on American Constitutional Development' in HE Malden (ed), *Magna Carta Commemoration Essays* (Royal Historical Society, London 1917)
HEBERT PM, 'The Nurnberg Subsequent Trials' (1949) 16 Ins Counsel J 226
HELLER KJ, *The Nuremberg Military Tribunals and the Origins of International Criminal Law* (OUP, Oxford 2011)
HENDERSON EF (ed) (tr), *Select Historical Documents of the Middle Ages* (G Bell and Sons, London 1905)
HERRMANN FR and SPEER BM, 'Facing the Accuser: Ancient and Medieval Precursors of the Confrontation Clause' (1994) 34 Va J Int'l L 481
HEUSTON RFV, *Essays in Constitutional Law* (2nd edn Stevens & Sons, London 1964)
HEVENER NK and MOSHER SA, 'General Principles of Law and the UN Covenant on Civil and Political Rights' (1978) 27 ICLQ 596
HINE HM (tr), *Seneca: Medea* (Aris & Phillips, Warminster 2000)
HO HL, *A Philosophy of Evidence Law: Justice in the Search for Truth* (OUP, Oxford 2008)
HODGSON J, 'Conceptions of the Trial in Inquisitorial and Adversarial Procedure' in A Duff and others (eds), *The Trial on Trial (2): Judgement and Calling to Account* (Hart, Oxford 2006)
HOLDSWORTH WS, *A History of English Law* (3rd edn Little, Brown and Co, Boston 1922) vol 1
HOLDSWORTH WS, *A History of English Law* (3rd edn Methuen, London 1923) vol 2
HOLT JC, *Magna Carta* (2nd edn CUP, Cambridge 1992)
HOWARD AED, *The Road from Runnymede: Magna Carta and Constitutionalism in America* (Virginia UP, Charlottesville 1968)
HOWARD AED, 'The Values of Federalism' (1993) 1 New Eur L Rev 143
HRUSCHKA J, 'Kant and Human Dignity' in BS Byrd and J Hruschka (eds), *Kant and Law* (Ashgate, Aldershot 2006)
HUMAN RIGHTS COMMITTEE, 'General Comment No 18: Non-discrimination' (1989) UN Doc A/45/40
HUMAN RIGHTS COMMITTE, 'General Comment No 32: Article 14: Right to Equality before Courts and Tribunals and to Fair Trial' (2007) UN Doc CCPR/C/GC/32
HUMPHREY JP, 'The International Bill of Rights: Scope and Implementation' (1976) 17 Wm & Mary L Rev 527
HUNT L, 'Introduction: The Revolutionary Origins of Human Rights' in L Hunt (ed) (tr), *The French Revolution and Human Rights: A Brief Documentary History* (Bedford/St Martin's, Boston 1996)

HUTTON M and PETERSON W (trs); OGILVIE RM, WARMINGTON EH and WINTERBOTTOM M (revised), *Tacitus: Agricola; Germania; Dialogus* (Harvard UP, Cambridge 1980) vol 1

INTER-AMERICAN COMMISSION ON HUMAN RIGHTS, 'Report on the Situation of Human Rights in Paraguay' OEA/Ser.L/V/II.43 doc 13 corr 1 (1978)

INTER-AMERICAN COMMISSION ON HUMAN RIGHTS, 'Report on the Situation of Human Rights in Uruguay' OEA/Ser.L/V/II.43 doc 19 corr 1 (1978)

INTER-AMERICAN COMMISSION ON HUMAN RIGHTS, 'Sixth Report on the Situation of Political Prisoners in Cuba' OEA/Ser.L/V/II.48 doc 24 (1979)

INTER-AMERICAN COMMISSION ON HUMAN RIGHTS, 'Report on the Situation of Human Rights in Argentina' OEA/Ser.L/V/II.49 doc 19 corr 1 (1980)

INTER-AMERICAN COMMISSION ON HUMAN RIGHTS, 'Report on the Situation of Human Rights in the Republic of Guatemala' OEA/Ser.L/V/II.53 doc 21 rev 2 (1981)

INTER-AMERICAN COMMISSION ON HUMAN RIGHTS, 'Seventh Report on the Situation of Human Rights in Cuba' OEA/Ser.L/V/II.61 doc 29 rev 1 (1983)

INTER-AMERICAN COMMISSION ON HUMAN RIGHTS, 'Second Report on the Human Rights Situation in Suriname' OEA/Ser.L/V/II.66 doc 21 rev 1 (1985)

IP J, 'The Rise and Spread of the Special Advocate' [2008] PL 717

IRVINE Lord, 'The Spirit of Magna Carta Continues to Resonate in Modern Law' (2003) 119 LQR 227

JACKSON J (tr), *Tacitus: The Annals Books 4–6, 11–12* (Heinemann, London 1986) vol 4

JACKSON JD, 'Managing Uncertainty and Finality: The Function of the Criminal Trial in Legal Inquiry' in A Duff and others (eds), *The Trial on Trial (1): Truth and Due Process* (Hart, Oxford 2004)

JACKSON JD, 'The Effect of Human Rights in Criminal Evidentiary Processes: Towards Convergence, Divergence or Realignment?' (2005) 68 MLR 737

JACKSON JD and SUMMERS SJ, *The Internationalisation of Criminal Evidence: Beyond the Common Law and Civil Law Traditions* (CUP, Cambridge 2012)

JACKSON P, *Natural Justice* (Sweet & Maxwell, London 1979)

JELLINEK G and FARRAND M (tr), *The Declaration of the Rights of Man and of Citizens: A Contribution to Modern Constitutional History* (Holt and Co, New York 1901)

JENNINGS A, 'Fair Trial' in K Starmer and others, *Criminal Justice, Police Powers and Human Rights* (Blackstone, London 2001)

JENNINGS I, *Magna Carta and its Influence in the World Today* (HMSO, London 1965)

JOHNSON MG, 'A Magna Carta for Mankind: Writing the Universal Declaration of Human Rights' in MG Johnson and J Symonides (eds), *The Universal Declaration of Human Rights: A History of its Creation and Implementation 1948–1998* (UNESCO, Paris 1998)

JOHNSON VR, 'The Declaration of the Rights of Man and of Citizens of 1789, the Reign of Terror, and the Revolutionary Tribunal of Paris' (1990) 13 BC Int'l & Comp L Rev 1

JONES JW, *The Law and Legal Theory of the Greeks* (Clarendon, Oxford 1956)

JÖRG N, FIELD S and BRANTS C, 'Are Inquisitorial and Adversarial Systems Converging?' in P Fennell and others (eds), *Criminal Justice in Europe: A Comparative Study* (Clarendon, Oxford 1995)

JOSEPH S and CASTAN M, *The International Covenant on Civil and Political Rights: Cases, Materials, and Commentary* (3rd edn OUP, Oxford 2013)

KANT I and GREGOR M (ed) (tr), *The Metaphysics of Morals* (CUP, Cambridge 1996)
KAUFMAN IR, 'The Essence of Judicial Independence' (1980) 80 Colum L Rev 671
KELLY HA, *Inquisitions and Other Trial Procedures in the Medieval West* (Ashgate, Aldershot 2001)
KELLY JM, '*Audi Alteram Partem*' (1964) 9 Nat LF 103
KELLY JM, *Roman Litigation* (Clarendon, Oxford 1966)
KIDD CJF, 'Disciplinary Proceedings and the Right to a Fair Criminal Trial Under the European Convention on Human Rights' (1987) 36 ICLQ 856
KNOOPS GJA, 'The Dichotomy Between Judicial Economy and Equality of Arms Within International and Internationalized Criminal Trials: A Defense Perspective' (2005) 28 Fordham Int'l LJ 1566
KOMMERS DP, 'German Constitutionalism: A Prolegomenon' (1991) 40 Emory LJ 837
KOVACS D (ed) (tr), *Euripides* (Harvard UP, Cambridge 1995)
KUIJER M, *The Blindfold of Lady Justice: Judicial Independence and Impartiality in Light of the Requirements of Article 6 ECHR* (EM Meijers Instituut, Leiden 2004)
LANGBEIN JH, 'The German Advantage in Civil Procedure' (1985) 52 U Chi L Rev 823
LANGBEIN JH, 'The Historical Origins of the Privilege Against Self-Incrimination at Common Law' (1994) 92 Mich L Rev 1047
LANGBEIN JH, 'The Prosecutorial Origins of Defence Counsel in the Eighteenth Century: The Appearance of Solicitors' (1999) 58 Cambridge LJ 314
LANSFORD T, 'Declaration of the Rights of Man and of the Citizen' in G Fremont-Barnes (ed), *Encyclopedia of the Age of Political Revolutions and New Ideologies, 1760–1815* (Greenwood, Westport 2007)
LAUTERPACHT H, 'The Law of Nations, the Law of Nature and the Rights of Man' (1943) 29 Transactions Grotius Society 1
LAUTERPACHT H, 'The Universal Declaration of Human Rights' (1948) 25 Brit YBIL 354
LAUTERPACHT H, *International Law and Human Rights* (Archon, Hamden 1968)
LAW COMMISSION, 'Evidence in Criminal Proceedings: Hearsay and Related Topics' Consultation Paper No 138 (HMSO, London 1995)
LAW DS and VERSTEEG M, 'The Declining Influence of the United States Constitution' (2012) 87 NYU L Rev 762
LEA HC, *A History of the Inquisition of the Middle Ages* (Macmillan, London 1908) vol 1
LEAMING A and SPICER J (eds), *The Grants, Concessions, and Original Constitutions of the Province of New Jersey* (2nd edn Honeyman, Somerville 1881)
LEMAY JAL, 'John Mercer and the Stamp Act in Virginia, 1764–1765' (1983) 91 Va Mag Hist & Biog 3
LIEBER F, *On Civil Liberty and Self-Government* (Lippincott, Grambo and Co, Philadelphia 1853) vol 2
LILLICH RB, 'Civil Rights' in T Meron (ed), *Human Rights in International Law: Legal and Policy Issues* (Clarendon, Oxford 1984) vol 1
LOCKE J, *An Essay Concerning Human Understanding* (Samuel Marks, New York 1825) vol 1
LOUCAIDES LG, 'Questions of Fair Trial Under the European Convention on Human Rights' (2003) 3 Hum Rts L Rev 27
LOVAT H and SHANY Y, 'The European Court of Human Rights' in Y Shany, *Assessing the Effectiveness of International Courts* (OUP, Oxford 2014)
LOWELL AL, 'The Judicial Use of Torture' (1897) 11 Harv L Rev 220

LUDWIKOWSKI RR, 'The French Declaration of the Rights of Man and Citizen and the American Constitutional Development' (1990) 38 Am J Comp L Supp 445

LUSTY D, 'Anonymous Accusers: An Historical & Comparative Analysis of Secret Witnesses in Criminal Trials' (2002) 24 Sydney L Rev 361

LUTZ DS (ed), *Colonial Origins of the American Constitution: A Documentary History* (Liberty Fund, Indianapolis 1998)

MACDONELL J, *Historical Trials* (Clarendon, Oxford 1927)

MACNAIR M, 'Vicinage and the Antecedents of the Jury' (1999) 17 Law & Hist Rev 537

MAFFEI S, *The European Right to Confrontation in Criminal Proceedings: Absent, Anonymous and Vulnerable Witnesses* (Europa Law, Groningen 2006)

MAITLAND FW, *Justice and Police* (Macmillan, London 1885)

MALSCH M, 'Victims on View: Are Victims Served by the Principle of Open Justice?' in H Kaptein and M Malsch (eds), *Crime, Victims and Justice: Essays on Principles and Practice* (Aldershot, Ashgate 2004)

MARSHALL HH, *Natural Justice* (Sweet & Maxwell, London 1959)

MASHAW JL, *Due Process in the Administrative State* (Yale UP, New Haven 1985)

MASSARO TM, 'The Dignity Value of Face-to-Face Confrontations' (1988) 40 U Fla L Rev 863

MAY R and WIERDA M, 'Trends in International Criminal Evidence: Nuremberg, Tokyo, The Hague, and Arusha' (1999) 37 Colum J Transnat'l L 725

MAYCOCK AL, *The Inquisition: From its Establishment to the Great Schism* (Constable, London 1926)

McCONVILLE M, SANDERS A and LENG R, *The Case for the Prosecution* (Routledge, London 1991)

McDOUGAL MS, LASSWELL HD and CHEN L-C, *Human Rights and World Public Order: The Basic Policies of an International Law of Human Dignity* (Yale UP, New Haven 1980)

McEWAN J, *Evidence and the Adversarial Process: The Modern Law* (Blackwell, Oxford 1992)

McGOUGH LS, 'Good Enough for Government Work: The Constitutional Duty to Preserve Forensic Interviews of Child Victims' (2002) 65 Law & Contemp Probs 179

McILWAIN CH, 'Due Process of Law in Magna Carta' (1914) 14 Colum L Rev 27

McINTYRE G, 'Equality of Arms – Defining Human Rights in the Jurisprudence of the International Criminal Tribunal for the former Yugoslavia' (2003) 16 LJIL 269

McKECHNIE WS, *Magna Carta: A Commentary on the Great Charter of King John* (J Maclehose, Glasgow 1914)

MEERNIK J, 'Equality of Arms? The Individual vs. The International Community in War Crimes Tribunals' (2003) 86 Judicature 312

MERON T, *Human Rights and Humanitarian Norms as Customary Law* (Clarendon, Oxford 1989)

MERRILLS JG and ROBERTSON AH, *Human Rights in Europe: A Study of the European Convention on Human Rights* (4th edn Manchester UP, Manchester 2001)

MICHELMAN FI, 'Formal and Associational Aims in Procedural Due Process' in JR Pennock and JW Chapman (eds), *Due Process* (New York UP, New York 1977)

MILL JS, *On Liberty* (2nd edn Ticknor and Fields, Boston 1863)

'MONTREAL STATEMENT of the Assembly for Human Rights, March 22–27, 1968' (1968) 9 J Int'l Comm Jurists 94

MOORE CH (tr), *Tacitus: The Histories Books 1–3* (Heinemann, London 1980) vol 2

MORAVCSIK A, 'The Origins of Human Rights Regimes: Democratic Delegation in Postwar Europe' (2000) 54 Int'l Org 217

MORRIS V and SCHARF MP, *An Insider's Guide to the International Criminal Tribunal for the Former Yugoslavia: A Documentary History and Analysis* (Transnational, Irvington-on-Hudson 1995) vol 1

MORRISON CA, 'Some Features of the Roman and the English Law of Evidence' (1959) 33 Tul L Rev 577

MOTT RL, *Due Process of Law: A Historical and Analytical Treatise of the Principles and Methods Followed by the Courts in the Application of the Concept of the "Law of the Land"* (Bobbs-Merrill, Indianapolis 1926)

MURPHY P and BADDOUR L, 'International Criminal Law and Common Law Rules of Evidence' in KAA Khan, C Buisman and C Gosnell (eds), *Principles of Evidence in International Criminal Justice* (OUP, Oxford 2010)

MURRAY AT (tr), *Demosthenes: Private Orations* (Heinemann, London 1939)

MUTUA M, *Human Rights: A Political and Cultural Critique* (Pennsylvania UP, Philadelphia 2002)

NADELMANN KH, 'Due Process of Law before the European Court of Human Rights: The Secret Deliberation' (1972) 66 AJIL 509

NATIONAL CONSTITUENT ASSEMBLY, *The French Constitution, Revised, Amended, and Finally Decreed, by the National Assembly* (W Young, Philadelphia 1791)

NAYAR MGK, 'Human Rights: The United Nations and United States Foreign Policy' (1978) 19 Harv Int'l LJ 813

NEGRI S, 'The Principle of "Equality of Arms" and the Evolving Law of International Criminal Procedure' (2005) 5 Int CLR 513

NEGRI S, 'Equality of Arms – Guiding Light or Empty Shell?' in M Bohlander (ed), *International Criminal Justice: A Critical Analysis of Institutions and Procedures* (Cameron May, London 2007)

NEILSON G, *Trial by Combat* (Hodge, Glasgow 1890)

NEW SOUTH WALES LAW REFORM COMMISSION, 'Questioning of Complainants by Unrepresented Accused in Sexual Offence Trials' Report 101 (Sydney 2003)

NIBLETT J, *Disclosure in Criminal Proceedings* (Blackstone, London 1997)

NOWAK M, *UN Covenant on Civil and Political Rights: CCPR Commentary* (Engel, Kehl 1993)

OSBORNE C, 'Hearsay and the European Court of Human Rights' [1993] Crim LR 255

OWEN T, 'Disclosure' in K Starmer and others, *Criminal Justice, Police Powers and Human Rights* (Blackstone, London 2001)

PACKER HL, *The Limits of Criminal Sanction* (Stanford UP, Stanford 1969)

PAINE T, *The Rights of Man; Being an Answer to Mr Burke's Attack on the French Revolution* (Sherwin, London 1817)

PARK RC, 'Adversarial Influences on the Interrogation of Trial Witnesses' in PJ van Koppen and SD Penrod (eds), *Adversarial Versus Inquisitorial Justice: Psychological Perspectives on Criminal Justice Systems* (Kluwer Academic/Plenum, New York 2003)

PARLIAMENTARY ASSEMBLY OF THE COUNCIL OF EUROPE: COMMITTEE ON LEGAL AFFAIRS AND HUMAN RIGHTS, 'Strengthening Subsidiarity: Integrating the Strasbourg Court's Case Law into National Law and Judicial Practice' AS/Jur/Inf (2010) 04

PENNINGTON K, *The Prince and the Law, 1200–1600: Sovereignty and Rights in the Western Legal Tradition* (California UP, Berkeley 1993)

PHARR C (tr), *The Theodosian Code and Novels and the Sirmondian Constitutions* (Princeton UP, Princeton 1952)

PHARR C (ed) and others, *Ancient Roman Statutes: A Translation with Introduction, Commentary, Glossary, and Index* (Texas UP, Austin 1961)

PHILLIPS R, *On the Powers and Duties of Juries, and on the Criminal Laws of England* (2nd edn Sherwood, Neely and Jones, London 1813)

PIKE LO, *A Constitutional History of the House of Lords from Original Sources* (Macmillan, London 1894)

PINCOFFS EL, 'Due Process, Fraternity, and a Kantian Injunction' in JR Pennock and JW Chapman (eds), *Due Process* (New York UP, New York 1977)

PITTMAN RC, Book Review (1960) 68 Va Mag Hist & Biog 109

PLOWDEN P and KERRIGAN K, *Advocacy and Human Rights: Using the Convention in Courts and Tribunals* (Cavendish, London 2002)

PLUCKNETT TFT, *A Concise History of the Common Law* (5th edn Butterworth, London 1956)

POLLITT D, 'The Right of Confrontation: Its History and Modern Dress' (1959) 8 J Pub L 381

POLLOCK F and MAITLAND FW, *The History of English Law before the Time of Edward I* (2nd edn CUP, London 1898) vols 1 and 2

POUND R, 'The Causes of Popular Dissatisfaction with the Administration of Justice' (1906) 40 Am L Rev 729

POUND R, 'What is a Profession? The Rise of the Legal Profession in Antiquity' (1944) 19 Notre Dame L 203

POWICKE FM, 'Per Judicium Parium vel per Legem Terrae' in HE Malden (ed), *Magna Carta Commemoration Essays* (Royal Historical Society, London 1917)

PRITCHARD MS, 'Human Dignity and Justice' (1972) 82 Ethics 299

RADICE B (tr), *Pliny: Letters and Panegyricus* (Harvard UP, Cambridge 1975) vol 2

RAITHBY J (ed), *The Statutes at Large, of England and of Great-Britain: From Magna Carta to the Union of the Kingdoms of Great Britain and Ireland* (G Eyre and A Strahan, London 1811) vols 6 and 7

RAKOVE JN, 'The Original Justifications for Judicial Independence' (2007) 95 Geo LJ 1061

RAWLS J, *A Theory of Justice* (OUP, Oxford 1999)

RAZ J, 'The Rule of Law and its Virtue' (1977) 93 LQR 195

RÉGNIER CA (ed), *Recueil des Loix Constitutives des Colonies Angloises, Confédérées sous la Dénomination d' États-Unis de l'Amérique-Septentrionale* (Cellot & Jombert, Paris 1778)

RIGGS RE, 'Substantive Due Process in 1791' [1990] Wis L Rev 941

ROBERTSON AH, *Human Rights in Europe* (Manchester UP, Manchester 1963)

ROBERTSON AH and MERRILLS JG, *Human Rights in the World: An Introduction to the Study of the International Protection of Human Rights* (4th edn Manchester UP, Manchester 1996)

ROGERS S, 'The Ethics of Advocacy' (1899) 15 LQR 259
ROLFE JC (tr), *Suetonius* (Harvard UP, Cambridge 1998) vol 2
RUSSELL MJ, 'Trial by Battle Procedure in Writs of Right and Criminal Appeals' (1983) 51 Tijdschrift voor Rechtsgeschiedenis 123
RUTLAND RA, *The Birth of the Bill of Rights, 1776–1791* (North Carolina UP, Chapel Hill 1955)
RYSSDAL R, 'The Coming of Age of the European Convention on Human Rights' [1996] EHRLR 18
SAFFERLING CJM, *Towards an International Criminal Procedure* (OUP, Oxford 2001)
SAPHIRE RB, 'Specifying Due Process Values: Toward a More Responsive Approach to Procedural Protection' (1978) 127 U Pa L Rev 111
SCHACHTER O, 'Human Dignity as a Normative Concept' (1983) 77 AJIL 848
SCHAEFER WV, 'Federalism and State Criminal Procedure' (1956) 70 Harv L Rev 1
SCHROEDER HJ, *Disciplinary Decrees of the General Councils: Text, Translation, and Commentary* (B Herder, St Louis 1937)
SCHWARTZ B, *The Roots of the Bill of Rights* (Chelsea House, New York 1980) vol 2
SCHWARTZ B, *The Great Rights of Mankind: A History of the American Bill of Rights* (Rowman & Littlefield, Lanham 1992)
SCOTT SP (tr), *The Civil Law* (Central Trust, Cincinnati 1932) vol 16
SELBY JE, *The Revolution in Virginia, 1775–1783* (Colonial Williamsburg, Williamsburg 2007)
SHACKLETON BAILEY DR (ed) (tr), *Cicero: Letters to Atticus* (Harvard UP, Cambridge 1999) vol 2
SHAPIRO AH, 'Political Theory and the Growth of Defensive Safeguards in Criminal Procedure: The Origins of the Treason Trials Act of 1696' (1993) 11 Law & Hist Rev 215
SHAPIRO M, 'Judicial Independence: The English Experience' (1977) 55 NC L Rev 577
SHULTZINER D, 'Human Dignity: Functions and Meanings' in J Malpas and N Lickiss (eds), *Perspectives on Human Dignity: A Conversation* (Springer, Dordrecht 2007)
SILVER JS, 'Equality of Arms and the Adversarial Process: A New Constitutional Right' [1990] Wis L Rev 1007
SIMMA B and ALSTON P, 'The Sources of Human Rights Law: Custom, Jus Cogens, and General Principles' (1992) 12 Aust YBIL 82
SOHN LB, 'The New International Law: Protection of the Rights of Individuals Rather than States' (1982) 32 Am U L Rev 1
SOLUM LB, 'Procedural Justice' (2004) 78 S Cal L Rev 181
SOMMERSTEIN AH (ed) (tr), *Aristophanes: Wasps* (Aris & Phillips, Warminster 1983)
SPENCER JR, 'Children's Evidence in Legal Proceedings in England' in JR Spencer and others (eds), *Children's Evidence in Legal Proceedings: An International Perspective* (Cambridge University Law Faculty, Cambridge 1990)
SPENCER JR, 'Orality and the Evidence of Absent Witnesses' [1994] Crim LR 628
STAVROS S, *The Guarantees for Accused Persons Under Article 6 of the European Convention on Human Rights: An Analysis of the Application of the Convention and a Comparison with Other Instruments* (Martinus Nijhoff, Dordrecht 1993)
STEPHEN JF, *A History of the Criminal Law of England* (Macmillan, London 1883) vol 1
STEPHEN JF, *A General View of the Criminal Law of England* (2nd edn Macmillan, London 1890)

STONE M, 'Instant Lie Detection? Demeanour and Credibility in Criminal Trials' [1991] Crim LR 821

STRACHAN-DAVIDSON JL, *Problems of the Roman Criminal Law* (Clarendon, Oxford 1912) vol 2

STRANGE M, 'Evidence' in K Starmer and others, *Criminal Justice, Police Powers and Human Rights* (Blackstone, London 2001)

SUMMERS RS, 'Evaluating and Improving Legal Processes – A Plea for "Process Values"' (1974) 60 Cornell L Rev 1

SUMMERS SJ, *Fair Trials: The European Criminal Procedural Tradition and the European Court of Human Rights* (Hart, Oxford 2007)

SWART B and YOUNG J, 'The European Convention on Human Rights and Criminal Justice in the Netherlands and the United Kingdom' in P Fennell and others (eds), *Criminal Justice in Europe: A Comparative Study* (Clarendon, Oxford 1995)

TAYLOR T, *Final Report to the Secretary of the Army on the Nuernberg War Crimes Trials Under Control Council Law No 10* (Government Printing Office, Washington 1949)

TAYLOR T, *The Anatomy of the Nuremberg Trials: A Personal Memoir* (AA Knopf, New York 1992)

THAYER JB, *A Preliminary Treatise on Evidence at the Common Law* (Little, Brown and Co, Boston 1898)

THIRLWAY H, 'The Sources of International Law' in MD Evans (ed), *International Law* (2nd edn OUP, Oxford 2006)

THOMPSON F, *Magna Carta: Its Role in the Making of the English Constitution 1300–1629* (Minnesota UP, Minneapolis 1948)

THORNBERRY P, *International Law and the Rights of Minorities* (Clarendon, Oxford 1991)

THORPE FN (ed), *The Federal and State Constitutions, Colonial Charters, and Other Organic Laws of the States, Territories, and Colonies Now or Heretofore Forming the United States of America* (Government Printing Office, Washington 1909) vols 1 and 3–7

TREBILCOCK MJ and DANIELS RJ, *Rule of Law Reform and Development: Charting the Fragile Path of Progress* (Edward Elgar, Cheltenham 2008)

TRECHSEL S, *Human Rights in Criminal Proceedings* (OUP, Oxford 2005)

TRIBE LH, *American Constitutional Law* (2nd edn Foundation Press, Mineola New York 1988)

TURNER RV, *Magna Carta* (Pearson Education, Harlow 2003)

TYLER TR, *Why People Obey the Law* (Princeton UP, Princeton 2006)

ULLMANN W, 'Medieval Principles of Evidence' (1946) LQR 77

ULLMANN W, 'Some Medieval Principles of Criminal Procedure' (1947) 59 Jur Rev 1

UN GENERAL ASSEMBLY, 'Report of the International Court of Justice: 1 August 2003–31 July 2004' 59th Session Supp No 4 UN Doc A/59/4 (2004)

US CONGRESS, *The French Declaration of the Rights of Man and of the Citizen and the American Bill of Rights: A Bicentennial Commemoration Issued Pursuant to SJ Res 317, 100th Congress* (Government Printing Office, Washington 1989)

VAN DIJK P, 'Universal Legal Principles of Fair Trial in Criminal Proceedings' in A Rosas and J Helgesen (eds), *Human Rights in a Changing East-West Perspective* (Pinter, London 1990)

VAN DIJK P and VAN HOOF GJH, *Theory and Practice of the European Convention on Human Rights* (3rd edn Kluwer Law International, The Hague 1998)

VAN DIJK P and VIERING M, 'Right to a Fair and Public Hearing (Article 6)' in P van Dijk and others (eds), *Theory and Practice of the European Convention on Human Rights* (4th edn Intersentia, Antwerp 2006)

VINCE CA and VINCE JH (trs), *Demosthenes: De Corona and De Falsa Legatione* (Heinemann, London 1926)

VINCE JH (tr), *Demosthenes: Against Meidias, Androtion, Aristocrates, Timocrates, Aristogeiton* (Heinemann, London 1935)

VINOGRADOFF P, 'Magna Carta, C. 39: Nullus Liber Homo, etc' in HE Malden (ed), *Magna Carta Commemoration Essays* (Royal Historical Society, London 1917)

VOUIN R, 'The Protection of the Accused in French Criminal Procedure' (1956) 5 ICLQ 157

WALDRON J, 'The Concept and the Rule of Law' (2008) 43 Ga L Rev 1

WALKER GQ, *The Rule of Law: Foundation of Constitutional Democracy* (Melbourne UP, Carlton 1988)

WALLACH EJ, 'The Procedural and Evidentiary Rules of the Post-World War II War Crimes Trials: Did They Provide an Outline for International Legal Procedure?' (1999) 37 Colum J Transnat'l L 851

WĄSEK-WIADEREK M, *The Principle of "Equality of Arms" in Criminal Procedure Under Article 6 of the European Convention on Human Rights and its Functions in Criminal Justice of Selected European Countries: A Comparative View* (Leuven UP, Leuven 2000)

WATSON A (ed) (tr), *The Digest of Justinian* (Pennsylvania UP, Philadelphia 1998) vols 1 and 2

WEISSBRODT D, *The Right to a Fair Trial Under the Universal Declaration of Human Rights and the International Covenant on Civil and Political Rights* (Martinus Nijhoff, The Hague 2001)

WELLBORN OG, 'Demeanor' (1991) 76 Cornell L Rev 1075

WELLS CL, 'The Origin of the Petty Jury' (1911) 27 LQR 347

WELLS CL, 'Early Opposition to the Petty Jury in Criminal Cases' (1914) 30 LQR 97

WHITE RCA and OVEY C, *Jacobs, White, & Ovey: The European Convention on Human Rights* (5th edn OUP, Oxford 2010)

WIGMORE JH, *A Treatise on the System of Evidence in Trials at Common Law* (Canada Law Book Co, Toronto 1905) vol 1

WIGMORE JH, *A Treatise on the Anglo-American System of Evidence in Trials at Common Law* (3rd edn Little, Brown and Co, Boston 1940) vols 5 and 8

WILLIAMS EN, *The Eighteenth-Century Constitution 1688–1815: Documents and Commentary* (CUP, London 1960)

WILTSHIRE SF, *Greece, Rome, and the Bill of Rights* (Oklahoma UP, Norman 1992)

WINTERBOTTOM M (tr), *The Elder Seneca: Declamations: Controversiae Books 1–6* (Harvard UP, Cambridge 1974) vol 1

WOOD AJ (ed), *The Statutes: Revised Edition* (Eyre & Spottiswoode, London 1870) vol 1

WOOLF Lord and CAMPBELL-HOLT C (ed), *The Pursuit of Justice* (OUP, Oxford 2008)

ONLINE MATERIALS

ATTORNEY GENERAL'S OFFICE, 'Attorney General's Guidelines on Disclosure (2005)' (Gov.UK) <https://www.gov.uk/guidance/attorney-general-s-guidelines-on-disclosure-2005-and-2011>

CONSEIL CONSTITUTIONNEL, 'Preamble to the Constitution of 27 October 1946' <www.conseil-constitutionnel.fr/conseil-constitutionnel/english/constitution/preamble-to-the-constitution-of-27-october-1946.105306.html>

CONSEIL CONSTITUTIONNEL, 'Constitution of 4 October 1958' <www.conseil-constitutionnel.fr/conseil-constitutionnel/english/constitution/constitution-of-4-october-1958.25742.html>

CROWN PROSECUTION SERVICE, 'Annual Report 2004–2005' (12 July 2005) <www.cps.gov.uk/publications/docs/annualreport05.pdf>

DOUCET JP, '*Ordonnance Criminelle du Mois D'Août 1670*' (Le Droit Criminel) <http://ledroitcriminel.fr/la_legislation_criminelle/anciens_textes/ordonnance_criminelle_de_1670.htm>

DOUCET JP, '*Code d'Instruction Criminelle de 1808*' (Le Droit Criminel) <http://ledroitcriminel.fr/la_legislation_criminelle/anciens_textes/code_instruction_criminelle_1808.htm>

DUFFETT B and others (trs), 'The German Code of Criminal Procedure' (Federal Ministry of Justice, 2014) <https://www.gesetze-im-internet.de/englisch_stpo/englisch_stpo.html>

EUROPEAN COURT OF HUMAN RIGHTS, 'Overview 1959–2011' (Council of Europe, Strasbourg 2012) <www.echr.coe.int/Documents/Overview_2011_ENG.pdf>

EUROPEAN COURT OF HUMAN RIGHTS, 'Inter-States Applications' (Council of Europe, Strasbourg 2016) <http://www.echr.coe.int/Documents/InterStates_applications_ENG.pdf>

GOVERNMENT OF CANADA JUSTICE LAWS WEBSITE (2016), Criminal Code of Canada RSC 1985 c C-46 <http://laws.justice.gc.ca/eng/acts/C-46/index.html>

OFFICE OF THE LAW REVISION COUNSEL, 'United States Code' <http://uscode.house.gov/>

SCOTTISH OFFICE HOME DEPARTMENT, 'A Literature Review of Public Defender or Staff Lawyer Schemes' (Legal Studies Research Findings No 19, 1998) <http://www.gov.scot/Publications/1998/12/39b894a7-b729-4715-901f-033fc34767a6>

SPENCER JR (tr), 'Code of Criminal Procedure' (Legifrance, 2006) <https://www.legifrance.gouv.fr/Traductions/en-English/Legifrance-translations>

TREATY SECTION, 'Multilateral Treaties Deposited with the Secretary-General: Status of Treaties: International Covenant on Civil and Political Rights' (UN, New York 2016) <https://treaties.un.org/Pages/Treaties.aspx?id=4&subid=A&clang=_en>

LIST OF CASES

EUROPEAN COURT OF HUMAN RIGHTS

AB v Slovakia (App 41784/98) ECHR 4 March 2003
Abbasov v Azerbaijan (App 24271/05) ECHR 17 January 2008
Abramyan v Russia (App 10709/02) ECHR 9 October 2008
Adolf v Austria (App 8269/78) (1982) Series A no 49
Ahorugeze v Sweden (App 37075/09) ECHR 27 October 2011
Airey v Ireland (App 6289/73) (1979) Series A no 32
Al Nashiri v Poland (App 28761/11) ECHR 24 July 2014
Albert and Le Compte v Belgium (Apps 7299/75; 7496/76) (1983) Series A no 58
Aleksandr Zaichenko v Russia (App 39660/02) ECHR 18 February 2010
Al-Khawaja and Tahery v UK (Apps 26766/05; 22228/06) ECHR 2011
Alvarez Sanchez v Spain (App 50720/99) ECHR 2001-XI
AM v Italy (App 37019/97) ECHR 1999-IX
Amirov v Russia (App 51857/13) ECHR 27 November 2014
Ananyev v Russia (App 20292/04) ECHR 30 July 2009
Andandonskiy v Russia (App 24015/02) ECHR 28 September 2006
APBP v France (App 38436/97) ECHR 21 March 2002
APEH Üldözötteinek Szövetsége and others v Hungary (App 32367/96) ECHR 2000-X
Aras v Turkey (No 2) (App 15065/07) ECHR 18 November 2014
Artico v Italy (App 6694/74) (1980) Series A no 37
Artner v Austria (App 13161/87) (1992) Series A no 242-A
Asch v Austria (App 12398/86) (1991) Series A no 203
Ashot Harutyunyan v Armenia (App 34334/04) ECHR 15 June 2010
Ashughyan v Armenia (App 33268/03) ECHR 17 July 2008
Atlan v UK (App 36533/97) ECHR 19 June 2001
Averill v UK (App 36408/97) ECHR 2000-VI
B v Finland (App 17122/02) ECHR 24 April 2007
Bakalov and others v Bulgaria (App 55796/00) ECHR 18 September 2007
Balčiūnas v Lithuania (App 17095/02) ECHR 20 July 2010
Balliu v Albania (App 74727/01) ECHR 16 June 2005
Balsytė-Lideikienė v Lithuania (App 72596/01) ECHR 4 November 2008
Bannikova v Russia (App 18757/06) ECHR 4 November 2010
Barberà, Messegué and Jabardo v Spain (App 10590/83) (1988) Series A no 146
Batsanina v Russia (App 3932/02) ECHR 26 May 2009
Beet and others v UK (App 47676/99 et seq) ECHR 1 March 2005
Belziuk v Poland (App 23103/93) ECHR 1998-II
Bendenoun v France (App 12547/86) (1994) Series A no 284

Benham v UK (App 19380/92) ECHR 1996-III
Benthem v the Netherlands (App 8848/80) (1985) Series A no 97
Bíro v Slovakia (App 57678/00) ECHR 27 June 2006
Birutis and others v Lithuania (Apps 47698/99; 48115/99) ECHR 28 March 2002
Blokker v the Netherlands (App 45282/99) ECHR 7 November 2000
Bocos-Cuesta v the Netherlands (App 54789/00) ECHR 10 November 2005
Boddaert v Belgium (App 12919/87) (1992) Series A no 235-D
Boner v UK (App 18711/91) (1994) Series A no 300-B
Bonev v Bulgaria (App 60018/00) ECHR 8 June 2006
Bönisch v Austria (App 8658/79) (1985) Series A no 92
Borgers v Belgium (App 12005/86) (1991) Series A no 214-B
Borisova v Bulgaria (App 56891/00) ECHR 21 December 2006
Botmeh and Alami v UK (App 15187/03) ECHR 7 June 2007
Brandstetter v Austria (Apps 11170/84; 12876/87; 13468/87) (1991) Series A no 211
Brennan v UK (App 39846/98) ECHR 2001-X
Bricmont v Belgium (App 10857/84) (1989) Series A no 158
Brogan and others v UK (App 11209/84 et seq) (1988) Series A no 145-B
Bulut v Austria (App 17358/90) ECHR 1996-II
Bykov v Russia (App 4378/02) ECHR 10 March 2009
Campbell v UK (App 13590/88) (1992) Series A no 233
Campbell and Fell v UK (Apps 7819/77; 7878/77) (1984) Series A no 80
Cardot v France (App 11069/84) (1991) Series A no 200
Castravet v Moldova (App 23393/05) ECHR 13 March 2007
Cebotari v Moldova (App 35615/06) ECHR 13 November 2007
Centre for Legal Resources on behalf of Valentin Câmpeanu v Romania (App 47848/08) ECHR 17 July 2014
Centro Europa 7 Srl and Di Stefano v Italy (App 38433/09) ECHR 7 June 2012
Cēsnieks v Latvia (App 9278/06) ECHR 11 February 2014
Chorniy v Ukraine (App 35227/06) ECHR 16 May 2013
Christine Goodwin v UK (App 28957/95) ECHR 2002-VI
Cipleu v Romania (App 36470/08) ECHR 14 January 2014
Cocchiarella v Italy (App 64886/01) ECHR 2006-V
Coëme and others v Belgium (App 32492/96 et seq) ECHR 2000-VII
Colozza v Italy (App 9024/80) (1985) Series A no 89
Corigliano v Italy (App 8304/78) (1982) Series A no 57
Correia de Matos v Portugal (App 48188/99) ECHR 2001-XII
Croissant v Germany (App 13611/88) (1992) Series A no 237-B
Cyprus v Turkey (App 25781/94) ECHR 2001-IV
Czekalla v Portugal (App 38830/97) ECHR 2002-VIII
Dallos v Hungary (App 29082/95) ECHR 2001-II
Daud v Portugal (App 22600/93) ECHR 1998-II
De Cubber v Belgium (App 9186/80) (1984) Series A no 86
De Haes and Gijsels v Belgium (App 19983/92) ECHR 1997-I
Delcourt v Belgium (App 2689/65) (1970) Series A no 11
Delta v France (App 11444/85) (1990) Series A no 191-A
Demicoli v Malta (App 13057/87) (1991) Series A no 210

Deweer v Belgium (App 6903/75) (1980) Series A no 35
Diallo v Sweden (App 13205/07) ECHR 5 January 2010
Dolenec v Croatia (App 25282/06) ECHR 26 November 2009
Dombo Beheer BV v the Netherlands (App 14448/88) (1993) Series A no 274
Doorson v the Netherlands (App 20524/92) ECHR 1996-II
Dorokhov v Russia (App 66802/01) ECHR 14 February 2008
Dowsett v UK (App 39482/98) ECHR 2003-VII
Duško Ivanovski v the former Yugoslav Republic of Macedonia (App 10718/05) ECHR 24 April 2014
Dvorski v Croatia (App 25703/11) ECHR 2015
Eckle v Germany (App 8130/78) (1982) Series A no 51
Edwards v UK (App 13071/87) (1992) Series A no 247-B
Edwards and Lewis v UK (Apps 39647/98; 40461/98) ECHR 2004-X
Efendiyev v Azerbaijan (App 27304/07) ECHR 18 December 2014
Eftimov v the former Yugoslav Republic of Macedonia (App 59974/08) ECHR 2 July 2015
Ekbatani v Sweden (App 10563/83) (1988) Series A no 134
El Haski v Belgium (App 649/08) ECHR 25 September 2012
Ellis, Simms and Martin v UK (Apps 46099/06; 46699/06) ECHR 10 April 2012
Engel and others v the Netherlands (App 5100/71 et seq) (1976) Series A no 22
Eraslan and others v Turkey (App 59653/00) ECHR 6 October 2009
Erdem v Germany (App 38321/97) ECHR 9 December 1999
Erdem v Germany (App 38321/97) ECHR 2001-VII
Escoubet v Belgium (App 26780/95) ECHR 1999-VII
Eskelinen and others v Finland (App 43803/98) ECHR 8 August 2006
Evrenos Önen v Turkey (App 29782/02) ECHR 15 February 2007
Ezeh and Connors v UK (Apps 39665/98; 40086/98) ECHR 2003-X
Fatma Tunç v Turkey (No 2) (App 18532/05) ECHR 13 October 2009
FC Mretebi v Georgia (App 38736/04) ECHR 31 July 2007
Ferrantelli and Santangelo v Italy (App 19874/92) ECHR 1996-III
Fitt v UK (App 29777/96) ECHR 2000-II
Foucher v France (App 22209/93) ECHR 1997-II
Franquesa Freixas v Spain (App 53590/99) ECHR 2000-XI
Frau v Italy (App 12147/86) (1991) Series A no 195-E
Fretté v France (App 36515/97) ECHR 2002-I
Frommelt v Liechtenstein (App 49158/99) ECHR 2003-VII
Gäfgen v Germany (App 22978/05) ECHR 2010
Galstyan v Armenia (App 26986/03) ECHR 15 November 2007
García Ruiz v Spain (App 30544/96) ECHR 1999-I
GB v France (App 44069/98) ECHR 2001-X
Georgios Papageorgiou v Greece (App 59506/00) ECHR 2003-VI
Gillan and Quinton v UK (App 4158/05) ECHR 12 January 2010
Göç v Turkey (App 36590/97) ECHR 2002-V
Goddi v Italy (App 8966/80) (1984) Series A no 76
Golder v UK (App 4451/70) (1975) Series A no 18
Gossa v Poland (App 47986/99) ECHR 9 January 2007
Granger v UK (App 11932/86) (1990) Series A no 174

Gregačević v Croatia (App 58331/09) ECHR 10 July 2012
Gurepka v Ukraine (App 61406/00) ECHR 6 September 2005
Gutfreund v France (App 45681/99) ECHR 2003-VII
Güveç v Turkey (App 70337/01) ECHR 2009
Hadjianastassiou v Greece (App 12945/87) (1992) Series A no 252
Hanif and Khan v UK (Apps 52999/08; 61779/08) ECHR 20 December 2011
Hanževački v Croatia (App 17182/07) ECHR 16 April 2009
Heaney and McGuinness v Ireland (App 34720/97) ECHR 2000-XII
Hermi v Italy (App 18114/02) ECHR 2006-XII
Hilden v Finland (App 32523/96) ECHR 14 September 1999
Hiro Balani v Spain (App 18064/91) (1994) Series A no 303-B
Hirst v UK (No 2) (App 74025/01) ECHR 2005-IX
Hirvisaari v Finland (App 49684/99) ECHR 27 September 2001
Hooper v UK (App 42317/98) ECHR 16 November 2004
Horncastle and others v UK (App 4184/10) ECHR 16 December 2014
Hozee v the Netherlands (App 21961/93) ECHR 1998-III
Hulki Güneş v Turkey (App 28490/95) ECHR 2003-VII
I v UK (App 25680/94) ECHR 11 July 2002
IJL and others v UK (Apps 29522/95; 30056/96; 30574/96) ECHR 2000-IX
Imbrioscia v Switzerland (App 13972/88) (1993) Series A no 275
Ireland v UK (App 5310/71) (1978) Series A no 25
Isgrò v Italy (App 11339/85) (1991) Series A no 194-A
Istratii and others v Moldova (Apps 8721/05; 8705/05; 8742/05) ECHR 27 March 2007
Janosevic v Sweden (App 34619/97) ECHR 2002-VII
Jasper v UK (App 27052/95) ECHR 16 February 2000
Javor and Javorová v Slovakia (App 42360/10) ECHR 15 September 2015
Jehovah's Witnesses of Moscow v Russia (App 302/02) ECHR 10 June 2010
Jelcovas v Lithuania (App 16913/04) ECHR 19 July 2011
JJ v the Netherlands (App 21351/93) ECHR 1998-II
John Murray v UK (App 18731/91) ECHR 1996-I
Jorgic v Germany (App 74613/01) ECHR 12 July 2007
Josef Fischer v Austria (App 33382/96) ECHR 17 January 2002
Jussila v Finland (App 73053/01) ECHR 2006-XIV
Kaçiu and Kotorri v Albania (Apps 33192/07; 33194/07) ECHR 25 June 2013
Kamasinski v Austria (App 9783/82) (1989) Series A no 168
Kangasluoma v Finland (App 48339/99) ECHR 20 January 2004
Karner v Austria (App 40016/98) ECHR 2003-IX
Kart v Turkey (App 8917/05) ECHR 2009
Kaste and Mathisen v Norway (Apps 18885/04; 21166/04) ECHR 9 November 2006
KDB v the Netherlands (App 21981/93) ECHR 1998-II
Kemal Kahraman and Ali Kahraman v Turkey (App 42104/02) ECHR 26 April 2007
Kemmache v France (No 3) (App 17621/91) (1994) Series A no 296-C
Kinský v the Czech Republic (App 42856/06) ECHR 9 February 2012
Kitov v Denmark (App 29759/96) ECHR 16 March 1999
Kjeldsen, Busk Madsen and Pedersen v Denmark (Apps 5095/71; 5920/72; 5926/72) (1976) Series A no 23

Klamecki v Poland (No 2) (App 31583/96) ECHR 3 April 2003
Klass and others v Germany (App 5029/71) (1978) Series A no 28
Klimentyev v Russia (App 46503/99) ECHR 16 November 2006
Kok v the Netherlands (App 43149/98) ECHR 2000-VI
Konstantin Markin v Russia (App 30078/06) ECHR 22 March 2012
Korellis v Cyprus (App 60804/00) ECHR 3 December 2002
Korellis v Cyprus (App 54528/00) ECHR 7 January 2003
Kostecki v Poland (App 14932/09) ECHR 4 June 2013
Kostovski v the Netherlands (App 11454/85) (1989) Series A no 166
Kovač v Croatia (App 503/05) ECHR 12 July 2007
Koval v Ukraine (App 65550/01) ECHR 19 October 2006
Krasniki v the Czech Republic (App 51277/99) ECHR 28 February 2006
Krasulya v Russia (App 12365/03) ECHR 22 February 2007
Kravtas v Lithuania (App 12717/06) ECHR 18 January 2011
Krčmář and others v the Czech Republic (App 35376/97) ECHR 3 March 2000
Kremzow v Austria (App 12350/86) (1993) Series A no 268-B
Kress v France (App 39594/98) ECHR 2001-VI
Kreuz v Poland (App 28249/95) ECHR 2001-VI
Krombach v France (App 29731/96) ECHR 2001-II
Kudła v Poland (App 30210/96) ECHR 2000-XI
Kuopila v Finland (App 27752/95) ECHR 27 April 2000
Lagardère v France (App 18851/07) ECHR 12 April 2012
Lagerblom v Sweden (App 26891/95) ECHR 14 January 2003
Lala v the Netherlands (App 14861/89) (1994) Series A no 297-A
Lanz v Austria (App 24430/94) ECHR 31 January 2002
Laska and Lika v Albania (Apps 12315/04; 17605/04) ECHR 20 April 2010
Laukkanen and Manninen v Finland (App 50230/99) ECHR 3 February 2004
Lauko v Slovakia (App 26138/95) ECHR 1998-VI
Lazariu v Romania (App 31973/03) ECHR 13 November 2014
Legillon v France (App 53406/10) ECHR 10 January 2013
Lloyd and others v UK (App 29798/96 et seq) ECHR 1 March 2005
Lobo Machado v Portugal (App 15764/89) ECHR 1996-I
Loizidou v Turkey (Preliminary Objections) (App 15318/89) (1995) Series A no 310
Lucà v Italy (App 33354/96) ECHR 2001-II
Lüdi v Switzerland (App 12433/86) (1992) Series A no 238
Luedicke, Belkacem and Koç v Germany (Apps 6210/73; 6877/75; 7132/75) (1978) Series A no 29
Lyons and others v UK (App 15227/03) ECHR 2003-IX
Maaouia v France (App 39652/98) ECHR 2000-X
Magee v UK (App 28135/95) ECHR 2000-VI
Malige v France (App 27812/95) ECHR 1998-VII
Marcello Viola v Italy (App 45106/04) ECHR 2006-XI
Maresti v Croatia (App 55759/07) ECHR 25 June 2009
Marpa Zeeland BV and Metal Welding BV v the Netherlands (App 46300/99) ECHR 2004-X
Mattoccia v Italy (App 23969/94) ECHR 2000-IX

Matyjek v Poland (App 38184/03) ECHR 2006-VII
Matyjek v Poland (App 38184/03) ECHR 24 April 2007
Maxwell v UK (App 18949/91) (1994) Series A no 300-C
Mayzit v Russia (App 63378/00) ECHR 20 January 2005
Meftah and others v France (Apps 32911/96; 35237/97; 34595/97) ECHR 2002-VII
Melin v France (App 12914/87) (1993) Series A no 261-A
Melnikov v Russia (App 23610/03) ECHR 14 January 2010
Mežnarić v Croatia (App 71615/01) ECHR 15 July 2005
Micallef v Malta (App 17056/06) ECHR 15 October 2009
Mikhaylova v Russia (App 46998/08) ECHR 19 November 2015
Mild and Virtanen v Finland (Apps 39481/98; 40227/98) ECHR 26 July 2005
Mirilashvili v Russia (App 6293/04) ECHR 11 December 2008
Mironov v Russia (App 22625/02) ECHR 5 October 2006
MM v UK (App 24029/07) ECHR 13 November 2012
Modarca v Moldova (App 14437/05) ECHR 10 May 2007
Moiseyev v Russia (App 62936/00) ECHR 9 October 2008
Monnell and Morris v UK (Apps 9562/81; 9818/82) (1987) Series A no 115
Morris v UK (App 38784/97) ECHR 2002-I
Mort v UK (App 44564/98) ECHR 2001-IX
MS v Finland (App 46601/99) ECHR 22 March 2005
Munjaz v UK (App 2913/06) ECHR 17 July 2012
Musa Karataş v Turkey (App 63315/00) ECHR 5 January 2010
Muttilainen v Finland (App 18358/02) ECHR 22 May 2007
Nasteska v the former Yugoslav Republic of Macedonia (App 23152/05) ECHR 27 May 2010
Nataliya Mikhaylenko v Ukraine (App 49069/11) ECHR 30 May 2013
Nejdet Şahin and Perihan Şahin v Turkey (App 13279/05) ECHR 20 October 2011
Neulinger and Shuruk v Switzerland (App 41615/07) ECHR 6 July 2010
Neumeister v Austria (App 1936/63) (1968) Series A no 8
Nideröst-Huber v Switzerland (App 18990/91) ECHR 1997-I
Öcalan v Turkey (App 46221/99) ECHR 2005-IV
Oferta Plus SRL v Moldova (App 14385/04) ECHR 19 December 2006
O'Halloran and Francis v UK (Apps 15809/02; 25624/02) ECHR 2007-III
Oleg Kolesnik v Ukraine (App 17551/02) ECHR 19 November 2009
Olujić v Croatia (App 22330/05) ECHR 5 February 2009
Opuz v Turkey (App 33401/02) ECHR 9 June 2009
Orlova v Russia (App 21088/06) ECHR 9 October 2008
Othman (Abu Qatada) v UK (App 8139/09) ECHR 2012
Öztürk v Germany (App 8544/79) (1984) Series A no 73
Pakelli v Germany (App 8398/78) (1983) Series A no 64
Pákozdi v Hungary (App 51269/07) ECHR 25 November 2014
Panovits v Cyprus (App 4268/04) ECHR 11 December 2008
Pavlenko v Russia (App 42371/02) ECHR 1 April 2010
Pedersen and Baadsgaard v Denmark (App 49017/99) ECHR 2004-XI
Pélissier and Sassi v France (App 25444/94) ECHR 1999-II
Pelladoah v the Netherlands (App 16737/90) (1994) Series A no 297-B
Pello v Estonia (App 11423/03) ECHR 12 April 2007

Perez v France (App 47287/99) ECHR 2004-I
Perić v Croatia (App 34499/06) ECHR 27 March 2008
Perks and others v UK (App 25277/94 et seq) ECHR 12 October 1999
Perna v Italy (App 48898/99) ECHR 6 May 2003
PG and JH v UK (App 44787/98) ECHR 2001-IX
Pham Hoang v France (App 13191/87) (1992) Series A no 243
Pierre-Bloch v France (App 24194/94) ECHR 1997-VI
Pishchalnikov v Russia (App 7025/04) ECHR 24 September 2009
Płonka v Poland (App 20310/02) ECHR 31 March 2009
Pobornikoff v Austria (App 28501/95) ECHR 3 October 2000
Poitrimol v France (App 14032/88) (1993) Series A no 277-A
Polufakin and Chernyshev v Russia (App 30997/02) ECHR 25 September 2008
Popov v Russia (App 26853/04) ECHR 13 July 2006
Pretty v UK (App 2346/02) ECHR 2002-III
Prežec v Croatia (App 48185/07) ECHR 15 October 2009
PS v Germany (App 33900/96) ECHR 20 December 2001
Pullar v UK (App 22399/93) ECHR 1996-III
Putz v Austria (App 18892/91) ECHR 1996-I
Quaranta v Switzerland (App 12744/87) (1991) Series A no 205
Ramanauskas v Lithuania (App 74420/01) ECHR 5 February 2008
Ravnsborg v Sweden (App 14220/88) (1994) Series A no 283-B
RD v Poland (Apps 29692/96; 34612/97) ECHR 18 December 2001
Reinhardt and Slimane-Kaïd v France (Apps 23043/93; 22921/93) ECHR 1998-II
Roman Zakharov v Russia (App 47143/06) ECHR 2015
Rowe and Davis v UK (App 28901/95) ECHR 2000-II
Rozhkov v Russia (App 64140/00) ECHR 5 February 2007
Rumyana Ivanova v Bulgaria (App 36207/03) ECHR 14 February 2008
Rutkowski v Poland (App 45995/99) ECHR 2000-XI
Ryakib Biryukov v Russia (App 14810/02) ECHR 17 January 2008
Rybacki v Poland (App 52479/99) ECHR 13 January 2009
S v Switzerland (Apps 12629/87; 13965/88) (1991) Series A no 220
S and Marper v UK (Apps 30562/04; 30566/04) ECHR 4 December 2008
Sabirov v Russia (App 13465/04) ECHR 11 February 2010
Sadak and others v Turkey (No 1) (App 29900/96 et seq) ECHR 2001-VIII
Şahin Çağdaş v Turkey (App 28137/02) ECHR 11 April 2006
Saïdi v France (App 14647/89) (1993) Series A no 261-C
Sakhnovskiy v Russia (App 21272/03) ECHR 2 November 2010
Salabiaku v France (App 10519/83) (1988) Series A no 141-A
Salduz v Turkey (App 36391/02) ECHR 2008
Salov v Ukraine (App 65518/01) ECHR 6 September 2005
Sannino v Italy (App 30961/03) ECHR 2006-VI
Sarkizov and others v Bulgaria (App 37981/06 et seq) ECHR 17 April 2012
Saunders v UK (App 19187/91) ECHR 1996-VI
Schädler-Eberle v Liechtenstein (App 56422/09) ECHR 18 July 2013
Schatschaschwili v Germany (App 9154/10) ECHR 2015
Schmautzer v Austria (App 15523/89) (1995) Series A no 328-A

Schönenberger and Durmaz v Switzerland (App 11368/85) (1988) Series A no 137
Scordino v Italy (No 1) (App 36813/97) ECHR 29 July 2004
Sejdovic v Italy (App 56581/00) ECHR 2006-II
Seleznev v Russia (App 15591/03) ECHR 26 June 2008
Selmouni v France (App 25803/94) ECHR 1999-V
Sergey Zolotukhin v Russia (App 14939/03) ECHR 10 February 2009
Shabelnik v Ukraine (App 16404/03) ECHR 19 February 2009
Sharomov v Russia (App 8927/02) ECHR 15 January 2009
Shilbergs v Russia (App 20075/03) ECHR 17 December 2009
Shulepov v Russia (App 15435/03) ECHR 26 June 2008
Sidorova (Adukevich) v Russia (App 4537/04) ECHR 14 February 2008
Sipavičius v Lithuania (App 49093/99) ECHR 21 February 2002
Skrobol v Poland (App 44165/98) ECHR 8 July 2003
SN v Sweden (App 34209/96) ECHR 2002-V
Solakov v the former Yugoslav Republic of Macedonia (App 47023/99) ECHR 2001-X
Somogyi v Italy (App 67972/01) ECHR 2004-IV
Stadukhin v Russia (App 6857/02) ECHR 18 October 2007
Stanford v UK (App 16757/90) (1994) Series A no 282-A
Štitić v Croatia (App 29660/03) ECHR 8 November 2007
Stoimenov v the former Yugoslav Republic of Macedonia (App 17995/02) ECHR 5 April 2007
Stran Greek Refineries and Stratis Andreadis v Greece (App 13427/87) (1994) Series A no 301-B
Šubinski v Slovenia (App 19611/04) ECHR 18 January 2007
Svinarenko and Slyadnev v Russia (Apps 32541/08; 43441/08) ECHR 2014
Svinarenkov v Estonia (App 42551/98) ECHR 15 February 2000
T v UK (App 24724/94) ECHR 16 December 1999
Taal v Estonia (App 13249/02) ECHR 22 November 2005
Taxquet v Belgium (App 926/05) ECHR 2010
The Sunday Times v UK (No 1) (App 6538/74) (1979) Series A no 30
Timergaliyev v Russia (App 40631/02) ECHR 14 October 2008
Titarenko v Ukraine (App 31720/02) ECHR 20 September 2012
TK and SE v Finland (App 38581/97) ECHR 31 May 2005
Tripodi v Italy (App 13743/88) (1994) Series A no 281-B
Tudor-Comert v Moldova (App 27888/04) ECHR 4 November 2008
Twalib v Greece (App 24294/94) ECHR 1998-IV
Twomey, Cameron and Guthrie v UK (Apps 67318/09; 22226/12) ECHR 28 May 2013
Tyrer v UK (App 5856/72) (1978) Series A no 26
United Communist Party of Turkey and others v Turkey (App 19392/92) ECHR 1998-I
Unterpertinger v Austria (App 9120/80) (1986) Series A no 110
V v Finland (App 40412/98) ECHR 24 April 2007
V v UK (App 24888/94) ECHR 1999-IX
Vacher v France (App 20368/92) ECHR 1996-VI
Van de Hurk v the Netherlands (App 16034/90) (1994) Series A no 288
Van Geyseghem v Belgium (App 26103/95) ECHR 1999-I
Van Mechelen and others v the Netherlands (App 21363/93 et seq) ECHR 1997-III
Van Orshoven v Belgium (App 20122/92) ECHR 1997-III
Vaudelle v France (App 35683/97) ECHR 2001-I

Vereinigung Bildender Künstler v Austria (App 68354/01) ECHR 25 January 2007
Vermeulen v Belgium (App 19075/91) ECHR 1996-I
Vidal v Belgium (App 12351/86) (1992) Series A no 235-B
Visser v the Netherlands (App 26668/95) ECHR 14 February 2002
Vladimir Romanov v Russia (App 41461/02) ECHR 24 July 2008
Vozhigov v Russia (App 5953/02) ECHR 26 April 2007
Weber v Switzerland (App 11034/84) (1990) Series A no 177
Wemhoff v Germany (App 2122/64) (1968) Series A no 7
Werner v Austria (App 21835/93) ECHR 1997-VII
Windisch v Austria (App 12489/86) (1990) Series A no 186
WS v Poland (App 21508/02) ECHR 19 June 2007
Yankov and others v Bulgaria (App 4570/05) ECHR 23 September 2010
Zahirović v Croatia (App 58590/11) ECHR 25 April 2013
Ždanoka v Latvia (App 58278/00) ECHR 2006-IV
Zhoglo v Ukraine (App 17988/02) ECHR 24 April 2008
Zhuk v Ukraine (App 45783/05) ECHR 21 October 2010
Zoon v the Netherlands (App 29202/95) ECHR 2000-XII

EUROPEAN COMMISSION OF HUMAN RIGHTS

Artico v Italy (App 6694/74) (1979) 2 Digest 836
Austria v Italy (App 788/60) (1961) 4 Yearbook 116
Bazil v UK (App 14385/88) EComHR 10 March 1989
Bell v UK (App 12322/86) EComHR 13 October 1987
Belziuk v Poland (App 23103/93) EComHR Report 26 February 1997
Biondo v Italy (App 8821/79) (1983) 64 DR 5
Bonzi v Switzerland (App 7854/77) (1978) 12 DR 188
Brown v UK (App 11129/84) (1985) 42 DR 269
Callaghan and others v UK (App 14739/89) (1989) 60 DR 296
Campbell v UK (App 12323/86) (1988) 57 DR 148
Can v Austria (App 9300/81) EComHR Report 12 July 1984
Cardot v France (App 11069/84) EComHR Report 3 April 1990
Croissant v Germany (App 13611/88) EComHR Report 7 March 1991
Drummond v UK (App 12917/87) EComHR 9 December 1987
Ensslin, Baader and Raspe v Germany (Apps 7572/76; 7586/76; 7587/76) (1978) 14 DR 91
F v Switzerland (App 12152/86) (1989) 61 DR 171
F v UK (App 11058/84) (1986) 47 DR 230
Glaser and others v Austria (App 834/60 et seq) EComHR Report 17 December 1963
Goddi v Italy (App 8966/80) EComHR Report 14 July 1982
Hardiman v UK (App 25935/94) EComHR 28 February 1996
Harper v UK (App 11229/84) EComHR 10 November 1986
Harward v Norway (App 14170/88) EComHR 12 March 1990
Herbert Huber v Austria (App 5523/72) (1974) 46 CD 99
Jespers v Belgium (App 8403/78) (1981) 27 DR 61
Jopkiewicz v Poland (App 24248/94) EComHR 17 January 1997

K v Denmark (App 19524/92) EComHR 5 May 1993
Kaufman v Belgium (App 10938/84) (1986) 50 DR 98
Kempers v Austria (App 21842/93) EComHR 27 February 1997
Köplinger v Austria (App 1850/63) (1966) 9 Yearbook 240
Köplinger v Austria (App 1850/63) (1969) 12 Yearbook 438
Kröcher and Möller v Switzerland (App 8463/78) (1981) 26 DR 24
Kurup v Denmark (App 11219/84) (1985) 42 DR 287
Luedicke, Belkacem and Koç v Germany (Apps 6210/73; 6877/75; 7132/75) EComHR Report 18 May 1977
M v UK (App 9728/82) (1983) 36 DR 155
Murphy v UK (App 4681/70) (1972) 43 CD 1
Nielsen v Denmark (App 343/57) (1961) 4 Yearbook 494
Ofner v Austria (App 524/59) (1960) 3 Yearbook 322
Ofner and Hopfinger v Austria (Apps 524/59; 617/59) (1963) 6 Yearbook 676
Östergren v Sweden (App 13572/88) (1991) 69 DR 198
Pakelli v Germany (App 8398/78) EComHR Report 12 December 1981
Pataki and Dunshirn v Austria (Apps 596/59; 789/60) (1963) 6 Yearbook 714
Perez Mahia v Spain (App 11022/84) (1985) 9 EHRR 145
Pfister v Germany (App 19512/92) EComHR 7 September 1993
Philis v Greece (App 16598/90) EComHR 11 December 1990
R v Belgium (App 15957/90) (1992) 72 DR 195
Ross v UK (App 11396/85) (1986) 50 DR 179
S v UK (App 11821/85) EComHR 12 December 1987
Schertenleib v Switzerland (App 8339/78) (1979) 17 DR 205
Struppat v Germany (App 2804/66) (1968) 27 CD 61
U v Luxembourg (App 10142/82) (1985) 42 DR 86
V v UK (App 11465/85) EComHR 3 March 1986
Wiechert v Germany (App 1404/62) (1964) 7 Yearbook 104
X v Austria (App 2370/64) (1967) 22 CD 96
X v Austria (App 2676/65) (1967) 23 CD 31
X v Austria (App 4338/69) (1970) 36 CD 79
X v Austria (App 4428/70) (1972) 40 CD 1
X v Austria (App 7138/75) (1977) 9 DR 50
X v Austria (App 8251/78) (1979) 17 DR 168
X v Belgium (App 1134/61) (1961) 4 Yearbook 378
X v Denmark (App 8395/78) (1981) 27 DR 50
X v Germany (App 509/59) (1960) 3 Yearbook 174
X v Germany (App 646/59) (1960) 3 Yearbook 272
X v Germany (App 599/59) (1961) 8 CD 12
X v Germany (App 722/60) (1962) 5 Yearbook 104
X v Germany (App 1169/61) (1963) 6 Yearbook 520
X v Germany (App 2646/65) (1966) 19 CD 89
X v Germany (App 3139/67) (1968) 26 CD 77
X v Germany (App 6946/75) (1976) 6 DR 114
X v Germany (App 7300/75) (1976) 2 Digest 857
X v Germany (App 9365/81) (1982) 28 DR 229

X v Germany (App 10098/82) (1984) 8 EHRR 214
X v Norway (App 5923/72) (1975) 3 DR 43
X v Norway (App 8202/78) (1979) 2 Digest 857
X v Sweden (App 434/58) (1959) 2 Yearbook 354
X v Switzerland (App 9127/80) (1981) 26 DR 238
X v UK (App 3852/68) (1969) 32 CD 38
X v UK (App 4042/69) (1970) 13 Yearbook 690
X v UK (App 5871/72) (1974) 1 DR 54
X v UK (App 6298/73) (1975) 2 Digest 831
X v UK (App 6956/75) (1976) 8 DR 103
X v UK (App 7413/76) (1977) 9 DR 100
X v UK (App 8295/78) (1978) 15 DR 242
X v UK (App 8386/78) (1980) 21 DR 126
X and Y v Austria (App 7909/74) (1978) 15 DR 160
X and Y v Belgium (Apps 1420/62; 1477/62; 1478/62) (1963) 6 Yearbook 590
X and Y v Germany (Apps 5217/71; 5367/72) (1972) 42 CD 139
X and Y v Ireland (App 8299/78) (1980) 22 DR 51
X and Z v Germany (App 3897/68) (1970) 35 CD 75
Y v Germany (App 11777/85) EComHR 13 October 1986

HUMAN RIGHTS COMMITTEE

Äärelä and Näkkäläjärvi v Finland (Comm 779/1997) UN Doc CCPR/C/73/D/779/1997 (2001)
Abdool Saleem Yasseen and Noel Thomas v Republic of Guyana (Comm 676/1996) UN Doc CCPR/C/62/D/676/1996 (1998)
Antonio Viana Acosta v Uruguay (Comm 110/1981) UN Doc Supp No 40 (A/39/40) 169 (1984)
Campbell v Jamaica (Comm 248/1987) UN Doc CCPR/C/44/D/248/1987 (1992)
Carlton Reid v Jamaica (Comm 250/1987) UN Doc CCPR/C/39/D/250/1987 (1990)
Delia Saldias de Lopez v Uruguay (Comm 52/1979) UN Doc CCPR/C/OP/1 88 (1984)
Devon Simpson v Jamaica (Comm 695/1996) UN Doc CCPR/C/73/D/695/1996 (2001)
Fei v Colombia (Comm 514/1992) UN Doc CCPR/C/53/D/514/1992 (1995)
Frank Robinson v Jamaica (Comm 223/1987) UN Doc CCPR/C/35/D/223/1987 (1989)
Henry v Jamaica (Comm 230/1987) UN Doc CCPR/C/43/D/230/1987 (1991)
Hervin Edwards v Jamaica (Comm 529/1993) UN Doc CCPR/C/60/D/529/1993 (1997)
Hezekiah Price v Jamaica (Comm 572/1994) UN Doc CCPR/C/58/D/572/1994 (1996)
Jansen-Gielen v the Netherlands (Comm 846/1999) UN Doc CCPR/C/71/D/846/1999 (2001)
John Campbell v Jamaica (Comm 307/1988) UN Doc CCPR/C/47/D/307/1988 (1993)
Lindon v Australia (Comm 646/1995) UN Doc CCPR/C/64/D/646/1995 (1998)
Little v Jamaica (Comm 283/1988) UN Doc CCPR/C/43/D/283/1988 (1991)
Michael Sawyers, Michael and Desmond McLean v Jamaica (Comm 256/1987) UN Doc CCPR/C/41/D/256/1987 (1991)
Miguel Angel Estrella v Uruguay (Comm 74/1980) UN Doc Supp No 40 (A/38/40) 150 (1983)
Morael v France (Comm 207/1986) UN Doc Supp No 40 (A/44/40) 210 (1989)
Oral Hendricks v Guyana (Comm 838/1998) UN Doc CCPR/C/76/D/838/1998 (2002)

Paul Kelly v Jamaica (Comm 253/1987) UN Doc CCPR/C/41/D/253/1987 60 (1991)
Robinson LaVende v Trinidad and Tobago (Comm 554/1993) UN Doc CCPR/C/61/D/554/1993 (1997)
Smith v Jamaica (Comm 282/1988) UN Doc CCPR/C/47/D/282/1988 (1993)
Wolf v Panama (Comm 289/1988) UN Doc CCPR/C/44/D/289/1988 80 (1992)
Wright v Jamaica (Comm 459/1991) UN Doc CCPR/C/55/D/459/1991 (1995)

INTER-AMERICAN COURT OF HUMAN RIGHTS

19 Merchants Case (Preliminary Objections) Inter-Am Ct HR Series C No 93 (12 June 2002)
Barrios Altos Case (Interpretation of Judgment on the Merits: Art 67 ACHR) Inter-Am Ct HR Series C No 83 (3 September 2001)
Cantoral Benavides Case (Reparations: Art 63(1) ACHR) Inter-Am Ct HR Series C No 88 (3 December 2001)
Castillo Petruzzi et al Case (Judgment) Inter-Am Ct HR Series C No 52 (30 May 1999)
Cayara Case (Preliminary Objections) Inter-Am Ct HR Series C No 14 (3 February 1993)
Gangaram Panday Case (Preliminary Objections) Inter-Am Ct HR Series C No 12 (4 December 1991)

AFRICAN COMMISSION ON HUMAN AND PEOPLES' RIGHTS

Avocats Sans Frontières (on behalf of Bwampamye) v Burundi (Comm 231/99) African Comm Hum & Peoples' Rights (2000)

INTERNATIONAL CRIMINAL TRIBUNAL FOR THE FORMER YUGOSLAVIA

Prosecutor v Aleksovski (Decision on Prosecutor's Appeal on Admissibility of Evidence) (Appeals Chamber) ICTY-95-14/1 (16 February 1999)
Prosecutor v Aleksovski (Judgement) (Appeals Chamber) ICTY-95-14/1-A (24 March 2000)
Prosecutor v Delalic (Decision on the Prosecution's Motion for an Order Requiring Advance Disclosure of Witnesses by the Defence) (Trial Chamber) ICTY-96-21 (4 February 1998)
Prosecutor v Delalic (Judgement) (Appeals Chamber) ICTY-96-21-A (20 February 2001)
Prosecutor v Halilović (Decision on Motion for Prosecution Access to Defence Documents Used in Cross-Examination of Prosecution Witnesses) (Trial Chamber) ICTY-01-48-T (9 May 2005)
Prosecutor v Krajišnik & Plavšić (Decision on Prosecution Motion for Clarification in Respect of Application of Rules 65 *ter*, 66(B) and 67(C)) (Trial Chamber) ICTY-00-39 & 40-PT (1 August 2001)

Prosecutor v Milutinović (Decision on Interlocutory Appeal on Motion for Additional Funds) (Appeals Chamber) ICTY-99-37-AR73.2 (13 November 2003)
Prosecutor v Šešelj (Decision on Appeal Against the Trial Chamber's Decision (No 2) on Assignment of Counsel) (Appeals Chamber) ICTY-03-67-AR73.4 (8 December 2006)
Prosecutor v Slobodan Milošević (Decision on Interlocutory Appeal of the Trial Chamber's Decision on the Assignment of Defense Counsel) (Appeals Chamber) ICTY-02-54-AR73.7 (1 November 2004)
Prosecutor v Tadić (Decision on the Prosecutor's Motion Requesting Protective Measures for Victims and Witnesses) (Trial Chamber) ICTY-94-1 (10 August 1995)
Prosecutor v Tadić (Separate Opinion of Judge Vohrah on Prosecution Motion for Production of Defence Witness Statements) (Trial Chamber) ICTY-94-1 (27 November 1996)
Prosecutor v Tadić (Judgement) (Appeals Chamber) ICTY-94-1-A (15 July 1999)

INTERNATIONAL CRIMINAL TRIBUNAL FOR RWANDA

Prosecutor v Akayesu (Judgement) (Appeals Chamber) ICTR-96-4-A (1 June 2001)
Prosecutor v Bagilishema (Judgement) (Trial Chamber) ICTR-95-1A-T (7 June 2001)
Prosecutor v Kambanda (Judgement) (Appeals Chamber) ICTR-97-23-A (19 October 2000)
Prosecutor v Kayishema and Ruzindana (Judgement: Reasons) (Appeals Chamber) ICTR-95-1-A (1 June 2001)
Prosecutor v Nahimana (Decision on the Motion to Stay the Proceedings in the Trial of Ferdinand Nahimana) (Trial Chamber) ICTR-99-52-T (5 June 2003)

INTERNATIONAL CRIMINAL COURT

Situation in the Democratic Republic of the Congo (Decision on the Prosecution's Application for Leave to Appeal the Chamber's Decision of 17 January 2006 on the Applications for Participation in the Proceedings of VPRS 1–6) (Pre-Trial Chamber I) ICC-01/04-135 (31 March 2006)
Situation in Uganda (Decision on Prosecutor's Application for Leave to Appeal in Part Pre-Trial Chamber II's Decision on the Prosecutor's Applications for Warrants of Arrest Under Article 58) (Pre-Trial Chamber II) ICC-02/04-01/05-20 (19 August 2005)

SPECIAL COURT FOR SIERRA LEONE

Prosecutor v Norman et al (CDF Case) (Decision on *Inter Partes* Motion by Prosecution to Freeze the Account of the Accused Sam Hinga Norman at Union Trust Bank (SL) Limited or at any other Bank in Sierra Leone) (Trial Chamber) SCSL-04-14-PT (19 April 2004)

INTERNATIONAL COURT OF JUSTICE

Application for Review of Judgement No 158 of the United Nations Administrative Tribunal (Advisory Opinion) [1973] ICJ Rep 166
Application for Review of Judgement No 273 of the United Nations Administrative Tribunal (Advisory Opinion) [1982] ICJ Rep 325
Application of the Convention on the Prevention and Punishment of the Crime of Genocide (Bosnia and Herzegovina v Yugoslavia) (Counter-Claims: Order) [1997] ICJ Rep 243
Continental Shelf (Libyan Arab Jamahiriya/Malta) (Judgement) [1985] ICJ Rep 13
Judgements of the Administrative Tribunal of the ILO upon Complaints made against the UNESCO (Advisory Opinion) [1956] ICJ Rep 77
Land and Maritime Boundary between Cameroon and Nigeria (Cameroon v Nigeria) (Order) [1999] ICJ Rep 983
Maritime Delimitation and Territorial Questions between Qatar and Bahrain (Qatar v Bahrain) (Jurisdiction and Admissibility: Judgement) [1994] ICJ Rep 112
Military and Paramilitary Activities in and against Nicaragua (Nicaragua v US) (Merits: Judgement) [1986] ICJ Rep 14
North Sea Continental Shelf Cases (Germany v Denmark; Germany v Netherlands) (Judgement) [1969] ICJ Rep 3
Oil Platforms (Islamic Republic of Iran v US) (Counter-Claim: Order) [1998] ICJ Rep 190
Request for an Examination of the Situation in Accordance with Paragraph 63 of the Court's Judgment of 20 December 1974 in the Nuclear Tests (New Zealand v France) Case (Order) [1995] ICJ Rep 288

INTERNATIONAL MILITARY TRIBUNAL AND NUREMBERG MILITARY TRIBUNAL

US v Alfried Krupp and others (1950) 9 TWC 1
US v Carl Krauch and others (1952) 8 TWC 1
US v Ernst von Weizsaecker and others (1949) 14 TWC 1
US v Friedrich Flick and others (1952) 6 TWC 1
US v Oswald Pohl and others (1950) 5 TWC 193
US v Otto Ohlendorf and others (1949) 4 TWC 1
US v Ulrich Greifelt and others (1950) 5 TWC 1
US v Wilhelm von Leeb and others (1950) 11 TWC 1
US and others v Hermann Wilhelm Göring and others (1947) 2 IMT 1; (1947) 3 IMT 1

NATIONAL

Allie Mohammed v The State [1999] 2 AC 111 (PC)
Attorney-General's Reference (No 3 of 1999) [2001] 2 AC 91 (HL)
Attorney-General's Reference (No 82a of 2000) [2002] EWCA Crim 215; [2002] 2 Cr App R 24
Barber v Page 390 US 719 (1968)

Bow Spring (Owners) v Manzanillo II (Owners) [2004] EWCA Civ 1007; [2005] 1 WLR 144
Brown v Stott [2003] 1 AC 681 (PC)
Bushell's Case (1670) 124 ER 1006 (CCP)
California v Green 399 US 149 (1970)
City of London v Wood (1701) 88 ER 1592 (CKB)
Coffin v US 156 US 432 (1895)
Coy v Iowa 487 US 1012 (1988)
Crawford v Washington 541 US 36 (2004)
Davie v Magistrates of Edinburgh 1953 SC 34
Day v Savadge (1614) 80 ER 235 (CKB)
Douglas v Alabama 380 US 415 (1965)
Dr Bonham's Case (1610) 77 ER 646 (CKB)
DS v HM Advocate [2007] UKPC D1; 2007 SC (PC) 1
Earl of Derby's Case (1613) 7 ER 1390 (CKB)
Edwards v Attorney-General for Canada [1930] AC 124 (PC)
Government of the Virgin Islands v Aquino 378 F2d 540 (3rd Cir 1967)
Hinds v Attorney-General of Barbados [2001] UKPC 56; [2002] 1 AC 854
Hurtado v California 110 US 516 (1884)
Kastigar v United States 406 US 441 (1972)
Kentucky v Stincer 482 US 730 (1987)
Klopfer v North Carolina 386 US 213 (1967)
Lilly v Virginia 527 US 116 (1999)
Malinski v New York 324 US 401 (1945)
Maryland v Craig 497 US 836 (1990)
Mattox v United States 156 US 237 (1895)
McKinley's Case (1817) 33 State Tr 275
McLean and another v Buchanan and another [2001] UKPC D3; [2001] 1 WLR 2425
McNabb v US 318 US 332 (1943)
Mechanical & General Inventions Co Ltd and Lehwess v Austin and the Austin Motor Co Ltd [1935] AC 346 (HL)
Miranda v Arizona 384 US 436 (1966)
Murray's Lessee v Hoboken Land & Improvement Co 59 US 272 (1856)
Ohio v Roberts 448 US 56 (1980)
Paul v Davis 424 US 693 (1976)
Pointer v Texas 380 US 400 (1965)
Powell v Alabama 287 US 45 (1932)
R v A (No 2) [2001] UKHL 25; [2002] 1 AC 45
R v Banks [1916] 2 KB 621 (CCA)
R v Bow Street Metropolitan Stipendiary Magistrate, ex p Pinochet Ugarte [2000] 1 AC 61 (HL)
R v Bow Street Metropolitan Stipendiary Magistrate, ex p Pinochet Ugarte (No 2) [2000] 1 AC 119 (HL)
R v Bow Street Metropolitan Stipendiary Magistrate, ex p Pinochet Ugarte (No 3) [2000] 1 AC 147 (HL)
R v Brown and others [2001] EWCA Crim 1771; [2001] All ER (D) 392 (Jul)
R v Brown (Winston) [1994] 1 WLR 1599 (CA)

R v Brown (Winston) [1998] AC 367 (HL)
R v Collins (1938) 26 Cr App R 177 (CA)
R v Davis [2008] UKHL 36; [2008] 3 WLR 125
R v DJX (1990) 91 Cr App R 36 (CA)
R v Forbes [2001] 1 AC 473 (HL)
R v H and others [2004] UKHL 3; [2004] 2 AC 134
R v Hulusi (Kolliari Mehmet) (1974) 58 Cr App R 378 (CA)
R v Marsh The Times 6 July 1993 (CA)
R v Owen (Martin James) [2001] EWCA Crim 1018
R v Puddick (1865) 176 ER 662
R v Remnant (1807) Russ & Ry 136
R v Sussex Justices ex p McCarthy [1924] 1 KB 256 (KB)
R v The Chancellor, Masters and Scholars of the University of Cambridge (1723) 93 ER 698 (CKB)
R v Wilson (1924) 18 Cr App Rep 108 (CCA)
Randall v The Queen [2002] UKPC 19; [2002] 1 WLR 2237
Re G Mayor Cooke (1889) 5 TLR 407
Re Pinochet Ugarte (No 4) [1999] All ER (D) 1371 (QB)
S v Leepile and others (5) (1986) (4) SA 187 (W)
Secretary of State for the Home Department v MB [2007] UKHL 46; [2008] 1 AC 440
Smith v Illinois 390 US 129 (1968)
The Queen v Palmer (Central Criminal Court, 14–27 May 1856)
United States v O'Keefe 128 F3d 885, 897 (5th Cir 1997)
United States v Turkish 623 F2d 769 (2nd Cir 1980)
Walker v Sauvinet 92 US 90 (1875)
White v Illinois 502 US 346 (1992)
Williams v Twomey 510 F2d 634 (7th Cir 1975)

LIST OF LEGISLATIVE INSTRUMENTS

INTERNATIONAL

Declaration by United Nations (adopted and entered into force 1 January 1942) 204 LNTS 381
Statute of the International Court of Justice (adopted 26 June 1945, entered into force 24 October 1945)
United Nations Charter (adopted 26 June 1945, entered into force 24 October 1945) 1 UNTS 16
Agreement for the Prosecution and Punishment of Major War Criminals of the European Axis, and Charter of the International Military Tribunal (adopted and entered into force 8 August 1945) 82 UNTS 279
Allied Control Council Law No 10 1945
Military Government Ordinance No 7 1946
Military Government Ordinance No 11 1947
Uniform Rules of Procedure, Military Tribunals, Nuernberg, Revised to 8 January 1948
Universal Declaration of Human Rights (adopted 10 December 1948) UNGA Res 217 A(III) UN Doc A/810 71
Statute of the Council of Europe (adopted 5 May 1949, entered into force 3 August 1949) ETS 1
European Convention on Human Rights (adopted 4 November 1950, entered into force 3 September 1953, as amended by Protocols Nos 11 and 14) ETS 5
Protocol No 1 European Convention on Human Rights (adopted 20 March 1952, entered into force 18 May 1954, as amended by Protocol No 11) ETS 9
International Convention on the Elimination of All Forms of Racial Discrimination (adopted 21 December 1965, entered into force 4 January 1969) 660 UNTS 195
International Covenant on Civil and Political Rights (adopted 16 December 1966, entered into force 23 March 1976) 999 UNTS 171
International Covenant on Economic, Social and Cultural Rights (adopted 16 December 1966, entered into force 3 January 1976) 993 UNTS 3
American Convention on Human Rights (adopted 22 November 1969, entered into force 18 July 1978) 1144 UNTS 123
Conference on Security and Co-operation in Europe: Final Act (adopted 1 August 1975, Helsinki) (1975) 14 ILM 1292
Rules of Court of the International Court of Justice (adopted 14 April 1978, entered into force 1 July 1978, as amended 29 September 2005)

Convention on the Elimination of All Forms of Discrimination against Women (adopted 18 December 1979, entered into force 3 September 1981) 1249 UNTS 13

African Charter on Human and Peoples' Rights (adopted 27 June 1981, entered into force 21 October 1986) 1520 UNTS 217

Protocol No 7 European Convention on Human Rights (adopted 22 November 1984, entered into force 1 November 1988, as amended by Protocol No 11) ETS 117

Convention against Torture and Other Cruel, Inhuman or Degrading Treatment or Punishment (adopted 10 December 1984, entered into force 26 June 1987) 1465 UNTS 85

Recommendation No R (85) 11 on the Position of the Victim in the Framework of Criminal Law and Procedure (adopted by Committee of Ministers 28 June 1985) (Council of Europe, Strasbourg 1985)

Declaration of Basic Principles of Justice for Victims of Crime and Abuse of Power (adopted 29 November 1985) UNGA Res 40/34 Annex 40 GAOR Supp (No 53) 214 UN Doc A/40/53 (1985)

Additional Protocol to the American Convention on Human Rights in the Area of Economic, Social and Cultural Rights (adopted 14 November 1988, entered into force 16 November 1999) (1989) 28 ILM 156

Convention on the Rights of the Child (adopted 20 November 1989, entered into force 2 September 1990) 1577 UNTS 3

Second Optional Protocol to the International Covenant on Civil and Political Rights (adopted 15 December 1989, entered into force 11 July 1991) UNGA Res 44/128 Annex 44 GAOR Supp (No 49) 207 UN Doc A/44/49 (1989)

Basic Principles on the Role of Lawyers (Eighth UN Congress on the Prevention of Crime and the Treatment of Offenders, Havana 27 August to 7 September 1990) UN Doc A/CONF.144/28/Rev.1 118 (1990)

International Convention on the Protection of the Rights of All Migrant Workers and Members of Their Families (adopted 18 December 1990, entered into force 1 July 2003) 2220 UNTS 3

Statute of the International Criminal Tribunal for the former Yugoslavia (adopted and entered into force 25 May 1993, as amended 7 July 2009)

Rules of Evidence and Procedure of the International Criminal Tribunal for the former Yugoslavia (adopted 11 February 1994, entered into force 14 March 1994, as amended 8 July 2015) UN Doc IT/32/Rev.50 (2015)

Protocol No 11 European Convention on Human Rights (adopted 11 May 1994, entered into force 1 November 1998) ETS 155

Statute of the International Criminal Tribunal for Rwanda (adopted and entered into force 8 November 1994, as amended 16 December 2009)

Rules of Procedure and Evidence of the International Criminal Tribunal for Rwanda (adopted 29 June 1995, as amended 13 May 2015)

Recommendation No R (97) 13 Concerning Intimidation of Witnesses and the Rights of the Defence (adopted by Committee of Ministers 10 September 1997) (Council of Europe, Strasbourg 1998)

Rome Statute of the International Criminal Court (adopted 17 July 1998, entered into force 1 July 2002) 2187 UNTS 90

Recommendation No R (2000) 2 on the Re-examination or Reopening of Certain Cases at Domestic Level Following Judgments of the European Court of Human Rights (adopted by Committee of Ministers 19 January 2000) (2000) 43 Yearbook 290

Rules of Procedure and Evidence of the International Criminal Court (adopted and entered into force 9 September 2002)

Convention on the Rights of Persons with Disabilities (adopted 13 December 2006, entered into force 3 May 2008) 2515 UNTS 3

Charter of Fundamental Rights of the European Union (adopted 12 December 2007, entered into force 1 December 2009) (2010) OJ C83/389

Standard Minimum Rules for the Treatment of Prisoners (the Nelson Mandela Rules) (adopted 17 December 2015) UNGA Res 70/175 UN Doc A/Res/70/175 (2015)

NATIONAL

Twelve Tables 449 BC

Codex Theodosianus 438 AD

Codex Justinianeus 529 AD

Digesta 533 AD

Novellae Constitutiones 535–564 AD

Constitutions of Clarendon 1164

Assize of Clarendon 1166

Canons of the Fourth Lateran Council 1215

Bull *Ad extirpanda* 1252

Magna Carta 1297

Statute of 28 Edward III (1354)

Maryland Act for the Liberties of the People 1638

Massachusetts Body of Liberties 1641

Rhode Island Acts and Orders of 1647

Connecticut Code of Laws 1650

French Criminal Ordinance 1670

The Charter or Fundamental Laws of West New Jersey 1676

New York Charter of Liberties and Privileges 1683

Treason Act 1696

Act Declaring Rights and Privileges of Subjects of East New Jersey 1698

Act of Settlement 1701

An Act for Punishing of Accessories to Felonies, and Receivers of Stolen Goods, and to Prevent the Wilful Burning and Destroying of Ships 1701

An Act for Improving the Union of the Two Kingdoms 1708

Maryland Declaration of Rights 1776

North Carolina Declaration of Rights 1776

Pennsylvania Declaration of Rights 1776

Virginia Bill of Rights 1776

New York Constitution 1777

Vermont Declaration of Rights 1777

South Carolina Constitution 1778

Massachusetts Declaration of Rights 1780
New Hampshire Bill of Rights 1784
US Constitution 1787
French Declaration of the Rights of Man and of Citizens 1789
French Constitution 1791, 1852, 1946, 1958
French Law of 16 September 1791
US Bill of Rights 1791
Delaware Constitution 1792
Kentucky Constitution 1792
French Code of Offences and Punishments 1795
Tennessee Declaration of Rights 1796
French Law of 7th Pluviôse Year IX (27 January 1801)
French Napoleonic Code of Criminal Procedure 1808
French Law of 4 March 1831
Prisoners' Counsel Act 1836
French Law of 17 July 1856
French Law of 19 June 1881
French Law of 8 December 1897
Administration of Justice (Miscellaneous Provisions) Act 1933
Basic Law for the Federal Republic of Germany 1949
Criminal Code of Canada 1985
German Criminal Procedure Code 1987
Special Immigration Appeals Commission Act 1997
Youth Justice and Criminal Evidence Act 1999
Special Immigration Appeals Commission (Procedure) Rules 2003 SI 2003/1034
Legal Aid, Sentencing and Punishment of Offenders Act 2012
US Code 2012

www.ingramcontent.com/pod-product-compliance
Ingram Content Group UK Ltd.
Pitfield, Milton Keynes, MK11 3LW, UK
UKHW051921100926
8556IPUK00021B/1304